Friedrich Max Müller

Contributions to the Science of Mythology

Vol. II

Friedrich Max Müller

Contributions to the Science of Mythology
Vol. II

ISBN/EAN: 9783337179755

Printed in Europe, USA, Canada, Australia, Japan

Cover: Foto ©ninafisch / pixelio.de

More available books at **www.hansebooks.com**

CONTRIBUTIONS

TO THE

SCIENCE OF MYTHOLOGY

BY THE

RIGHT HON. PROFESSOR F. MAX MÜLLER, K.M.
MEMBER OF THE FRENCH INSTITUTE

IN TWO VOLUMES

VOL. II

LONGMANS, GREEN, AND CO.
39 PATERNOSTER ROW, LONDON
NEW YORK AND BOMBAY
1897

All rights reserved

CONTENTS.

CHAPTER VI.

Vedic Mythology.
	PAGE
In what sense is the Veda primitive?	427
Lettish Mythology	430
The Sky-tree	434
Jason and the Golden Fleece	436
Antecedents of Vedic Mythology	440
Composite Character of Mythology	441
Character of Vedic Gods predominantly physical	444
Age of Vedic Literature	445
Sraddhâ	448
Relation between the Vedic and other Aryan Mythologies	451
More Modern Ingredients in Vedic Mythology	452
Ceremonial Ideas in Vedic Hymns	452
Sacrifice and Prayer	453
Magic and Witchcraft	458
Von Ihering's Rationalism	460
Atharva-veda	461
Mordvinian and Wotjakian Sacrifices	462
Société Finno-Ougrienne	463
Vedic Deities	472
Yâska's Classification of Vedic Devatâs	472
Devatâ	473
Three Classes of Vedic Deities	473
Triad of Vedic Deities	475
Number of Gods	475
The Thirty-three Gods	475
I. Agni	480
II. Indra	483

	PAGE
III. Âditya	485
Vedic Deities not restricted to one Locality	487
Gods by Birth and by Creation	488
The Pantheon of the Rig-veda Hymns	488
Yâska's Pantheon	491
Earlier and Later Gods	492
The Reign of Dyaus	492
Dyâvâ-prithivî	493
Parallel Development. Ζεὺς Γελέων	499
Limits of Mythological Comparisons	500
Manifold Character of the Ancient Gods	502
Hêre	504
Európe	506
Kronos	507
Akmon	507
Kronos	510
The Wives of Zeus. 1. Eurynome	513
2. Zeus, Lêto, Apollon and Artemis	514
3. Zeus, Lêda, Helena	515
4. Zeus, Aigina, Aiakos	518
5. Zeus, Kallisto, and Arkas	519
6. Zeus, Alkmênê, and Hêrakles	520
7. Zeus and Semele	520
Twin Deities	521
8. Zeus, Antiope, Amphion and Zêthos	522
9. Zeus, Diônê, Dia	522
10. Zeus, Protogeneia, Aëthlios	524
11. Zeus, Êlektra, Harmonia, Dardanos, and Jāsion	524
12. Zeus, Danae, and Perseus	524
Vedic and other Aryan Mythologies	527
Indian Myths	527
Dêmêter. Earth	530
Gaia and Dêmêter	533
Dêo. Erînys	537
Varuna	545
Varuna as Moon	554
Âdityas	555
Aditi	556
Asvinau and other Dual Gods and Heroes	558
The Relations of the Asvins	558

CONTENTS. vii

	PAGE
Names and Legends of the Asvins	559
The Dawn as the Mother of Twins	562
Yama, the Twin	562
Sun and Dawn as Horse and Mare	563
Sara*ny*û as the Dawn	564
Meaning of the Old Myth	565
Yama	566
Yama as Agni	566
Yama as the Firstborn and the first to die	568
Was Yama=Adam?	569
Greek and Roman Twins	577
Other Names of the Asvins	579
Nâsatyâ	580
Asvins as Temporal Gods	583
Achievements of the Asvins	583
Vartikâ	584
*K*yavâna	587
Atri	589
Vandana	590
Bhu*g*yu Taugrya	591
V*r*ika	591
Kali	591
Vispalâ	592
Parâv*ri*g	593
Rebha	594
Vimada	595
Vadhrimatî	595
Ghoshâ	596
Sayu	597
Pedu and the Horse Paidva	597
Serpent-worship in the Veda	598
True and undefined Character of the Asvins	600
Rudra and the Rudras	605
Rudra as *S*iva	606
Yâska's Mythology	608
Differences and Similarities	609
The Children of Sara*ny*û	612
Hêrakles and Îphiklês	612
Amphitryon	614
Perseus	615

Karna, son of Prithà	616
Labours of Hêrakles	617
Adversaries of Hêrakles	623
The Golden Apple	624
The Hind of Keryneia	625
Kerberos	627
The Two with the One	633
Antiope	642
Harmonia	645
Hahn's Sagwissenschaft	650
Mundilföri	651
Hêlios	652
Sûrya	653
Rohita	655
Threefold Character of Sûrya and Agni	656
Olympos	657
Poseidon	658
Trita and Trita	661
Trita in Greek Mythology	668
Hermes and Apollon	673
Hermes. Saramà	673
Sàrameyau	675
Cognate Gods	680
Apollon	681
Aphrodite	682
Athêne	682
Zeus and Maia	684
Apollon	685
Ilithyia or Eileithyia	696
Greek and Italian Gods	707
Apollon and Mars	710
Mamurius	714
Athêne	725
Name of Athêne	726
Aphrodite = Charis	728
Artemis	732
Indra	743
Importance of Names	750
Indra in the Veda	751
Andra	756

CONTENTS.

	PAGE
Indra, an Agent	757
Indra Supreme	757
Vritra, Ahi	758
Dàsas	760
Conquest of Cows	764
Cacus and Hercules	766
Indra, Ushas, &c.	769
Indra, as Deliverer of Women	771
Hèrakles and his Heroines	772
Dawn. Fors	774
Agni	780
Agni in India and Persia	784
The Five Agnis in India and Persia	785
Agni in the Veda	786
Fire in other Mythologies	790
Héphaistos. Vulcan	791
Bhuranyu = Phorôneus	796
Vulcanus. Ulkà	799
Fèronia	800
Héphaistos and Yávishtha	801
Fire-totems	804
Atharvan	806
Angiras	806
Bhrigavàna	807
Promêtheus	810
Minys, Manu	813
Manu	814
Abstract Deities	817
Savitri	819
Brihaspati and Brahmanaspati	825
Comparison of Myths in unrelated Languages	830
Belief in another Life	831
INDEX	835

CONTRIBUTIONS

TO THE

SCIENCE OF MYTHOLOGY.

CHAPTER VI.

VEDIC MYTHOLOGY.

WE now approach the mythology of the ancient Aryan inhabitants of India, to see whether their mythology and likewise those of the other closely related Aryan nations, particularly the Greeks and Romans, will yield to the same solvents and disclose the same elements which we found without much effort in the mythological language of Mordvinians and Fins, people entirely unconnected by blood or language with the Aryan family of speech.

In what sense is the Veda primitive?

The chief superiority which Vedic mythology may claim over all mythologies consists in the great wealth of traditional literature handed down to us by an almost miraculous process, and dating from a period during which the mythopœic process was still in full operation. The question of the exact date of Vedic literature, does not concern us here, though I may as well state for the benefit of those who accuse me of having exaggerated its antiquity that among Sanskrit scholars I have always been blamed for assigning far too modern a date to the Veda, about 1200 B.C., while the late Professor Whitney claimed 1500 B.C., others 2000 or even 5000 B.C. as more likely dates. I have gone even further, and have repeatedly declared that I should be extremely glad to be able to escape from the stringency of my own arguments, and to be able to assign a more recent date to the Vedic age. But whatever the chronological date of the Veda may be, I have always felt that without a knowledge of the period of mythological fermentation which is presented to us in the Vedic hymns and Brâhma*n*as, it would have been almost impossible to understand the mythology of any of the Aryan languages, more particularly of the Greeks and Romans. Does any one deny this now? Does any one deny that for catching the faint voices of the most distant Aryan antiquity, we have nothing to place by the side of the Veda? We must not exaggerate, and I am afraid that of late the depth to which the shaft of the Veda can lead us, has sometimes been exaggerated. It may enable us to listen 'to the voices of the earth-born sons of Manu,' if such a metaphor is allowed with reference to the original meaning of Manu; but it will hardly enable us to hear the inarticulate shouts of the sons of nature, the Naturvölker, who were supposed to lurk closely behind the backs of the Vedic *R*ishis. This would be claiming too much for the Veda. We may, for instance, learn from the ancient Sanskrit name of daughter, that daughter, duhit*ri*, meant originally milker. But to discover behind this charming Aryan idyll a still more distant idyll when cows were not yet milked, or, because duhit*ri* is masculine in form, were milked by men only, as the heavenly cows were by Indra, requires a power of vision or imagination that is not given to many. Possibly a future Mannhardt may prove that the daughters of the house were not too proud to milk the cows even in much more recent times, just as unmarried women continue to be called spinsters, even after spinning has long gone out of fashion.

Many things which seem incredible to classical scholars exist as simple facts in the Veda. What from a Greek point of view is a distant past is here placed before us as still actually present. What to the Greek scholar seems wild and fanciful is simply a matter of fact before the eyes of the student of the Vedic hymns. It has been doubted whether Zeus had anything to do with the sky, Apollon with the sun, Athêne with the morning, but no one could question that in the Veda Dyaus sprang from the sky, Savit*ri* from the sun, Ahanâ from the morning light. Some of the greatest horrors of Greek mythology, incestuous relations between sisters and brothers, nay between mothers and sons, betray their physical origin in the Veda, so as to exclude any possibility of doubt. We must not imagine that Greek and Roman mythology are Vedic mythology in a later stage. There is no such direct continuity between the two, as little as there is between the languages of Greece and India. Greek gods have never been Vedic gods, but both Greek and Vedic gods have started from the same germs, and it is with these germs, not with the full-grown trees, that Comparative Mythology is chiefly concerned. Looking upon Vedic and Greek mythology as two parallel streams which start from the same source, we can clearly see that the Vedic stream offers an immense advantage by enabling us to follow it much further back, and much nearer to what seems to have been its source than the Greek stream; nay, I should say, so far that in the Veda we sometimes see the stream of mythological thought welling up before our eyes from its true source, the human heart. The merely chronological antiquity of the Veda is therefore of little consequence to us. For what should we gain if we could date the Veda back to 6000 or 4000 B.C.? Beyond 2000 B.C. all is tohu va bohu, emptiness and darkness, mere vanity and vexation of spirit, without a ray of light from anywhere. The hallucinations about the Vedic poets being separated by a few generations only from a race of Homines alali, 'who had listened to the music of the morning stars and the shouts of the sons of God,' or who can represent to us man in his most primitive state, as he came direct from the mind and the hands of God, or if we may believe Darwin, from the womb of his Simian mother, if they ever existed among scholars, exist no longer, nor is there any valour in once more slaying the slain. All that can be seriously maintained is that we possess nothing more primitive in Aryan literature than the Veda, and that it would seem useless to look in any other literature for the antecedents of that intellectual world which is opened before us in the Veda.

Lettish Mythology.

We should perhaps make one exception in favour of the popular poetry of a small branch of the Aryan family of speech which has hitherto been too little regarded by students of mythology, but the importance of which was pointed out many years ago by Mannhardt—I mean the Lettish. The Lets who with the Lituanians represent an independent division of the Slavonic branch, show, as was pointed out by Bopp and Pott, several remnants of a very primitive character in their grammar, though mixed up with formations of a much later age. These primitive forms preserved in the language of the Lituanians have misled several scholars into a belief that the whole of that language has retained its primitive stamp. This, however, is not the case, and we must guard against committing the same mistake with regard to the mythological elements preserved in the popular songs of the Lets. It cannot be denied, however, that by the side of much that is decidedly modern, full of Christian and even Mohammedan ideas, we meet there at the same time with thoughts and expressions which are not only Vedic in their simplicity, but seem to carry us in some cases to a stage more simple, more primitive, and more intelligible than the mythological phraseology of those ancient hymns. We must not exaggerate, and not knowing much of Lettish myself, I ought to speak with great reserve. It seems to me a very great loss that the Collectanea which Mannhardt left on Lettish and Lituanian mythology, which Dr. Berkholz of Riga undertook to publish (see Quellen und Forschungen, p. xxix), have never appeared. His Lituanian researches would of course be more valuable even than what he has left us on the Lettish Solar Myth, for Lituanian is to Lettish what Old Norse is to Middle High German, and would probably give us the key to many secrets not only in Lettish, but also in Greek and Roman mythology. A great treasure lies hidden there; will no one lift it? Trusting in Mannhardt's statements, I may at least say so much, that there are cases in which the phraseology of the Veda seems strange or bold to us, but where it is nevertheless supported by the phraseology of Lettish and other Slavonic popular songs. It has been doubted whether when the Vedic poets speak simply of the cow, or the mother of the cows (Rv. IV, 52, 3), we are justified in translating these names by the Dawn; and whether instead of saying 'it is morning,' anybody in his senses could have said, 'the red cow lies among the black cows.' But in Russian songs (see Mannhardt, p. 308), the black cow is simply a name for the night, the day is called the grey or the white ox, and the twilight the grey bull [1]. The Dawn in the Veda is constantly called Divo duhitâ, the daughter of Dyaus or the Sky. If we could doubt as to the meaning of this name, the Lettish name for the Dawn, Diewodukte, would certainly remove all uncertainty. She is distinctly said to be Saulyte, the sun (i.e. of the morning), or Saules meita. In the Veda we often hear of many Dawns or Dawn-maidens, and the poets of the Lets speak likewise of many beautiful Sky-daughters or God-daughters, Diewo

[1] Afanasieff in his Poetische Naturanschauungen, I, 659, gives a number of riddles, full of mythological germs, such as: The black cow has tossed and killed the people, the white cow has made them alive again; the black cow has imprisoned the people, the white cow has brought them out again; the black cow has barricaded the door; the grey bull looked through the window, &c. Mannhardt, p. 308, note.

Dukruzeles. It has been doubted whether this daughter of Dyaus, the Ushas of the Veda, could be represented in Greece by Charis or Aphrodite. But the Lettish songs tell us of the Dawn brilliant in her golden crown, and holding her golden horses with her golden rays. She has clearly in the eyes of the Lets become a goddess of beauty and love, wooed by the Moon and the God-sons. In the morning, we are told that her fire is lit by the Morning Star, in the evening the Evening Star is said to make her bed. She is also represented as crying over the golden apple that has fallen from the apple-tree, and over the golden boat that has sunk into the sea. These are some of the mythological germs out of which grows in time the rank vegetation of mythology. What the golden boat is that sinks into the sea and is mourned for by the daughter of the sky (No. 33), however doubtful it may be elsewhere, is not to be mistaken in the mythology of the Lets. It is the setting sun which in the Veda has to be saved by the Asvins; it is the golden boat in which Hêlios and Hêrakles sail from West to East. Sometimes it is the Sun-daughter herself that is drowned, like Kyavâna in the Veda, and as Kyavâna and similar heroes have to be saved in the Veda by the Asvins, the Lets also call upon the God-sons (Διόσκοροι) to row in a boat and save the Sun-daughter (No. 35). All these are only disjointed elements of mythology, but that is their greatest interest; they are still chaotic, but they afterwards gather round a centre and are reduced to some kind of order, regardless often of their original character and intention. We may observe contradictions between these mythological aphorisms from the very beginning. How could it be otherwise when it was open to every poet to interpret the phenomena of nature according to his own sweet will? Thus the Lettish songs tell us that the God-son who woos the Sun-daughter has grey horses. But these grey horses are elsewhere called the horses of the Moon, and ridden by the God-sons when wooing the daughter of the Sun (Sûryâ). Then again we are told that the Moon has no horses of his own, or that the Morning and Evening Stars are his horses. In other songs the stars are called the suitors of the Sun-daughter, and they also seem to carry her off, while the Moon, after having carried her off, seems to have forsaken her, and to have been punished by Perkun for his faithlessness. There are similar contradictions with reference to the suitors of Sûryâ, the Sun-daughter, in the Veda, and some of these contain the germs of those very tragedies which surprise us in most mythologies. When the Sun had promised her daughter to the God-son, and afterwards given her to the Moon, Perkun, who was invited to the wedding, cut the Moon in pieces and destroyed the great oak-tree. In other songs the Sun is represented as having cut the Moon in pieces because he had taken away the betrothed bride from the Morning Star (No. 716). But after the Moon had wedded the Sun he is said to have fallen in love with the Morning Star, and for that to have been cut in two by Perkun (No. 77).

The Sky-tree.

There is a great oak-tree or apple-tree or rose-tree, often mentioned in the Lettish songs, and there seems to me little doubt that it was meant for an imaginary tree on which every day the sun was supposed to grow up in the East. The sun is called the rose as well as the golden apple, and as a rose or an apple always requires a stem to grow on, an invisible tree was supposed to spring up every morning, to grow higher and higher till noon, and then to come down again or to be cut down in the evening, so that all its branches were scattered about. This would lend some meaning to what has hitherto been a great puzzle to many students of mythology, namely the Weltbaum, of which Kuhn and other scholars speak as if everybody knew what it meant, while it has always seemed to me very difficult to connect any clear idea with that name. If the clouds also were supposed to belong to that tree, it would come very near the German Wetterbaum, the tree of the thunderclouds, which seems to have been imagined because the clouds also, like the foliage of a tree, presupposed a support, or a stem from which they could spring and on which they were supposed to rest. If then we accept this Lettish conception of a sun-tree, whether a rose (No. 84) or an apple-tree or an oak, we shall understand how the Sun-daughter could have been fabled to ascend on the rose-tree to the sky (No. 83), like Jack on the beanstalk, and how the same Sun-daughter should have cried over the apple that fell from the tree (No. 28), that apple being the daily sun which drops in the West, and was supposed to lie there till it could be recovered by some god or powerful hero [1].

---

[1] The Sun-daughter is told not to cry over the apple, because the God-sons will come in the morning to roll the golden apple (No. 29), or to hurl it on high.

Here it seems to me we get an intelligent background for the apple or the apples of the Hesperides, which had to be brought back by Hêrakles, as the heroic representative of the sun. The story would have been originally no more than that the sun of the morning was the apple that had fallen from the tree in the evening, and which no one could bring back except some powerful hero, some Hêrakles, himself of solar origin. This outline once given, anything else that we hear of the labours of Hêrakles in recovering the apple or even the apples of the Hesperides would become more or less intelligible.

Jâson and the Golden Fleece.

The same tree as the great oak-tree, watched by dragons, may help us to interpret the exploit of another hero, namely Jâson ('Ιάσων). We must of course distinguish, as the Greeks did, between 'Ιασίων, the son of Zeus and Electra (or Hêmera) and brother of Dardanos, who on the thrice-ploughed field begat with Dêmêter Plouton or Ploutos, and was killed by the thunderbolt of Zeus, and 'Ιάσων, the son of Aison and Polymêde, the grandson of Krêtheus of Jolkos, and the famous conqueror of the golden fleece and of Mêdeia, the daughter of Aiêtes. But the names and their varieties are difficult to keep apart, except that 'Ιάσων, the Argonaut, has short ι and long â, while (if I am not mistaken), 'Ιασίων, Ίασος, 'Ιάσιος, 'Ιασεύς have long ι and short a, because the name corresponds to Sk. Vivásvân, the sun, which transliterated into Greek would become ϜιϜάσϜων, i.e. 'Ιάσων or 'Ιασίων. The tradition was that Jâson had been instructed by Cheiron, and had received from him the name of Jâson, i.e. the healer, instead of his former name of Diomêdes. Here therefore the long a of ἰᾶσθαι would be right, though it does not follow that 'Ιάσων was originally meant for healer. But the beloved of Dêmêter who is called not only Jăsion, but Jăsos and Jăsios, had originally a short a, and its i was lengthened in order to make the name possible in hexameters. This Jăsion then, originally Jăson, would be meant for Vivâsvân the sun, and who could with Dêmêter beget the wealth of the fields, if not the sun?

As to the other Jâson, unless originally he was likewise Vivâsvân, the sun, and afterwards misinterpreted as a healer, ἰατρός, he would lend himself readily as the chief actor in several of the adventures of the Argonaut Jâson. Let us remember that Phrixos, after losing Helle (another Sûryâ), had carried the golden fleece to Aia, the country ruled by Aiêtes, who was the husband of Idyia (the knowing, another name of Hekate), and the father of Mêdeia (the wise). It is true it is difficult to suggest an etymology for Aia. Even if it could stand for Gaia, that would help us very little. Mimnermos, however, as quoted by Strabo, i, 2, gives us an important hint by telling us that Aia was the country where the rays (ἀκτῖνες) of the swift Hêlios are kept in a golden chamber on the shore of Ôkeanos. If this was the popular belief in his time, then Aia was the West where Hêlios deposits every day his rays, as the Sun-daughter deposits her crown, and where he dwells till he appears again with his rays in the East. Later poets speak of one Aia in the West which they assign to Kirke, and another Aia in the East which belongs to the brother of Kirke, Aiêtes, both children, it should be observed, of Hêlios and Perse. In the Odyssey Aia is clearly the Aia [1] in the West.

The next question is, what could be meant by the golden fleece? It was the fleece of the golden ram on which Helle and Phrixos, children of Nephele, had crossed the Hellespont. Helle (Sûryâ) was drowned, like the Sun-daughter, while her brother Phrixos (ripple) when arriving in Aia hung the fleece of the ram [2] on which he and his sister had been riding on a great oak-tree which was guarded by a dragon. The Lets seem to know nothing of the dangerous journey of Phrixos and Helle, but they know of a woollen cloth which Maria, here the Sun-daughter, had hung on the great oak-tree, and which had been bespattered with the blood of the oak-tree when it was struck down by Perkun (No. 72). This woollen cloth is often mentioned in the Lettish songs, it had to be cleaned, washed, and dried. We have seen already that the great oak-tree which grew in the West is really the same as the sun-tree [3] that springs up in the morning and is cut down every evening. The branches of it were not to be gathered, but the Sun-daughter is said to have carried off one golden bough (Nos. 45, 82) [4]. The

---

[1] There is a name of the dark half of the moon which occurs in the Satapatha-brâhmaṇa VIII, 4, 2, 11, and might be identified with aiu, namely ayava. But even if phonetically possible, it would not help us for discovering the original conception of the country of Aiêtes.

[2] Cf. Babr. 93, 7, κριὸς βαθείῃ φρικὶ μᾶλλον ὀρθώσας.

[3] Sun-beam = Zounenboom (Willams, Belg. Museum, i, 326).

[4] The same tree is called in Finnish puu Jumalan, the tree of God, in Est. Taara tamme, the oak of Taara, planted by the Sun-son, Eston. Paiwapoega or by Taara's son. When, how-

red woollen cloth that was hung on it by the Sun-daughter can hardly have been meant for anything but the red of the evening or the setting sun, sometimes called her red cloak. When it is said that this woollen cloth when gathered up was full of silver pieces (No. 37), this can only have been meant for the silver stars which had risen where the red of the evening had been spread out before.

If then we take this red cloth on the oak-tree for the original form of the fleece hung on the oak-tree in Aia, i.e. in the West, its recovery by some hero would simply be the repetition of the recovery of the golden apple by Hêrakles. This recovery could only be the work of a solar hero, who brings the next day, and might well have been called Vivâsvân or Jâson, the sun (not yet Jâson, the healer), being the father of the two Asvins, and the husband of Erînys (Saranyû). The fundamental idea of this expedition of Jâson as of several of the labours of Hêrakles, such as the fetching of the apples of the Hesperides, the recovery of the girdle of Hippolyte (the Sun-daughter also has her girdle), the chase of the golden-horned Kerynean doe (generally taken for a representative of the moon), seems to have always been the same, the bringing back of the western sun. At first we must suppose that there were ancient sayings among the people such as 'the great oak-tree has been cut down,' 'the red woollen cloth has been spread out,' 'the girdle has been brought back,' 'the golden apple in the West has

---

ever, it is said that this tree overshadows the whole sky and does not allow sun and moon to shine, it would seem to be the Wetterbaum, thunder-tree, rather than the sun-tree.

been found,' ' the gold-horned doe has been caught '
—all meaning no more than what we mean when we
say the bright sunlight has come back. As this
return or recovery could not be achieved by itself,
some agent had to be supplied to do the work, and
the agent could only be the sun again in his diurnal
and half-humanised character. All this may sound
very strange, but to the student of ancient language it
is so by no means, only we must wait till we get more
light from ancient Lituanian sources in addition to
what Mannhardt has already obtained from more
modern Lettish poetry. What with proverbial sayings and popular riddles, mythology would spring up
in abundance, and answers would readily be given by
imaginative grannies to any questions that might be
asked. If, for instance, the old people were asked
who made crowns and girdles for the Sun-daughter
and the God-sons, they would soon tell of a Heaven-
smith who makes crowns and girdles and rings and
spurs, while they would point to the stars as the
sparks that come flying from his smithy, and fall
into the great waters [1].

Antecedents of Vedic Mythology.

This must suffice to show in what sense Lettish
sagas may be said to allow us a glance into the
antecedents even of Vedic mythology. If that is
so, we shall of course be told that the study of the
mythology of Tasmanians or Andaman islanders
will carry us still further back. This may be quite
true, though we must never forget that the Lituanians are Âryas, the Mincoupies are not. But

---

[1] See Mannhardt, Lettische Sonnenmythen, Nos. 36-38.

I have not a word to say against any attempts to find the right key to mythological riddles, wherever it can be found.

I have fully dealt with these speculations and I shall only add here, that what seems to me surprising is that no one who holds those views should have perceived the necessity of first proving that the palaeolithic savages of to-day or yesterday began their life or their historical development on earth one day, nay one hour, later or earlier than the Âryas of India or Lituania. We know from the languages and from some of the complicated customs of uncivilised races that those so-called sons of nature have had many ups and downs before they became what they are now, yet no one has attempted to prove that their ups and downs were exactly the same as the ups and downs of the Âryas. We must try to think clearly, and must not allow ourselves to be carried away by mere plausibilities. Granted that the Âryas must have been savages, does it really follow that all savages, any more than all civilised races, were alike, or that the Âryan savages in their elaboration of myths and customs acted exactly like other savages? Even modern savages differ most characteristically from each other. As Dr. Bleek has pointed out, the mere fact that the Bântu languages have no masculine and feminine gender, accounts for the poverty of their mythology. Who then is to determine what phase of savagery, Red Indian, African, Tasmanian, or Andaman, underlies, directly or indirectly, the childhood of the Âryas?

Composite Character of Mythology.

Ancient languages, ancient beliefs and customs

were not formed according to rule. Even if we were to admit that all human beings were born alike, their surroundings have always been very different, and their intellectual productions must have differed in consequence. Mythology is not a thing that is what it is, by necessity. It is determined in its growth by ever so many accidental circumstances, by ever so many known and unknown influences, even by individual poets or sages. When it reaches us, it has passed through ever so many hands. It forms then an immense conglomerate which excludes hardly anything that has ever passed through the mind of man. What should we say if some geologists, after discovering shells or flakes of flint in one of their pudding stones, were to say that these conglomerates consisted by necessity of shells and flints? Yet, that is exactly what many of our comparative mythologists have lately been doing. When they had discovered, for instance, that some mythological gods and heroes were historical characters, at once they started a theory that all gods and all heroes were originally real men and women. We saw how the story of Daphne fleeing before Phoibos was explained as the recollection of an adventure, such as might happen any day, of a damsel of the name of Miss Dawn being pursued by a ruffian of the name of Mr. Sun.

When ethnologists saw that reverence was paid by certain tribes to a stone or a shell or the tail of a lion, at once fetishism was made the solvent of all mythological and religious puzzles. The difference that fetishes are objects worshipped, as far as the worshippers are concerned, without any rhyme or reason, while other objects, now often classed as fetishes, such as amulets, crosses, relics, palladions, yûpas, or maypoles, if they are worshipped at all, are worshipped for a very intelligible reason, was completely ignored.

As soon as it became known that in several languages, both ancient and modern, the names of some divine or half-divine beings meant originally lions or bulls, totemism became the order of the day, and was preached most persuasively as the foundation of all religious and mythological worship. The objection that a totem meant originally a clan-mark was treated as scholastic pedantry, till at last the totemistic epidemic attacked even those who ought to have been proof against this infantile complaint.

It is a well-known and easily understood fact that many nations, both civilised and uncivilised, preserve the memory of their fathers, grandfathers, and great-grandfathers, that they revere their names, and often at their meals and on other occasions honour them with simple offerings.

All this is human, and intelligible, and, in that sense, primitive. If earlier traces of such customs can be found among modern savages, by all means let us have them. Only we must not allow ourselves to be carried away into a blindfolded acceptance of ancestor-worship, as explained by Mr. Herbert Spencer, or of totemism or fetishism or animism, when used as the solvents of all the problems of religion and mythology.

On the other hand, after we have once understood the comprehensive character of mythology, it would be folly to deny that there may be instances of what by these most ill-defined terms are called fetishism, totemism, and ancestral spiritism in the Veda, in

Homer, or even in the Bible; but if there are such, they must be treated each on its own merits. It would be altogether begging the question to say that these isolated instances are remnants or so-called survivals from a complete period of ancient thought and worship, which consisted of nothing but fetishism, totemism, or spiritism, as practised by the ancestors of all the Aryan races, nay of all mankind. It would be easy to produce instances even in our own times of what we are invited to comprehend under these vague terms.

Are there not priests and nuns among us who wear amulets (fetishes)? Are there no soldiers ready to die for their colours (totems)? Are there no commemorative services in honour of ancestors departed long ago? But the truth is that even among the most backward savages we never find a religion consisting exclusively of a belief in fetishes, in totems, or in ancestral spirits [1]. A closer study has always shown that these are ingredients or accretions or excrescences of a more comprehensive and comprehensible faith, and that the influence of natural phenomena is visible in the religious traditions of most, if not of all so-called fetish-worshippers, totemists, and spiritists [2].

Character of Vedic Gods predominantly physical.

I do not believe, though we have been told so, that any serious students of Vedic literature have ever denied the physical origin of the Vedic gods,

---

[1] Hibbert Lectures, 1878, p. 107: 'No religion consists of fetishism only.'

[2] See M. M., Presidential Address at the Anthropological Section of the British Association in 1891, p. 12.

and have joined the ranks of those who represent them as ancestral spirits, as fetishes, or totems. Professor Tiele has strongly protested against the supposition that he had ever joined the school of M. Gaidoz. As to M. Barth, he declares in no uncertain tone : ' No one contests any longer that myths are from the first the natural and popular expression of very simple facts, that particularly the most ancient have reference to the most common phenomena of nature, and that they depend very closely on language [1] ;' while Professor Oldenberg in his Religion des Veda, p. 53, though he seems to me in some places far too sanguine in his hopes of finding antecedents and explanations of Vedic myths and customs among the lowest of the low, states without hesitation that 'the fundamental stock of Vedic myths may be expected to consist of physical events.' What more can we want? At a later time Professor Oldenberg has guarded himself even more carefully against being supposed to have joined our so-called adversaries. He shows clearly the evolution of Aryan mythology through the three successive historical periods, the Indo-European, the Indo-Iranian, and the Vedic, and if he admits a more distant stage of savagery before the beginning of the Aryan period, this is what no one would deny as a possibility, though as yet it seems outside the sphere of practical politics, and need not disturb us for the present.

Age of Vedic Literature.

There are many things which are perfectly understood among Sanskrit scholars, though they are not

---

[1] Anthropological Religion, p. 424.

often discussed in public, for the simple reason that there are no definite facts on which these understandings could be shown to rest. We speak, for instance, of the date of Vedic poetry as about 1200 to 1500, but all we mean by this is that we have no authority to enable us to fix on any earlier or later date. But whoever knows the Vedic hymns knows that they presuppose, nay that they necessitate, indefinite periods of intellectual and linguistic growth which no merely chronological plummet can ever fathom. It may be said that children learn quickly to perceive, to conceive, and to speak, and that the same may have been the case in the childhood of our race. But it is not a question of years, it is a question of vast periods of intellectual growth, that must have passed before any noun could be formed and declined, before any verb could have been elaborated and conjugated. As to the growth of religious thought, we can clearly see how in the Vedic hymns a race of old gods, the Asuras, such as Dyaus and Varuna, are vanishing, and the new gods, the Devas, are still uncertain between their physical and their moral meaning. Some of the commonest words, such as yagña, sacrifice, brahman, word and prayer, rita, law and order, Aditi, the Beyond, have already in the Veda lost their etymological meaning, and leave on us the impression that even their traditional meaning had become very uncertain. The period during which these words spoke, as it were, for themselves, lies far beyond the period of the Vedic Rishis. There is besides a whole stream of thought and language in India, which in its literary embodiment is treated and rightly treated as post-Vedic, but which requires antecedents which, as they are not found in Vedic literature, must be allowed to have existed elsewhere, and to have passed through a parallel development, going back to Vedic or even pre-Vedic times. The epic elements collected in the Mahâbhârata and Râmâyana required time to grow up before they could have been gathered in these gigantic poems. And the same applies to the laws, and to many popular stories which meet us for the first time in the Sâstras of the Brâhmans and the Gâtakas of the Buddhists, not as recent productions, but as old, or, as what is called Smriti, re-collection, as distinct from Sruti, revelation.

But even this is not all. We know that there was a time when the Âryas of India and Persia were not yet separated, and we have historical remains of that period in what the Veda and Avesta share in common, whether in language, in religion, ceremonial, or mythology. In that period the old name of god, asura, must have been the recognised name for gods, ahura = asura being the principal element in the name of the supreme deity Ahurô-mazdâo, while deva was not used at all as a name of god or gods.

Then again, before that Indo-Iranian period there was that equally real period which preceded the Aryan Separation, and which has its history in the annals of words common to the two great divisions of that family, the Southern and the Northern. If we consider the intellectual work assigned to that period, we shall hesitate indeed before assigning to it any definite chronological limits.

And if then we ask ourselves the question whether that Pan-Aryan period could have been immediately preceded by a period of what is called savagery, or rather by any special kind of savagery, whether North American or South African, I feel sure that all true scholars will hesitate before committing themselves to any of these far-reaching theories.

Sraddhâ.

An instance will explain what I mean. If we take such a word as faith, or 'to believe,' it may seem to us very simple and natural; but that the idea of believing, as different from seeing, knowing, denying, or doubting, was not so easily elaborated, is best shown by the fact that we look for it in vain in the dictionaries of many uncivilised races. Even the Greeks do not say much of faith, though they have the word. What they recommend is εὐσέβεια, reverence, piety, rather than πίστις, faith. Mere vague belief, οἴησις, was called by Heraclitus ἱερὰ νοῦσος, a sacred malady. Now when we find in Sanskrit Srad-da-dhâmas and in Latin crêdimus, in Sk. srad-dadhau and in Latin crêdidi, in Sk. srad-dhitam and in Latin crêditum, we cannot doubt that these words existed before the Brâhmans came to India, before the Âryas of India and Persia separated, nay before the original Aryan family broke up into its two branches. And if the word had been elaborated, the idea of faith also, in its simplest form, must have been realised before that early date. But what was meant by this srat in srad-dadhau, i.e. I make or take as srat, a word of which little trace is left in crêdo for cred-do? Darmesteter identified srat or srad with hrid, heart, Lat. cor, Gr. καρδία, Goth. hairtô, Irish, cride, which would give us the original concept of putting in the heart or taking to heart. But is this the germ of the idea expressed by 'to believe'? The phonetic difficulty of s (srat) taking the place of h (hrid) in two contemporaneous words in Sanskrit might possibly be got over, but there is a passage in the Rig-veda, not considered by Darmesteter, which makes it impossible to assign to srat the original meaning of heart. In Rv. VIII, 75, 2 : srát vísvâ váryâ kridhi, 'Make all things wished for, true, O Agni.' Here the meaning of heart would be clearly impossible ; srat seems to mean true, sratkri to make true, srat-dhâ, to hold true. In some passages sraddhâ would bear the meaning of promise or troth, for instance, Rv. I, 108, 6 :—

Yát ábravam prathamám vâm vrinânáh
Ayám sómah ásuraih nah vihávyah |
Tám satyám sraddhâm abhí â hí yâtám
Átha sómasya pibatam sutásya ||

'What I said, when first adoring you, "this Soma of ours is to be called for by the gods," on this true promise come near, and then drink of the Soma that has been pressed for you.'

In VI, 26, 6, also, tvám sraddhâbhih mandasânáh sómaih, the only sense possible seems to be, 'Thou, rejoicing in our vows and offerings of Soma.' Most frequently both the verb and the substantive are used in the sense of trusting and believing in the gods and in their power, and are construed then with the dative. Rv. I, 55, 5 :—

Ádha kaná srát dadhati tvíshimate
Índrâya vágram nighánighnate vadhám.

'Then indeed men believe in Indra, the fiery warrior who again and again hurls down the thunderbolts.'

In Latin we have already the accusative in 'Alte tonantem credidimus Jovem.' The Vedic poets actually appeal to the mighty works of Indra to make people believe in him. Rv. I, 103, 5 :—

Tát asya idám paṣyata bhū́ri pushṭā́m
Srát índrasya dhattana vîryâya.

'Look at this, his great and mighty work, and believe in the power of Indra.' The regular succession of the heavenly phenomena is sometimes pointed out as a warrant for seeing and believing. Rv. I, 102, 2 : Asmé sûryâḳandramásâ, abhi-ḳákshe sraddhé kám Indra ḳarataḥ vitarturám, 'Sun and Moon move on alternately, that we should see and believe.'

In the sense of trusting or relying, sraddhâ is also construed with the accusative. Rv. I, 103, 3 : Sáḥ gátûbharmâ sraddádhânaḥ ógaḥ púraḥ vibhindán aḳarat ví dásîḥ, 'He, the bearer of the thunderbolt, trusting in his strength, moved along, cutting the hostile strongholds to pieces.' I mention all this in order to show through how many successive phases of thought the Aryan mind must have worked its way, before such a concept as faith could have been finished as embodied in one of the oldest Aryan compounds srat+dhâ. And yet all this must have been finished long before the Vedic, long before the Indo-Aryan, long before the end of the Pan-Aryan period, because thus only can we explain the co-existence of sraddhitam in Sanskrit and créditum in Latin. Into what distant past the history of this Aryan compound carries us would be difficult to say chronologically ; psychologically, however, we may be certain that it was a good deal later than what is represented by their period of mere savagery. Before people could be asked to believe in the gods, the gods (whether asuras or devas) must have been elaborated, nay a period of primitive scepticism must have intervened, before faith could be required and represented almost as a virtue (Rv. II, 26, 3; I, 104, 7). The gods whom men were asked to believe in were in the Veda the gods of nature. No one who knows the Veda can doubt this; no one, even with the greatest tenderness for ethnological speculations, would, I feel sure, ever make the slightest concession on this, the fundamental principle of Comparative Mythology. Our first duty therefore is to try to interpret the Veda from itself. The next step is to look for light in cognate languages and cognate mythologies. If all this fails, it will be time to cast a loving glance at the folklore of unrelated and uncivilised races, though I am bound to say, I know, as yet, of few cases only where Tasmanians, Mincoupies, or Blackfeet have proved half as useful to us as even Sâyana's much abused commentary.

Relation between the Vedic and other Aryan Mythologies.

It has been questioned whether the mythology of the Veda is really so intimately connected with that of other Aryan nations as its language has been proved to be, and whether it is more primitive than all the rest. Here again we must try to come to a clear understanding. That the Aryan mythologies spring from a common source, the one equation of Dyaush-pitar, Ζεὺς πατήρ, and Ju-piter has placed once for all beyond the reach of reasonable doubt. And when we say that Vedic mythology represents a period of thought which had almost entirely passed away before we can conceive the possibility of the Olympian Pantheon, or of the mythological creations of Italy and Germany, we do not speak simply of chronological priority. What chronology is there that could settle the dates of the birth and the death of the Aryan gods? Some myths die soon and are forgotten, while others possess so peculiar a vitality that they survive from age to age in all their freshness and youthfulness, that is, in their intelligibility, or what has been called their transparency. If the Vedic mythology, such as it is, could be proved to have sprung up but yesterday in a desert island or in the moon, its psychological priority and its psychological interest would remain just the same.

Still, however simple in its conceptions Vedic mythology may be, as compared to Greek and Roman mythology, it would not be right to claim for it a primordial character, whatever that may mean.

More Modern Ingredients in Vedic Mythology.

Even the oldest Vedic hymns and the oldest Vedic gods often exhibit a decidedly secondary and tertiary character. As we find here and there in Greek, Latin, or Lituanian grammatical forms more primitive than their corresponding forms in Sanskrit, we find in their mythologies also some names and legends less disturbed than what corresponds to them in the Veda. This has always been admitted by all serious scholars.

Ceremonial Ideas in Vedic Hymns.

But some of them seem to me to have gone a great deal too far in maintaining that all Vedic hymns are productions of a modern or secondary age, compositions in fact of priests, and solely intended as accompaniments to a highly developed sacrificial ceremonial. The reason of this misconception is that some scholars have formed to themselves a kind of ideal of what primitive poetry ought to be, and starting from this ideal, which has no existence except in their brain, of a pre-adamite or half-angelic childhood of the human race, they declare even the most ancient poems as time-worn and effete. The question is, do we know any Aryan poetry less time-worn and more ancient than that of the Veda? That a considerable portion of our Vedic hymns was preserved simply because they could be fitted into the sacrificial framework of the Brâhmans, no Vedic scholar has ever doubted. But this is very different from asserting that we possess no Vedic poetry, nay that no Vedic poetry existed before the institution of the Vedic ceremonial.

Sacrifice and Prayer.

Some theorists went even further and maintained that by some inward necessity sacrifice everywhere comes first and sacred poetry second. Such general assertions carry little weight. All depends here on what we mean by sacrifice. If, as the Vedic poet says, it is a sacrifice to Agni, the god of fire, to put but one log of wood on the hearth [1], if to bend the knee before the rising sun, or to lift the hands towards heaven during a thunderstorm is to be called worship, then it would certainly be difficult to say which comes first, praise or worship. But if sacrifice means what the Brâhmans meant by their Ya*gñ*a, a most complicated ceremonial, though presupposed even in many of the hymns, then to suppose that no

---

[1] Âpast. Sûtras II, 9, 21.

word of prayer or praise did ever proceed in measured cadence from the lips of the Brâhmans, till they had elaborated their minute sacrificial ceremonial, their Srauta sacrifices, is opposed to all we know, whether from psychology or from history. Who is competent to settle who came first, the priest or the poet, if not the priest himself? Yet the author of Hymn 88 in the tenth Ma*n*/*d*ala, whether we call him priest or poet, says, Rv. X, 88, 8 :—

Sûktavâkâm prathamâm ât ít agním,
Ât ít haví*h* a*g*anayanta devâ*h*.

'The gods created first the reciter of hymns, then Agni (the sacrificial fire), then the sacrificial offerings.'

This looks almost like an intentional protest against the opposite theory; at all events, it cannot be treated as a merely casual and unimportant remark. There are in the Rig-veda hymns utterly inappropriate for sacrificial purposes, and there are other hymns that had actually to be altered in some minute points (ûha) in order to suit the requirements of a complicated liturgy. If former students of the Veda neglected the liturgical elements, those who have since called attention to their existence and importance have, as usual, allowed themselves to be carried away much too far in the opposite direction. It is true, no doubt, that in very early times the sacrifice has taken a larger development in India than anywhere else. Only we should be careful. If we are told that karman must be translated by sacrifice, this is true; but the reason is that sacrifice in early times was simply any act that accompanied a prayer. Nor must we imagine, because we translate ya*g*ña, kratu, adhvara by sacrifice, that therefore the ancient sacrifices in India were the same thing as the sacrifices of which we read among the Jews, Greeks, and Romans, or, it may be, the sacrifices and orgies of uncivilised and savage races. The growth of sacrificial customs has to be studied separately in every country. If we found the minute sacrificial rules which have been preserved to us in the Brâhma*n*as and Sûtras in India, repeated in Greece and Rome, or even in the canons of the Christian Church, we should say at once that such rules could only be the result of a long continued, and therefore of a far advanced and very modern civilisation, and that they prove the existence of a long established and powerful priesthood. I pointed out many years ago, 1859, in my History of Ancient Sanskrit Literature, p. 493, how perplexing it was to see the most minute ceremonial distinctions recognised not only in the Brâhma*n*as and Sûtras, but already in the hymns of the Rig-veda. I showed how the names of the seven different classes of priests, intended each for their own special sacrificial acts, such as Hot*ri*, Pot*ri*, Nesh*tri*, Agnîdh, Prasâst*ri*, Adhvaryu, and Brahman, occurred in the hymns, and had become so familiar that some of them had actually been transferred to Agni, the god of the sacrificial fire. I have nothing to retract from what I said then, and I can only repeat that, in order to account for the apparently artificial and modern ideas occurring in these hymns, I should give anything to be able to assign to the final collection of the hymns of the Rig-veda a much later date than what is commonly assigned to it. But I see as yet no chance of escape from my own arguments, and I often wish that those who repeat again and again that Vedic literature has been proved to be much more modern than I supposed it to be, would give me their proofs. No one would be more grateful for them than I. But as the case stands at present, I am afraid that nothing remains but to try to learn a new lesson, namely that religious acts, and even minute ceremonial rules and distinctions, may under favouring circumstances spring up in a much earlier stage of civilisation than we were led to suppose from a study of the religion of the Jews, the Greeks and Romans, or even of savage races. At all events, the fact that many of the Vedic hymns presuppose on the part of the poets a familiarity with senseless ceremonial minutiae, cannot possibly justify the historian of religion in maintaining that in India ceremonial came first, and sacred poetry second, still less, as has been asserted by some writers who are not Vedic scholars, that there are no hymns in the Rig-veda which were not from the first composed by priests, and exclusively for sacrificial purposes. One cannot well prove what stands written on so many pages of the Rig-veda. If we call every petition addressed to the Devas, every praise of their power and majesty, which was afterwards employed in the course of certain sacrifices, a sacrificial hymn, then no doubt the majority of the poems collected in the Rig-veda may go by that name. If we imagine that no gift of water, honey, milk, butter, or cake could be made to the gods except by a priest, or that every libation at the beginning or end of a meal, every surrender of a valued possession on the funeral pile or on a fresh grave, is a sacrifice, then most of the hymns of the Vedic *Ri*shis, though even then by no means all, may be called mere accessories of sacrificial performances. But there are surely recurrent, and more or less solemn acts in the morning and the evening, if consisting only in the stirring and lighting of the fire on the hearth in the morning, and its careful making up in the evening, there is the glory of the full moon, and the return of the new moon which call forth religious feelings, and become an excuse for more or less boisterous festivities. There was even a definite practical purpose in the celebration of the return of the seasons, whether three or four or five or six, in the observation of the four stations of the sun at the time of the shortest and the longest days, and, later on, at the vernal and autumnal equinoxes. All this is natural, and indispensable, simply for the sake of keeping time, though it does not presuppose a priesthood or a ceremonial canon. I feel more and more convinced that the true origin of the solemn public sacrifices must be sought for in the necessity of establishing and maintaining a kind of calendar for reckoning days, sennights, fortnights, months, seasons, and years. This would naturally lead to the establishment of festivals on certain days of the year, but these need not have been more at first than gatherings and feastings of families, clans, or villages, with praises of certain gods who are more intimately connected with certain days or seasons, and with friendly recollections of departed members of the family. But when we meet with a fixed number of priests and their various offices, an elaborate construction of the altars intended for various fires, a large number of sacrificial implements, and the preparation of every kind of sacrificial offering, we feel no doubt that we have reached a new and comparatively modern stage. Only need we suppose that such a stage was never reached, before some poetical expression had been given to the motives which, we cannot doubt, inspired every one of these solemn performances? It is quite possible that such poetical utterances had an intimate relation to such acts as the lighting of the fire in the morning and its protection in the evening; but an expression of gratitude for the genial warmth of the fire on the hearth, or a praise of the sun at the return of spring, need surely not have waited till there was a special priest to perform the act of kindling the fire, till the logs that should be used for such a purpose had been carefully measured and numbered, &c.

I am always most reluctant to differ on questions of this kind from Grimm. Grimm (Kleinere Schriften, ii, p. 460) admits, as is well known, three successive periods, the first where people sacrificed only, the second where they sacrificed and prayed, the third where they prayed only. I do not see, however, that this was more than a postulate with Grimm, and I doubt whether there are facts to support it.

Magic and Witchcraft.

It has been said, and I think truly said, that much of the Vedic ceremonial savours of magic and witchcraft, and bears a certain likeness to the sorcery and black art practised by savage races in ancient and modern times. It could hardly be otherwise, for every sacrifice contains the germs of magic within it. Sacrifices even of the simplest kind were supposed to produce an effect indirectly through the intervention of divine beings. This too may be called superstitious, but at the time and to the persons most concerned, it was not without a certain logic. Believing in gods as they did, they naturally believed that their gods were accessible to the same arguments and the same bribes which produced an effect on their friends on earth. As soon, however, as these Devas were left out of consideration, sacrifice and prayer by themselves were supposed to exercise a direct and constraining influence on nature in producing the events that were desired. They may then be said to have assumed a magical character. It is difficult to draw a sharp line of demarcation between these two kinds of ceremonies, and between the psychological dispositions that gave rise to them. The very words we use are ill-defined. In German the word commonly used for magic is Zauber, but it is by no means easy to say under what circumstances Zauber comprehends sorcery, witchcraft, enchantment, and black art. If a priest implores the help of the god of rain, or offers presents to Par*g*anya, this would probably be called a sacrifice, but if by his spells and contortions he pretends to force par*g*anya, the rain-cloud, to send down rain, it would seem at once to become magic or Zauber[1]. Still there is clearly a transition between the two. Magic, in fact, seems to stand to sacrifice in the same relation in which superstition stands to faith, or logos to myth, and it may be stated without fear of contradiction, that every sacrificial act, the original purpose of which

---

[1] Oldenberg, l. c., pp. 435, 448, 459 seq.

has been forgotten, is very apt to become magical. Or if this seems to be too wide a generalisation, we may say at all events that every magical act which now seems irrational, must originally have had a reason, and that it is the highest object of our studies to discover that reason.

Von Ihering's Rationalism.

In this respect Prof. Ihering has set us a splendid example to follow, showing us how there must be and how there is reason at the bottom of everything, however unreasonable it seems to us, in the customs and laws of the ancient world. What could seem more magical than the auguria taken by an army on its march? Why did they throw grain before the fowls and watch their movements? Because originally, as Prof. Ihering has shown, when entering into an unknown country, it was often a question of life and death whether the grain and berries that were found growing wild were poisonous or wholesome. The only way to find this out was to throw some of these grains before the fowls which had been brought on purpose, and to watch the result. As soon as the real purpose was forgotten, this augurium became a purely magical art, kept up by the augurs for their own purposes, but deprived of its original purpose (Zweck). We are told that in some of the islands of the Southern Sea the natives will eat no berries unless some of them have been pecked by the birds.

It is clear that such acts, which had dwindled down to mere superstitions, are far more likely to receive some kind of explanation in countries which possess an ancient literature or tradition

than among African or Australian savages, where
we never get beyond the surface of the day. In
India, in Greece, in Italy we may catch a glimpse
now and then through the twilight of a more or less
continuous tradition; in Africa and Australia we
move in complete darkness. It is much more likely,
therefore, that a study of such works as the Atharva-
veda, the Kauśika-sûtras, the Adbhuta-brâhmaṇa,
the Gṛihya-sûtras, &c., may help us to understand
the magical practices of Zulus and Red Indians than
vice versâ, and nothing can be more useful to the
anthropologist by profession than a careful study
of the Vedic age, with its prayers, its sacrifices,
its imprecations and superstitions, if he wishes to
understand some of the secret springs of magic and
witchcraft as practised by Red Indians or Maoris.
A study of the Srâddha sacrifices, of the cult of the
Pitṛis in India, and of the Fravashis of Persia, has
helped us to understand for the first time the
true meaning of ancestor-worship, so widely spread
among civilised and uncivilised races of the present
day; why should not more light come from the same
quarter in elucidation of Shamanism or Hwang-kiao?

Atharva-veda.

I know there are many scholars who would protest against studying what they mean by Vedic
Religion in such works as the Atharva-veda, the
Kauśika-sûtras, or the Adbhuta-brâhmaṇa, and it
is generally agreed that the Atharva-veda is very
modern as compared to the Rig-veda. Even those
who stand up for the antiquity of the Atharva
hymns, would probably admit that they belong to
a totally different stratum from that which gave

rise to the hymns of the Rig-veda. Still we know of nothing nearer to the other Vedas than the Atharva-veda, and though most scholars would agree that the Atharva-veda should at first be studied by itself, and not be mixed up with the other Vedas, many of the superstitions and purely magical mantras of the Atharvâṅgirasas can only be explained by a reference to the Rig-veda, and not by consulting the accounts of travellers among the tribes of Northern Asia and Northern America.

Mordvinian and Wotjakian Sacrifices.

But though I am not very sanguine of our ever gaining complete light on the origin of sacrificial and magical performances from the lowest of savages, from Bushmen or Australians, I have always been ready to learn a lesson from the ceremonial customs of such races as Mordvines and Wotjakes, who possess something like trustworthy traditions of the past, and whose language has been carefully studied by real scholars. We all know how precarious and how perplexing the study of ancient customs is, how rarely we can find competent and trustworthy authorities, and how almost impossible it is to get any historical information extending beyond the present generation, and laying bare the roots from which certain customs have sprung. The explanation given by a native is generally considered as settling such matters, but it is only too well known by those who have trusted to that kind of evidence, how readily a native supplies whatever is wanted, and how innocently he tenders his own private impressions as representing the opinion of a whole clan or a whole people.

Société Finno-Ougrienne.

We ought to be all the more grateful, therefore, to the Société Finno-Ougrienne for having sent from time to time competent scholars to report not only on the poetry but likewise on the customs, sacrificial or otherwise, of races still in a transition state, and without a sacred literature of their own, and, even when acquainted with and partially converted to Christianity, still performing their pagan sacrifices and worshipping their pagan deities. Such are, for instance, the Mordvinians, scattered in the district of Astrakhan on the upper course of the Volga, as lately described by M. W. Mainof in the fifth volume of the Journal de la Société Finno-Ougrienne, 1889. Such are the Erzjanians, a branch of the Mordvinians, whose prayers, riddles, and incantations have been studied by M. H. Paasonen in the twelfth volume of the same Journal, 1894. And such are the Wotjakians, specimens of whose popular and sacred poetry have been collected and published by M. Yrjö Wichmann in the eleventh volume, 1893. These Wotjakians are chiefly found in the governments of Wjatka, Kasan, and Perm.

Among such races, if anywhere, we may hope to learn something of the true origin of sacrificial acts and sacrificial poetry and of the mutual relation of the two. The authorities which I shall quote are all Finno-Ugrian scholars, and in their hands we may feel safe against such blunders and misunderstandings as are but too common in the works of casual travellers, and missionaries, even if stationed for years in the same places. Anyhow it will be seen that I have not neglected to study collateral evidence, even if taken from non-Aryan races, if only the authorities we have to follow are trustworthy and vouched for by so eminent a body as the Société Finno-Ougrienne.

We found before how the mythology of these Finno-Ugrian races offered striking analogies to the mythology of the Veda, and it is possible, therefore, that their sacrificial customs also may exhibit some useful parallels to the early ceremonial of the Vedic priesthood.

In examining the papers published in the Journal de la Société Finno-Ougrienne we can still catch a few glimpses of the earliest periods of religious thought, and we find there hymns and formulas accompanied by the simplest sacrificial or superstitious acts which often remind us of similar mantras in the Atharva-veda. Thus in the collection of Erzjanian incantations in volume twelve, we read the following lines, intended to cure an illness caused by a fall (p. 5): 'O free light, Darija, the gloaming, and Marija, the dawn, and thou light, Nastasija, assist us, help us! Goddess of the Earth, I place before thee bread and salt, and ask for thy grace. Where that man, Andrej, fell, cure him, make him whole, assist him, help him, thou earth-ruling goddess Uljana.

'Thanks to thee that thou gavest help. I have given thee food and drink. I have placed before thee sweet bread and salt, I have offered thee good eggs and cake as a reward for thy help. I scrape together a twokopek piece, I dedicate to thee a pud of silver, a pud of copper, and a hundred roubles of money.'

Here we see a strange mixture. The very name

of Andrej, i.e. Andrew, shows the presence of Christianity, the two kopeks are of a still more modern date, but the invocations of the Dawn, the Gloaming, and the Earth as goddesses are pure paganism. The petition was inspired by anxiety for the life of Andrew, and by a belief in the healing power of these pagan deities [1]. We sometimes find a cartwheel used by these Ugrian tribes for healing diseases (p. 182), just as it was in Vedic times and among the Germans. In the offerings of eggs, cake, and money, we may discover germs of sacrificial acts, but we can also clearly perceive that these acts would have been inconceivable without the thoughts contained in the prayer, whether uttered outwardly or felt inwardly. Prayer alone gives significance to the act; we can imagine the prayer without the cake, but hardly the cake without the prayer.

When after a thunderstorm the sky begins to clear, the Erzjanians recite the following words, which might perfectly well have formed part of a hymn of the Yaǵur-veda, addressed to Indra or to Ushas (p. 21): 'Manej, come forth, come forth! I shall give thee a beautiful egg, I shall kill for thee a white cock.'

Among the Wotjakian linguistic specimens (vol. xi), we find many prayers, most of them accompanied by offerings or what may be called simple sacrificial acts. Some are actually addressed to Christ, others begin with Bismillah (p. 167), but most are addressed to pagan deities such as Inmar, Mużjem Mumi̯ (Mother Earth), Šundi̯-Mumi̯ (Sun-mother), Mother Vožo, &c.

---

[1] See Kuhn, Indische und Germanische Segenssprüche, K. Z, xiii, 49.

Thus we read (p. 122): 'My osto Inmar, my great Inmar, creator Inmar, give a good year, give thy warm rain, give thy warm nights, give thy dew. Hear our prayers. We sacrifice old bread, give us still more of new bread!'

P. 124. 'We place offerings in the lap of the great Inmar, the Kiu̯ud'źiń, the fertile Sky, the D̦ukiu̯ud'źiń, the corn-creating Sky, the Mu-kiu̯ud'źiń, the earth-fertilising Sky, and the Muźi̯em Mumi̯[1], the Mother Earth, that we may have good luck. Give us a good year, give thy warm nights, give thy warm rain, give thy dew, give thy flowers.

'My Gudiri-Mumi̯, Thunder-Mother, and my Šundi̯-Mumi̯, Sun-Mother! We remember you with good broth and with bread. Give us warm days, and fair summer, and warm rain.'

Ancestral spirits also are invoked, as in the next prayer (p. 126):—

'There thou hast something. May it fall before thee! We shall give thee a horse. Grandfather, grandmother, father, mother, all members of our family! May the sacrifice fall before you!

'We give a horse to the father, and may it please him. May the other horses prosper. Give good life to the whole herd! Let the whole herd prosper!'

Or again, p. 143, after an invocation of the great deities, the ancestors are invoked: 'And you also, departed fathers and mothers! Do not forsake us

---

[1] May I take this opportunity of repeating once more what I have often said, that the introduction of many diacritical marks makes printing, nay even intelligent reading, almost impossible. We should in writing keep, as much as possible, to broader phonetic categories, and leave the proper pronunciation to those who know each special language.

young people! Bring up our good flock! Make the corn we have sown heavy and good. Protect us against hatred and troubles!'

The great gods also are sometimes addressed as parents, and Inmar is invoked to look down from on high on his children (p. 155).

The Wotjakes in the district of Jelabuga sacrifice to Mardan as their ancestor (p. 130): 'We bring a horse as an offering to thee, Father Mardan, because thou hast given us good children, because thou hast given us good corn and good bread. We thank thee, Father Mardan.'

Sometimes we find the Rivers invoked as mothers (p. 134), just as in the Veda: 'Of one mind with our good neighbours, we came to thy shore with beer and kumyschka. Tśupt́si and Pi̇zep, you fertile mothers, give to our people an easy year, luck and well-being in all things! O mothers who never run dry, carry off with your waters all sicknesses. O my Vu-murt [1] (water spirit), carry our good cattle and our flock well across the stream, across the ford. If thou carry them well across, if thou takest great care of them, there will be something for thee also, something of the sacrifice will be left for thee. You fast-running, fertile mother-streams, give to the grass and to the seed something of your moisture.'

On p. 160 we read: 'O mother Vožo! Do not go away angry. Let thy warm, mild rain pour down on our field! Do not frighten thy people! Do not be angry with us even though we came along noisily! Thou also, Inmar, do not forsake us!'

All this is full of the spirit of Vedic poetry, and it is very simple and childlike.

---

[1] On Vu-murt, see also p. 163.

The Wotjakes, even after their conversion, were evidently afraid to leave their old gods altogether, and at the same time they did not wish to offend Christ. Thus we read (p. 141): 'My Christus, do not be angry, though we do not all keep the fast. Guard our good flock, and also ourselves! May the corn we have sown grow well, O my Christ!'

Sometimes it was not a simple horse or an ox or a goose that was slaughtered for gods and ancestors, but the victim had to be carefully prepared so as to have silver hoofs, and golden hair (p. 145). Those who sacrificed had to be clean, and after having washed in the bath-room, they had to appear in white shirts and white clothes. The broth had to be put into cups and the cups to be placed on the table in rows of three (p. 145). And when it was scattered on the fir-wood board, invocations like the Vedic nivids had to be used, such as, 'My Inmar, send us warm, mild rain at the right season!'

Nor was the ceremonial always so simple. Sometimes it sufficed that the worshipper should turn towards the rising sun, take his spade and scatter the grain against the wind, saying, 'O Inmar, let the grains sparkle like silver and gold; we ask thee for good luck and well-being.' Sometimes, however, a large number of priests were wanted, as in the Veda, priests of different names and different occupations, and mostly old men who knew how to pray and how to perform the ancient sacrifices. Mistakes at a sacrifice were evidently fatal, and there is one prayer (p. 152) where we read:—

'We young men may say at the beginning what ought to be said at the end. But do thou correct us, O Inmar! There are many things which we, young people, cannot say and pronounce properly. But even if we say three words only, be thou gracious to us!'

Who does not here remember similar warnings against false pronunciations in the Veda?

We get much fuller descriptions of the Mordvinian sacrifices in Mainof's paper. There (p. 11) we meet with an account of a horse-sacrifice as seen by Barbaro, an Italian, in the sixteenth century. The horse was fastened by the neck and the four feet to sticks stuck in the earth; the people then killed it with arrows, tore off the skin and ate the flesh, observing most complicated rules. The skin was then stuffed with straw and lifted to the top of a tree to receive the prayers of the multitude. The tree was adorned with rags, ribands, and other offerings, like the sacred trees in India, and like many trees which may be seen even now in Mohammedan countries. Something of this ceremony has been preserved among the Mordvinians to the present day, only that the horse is now represented by two men hidden under the skin of the horse. In the province of Penza people still recollect the sacrifice of a stallion dedicated to Chkaï, the god of the sun, and the sacrifice of a white bull who must have a black mark on the forehead and on the stomach. Other gods, such Chim-Paz (the sun), required a red bull (v, p. 36).

Although the rules of the sacrifice were known to the old people in a village, we are told by the Archimandrite Makarius (Journal, v, p. 24), that he knew a Mordvine, Kouzma by name, who had collected a complete ritual. This took place not more than sixty years ago, and his descendants still enjoy considerable veneration, and possess some of the implements used by him, among the rest the stone knife or stone saw which was used at the sacrifice long after steel knives had come into use (v, p. 26). This knife was considered sacred, and drops of water that had been poured over it were given as medicine (p. 38). As in the Vedic sacrifices, we find among the Mordvines also the brewing of an intoxicating beverage, some kind of Soma, containing hops and honey, as an essential part of their sacrificial festivals. Small cakes were baked to be eaten at the same time.

When the victim, whether a horse or a bull, was to be killed, the priests knelt down and said: 'O Bull, our father! be not angry with us and do not complain! Die for us, for the glory of the gods and for our welfare! If thou die, we shall live.' This is supposed to be the survival of a human sacrifice, and there are certainly some traces left of human victims having been immolated in former times. But even apart from that the custom of asking forgiveness of the animals before they were killed was very general. The following is a prayer of women addressed to Angué-Patay: 'Give us benches full of children, and let them be in perfect health! We ought to immolate two women in thy name, and we kill only two sheep.' How old these sacrifices and the hymns which the Mordvinians recited to Mainof must have been, we may gather from the fact that the people confessed they did no longer understand them. 'Ce sont de bonnes paroles,' they said, 'mais nous ne savons plus ce qu'elles veulent dire' (p. 37). Might not the Brâhmans even during the Brâhmaṇa period have said the same? Some of the

invocations are only whispered (upâṃsu, like some
of the nivids of the Yagur-veda), such as (p. 37) :—

'Chim-Paz, Sun-god,
'Vany-Paz, guardian-god,
'Mastorom-Paz¹, Earth-god,
'Vanymizton, save us!'
'Nichké-Paz, Great god,
'Svet Vernichké, blood-red light,

'Velen-Paz, God of the fields,
'Vanymizton, save us!'
'Anguépatiaï-Paz, Goddess mother,
'Oznymizton, pray for us!'

We see, therefore, among the half-civilised Finno-Ugrian tribes many residua, preserved almost to the present day, of a system of sacrifices intelligible in their origin, but in their present form often merely traditional, artificial, complicated, and unintelligible. We see that prayers addressed to the deities of nature were perfectly possible without sacrificial gifts, while sacrificial gifts without prayers, or without some words addressed to those for whom they were intended, are nowhere to be met with. A mute sacrifice is no sacrifice at all, a prayer unaccompanied by any sacrificial demonstrations is perhaps the best, certainly the most natural, and therefore probably the earliest manifestation of religious sentiment.

If, therefore, we may learn some lessons from a comparative study of other religions, and if even Vedic poetry and Vedic sacrifices are not so entirely different from the poetry and the ceremonial of other religions as to withdraw themselves from comparison, we may in future treat the religious poetry of the Veda as antecedent to the ceremonial of the Brâhmaṇas, though fully admitting that the priests who employed these hymns, even after they had lost

---

¹ Also Mastor-Paz, p. 46, and Mastyr-Paz.

a perfect understanding of them, modified them, corrupted them, and imitated them without any misgivings.

We owe much to the Brâhmana priests. To them, and more particularly to the Hotri priests, who had to learn the whole collection of the hymns by heart in order to recite them at the great sacrifices, we probably owe the almost miraculous preservation of Vedic poetry, but certainly not its first creation. We must be grateful to the sacrificial age, the age of the Brâhmanas, for having preserved by means of a most perfectly organised oral tradition whatever was left at their time of genuine ancient poetry, just as the Mordvines are grateful to Kouzma for having collected a kind of prayer-book and sacrificial guide for their priesthood.

Vedic Deities.

It has sometimes been maintained that whatever the origin of the Vedic gods may have been, the poets of the Veda knew nothing about it, as little as Homer knew the origin of Apollon or Athêne.

Yâska's Classification of Vedic Devatâs.

But when we consult Yâska, one of the earliest Indian theologians, who lived before Pânini, and probably before the rise of Buddhism, we find him not only fully aware of the physical character of the Vedic gods, but classifying them at once according to the various places and spheres of activity which each of them occupied in nature. He divides them into three classes, gods of the earth, gods of the air, and gods of the sky.

Devatâ.

In examining Yâska's ancient catalogue of the gods, we must bear in mind that with him deity or devatâ means something different from what it means with us. Every object that is praised by a poet in a hymn or even in a single verse, is in his technical language a devatâ, a deity. We should simply say it was the object of worship or praise. Thus, if a horse is praised, or a bird, or frogs, or a stone, a chariot, a bow, a bowstring, a whip, or a mortar, they are all put down as devatâs. I wonder that this has not been used as a proof of the existence of fetish-worship among the Vedic *R*ishis. Would not the existence of stones, chariots, bows, &c., as Devatâs seem to settle once for all the existence of fetish-worship in the Veda? It would certainly be a stronger argument than many that have been produced for that purpose, though we see that the name of devatâ, deity, owes its origin simply to a theory of a theological school, and meant with them no more than an object praised, magnified, or sanctified.

The Three Classes of Vedic Deities.

In the arrangement which Yâska gives of the principal deities of the Veda, it is not always easy to distinguish between ancient tradition and later theory. If I say later theory, I mean, of course, later in comparison with the Vedic hymns and the Brâhma*n*as. We must always remember that what we call the Nirukta, which is ascribed to Yâska, presupposes the Nigha*n*tu or the Nigha*n*tus, the lists of words of which the Nirukta forms but a kind of commentary.

Now these Nighan*t*us are certainly ancient; they are actually mentioned in an important passage of the Dîpavaṁsa, V, 62. Here the young Tissa is introduced as asking the Thera Siggava a difficult question concerning the Rig-veda, the Ya*g*ur-veda, the Sâma-veda, and also the Nighan*t*u (not yet the Nirukta), and fifthly the Itihâsa. This is supposed to have taken place in 359 B.C. It is true that the Dîpavaṁsa cannot be older than the beginning of the fourth century A.D., but it rests on older authorities, particularly on the A*tth*akathâ of the Mahâvîra fraternity; and the absence of any mention of the Atharva-veda would seem to assign to the statement in question a very considerable antiquity. Anyhow we see from this passage the high authority assigned to the Nighan*t*u even by the early Buddhists, and we may gather from it at all events that the Nighan*t*us were pre-Buddhistic.

Yâska, the author of the Nirukta, quotes representatives of his own theories, the so-called Nairuktas, who had lived before his time, and if Yâska is older than Pâ*n*ini, this would bring us to at least 500 B.C. But many of these Nairukta theories are based on passages in the Brâhma*n*as, nay even in the hymns, and would therefore prove a still more remote antiquity for the period in which theological speculation, as represented in the Brâhma*n*as, was rife in India. It can also be proved by independent evidence that the fundamental theory on which Yâska's division of the Vedic deities is based, namely the three localities to which the principal deities are referred, dates certainly from the Brâhma*n*a period, nay has, as we shall see, certain warrants even in the hymns.

Triad of Vedic Deities.

Apart from the philosophical doctrine that all gods are only manifestations of the supreme Self, the Âtman, Yâska quotes, as we saw, the Nairuktas in support of a triad of gods, (1) those of the earth, (2) those of the air, and (3) those of the sky. Agni (fire), as Yâska says, has his place on earth, Vâyu (wind) or Indra in the air, and Sûrya (sun) in the sky.

Number of Gods.

This triad of deities is not Yâska's invention. It is clearly indicated already in the Brâhmaṇas. Thus we read in the Aitareya-brâhmaṇa that Praǵâpati created three greatnesses, Agni, Vâyu, Sûrya. In the Khândogya-Upanishad (IV, 17, 1) we read: 'Praǵâpati brooded over the worlds, and from them thus brooded over he squeezed out the essences, Agni from the earth, Vâyu from the sky, Âditya (the sun) from heaven.'

Even in the hymns this threefold division of earth, air, and sky, or, as sometimes translated, earth, sky, and heaven, is well established. Thus we read in Rv. X, 65, 9, of terrestrial gods, pârthiva, of celestial, divya, and of those who dwell in the waters (clouds), ye apsu. Their number is given as thirty-three (Rv. I, 45, 1; III, 6, 9; VIII, 28, 1), divided into three classes of eleven each.

The Thirty-three Gods.

This number of thirty-three must be old, for it occurs in the Avesta also. According to another division, however, the gods were not thrice eleven, but were twelve Âdityas, eleven Rudras, and eight Vasus. The names of these three classes occur in the hymns (I, 45, 1), but not their respective numbers, except that of the Âdityas, which in the hymns is given as seven, not yet as twelve. In the Satapatha-brâhmana IV, 5, 7, 2, their numbers are given, and Dyaus and P*r*ithivî, or Indra and Pra*g*âpati, are added in order to bring the number up to thirty-three. A similar account is given in the Aitareya-brâhma*n*a II, 18, where the two additional gods are Pra*g*âpati and Vasha*t*kâra. There are other classifications of these gods in the hymns of the Rig-veda, such as:—

 II, 3, 4. Vasus. Visve Devas, Âdityas,
 III, 20, 5. I, 45, 1, Vasus. Rudras, Âdityas,
 IV, 8, 8, Âdityas, Rudras, Vasus,
 VII, 51, 3, Âdityas, Maruts, Devas,
 X, 25, 1, Rudras, Vasus, Visve.

Sometimes the number of the gods seems to be raised at random, though the number three prevails throughout. Thus in Rv. IV, 9, 9, we read of 3,339 gods who worshipped Agni, while there is a curious passage in the B*r*ihad-âra*n*yaka-Upanishad III, 9, where the number of the gods is first stated as 3,306, and then, step by step, reduced to thirty-three, to six, to three, to two, to one-and-a-half, and finally to one.

According to Yâska the three principal deities dwelling on earth, in the air, and in the sky, i.e. Agni, Indra, and Âditya, receive different names according to their different activities which are celebrated by the Vedic poets. They are conceived also as endowed with various forms. The Supreme Self (Âtman) at the root of all the gods is, of course, without any form whatever, but the individual deities are supposed to be endowed with form, nay, in many cases with human form. In the case of deities like Fire, Wind, and Sun, the form is indicated by the name; in the case of deities like Gâtavedas, Rudra, Indra, Pargaṇya, and Asvinau, who do not exhibit so clearly the visible objects in nature from which they sprang, it is clear at least that they are praised as if they were not only sentient, but intelligent also, and capable of understanding what is said to them and of them. They are conceived, in fact, as manlike, and as possessing the ordinary members of human beings. The Vedic poets mention, for instance, the arms of Indra (IV, 31, 3), the fist of Indra (III, 1, 5); they also ascribe to them such things as belong to men only. Thus Indra is said to have a beautiful wife (III, 20, 1), and his two horses are the Haris, 2, 4, 6, 8, or 10 in number. Vâyu (wind), too, has his Niyuts (steeds), Sûrya (sun) his Harits, Pûshan (sun) his Agâs (goats), Ushas (dawn) her Aruṇis (reddish horses). The acts, again, which they are said to perform are like the acts of men. They hear and see, they eat and drink, and this not only like animals, but like men who understand, and are conscious of what they are doing.

There have, however, been differences of opinion on this point. Some ancient interpreters of the Veda seem to have argued that the gods, such as Fire, Wind, Sun, Earth, and Moon, were not endowed with a human form, and that their being addressed as if they were intelligent beings, proves nothing, because rivers, plants, dice, and other things also are addressed in the same way, as if performing human acts, and as if possessed of a human body. This is explained as metaphorical (rûpaka) language. If a river is addressed as driving on a chariot, it would be impossible to take this literally, and hence it is to be taken as a rûpaka-pravâda. The prevalent opinion, however, seems to have been that the gods had to be conceived as endowed with a human form, though, from the old Vedânta point of view, they were various manifestations only of the Âtman or the Supreme Self.

The classification of the Vedic deities in three classes according to the localities in which they are supposed chiefly to dwell, though very imperfect in its details, deserves nevertheless to be carefully examined as a first attempt at theological speculation.

We shall see that for a proper understanding of the Vedic gods and their relation to each other, this view of their activity, nay of their very essence, as determined by the sphere in which they act, is extremely important and useful. At first sight the idea that there were originally three gods only, Agni, Indra, and Âditya, representing certain phenomena on earth, in the air, and in the sky, and that these received different names according to the special work assigned to them, seems very artificial, and therefore wrong. And yet there is some truth in it, if we do not take it in too literal a sense. We must not suppose that Agni, after having been named and recognised as a special deity, was afterwards changed into Dravinodas, Tanûnapât, Tvash*tri* or Sûrya, or that Indra was named at a later time Vâyu, Rudra, Par*g*anya, or that Âditya assumed the form of Ushas, the Asvinau, of Vish*n*u or

Varuna. Yet there is truth hidden in Yâska's theory, namely this, that though Agni may have started from the fire on the hearth, he was not restricted to it, but was recognised in all the manifestations of light on earth and in the sky. Indra, again, though originally the giver of rain, could be recognised not only as the conqueror of the clouds, but as the agent in all that takes place in the air, while Âditya was accepted not simply as the sun, but as the active power in the whole sky. The fault of Yâska's threefold division is not that it is too general, but that in some cases it is really too narrow, because there are Devatâs who extend their influence over more than one of these three spheres of nature. Agni, for instance, though originally recognised in the house-fire, and therefore belonging to the earth, is likewise seen by the Vedic poets as present in the lightning of the air, in the brightness of the sky, nay, according to a very common conception, in the waters also, whether the clouds or the sea, into which he plunges every evening, and from which he rises in the morning. In some cases the names given to the divine agents in the three realms of nature vary according to the special work performed by each of them, in others the general names of Agni, Indra, Âditya are retained throughout. In these cases Agni, Indra, and Âditya often overshadow the special gods of their own spheres, nay they encroach even on the spheres not specially their own, and thus produce a confusion which is often very perplexing to those who want to find in the Veda their own views, or those which they have derived from the more specialised mythology of other nations.

I. Agni.

Following, therefore, the guidance of Yâska, we begin with Agni, whether he belongs to the earth or the earth belongs to him. To him, according to Yâska, belong also the Morning libation (prâta*h*-savanam), the spring among the seasons, the Gâyatrî among the metres, the Triv*r*it among the stomas (praises), the Rathantara among the Sâmans (songs). Much of this is of course secondary and artificial, but it rests on a true principle. Agni is supposed to have associates and followers (Devaga*n*as), and these are not only gods and goddesses, but likewise a number of objects with which he is thought to be more or less intimately connected. Thus the deities invoked in the Âprî hymns[1], are all supposed to be his, or he is supposed to be connected with every one of them.

First of all, two names of Agni, the god of fire, are given as synonymous, viz. 2. *G*âtavedas (knowing all things [2]), and 3. Vai*s*vânara (belonging to all men). Then follow the names of the Âprî deities[3]:—

I. 4. Dravi*n*odas (giver of wealth).	7. Narâsa*m*sa (man-praise).
5. Idhma (fuel).	8. I*l*a, also called Î*l*ita*h* (implored).
6. Tanûnapât (self-born).	

[1] Vedic Hymns, S. B. E., vol. xlvi, p. 10.

[2] With reference to Rv. VI, 15, 13, vísvâ veda *g*ánimâ *g*âtávedâ*h*, I translate omniscient, not all-possessor. That vedas does not occur by itself, is no objection, see compounds with *g*oshas, oshas, &c. See, however, Vedic Hymns, vol. xlvi.

[3] See History of Ancient Sanskrit Literature, p. 413 seq. Modern as these Âprî hymns seem to us, âfri hymns are known in the Avesta.

9. Barhis (the turf-altar).
10. Dvâra*h* (the doors of heaven, the East).
11. Ushâsânaktâ (dawn and night).
12. Daivyâ Hotârau (the two divine priests).
13. Tisro Devî*h* (the three goddesses, Agnâyî, P*ri*thivî, Ilâ, or Bhâratî, Il*â*, Sarasvatî)[1].
14. Tvash*tri* (the carpenter, creator).
15. Vanaspati (the sacrificial tree).
16. Svâhâk*ri*tis (the invocations).

Many of these names refer to various objects invoked by the poets in the so-called Âprî hymns. Agni, if not exactly identified with them, was supposed to be represented by them, and to take cognisance of the invocations addressed to their names. Then follows a long list of other names which are likewise considered as names of objects sacred to Agni, as we should say, and often mentioned in hymns addressed to this deity. Such are :—

II. 1. Asva (the horse).
2. *S*akuni (the bird).
3. Ma*n*dûka (the frog).
4. Aksha (the dice).
5. Grâvan (stones, sacrificial).
6. Nârâsa*m*sa (panegyric hymn, or the object of it).
7. Ratha (chariot).
8. Dundubhi (drum).
9. Ishudhi (quiver).
10. Hastaghna (arm-bandage).
11. Abhîsu (reins).
12. Dhanus (bow).
13. *G*yâ (bowstring).
14. Ishu (arrow).
15. Asvâ*g*anî (horse-whip).
16. Ulûkhala (mortar).
17. V*ri*shabha (bull, a tool).
18. Drughana (hatchet).
19. Pitu (food).
20. Nadî (rivers).
21. Ap (waters).
22. Oshadhi (shrubs).
23. Râtrî (night).
24. Ara*n*yânî (forest-spirit).
25. *S*raddhâ (faith).
26. P*ri*thivî (earth).
27. Apvâ (disease).
28. Agnâyî (wife of Agni).

---
[1] Vedic Hymns, S. B. E., vol. xlvi, p. 12.

29. Ulûkhala-musale (mortar and pestle).
30. Havirdhâne (waggons for Soma-offerings).
31. Dyâvâ-p*r*ithivî (heaven and earth).
32. Vipâ*tkh*utudri (the two rivers, Vipâs and Sutudrî).
33. Ârtnî (the two ends of a bow).
34. Sunâsîrau (wind and sun, or Indra and Vâyu).
35. Devî *g*osh*t*rî (the two loving goddesses).
36. Devî ûr*g*ahutî (the two food-giving goddesses, Heaven and Earth, Day and Night, Autumn and Year).

It is clear that these so-called deities were put together by Yâska without much system. Those from 29 to 36, however, are classed together as Dvandva or dual deities, and some, such as the Three Goddesses (Agnâyî, P*r*ithivî, and I*l*â, or Bhâratî, I*l*â, and Sarasvatî), are classed together as the wives of Agni.

In what sense these 36 Devatâs may be regarded as deities may easily be seen from any of the invocations addressed to them. Thus the Ârtnîs, the two ends of a bow, are praised in Rv. VI, 75, 4:—

'The two ends of the bow darting asunder of one accord may strike away the enemies, the fiends.'

The bow is praised in the Rv. VI, 75, 2 :—

'Let us win cows with the bow, let us win the race with the bow, let us win hard battles with the bow ; the bow does injury to the enemy, let us win all countries with the bow !'

The bowstring is praised in Rv. VI, 75, 3 :—

'Like one who is going to whisper she comes near to the ear ; like a woman embracing her dear friend she hums, stretched along the bow, helpful in battle.'

It is clear that if such addresses were supposed to change a bow and a bowstring into a deity or into a fetish, there would be no poet even in our days who was not an idolator or a fetish-worshipper. But suppose we were to call the bowstring, as addressed by the Vedic poet, a fetish, instead of a poetical fancy, what should we gain?

The principal activity of Agni consists, according to Yâska, in carrying oblations to the gods or bringing the gods to the sacrifice.

There are certain gods who are praised together with Agni, viz. Indra, Soma, Varu*n*a, Par*g*anya, the *R*itus (seasons). Vish*n*u and Pûshan, though they share in the same offerings with Agni, were not praised together with him in the same verses [1].

II. Indra.

Indra belongs to the air, or the air to Indra. He and Vâyu (wind) are taken by Yâska for the same being. His are the Noon-libation (mâdhyandinasavana), the summer, the Trish*t*ubh-metre, the Pañ*k*ada*s*a Stoma, and the B*r*ihat-Sâman. His companions are the Maruts, the Rudras, besides a number of deities recorded in the Nigha*nt*u, V, 4, 5. I give them as they are found there:—

III.
1. Vâyu (wind).
2. Varu*n*a (sky).
3. Rudra (storm).
4. Indra (rain-giver).
5. Par*g*anya (cloud).
6. B*r*ihaspati (lord of speech).
7. Brahma*n*aspati (lord of prayer).
8. Kshetrasya pati (lord of the land).
9. Vâstoshpati (lord of the house).
10. Vâ*k*aspati (lord of speech, breath).
11. Apâm napât (offspring of the water, or Agni).
12. Yama.
13. Mitra.
14. Ka.
15. Sarasvat.
16. Vi*s*vakarman (maker of all things).
17. Târkshya (giver of rain).

---

[1] See, however, Rv. X, 17, 3.

18. Manyu (anger).
19. Dadhikrâvan (racer).
20. Savit*ri* (sun).
21. Tvash*tri* (maker, sun).
22. Vâta (wind).
23. Agni (fire).
24. Vena.
25. Asuniti (spirit, breath).
26. *R*ita (right, law).
27. Indu (rain, moon).
28. Pra*g*âpati (lord of creatures).
29. Ahi (dragon).
30. Ahirbudhnya (dragon of the deep).
31. Supar*n*a (bird).
32. Purûravas (a hero).

Another class of gods likewise belonging to the air are :—

IV. 1. *S*yena (falcon, horse).
2. Soma (moon or Soma plant[1]).
3. *K*andramas (moon).
4. M*ri*tyu (death).
5. Visvânara (also Vaisvânara, belonging to all men).
6. Dhât*ri* (creator, as rain-giver).
7. Vidhât*ri* (creator, as rain-giver).
8. Marut (storm-gods)[2].
9. Rudra (storms).
10. *R*ibhu (the *R*ibhus).
11. A*n*giras (the A*n*giras, *R*ishis).
12. Pit*ri* (Fathers, Manes).
13. Atharvan (the Atharvans, *R*ishis).
14. Bh*ri*gu (the Bh*ri*gus, *R*ishis).
15. Âptya (*R*ishis).
16. Aditi[3] (fem.).
17. Saramâ[3] (fem.).
18. Sarasvatî[3] (fem.).
19. Vâ*k* (Speech, thunder).
20. Anumati (moon, when nearly full).
21. Râkâ (full-moon).
22. Sinîvâlî (new moon).
23. Kuhû (moon, nearly invisible).
24. Yamî (fem. Ushas).
25. Urvasî (fem.).
26. P*ri*thivî (fem.).
27. Indrâ*n*î (wife of Indra).
28. Gaurî (fem., cloud ?).
29. Go (cow).
30. Dhenu (cow).
31. Aghnyâ (cow).
32. Pathyâ (salvation).
33. Svasti (well-being).
34. Ushas (dawn).
35. Ilâ (earth).
36. Rodasî (wife of Rudra).

All these gods and goddesses are said to belong to

---

[1] Haimavato Mau*g*avato vâ.
[2] Devaga*n*as, companions of gods.
[3] Wives or companions of Indra.

the air and to the clouds where Indra performs his principal work in killing V*ri*tra and other demons of darkness, in sending down dew and rain, and in performing other acts of valour. Though all the gods dwelling in the air between earth and heaven are looked upon as his staff, his ga*n*as, companions properly so called, are such bodies as the Maruts, Rudras, &c., while the feminine deities are looked upon as under his protection.

The gods with whom Indra is praised in the same hymns, are Agni, Soma, Varu*n*a, Pûshan, B*ri*haspati, Brahma*n*aspati, Parvata, Kutsa, Vish*n*u, and Vâyu. Other gods of the middle sphere praised together are, Mitra with Varu*n*a, Soma with Pûshan, Soma with Rudra, Pûshan with Agni, and Par*g*anya with Vâta.

III. Âditya.

Âditya (sun) belongs to yonder world (heaven). His is the third Savana, the autumn, the Gâyatrî metre, the Saptada*s*a Stoma, and the Vairûpa Sâman.

His assistant gods are:—

V. 1. A*s*vinau (day and night)[1].
2. Ushas (dawn).
3. Sûryâ (sun, fem.).
4. V*ri*shâkapâyî (wife of V*ri*shâkapi, the sun).
5. Sara*n*yû (end of night, dawn).
6. Tvash*tri* (maker), cf. I. 14.
7. Savit*ri* (sun).
8. Bhaga (sun).
9. Sûrya (sun).
10. Pûshan (sun).
11. Vish*n*u (sun).
12. Vi*s*vânara, cf. IV. 5.
13. Varu*n*a, cf. III. 2.
14. Kesin (sol crinitus).
15. Kesins (three Kesins, Agni, Vâyu or Vidyut, and Sûrya).
16. V*ri*shâkapi (sun).
17. Yama, cf. III. 12.
18. A*g*a ekapâd (sun).
19. P*ri*thivî (earth or sky), cf. II. 26; IV. 26.

---

[1] Vâsâtya, a son of Ushas, p. 608, and Nâsatya.

20. Samudra (sea).	26. Devas (the gods).
21. Dadhyan (*R*ishi).	27. Visve devâ*h* (the All-gods).
22. Atharvan (*R*ishi).	
23. Manu (*R*ishi).	28. Sâdhyas.
24. Âdityas (the sons of Aditi).	29. Vasus.
	30. Vâ*g*ins.
25. Sapta *R*ishaya*h* (the seven *R*ishis).	31. Devapatnîs (the wives of the gods).

The chief work of Âditya is the lifting of moisture, and whatever deed is most pre-eminent, may be supposed to be done by him. The gods praised together with him are *K*andramas, Vâyu, Sa*m*vatsara (the year).

We are also informed that whenever there is any reference in a verse to autumn, when the metre is Anush*t*ubh, the Stoma Ekavi*m*sa, the Sâman Vairâ*g*a, we may conclude that the verse is addressed to Agni.

When the season is winter, the metre Pankti, the Stoma Tri*n*ava, and the Sâman *S*âkvara, the probability is that the verse is intended for Indra, as dwelling in the air.

When the season is *S*isira (spring), the metre Ati*kkh*andas, the Stoma Trayastri*m*sa, the Sâman Raivata, the verse is supposed to refer to Âditya, as dwelling in the sky. All this is artificial, but interesting, as giving the systematised views of later Brâhmanic theologians.

This gives us the following scheme:—

Agni.	Indra.	Âditya.
Worlds: Earth	Air	Sky
Libations: Morning	Noon	Third
Seasons: Spring	Summer	Rains
(and Autumn)	(and Winter)	(and *S*isira)
Metres: Gâyatrî	Trish*t*ubh	*G*agatî
(and Anush*t*ubh)	(and Pankti)	(and Ati*kkh*andas)
Stomas: Triv*r*it	Pa*n*kadasa	Saptadasa
(and Ekavi*m*sa)	(and Tri*n*ava)	(and Trayastri*m*sa)

AGNI.	INDRA.	ÂDITYA.
Sâmans: Rathantara (and Vairâga)	Brihat (and Sâkvara)	Vairûpa (and Raivata)
Attendants:		
See Nigh. V, 1–3	V, 4–5	V, 6
Women: ibid.	ibid.	ibid.
Work done:		
Carrying oblations	Giving forth of moisture	Taking up moisture
Bringing the gods	Killing Vritra	Holding moisture
Making things visible	Any powerful act	Pre-eminent deeds

Although much in these classifications of Yâska is clearly modern, yet it is not very far removed from the theology of the Brâhmaṇas. Whether rightly or wrongly, we cannot doubt that in Yâska's time, let us say 500 B.C., the Vedic gods were looked upon, as he represents them, as residing in the three worlds, earth, air, and sky; that is to say, they were recognised not only as gods of nature in general, but as active beings, each active in his own special sphere.

Vedic Deities not restricted to one Locality.

But, as I pointed out before, the ancient Hindu theologians knew also that certain gods were not restricted to their own special locality, but that they manifested themselves at the same time on earth, in the air and in the sky. Thus, besides the Agni on earth, who was the principal Agni, they admitted an Agni in the air (madhyama), and another (uttama) in the sky, that is to say, the ordinary fire, the lightning, and the sun. Agni was actually called trimûrdhan, having three heads, possibly occupying three places. The Dawn also was not only a goddess of the sky as a companion of the sun, but likewise a goddess of the air in her connection with the clouds. (Nirukta, ed. Satyavrata, vol. iv, p. 241.)

Gods by Birth and by Creation.

The ancient Hindu theologians knew that some of these deities had been raised to a divine rank (Karmadevatâ*h*)[1], while others were divine by birth (Âgânadevatâ*h*), and they distinguished between gods who were only celebrated by hymns, and others who were both celebrated by hymns and honoured by oblations (havirbhâg and sûktâbhâg). All these may be later theological speculations, but they show nevertheless that these Nairuktas had carefully thought about the true character of their gods, far more than, for instance, the Greeks at the time of Sokrates. This is a lesson which ought not to be neglected. We ought, no doubt, to preserve our own independent judgment, but we ought not to imagine that the ancient authority of the Nairuktas can be lightly set aside in favour of mere a priori theories, however ingeniously invented and learnedly defended.

The Pantheon of the Rig-veda Hymns.

The Pantheon set before us by Yâska may safely be accepted as the Pantheon of the Brâhmanas, though not as that of the ancient poets of the Rig-veda.

It is, in fact, almost impossible to speak of the religion of the poets of the Rig-veda as a whole, or to assert anything general about them; and this for a very good reason. Let us accept the date of 1000 B. C. as the time when the Samhitâ, the

---

[1] See Nirukta, ed. Satyavrata, vol. iv, p. 322, note. Satapatha-br. XIV, 7, 1, 34.

collection of the Vedic hymns, had been completed. Even then there are ever so many periods beyond, during which the Vedic hymns were composed and collected in different families. Attempts have been made by different scholars to establish certain chronological divisions between the ten books of the Rig-veda, but as yet with little success, for we have to contend with two difficulties. The first arises from the individual freedom with which each poet utters his thoughts and feelings, without as yet any restraints, such as arise from tradition or from constituted authorities; the second is due to the long continuance of oral tradition which, though most tenacious of minute niceties, opposes but slight barriers to later changes, and additions or omissions, whenever they seemed useful or desirable. I do not hint at anything like intentional fraud. I only mean that the same free handling which has been observed in our own time among the reciters of Finnish epic poetry, could hardly have been entirely absent in India. That there are modern, middle, and ancient hymns in the Veda, no European scholar would doubt, though few would venture to assign chronological dates to these classes. We know that the ten collections or Ma*n*dalas are claimed as their property by different families. Every one of these families, if settled in neighbouring valleys, would soon develop their own poetry, and we must remember that what seems to us more modern or more ancient, may be no more than the result of that individuality which at all times and in all places distinguishes different poets, different families, different clans, and different colonies.

But though it would be difficult to introduce

chronological order into the collection of hymns which go by the name of the Rig-veda-Samhitâ, there are a few facts, to which I called attention in 1859 in my History of Ancient Sanskrit Literature, and which seem to me to show that the ten books or Mandalas of which this collection consists were collected according to one and the same system. Eight out of the ten Mandalas begin with hymns addressed to Agni, and these hymns, with the exception of the tenth Mandala, are invariably followed by hymns addressed to Indra. Afterwards follow hymns to the Visve Devas, and other gods, who are not, however, arranged according to one and the same system. It is not likely that the hymns addressed to Agni and Indra would have occupied this prominent place in every one of these eight Mandalas, unless there had been an understanding between the collectors. Secondly, we find the so-called Âprî hymns in seven of the ten Mandalas, which proves that each of the principal Vedic families for whom these Mandalas were collected thought it necessary to possess such a hymn in their own private collection. All these hymns are made after one and the same pattern, and this proves again that the compilers of the Mandalas worked according to a common plan.

Thirdly, it is easy to see from the Anukramanikâ or Index, that the succession of hymns in each of the Anuvâkas or sections of the Mandalas follow each other according to the number of their verses. This is again a principle followed by the compilers of each Mandala, and requires the admission of an understanding between them. It is true that this numerical principle is often violated in the collection of the Rig-veda as we possess it, but the principle itself is so clearly established that scholars have felt justified in rearranging the order of the hymns, and removing later additions by simply carrying out the fundamental principle, such as it must have been conceived originally by all the collectors of the ten Ma*n*dalas, namely, to arrange the hymns in each Anuvâka according to the decreasing number of their verses. There is one more point to which I called attention many years ago, and which shows in the clearest way that at the time when the Pada text of the hymns was constituted the Sa*m*hitâ text existed in its completeness. In that text the iterata in the hymns are not repeated, but are left out (galita), and this according to special rules as detailed in the Galita-pradîpa. From this we learn two things, first, that the Sa*m*hitâ was considered at the time as one corpus of Vedic poetry, and secondly that these verbatim iterata affected alike all the Ma*n*dalas of the Sa*m*hitâ, and therefore presupposed the existence of a recognised Sa*m*hitâ text.

Yâska's Pantheon.

Though we may accept Yâska's Pantheon, not only for his own time, but for the time of the Brâhma*n*as also, we cannot accept it for the hymns of the Rig-veda, still less for that period which preceded our hymns, and which we may partially reconstruct from what we know of the gods of the Indo-Iranic and of the Aryan periods. We saw that according to Yâska the three principal deities were Agni, Indra, and Âditya, or as they are sometimes called, Rv. I, 158, 1, Agni, Vâta, and Sûrya, the unseen powers active in light, in air, and the highest sky.

Earlier and Later Gods.

But in the hymns of the Rig-veda we can still discover clear traces of a more ancient supreme deity, namely Dyaus, whom Yâska does not even mention as a separate god, but whose existence is proved by several hymns of the Rig-veda, and by the evidence of Greek, Latin, and Germanic mythology. Perhaps it is hardly fair to charge Yâska with ignorance of this god, for he mentions him at least in the compound names of the deity Dyâvâ-prithivyau, Heaven and Earth, Dyâvâ-bhûmî, the same, and Dyunisau, day and night. It is wrong to say that the Anukramanî passes him by; for he is mentioned there once at least as the optional deity of one verse, I, 94, 16, by the side of Agni, with Mitrâ-Varunau, Aditi, Sindhu, and Prithivî; and these gods, together with Dyu (or Agni), are said to form six gods.

The Reign of Dyaus.

In the hymns of the Rig-veda, however, we can clearly distinguish a period during which Agni or Indra were not yet the principal or representative deities, but when such gods as Dyu (nom. Dyaus) and Varuna occupied a far more important place. That this period was antecedent to the Agni and Indra period we may, I think, conclude from the fact that the names of neither Agni nor Indra, as gods, can be discovered in the mythology of other Aryan nations, while Dyu has retained his place in Greek, Roman, and Teutonic mythology, and Varuna has left clear traces of himself in Persia and Greece. Dyu has long been represented as the supreme god of the Âryas, and I know of no real argument why he should not. The god of the sky is, according to his very nature, supreme, and is so, as a matter of fact, in most of the ancient religions. He must certainly have existed before the separation of the South-Eastern and North-Western branches of the Aryan family, because he exists both in Sanskrit and Greek, and his former superiority over Indra is recognised even in certain of the hymns of the Rig-veda[1]. Besides, if he was not supreme among the other gods, who was?

Dyâvâ-p*r*ithivî.

I have so often discussed the origin and history of this the most ancient of Aryan gods, Dyaush-pitâ(r), Zeus patêr, Ju-piter (and Týr)[2], that I need not in this place give more than the salient facts.

In India Dyu, as a masculine deity, is wellnigh forgotten, while in ordinary Sanskrit Dyu has become an appellative, is a feminine, and means sky. For a long time dyu in the Veda also was translated throughout by sky or day, and it was supposed that Dyu hardly deserved a place of his own among the Vedic deities. I believe it is true that in the Veda Dyu is not one of the havirbhâ*g*, sacrifice-receiving deities. But though he receives no special oblations, he receives praise (stomabhâ*g*), and the very highest that could be bestowed on any god. Nor is it quite true that he belongs to a very ancient period only. At all events in the Atharva-veda, which is generally considered as far more modern than the Rig-veda,

---

[1] Science of Language, vol. ii, p. 542.
[2] Ibid. (1891), vol. ii, p. 537.

Dyu occurs, and is evidently a familiar and popular deity. Thus we read Ath. VI, 4, 3, in a hymn to various deities: Urushyā́ na uru*g*mann áprayu*kkh*an Dyaúshpítar yāváya du*kkh*únâ yā́, 'Protect us, Wide-Ranger, without fail, Heaven-father, remove all disasters.'

I had pointed out many years ago what seemed to me a decisive fact, that when Dyu occurs in the Rig-veda together with other gods, he generally occupies the first place. It should also be remembered that he is represented as the father and grandfather of other gods, even of Indra, who afterwards supplanted his father, so that the father had to bow before his son.

Most frequently, however, Dyu is connected with P*r*ithivi, earth, and, although Heaven and Earth form a divine Dvandva or pair, Dyu is invoked separately also by the side of P*r*ithivi, e.g. VI, 20, 2: Námo Divé náma*h* p*r*ithivyái náma óshadhíbhya*h*, 'Reverence to Dyu, reverence to the earth, reverence to the plants.' Here, no doubt, it might be said that Dyu was meant for the sky, not yet personified, and dyu certainly occurs now and then with this purely local meaning, but in most cases where heaven and earth are similarly invoked, Dyu has clearly a personal and a masculine character. For instance, I, 32, 4: Divé *k*a vi*s*vávedase p*r*ithivyaí *k*a akaram náma*h*, 'To the all-knowing Dyu and to the Earth have I paid adoration.'

Here the adjective vi*s*vávedase shows that Dyu is taken as a deity, united with, yet independent of, the Earth; just as in other cases the addition of an adjective in the feminine gender forces us to take dyu as a feminine and as an appellative, e.g. VI, 6, 3,

Yó na*h* Soma abhidā́sati sánābhir yá*s* *k*a níshtya*h*
Ápa tásya bálam tira mahíva dyaúr vadha tmánā,
'O Soma! whoever attacks us, a relation or a stranger, draw thou away his strength, strike him thyself. like the great sky!' Here, no doubt, we expect Dyu as a masculine, and both Ludwig and Griffith translate 'like the mighty Dyaus.' But mahî can only be a feminine, and is so intimately connected with dyaus that there is no excuse for changing the text. The true relation between Dyu and Prithivî is seen in passages like IX, 10, 12, Rv. I, 164, 33:—

Dyaúr na*h* pitā́ *g*anitā́, nā́bhir átra,
Bándhur no mātā́ p*r*ithivī́ mahī́yám.

'Dyu is the father who begat us, our origin is there, this great Earth is our parent mother.'

In the Rig-veda, where Dyâvâ-prithivî are often celebrated together, there is no hymn addressed to Dyu singly, though there is to P*r*ithivî (V, 84). In the verses addressed to Dyâvâ-p*r*ithivî or to Dyâvâ (dual)[1] and P*r*ithivî (dual), it is difficult to say why Dyu was changed to Dyâvâ, while it remained unchanged in dyunis̀au. Dyâvâ cannot be a feminine formed of Dyu like Ushasâ of Ushas, and in the compound Dyâvâ-p*r*ithivî it certainly represents the sky as a male deity and in a dual form. (See Pâ*n*. VI, 3, 29.) In the hymns addressed to Dyâvâ-p*r*ithivî (also Rodasi), Dyu is always spoken of as the father, P*r*ithivî as the mother, according to a world-wide metaphor which represents heaven and earth as the parents of the human race (Rv. I, 159, 2).

---

[1] This Dyâvâ has to be taken as originally a dual of dyu, like Agni-shomau, Sûryâ-mâsâ, &c. In the gen., however, the form Divas-p*r*ithivyo*h* is found (Pâ*n*. VI. 3, 30).

But they are likewise, like Zeus and Hêre, looked upon as brother and sister (*gámî sáyonî*, Rv. I, 159, 4). A son is mentioned of Heaven and Earth who can hardly be any one but Sûrya or Agni, the sun, said to be moving along between them (I, 161, 1). Still this is not quite clear, particularly as the same son is soon after said to have himself shaped heaven and earth (I, 160, 3), while in other places Indra is called the son of Dyu. Such incongruities, however, do not disturb the Vedic *Ri*shis, on the contrary, they delight in them. The story of the marriage union and of the separation of Heaven and Earth with all its consequences is so widely spread, that the late Professor Munro might well have said: 'From the Veda to the Pervigilium Veneris poets and philosophers have loved to celebrate this union of ether and earth, ether as father descending in showers into the lap of mother earth.'

Though Dyu and P*ri*thivî together are addressed as all-powerful and all-embracing, yet in certain places they seem subject to other gods. They are even said to obey the law of Mitra (IV, 56, 7), and the command of Varu*n*a (VI, 76, 1).

The former supreme position of Dyu has indeed faded away almost entirely from the memory of many of the Vedic poets, yet there are passages which leave no doubt that there was a time, less removed from the Aryan Separation than the Veda, when Dyu was supreme, was before Indra, was greater than Indra, was in fact like Zeus, the lord of gods and men. Thus we read in a hymn addressed to Indra (Rv. IV, 17, 4): 'Dyu, thy father, was reputed strong, the maker of Indra was mighty in his works; he who begat the heavenly Indra, armed with the thunderbolt, who, like the earth, is immovable from his seat.' This, considering the whole tenor of the hymn, which is a panegyric of Indra's power, would seem to show that the poet considered the greatness of Dyu as a matter of the past. And this appears even more clearly from ver. 12, where the poet says: 'How much does Indra care for his mother, or for the father that begat him?' Nay, in I, 131, 1, we read: 'Before Indra the divine Dyu (masc.) bowed, before Indra bowed the great Earth.' And in I, 61, 9, it is said that the greatness of Indra exceeded heaven (dyaus), earth, and sky, while in X, 54, 3, the poet is so overwhelmed by Indra's greatness that he exclaims[1]: 'What poets living before us have reached the end of all thy greatness? for thou hast indeed begotten thy father and thy mother together from thy own body!' This gives an idea of the floating character of Vedic mythology, when the son may be the father of his parents, nay the lover of his daughters, according as the relations between the phenomena, originally signified by their mythological names, change and present themselves under different aspects to the minds of their worshippers.

Passages like these leave hardly any doubt that there was a time when among the Âryas of India as among the Âryas of Greece, Dyu was supreme among the gods, while such epithets as IV, 17, 13, vibhañganúh and asániman, the destroyer who wields the thunderbolt, place the old Dyu before our eyes as a fighting god, and as a wielder of the thunderbolt like Indra and like Zeus.

---

[1] M. M., India, p. 161.

I need not go further into the evidence which supports the original character which I ascribe to Dyu in the ancient, and in the pre-Vedic times of India. I may refer to my former contributions [1] to this, the most important chapter of Comparative Mythology. I believe that the objections which were once raised against the equation of Dyaus and Zeus, on the ground that Dyaus was simply a name of the sky, have now been surrendered. Even the most stubborn opponents of all attempts at tracing Greek and Indian gods back to a common source seem to have yielded an unwilling assent to the relationship between the Greek $Ζεὺς\ πατήρ$, the Vedic Dyaush-pitar, the Latin Jupiter, and the Teutonic Týr. But they do not seem to have perceived that in making this concession they have really conceded everything, or at all events the fundamental principle of scientific mythology. If it is once admitted that the Supreme God of the ancient world was known under one and the same name before the ancestors of Hindus, Greeks, Romans, and Germans became permanently separated, and that the ancient Aryan name of that deity has survived in the most ancient literary relics of every one of these nations, it would surely seem to follow that this could not have been the only name which thus survived. If the word for ten is the same in the principal Aryan languages, should we not be surprised to find that all the other numerals were different? If the stem of the pronoun of the first person was identical in Sanskrit and Greek, should we not be surprised if the second person showed

---

[1] 'Lesson of Jupiter,' Nineteenth Century, Oct., 1885.

no similarity whatever? It is true that in Comparative Mythology we must not expect to discover more than the original starting-points from which two or more streams of mythological fancy took their beginning. We must be satisfied if the root is the same, however much the derivation suffixes may differ, for we know how they vary in Greek itself. When we have once discovered the common starting-point, as in the case of Dyaush-pitar and Ζεὺς πατήρ, we ought to be satisfied. What has grown up afterwards on Greek soil or on Indian soil can hardly be expected to be found in the hymns of the Veda; the utmost we can expect is that these parallel developments may sometimes help to explain one another.

Parallel Development. Ζεὺς Γελέων.

We have, for instance, in Greek inscriptions, a Ζεὺς Γελέων[1]. What can this γελέων mean? Benfey has shown that γελεῖν, which Hesychius explains by λάμπειν, was connected with Sk. *gval*, to flame, and likewise the accusative γέλαν, which Hesychius explains by αὐγὴν ἡλίου. From the same root comes of course the Gr. γελᾶν in the sense of laughing, and this laughing must have meant originally beaming. The close connection between these two verbs, beaming and laughing, is brought out very clearly in the Vedic expression (II, 4, 6): Dyáuh iva smáyamánah nábhobhih. Here Agni is compared with Dyu, the sky, when laughing in the clouds, this laughing in the clouds being evidently

---

[1] Cf. M. H. E. Meier, Die Demen von Attica, nach Inschriften von Ludwig Ross, 1846; Benfey, Nachrichten der K. Gesellschaft zu Göttingen, Jan. 17, 1877.

meant for lightning[1], as Benfey has proved in one of his most ingenious articles on *gaghghatîs* (for *y*akshatîs, from *has*, to laugh)[2]. We read, Rv. I, 168, 8, áva smayanta vidyúta*h* p*r*ithivyā́m, 'The lightnings laughed down on the earth:' and in I, 79, 2, *s*ivā́bhi*h* nā́ smā́yamā́nā̂bhi*h* ā́ agât pátanti míha*h* stanáyanti abhrā́, 'He came with the smiling (lightnings, fem.), the rain-drops fall, the clouds thunder.'

All this shows that in India at all events lightning was sometimes conceived as laughing, and that therefore the god who held the thunderbolt (Dyáus asánimân) might be conceived as the laughing Dyaus. If then the Greek Ζεὺς Γελέων is, according to Hesychius, the beaming Zeus, we may carry the interpretation a step further and explain the beaming as lightning, and the Ζεὺς Γελέων as Ζεὺς τερπικέραυνος or κεραυνοφαής. This peculiar development of Dyaus and Zeus probably took place independently in India and Greece, still the tendency was due to a common impulse carried away from the common Aryan home.

Limits of Mythological Comparisons.

I should always look upon such a coincidence as between the smiling Dyaus and the Zeus Geleôn as really more than we have any right to expect, and it is due to repeated attempts to discover more and more of such very minute coincidences between Vedic and Greek gods that many scholars have withheld their assent even to the far more important fundamental,

---

[1] Senart, La Légende du Buddha, pp. 323-4.
[2] Nachrichten der K. Gesellschaft zu Göttingen, June 28, 1876.

but naturally more general similarities which have been pointed out by Vedic scholars. In comparative mythology also there are some things which are too good to be true. We do not expect myths such as we meet with in the Purâṅas to have left traces in Greek and Latin, neither should we expect later Greek myths, such as, for instance, the peacock of Juno, to find their counterparts in the Veda. It is evident that both in India and in Greece many myths have sprung up after the Aryan Separation, and any comparison between them would either be an anachronism, or lead us from a genealogical to a purely analogical or psychological study of mythology. When we have discovered in Varuṅa and Ouranos the original idea of the covering sky, we have done enough. When we have discovered in the Haritas and Charites the representatives of the brightness of the morning sun, we need go no further. We shall never find the Charites as horses in Homer, nor the Haritas as the Graces in the Veda. If we find in the Veda the seven Haritas assuming a feminine character as maidens or sisters, we have really gained more than we had any right to expect. There is no Svârâ in the Veda, no βοῶπις πότνια ῞Ηρη, no cow-eyed wife of Dyaus. All we can say is that Hêre presupposed Svârâ, the heavenly, whether recognised as the wife of the sky or not. The germ was in the Veda, but not the flower which grew up under the sky of Greece. Bharaṅyu in the Veda is not what Phorôneus is in Greece; all we can say is that they started from the same root, bhar, here used in the sense of bearing or being borne along, and applied in both countries to the nimble and swiftly-moving fire. So far they had a common origin and growth, but no further. So far they prove the common beginnings of an Aryan mythology before the Aryan Separation. Everything else beyond this should be gratefully accepted whenever it exists, but should not be postulated as a matter of right.

Manifold Character of the Ancient Gods.

We must also bear in mind that in the beginning, before a name grew into the name of a definite deity, it had often been used in a more general and less definite sense. Dyaus, before it became the name of a god, meant sky, but before it meant sky it probably had the even more general meaning of light. And even after Dyaus had become the name of an active and personal power, it or he might be conceived in many various ways.

Dyaus might be conceived as the sublime brightness on high (hoc sublime candens), and share in the character of serenity, sublimity, and infinity, which distinguish the Greek Zeus in his highest conception. But the sky might also be adored as the giver of rain, as the light of the morning, as the dispeller of darkness, as fighting the night, as hurling the lightning, as tearing the clouds; nay, whatever work can be ascribed to the sun or the moon, to the storms and the seasons, may all directly or indirectly be referred to the representative of the sky, that is, to Dyaus. In India the dramatic character of Dyaus had almost passed away before the hymns of the Veda in which he is mentioned were composed. We only catch some faint reminiscences of his former greatness, but most of the acts that might be ascribed to him, have been transferred to other deities, such as Indra, Mitra, Varuna, Vish*n*u, Pûshan, &c.

In Greece Zeus stands before us not only as the supreme deity, the father of gods and men, but every physical event that can be more or less distantly referred to the sky, is represented as coming within the sphere of his activity. His brothers, Poseidon and Hades, have long been recognised as merely localised repetitions of Zeus, as Ζηνοποσειδῶν and Ζεὺς καταχθόνιος or Ζεὺς ἄλλος. And as Zeus is not only the god of all the Hellenes (Pan-Hellenic), but enjoyed also special local worship in ever so many parts of the country, in hills and valleys, near rivers or on the sea-shore, his character took every kind of local colouring, nay he became responsible for many of the adventures that happened in towns and colonies supposed to be under his special protection. Many of these have a character of historical reality, which ought at once to discourage any attempt at mythological analysis.

One side in the character of Zeus is totally absent in the Veda. We can match his physical qualities in these ancient hymns, we may easily translate some of his epithets into Sanskrit, such as ὑέτιος, Jupiter pluvius, ὄμβριος, sender of rain, τροφώνιος, nourisher, κελαινεφής, wrapped in dark clouds, κεραύνιος, wielding the thunder, νεφεληγερέτης, cloud-gatherer, αἰγίοχος, Aigis-bearing and storm-sending, εὐήνεμος, serene. But we should look in vain for the moral qualities of Zeus, as expressed in such epithets as πίστιος, Jupiter Fidius, ὅρκιος, protector of oaths, ξένιος, protector of the rights of hospitality. Ideas such as that of Mêtis, wisdom, being the first wife of the god of heaven, or of Themis, Law, acting as his assistant, or of Dike, Justice, being his daughter, were foreign to the *Ri*shis in their praises of Dyaus.

Hêre.

The recognised wife of Zeus in Homer is Hêre, according to Greek mythology, his sister. Considering the character of her husband she could hardly be anything but either the sky, conceived as a woman, and in that case often specialised as the Dawn, or even the Earth.

Her name of Hêre, however, leaves little doubt on this point. It is true that it has been connected with ἔρα, the earth, but there would be both phonetic and material difficulties in the way. She is conceived as sitting on a golden throne (χρυσόθρονος), as mother of the Charites, which points to a celestial rather than to a terrestrial being. It is natural therefore to look upon Ἥρη as representing a Sanskrit *Svârâ, as a feminine of svar, the sun and the bright sky.

Originally she might have been the bright air between sky and earth, a kind of antarikshaprâḥ, or sky-pervading goddess, an epithet applied in the Veda to Urvaśî (X, 95, 17), as a well-known representative of the dawn.

Much might be said, however, for another etymology from the root vas, to shine. From this we have in Greek ἔαρ (vasar), and ἦρ, spring, and in her marriage[1] with Zeus (the ἱερὸς γάμος) she distinctly shows the character of a vernal goddess. The fact also that Zeus is first united with her, after assuming the form of a cuckoo, might be interpreted in favour of a spring goddess[2]. On the other hand, the frequent quarrels between Zeus and

---

[1] Il. xiv, 152 seq. [2] Hesiod, Op. et Dies, 486.

Hêre find a better explanation in the storms in which the god of the highest heaven seems to be fighting with the clouds. Hêre, suspended in the sky by Zeus with her hands tied by golden fetters and her feet weighted with anvils, would seem to be a more appropriate image for a cloud, than for a vernal deity or for the earth. Typhâon, also, the child which she bore by herself, could only have been meant for a hurricane, the offspring of the cloudy atmosphere which is near ($ὁμόθρονος$) to the brilliant sky, but submissive to Zeus. We must be satisfied with these general outlines of Hêre. It is the identity of the germ which gives us the conviction that the common beginning of Greek and Vedic mythology is a historical fact, and it is this historical fact which is of supreme importance to the student of Comparative Mythology, as the beginning of the history of the human mind. If we are able to discover more far-reaching similarities or identities, as Dyaush-pitar and Jupiter, as sárdho márutas and çerfo Martio [1], dâtâro vasûnâm = $δωτῆρες ἐάων$, we ought to be thankful, but we ought never to forget that our real object is to make the foundation sure, to establish the fact of a common beginning of mythology, and to fix that beginning as antecedent to the Aryan Separation. The fact therefore that Hêre does not exist in the Veda as a goddess called Svârâ, ought to be no disappointment, particularly if we see how her place is occupied there by other names such as Aditi or Ushas or Urvasî, who is called rágasa*h* vimânî, traversing the clouds, like Hêre traversing the sky on her chariot prepared by

---

[1] S. B. E., vol. xxxii, p. xxv.

Hêbe and by the Horae. The later development of Hêre, as protectress of marriage, as assisting with Eileithyia at the birth of children, as representing the dignity of married womanhood, all this does not and could not exist in the Veda. Still, if the oak images of Hêre in the grove of Alalkomenae, and the wooden statues of Smilis could grow into the Juno Ludovisi, why should not a cloud or air goddess of India, whether called Svârâ or Urvasî or any other such name, have supplied the first germs from which the Βοῶπις πότνια Ἥρη, in all her majesty, descended?

Európe.

Among the many epithets of Hêre there is one that sheds more light on her character. If we are right in supposing that names beginning with εὐρυ, wide, are generally names of sun-gods or dawn-goddesses, and if in several of the heroines carried off by Zeus, we have recognised ancient representatives of the dawn, we can hardly be wrong in taking Zeus Euryopa, the wide-seeing Zeus, for Zeus in his solar character, and if so, then Európe, the wide-seeing, or wide-shining, carried off by Zeus in the shape of a white bull, as a slightly disguised dawn-goddess. But if that is admitted, it becomes important to observe that Hêre also is called Eurôpia, and thus betrays her character as originally a matutinal apparition, though afterwards extending her sway through the air (antarikshaprâ) over heaven and earth. If some scholars maintain that none of these arguments is clinching, and that a mere incredulous smile can dispose of them all, have they never thought what an extraordinary state of things it would be if all these coincidences were the result of mere accident? There was a time when in geology Ammonites and similar petrifactions were treated as mere lusus naturae, but that time is over, and ought to have been over long ago in mythology also. The organic nature of myths ought to be recognised once for all, and if we cannot as yet discover the original life in all myths, as little as in all geological petrifactions, the general principle ought to remain unshaken that there is nothing in mythology that had not originally a meaning, a purpose, an organic, that is a rational structure.

Kronos.

Kronos, who was the father of Zeus, of Hêre, Hestia, Dêmêter, Hades, and Poseidon, is unknown in India. Even in Greece he was a god without a history, and I still, with Welcker, hold it to be most likely that he was invented ex post, in order to account for the name of the Κρονίωνες or the Κρονίδαι. Κρόνος may, whatever may be said to the contrary, stand dialectically for χρόνος, time, and as aeviternus, from aevum, time, came to mean aeternus, eternal, κρόνιος, too, may have been a name of the eternal gods, οἱ ἀεὶ ἐόντες, and when no longer understood may have suggested a Κρόνος, as the father of the Κρονίωνες, as Οὐρανός was the father of the Οὐρανίωνες. This, of course, may be called a mere hypothesis, but what else could it be? Only, until a better hypothesis can be framed, it may well be allowed to hold the ground.

Akmon.

Though in the Veda we hear neither of a father or grandfather of Dyaus, corresponding to Kronos or

Ouranos, for Varuna is not called the father of Dyaus, it may be that the language of the Veda and Avesta can help us to explain the name of one who, according to Eustathius, was the father of Ouranos, nay, who was also called the father of Kronos[1]. This is Akmon, which in Greek means meteoric stone, thunderbolt and anvil. But how could Akmon in any of these senses be called the father of Ouranos? The riddle, like many other mythological riddles, has been solved by etymology. Akmon is clearly the Vedic asman, which means stone, and afterwards thunderbolt, but also heaven, so that its dual is actually used in the sense of heaven and earth (Rv. II, 12, 3)[2]. It is clear therefore that the sky had once been conceived as a stone vault, and this is confirmed by the fact that in the Avesta also asman means sky, and has remained the name of sky to the present day in the modern Persian word for sky, which is âsmân.

From asman in the sense of sky, or from ἄκμων in the same sense, was derived Ἀκμονίδαι, according to Hesychius, another name for Οὐρανίδαι. As the Ouranidae required an Ouranos, the Kronidae a Kronos, and, as we are told, the Âdityas an Aditi, the Akmonidae required a personified Akmon, not in the sense of either stone, thunderbolt, or anvil, but

---

[1] Eust. Comm. 1154, 23; 1150, 59. Roth, in Z. D. M. G. ii, p. 44.

[2] Yáḥ ásmanoḥ antáḥ agním gagâna, 'He who produced Agni from between the two asmans.' We cannot translate this by 'he who produced fire from between two flints,' because it occurs among the heroic achievements of Indra, such as killing the serpent Agni, and driving the cows out of the cave of Vala, while striking sparks out of a flint is hardly an heroic achievement for a god.

in the sense of οὐρανός, sky, and therefore, like Ouranos, sometimes represented as a son of Gaia.

In Sanskrit the sun also is conceived as a stone, for instance in the Sat.-br. IX, 2, 3, 14, asau vâ âdityo ̓smâ prismi/, 'That sun is a dazzling stone.'

It is in this way that names of Greek gods, such as Zeus, Hêre, or Akmon, can be rendered intelligible, whether their prototypes in Sanskrit had assumed a personal mythological character, as in the case of Zeus, or whether they existed in the shape of nouns only, but of nouns intelligible in their etymological structure, and sometimes in the Veda still used in their original meaning.

When we are dealing with the poetical creations of an age beyond the beginnings of history, we must not expect absolute certainty, we must be satisfied with probability. Who was present at the naming of Kronos, of Zeus, or Hêre? Still we may be satisfied of one thing, that every one of the names of the Aryan gods had a beginning, had a reason, or, what is the same thing, an etymology. If such a reason can be discovered we should not think that it must be wrong because it is not absolutely convincing, not altogether beyond the reach of doubt. That some rays of light have fallen from the Veda to light up the dark recesses of Greek mythology, no one who has eyes to see can have failed to see. Several comparisons of Vedic and Greek deities which at first seemed incredible have year after year become more and more evident. Scepticism is most useful in all scientific researches, but scepticism may become as pernicious to the progress of learning as dogmatism, if at the very beginning of new inquiries it demands the same degree of certainty which can only be the result of a long accumulation of evidence. I can still remember the time when it was stoutly denied by many classical scholars that the language of India could claim any relationship with the classical languages, Greek and Latin. Who doubts it now? If a comparison of Indian and Greek deities was treated, nay is still treated, with flippant contempt by certain scholars, is that any reason why we should not persevere? Is it likely that a mine which has yielded what even the most ignorant must accept as sterling gold, should yield nothing else, if only we persevere, undaunted by disappointments, undismayed by gibes and jeers?

Kronos.

If there is another explanation of Kronos which would make of him a primary, not a merely secondary deity, why should we not examine it dispassionately, and if it seems preferable, accept it? I do not look upon Welcker as infallible, still less upon myself. All I ask for is a certain amount of seriousness and scientific temper.

It has been maintained by several scholars, and apparently approved by Curtius, whom in matters of Greek scholarship I still venture to consider as an authority, that Kronos may be connected with κραίνω (κραιαίνω), to perform. G. Hermann for the same reason had rendered Kronos by Perficus. This κραίνω (κράντωρ) has been connected with the Sanskrit k*ri* (k*ri-n*omi, karman), and this k*ri* has in Sanskrit already assumed the general meaning of to make, to do. In this way Kronos would mean the maker, possibly the creator of the world. Now I ask, first of all, is Kronos ever represented as the maker or creator of the world; I might even go on to ask, was any one of the Greek gods originally conceived in that character? Others have pointed to the Vedic krâna, strong, as the nearest approach to Kronos. There would be no phonetic difficulty, but is Kronos the strong god in any sense of the word?

Besides, roots of such faded meaning as kri, to make, may always be accepted as belonging to a secondary phase of thought. We know that even in Hebrew, barâ, to create, meant originally to cut, to hew, to shape, and this, I should think, was also the original meaning of kar. In some forms, such as the aor. askrita, we can clearly see that kar was originally skar¹, and corresponds to Greek κείρω for σκείρω, Zend kar. In Latin we find cul-ter, knife, but scarifico, to scrape, and if curtus, short, and scortum, hide, are referred to krit, to cut, rather than to kri, we must remember that krit itself is only a differentiated form of kri. And here we see the natural development of thought, beginning with cutting, shearing, scraping, and tanning a hide (cf. gerben), and ending with preparing, making, and creating. The sense of cutting and scraping appears again in Sk. kritti, hide, in cortex, bark, &c.

For the same reason which makes me hesitate to see in Kronos a mere maker or even creator, I should feel most unwilling to see in Cerus manus, a mere bonus creator, or to admit that Ceres was a creando dicta. To make and to create are far too abstract, nay too metaphysical ideas to find a legitimate place in the mythopœic age, which lived on far more

---

¹ Curtius, Grundzüge, p. 429.

palpable and substantial ideas than those of making or creating.

These are my reasons why I am unwilling to see in Kronos a creator, but why I still adhere to Welcker's view that Kronos was not a primary but a secondary deity, formed to account for the Κρόνιοι or Κρονίωνες or Κρονίδαι, while I see in Κρόνος a dialectic variety of χρόνος, and in χρόνος a word possibly connected with kshana, a moment (καιρός), afterwards time in general, by the ordinary transition from the special to the general, from a time to the time, and all time.

Of course, if certain scholars say that all this is pure rationalism, and that we must not attempt to rationalise mythology, it is impossible to rationalise or to reason with them.

What argument, what real reason has ever been brought forward against Zeus as the husband of Dêmêter (who shares with Hêre the name of Europe) being Dyaus, the bright sky, fertilising the earth, and begetting of her that young vegetation, that (κόρη) which returns every spring to her mother, and every winter is carried away by the unseen god of the lower world? Was not the same story told of Dêmêter and Jāson (vivasvân), only that their child was called Ploutos, or wealth? It was surely no very great stretch of poetical fancy if that young vegetation was called Kore, the child[1], and was represented as carried off in winter by Hades, the invisible, the god of the subterraneous regions. I do not say that this is perfectly certain, but it is

---

[1] See Mannhardt, on the parallelism between child and corn, Quellen, p. 307 and chapter vi, Kind und Korn, p. 350 seq.

an interpretation more or less remembered by the Greeks themselves, and till a better one can be discovered, it may teach us at all events that the Greeks also were fully aware that behind their mythological stories there must be something real, something tangible, something intelligible. The myth of Dêmêter and Kore is perfectly intelligible to any one who has a feeling for poetry. It is poetry which appeals even to us when in the first warm days of spring we watch the marvellous return of our favourite flowers, and ask ourselves, as we see them breaking forth from the hard soil or from the dark dry branches of our shrubs and trees, where they can have been hidden, unseen by mortal eyes. Nor is the sadness and the wailing of Dêmêter beyond our sympathy when day after day the flowers and leaves wither and fall, and the trees stand again before us dead and dark, and we ask ourselves whether we shall live to see them again. We may know where the germs of a new life, of a new beautiful spring are hiding, but can we say more than that they are in invisible hands, or in the hands of Hades, the invisible, and that the child or the spring will return whenever Dêmêter or the earth is embraced by Zeus, the brightness of the sky? Zeus, as united with Hêre, with Dêmêter and with many other goddesses and heroines, is always the same Zeus, and in the background we may always discover the same Dyaus.

The Wives of Zeus. 1. Eurynome.

Let us examine some of these wives of Zeus. When Zeus is called the husband of Eurynome, the very name of Eurynome (beginning with εὐρύ, Sk. uru, wide) suggests her meaning as the Dawn. She is said to have been an old goddess who had ruled on Olympos before Kronos and Rhea [1]. If she is said to have become by Zeus the mother of the Charites, what is that again but the often repeated story of Dyaus, as the lover of Ushas, the dawn, surrounded or carried along by the Haritas, the bright rays or horses of the morning sun? If she, as Basileia, is called the wife of Hyperion and mother of Hêlios and Selêne (Diod. iii, 57), can we doubt of her original character?

2. Zeus, Lêto and Apollon and Artemis.

Next, if Zeus with Lêto begets Apollon and Artemis, why should we doubt that Lêto was the night, from λανθάνειν, latere [2], the sister of Asteria, the starry sky, or that Dêlos, the birthplace of Apollon, was the bright East, while Ortygia, the birthplace of Artemis, is explained by the Sanskrit vartikâ, the quail, i. e. the returning morn or spring [3]?

---

[1] Of course all these myths sprang up independently, not one from the other, and were afterwards arranged genealogically and chronologically. When Kronos was said to be the husband of Rhea, or Rheia, Rhoia was not yet the Magna Mater, nor Hekate. She probably was nothing but an earth-goddess, and her name might well be accepted as corresponding to urvî, the broad, a Vedic name for the Earth. Urvî stands for *varvî (cf. variyasi), and the initial e of *ἐρεια is lost in Greek, see Lobeck, De prosthesi et aphaeresi vocalis e, Pathologia I, p. 46. When afterwards Rhea became mixed up with Dêmêter, with Hekate and with the Magna Mater and Kybele it is difficult, if not impossible, to follow her development. She becomes an Asiatic rather than a Greek goddess, and few traces, beyond her name, are left of her Aryan origin.

[2] See the argument elaborated by Fay, l. c., p. 4, note.

[3] Science of Language, ii, 626.

In the Veda this Vartikâ is represented as swallowed by a wolf, but delivered from his mouth by the Asvins, the gods of the early morning. What the meaning of such a myth was, is surely not difficult to see, if we have once learnt that the chief subjects of ancient mythological language were taken from the changes of day and night, of light and darkness, of spring and winter. It may be quite true that such words as Lêto and Latona, as derived from λαθεῖν and latere, are not in accordance with the phonetic rules which determine the formation of appellative nouns. It would indeed be extraordinary if they were, and if in mythology alone proper names were free from all the accidents which befall them everywhere else. Besides, the principal strength of our arguments in support of these comparisons lies in the facts, while the names supply us with confirmatory evidence only, and would leave the facts to speak for themselves, even if no linguistic evidence were forthcoming in support of them. We are never surprised if we see the gods called the children of Zeus, the god of the sky, and if these children must have mothers, what is more natural than that they should be goddesses or representatives of the earth, or of the dawn, or of the air?

3. Zeus, Lêda, Helena.

I therefore have no hesitation in seeing in the heroine called Lêda also another representative of the first grey dawn, the Vedic Saraṇyû. If Zeus was supposed to have approached her in the shape of a swan, we know that in the Veda, as well as in the later mythological language of India, haṃsa, swan, was a well-known representative of the sun. If her sons are the twins, the Dioskouroi, i. e. the Aśvins, day and night, her daughter, Helena, can be nothing but the beautiful morning, the offspring of the dark twilight. I do not attempt at present any etymological explanation of Kastor and Polydeukes, but I am as strongly convinced as ever that in the name of Helena we have a remnant of the Vedic Saramâ, a near relation of Saraṇyû. She is represented as a dog, as Saraṇyû is represented as a horse, and if the Haritas, the horses of the sun, became Charis (Aphrodite) and the Charites, why should not Saramâ, the dog, have become Helena? If we read that Saramâ was the first to discover the cattle in the cave (the night), which Indra breaks open every morning, what can she be in the ancient mythological phraseology of India, if not the morning light? I am fully aware that the change of m into n in the middle of a word is conditioned, as in $\beta a \acute{\iota} \nu \omega$ = gamya, &c., by a following y. But I hold that in a proper name such an irregularity as n for m is admissible. Besides we should not forget that the root sar is used with special reference to the rays of light (Rv. V, 1, 1), and that derivative suffixes vary, most of all in Greek, so that out of many derivatives of the root sar, Saraṇâ would have been quite as possible a form as Saramâ or Saraṇyû (ushṇa = ushma, fornus = formus). But the real question is this. We have in the Veda a Saramâ who is carried off by the Paṇis, but is restored to her rightful liege; and we have in Greece a Helena who is carried off by Paris, but restored in the end to her rightful husband. The same person is in the Veda in close relation with twins; Saramâ as mother of the Sârameyau, Helena as sister of the Dioskouroi. In the Gṛihya-sutras of Pâraskara,

I, 16, 24, we actually read of twin brothers of Saramâ, viz. Syâma-Sabalau. Is it likely then that these two persons should bear a name, the same in every vowel and consonant except the m, which ought not to appear as n in Greek, except when final (tam = τον), or when followed by y (gamyate = βαίνω)? No doubt it should have been Ἐλέμη, not Ἑλένη, though it might surely have been in Sanskrit Saranâ as well as Saramâ. Is all this mere accident, and was there no thought-relationship whatever between Saramâ and Helena in the far distance? It is no doubt a mere accident, still it is curious that Helena has regained the m in her most recent form, for it is well known that the Feu de St. Elme was originally the fire of Helena. Cf. Lydus (De Ostentis), τὸ δὲ τοιοῦτον, σχῆμα ... οἱ τὴν θάλατταν πλέοντες Ἑλένην καλοῦσιν. (Decharme, l.c., p. 609.) It has been argued very gravely that Saramâ is only a bitch, and Helena the most beautiful woman of Greece. Yes, but the Haritas in the Veda are only horses, the Charites in Greece are the Graces! And why is Saramâ a sunî or κύων? Not, like Helen, for her shamelessness [1], but simply because she was conceived as hunting round the ends of the sky to discover the stolen cattle of Indra [2].

More difficult than the marriages of Zeus hitherto mentioned, is his union with Maia (Μαῖα) and her becoming through him the mother of Hermes, the Sârameya. Maia has been taken for a representative of the earth or of the dawn (mahî), an etymology which we shall have to discuss hereafter, when we have first cleared up the character of Hermes, her son.

---

[1] Il. vi, 344, 356.   [2] Rv. X, 108, 5.

4. Zeus, Aigîna, Aiakos.

To explain all the love affairs of Zeus would be difficult, if not impossible. Many of them are mere variations of one and the same theme. Some of them are clearly of local origin. Thus when a royal family had once assumed the title of Διογενεῖς, or Zeus-born, Zeus was soon fabled to have been their real ancestor, and his wife would naturally be the country over which they reigned, or the river running by the side of the royal castle. Thus if Aiakos was king of Aigîna by the grace of Zeus, Aigîna would naturally become his mother, and Zeus her husband. Hence arose without any effort the legend that Zeus, whose character as a true pater patriae was well known all over Greece, had in the form of an eagle carried off Aigîna. She was the daughter of Asôpus, one of the many rivers of that name, a name probably transferred from the river in the Peloponnesus to that in Aigîna, Aigîna having been colonised by emigrants from the Peloponnesus. Asôpus, offended by the violence of Zeus, fought against him, but was driven back by the thunderbolt of the god. Aiakos, the son of Zeus and Aigîna, ruled in Aigîna which, before it was colonised, had the name of Oinône or Oinôpia. It is clear therefore that the myth of Aiakos and of his parents, Zeus and Aigîna, contains a number of local or historical elements which cannot be expected to yield to any linguistic analysis. If we call them historical, we must remember that Aiakos was the father of Pêleus, and Pêleus the father of Achilles, both belonging to pre-historic and mythological rather than to historic ages. Still in the case of Aiakos facts and myths seem to confirm each other, and we may be satisfied that the story of the marriage between Zeus and Aigîna is no more than a legendary tradition that Oinône was colonised by Greeks from the Peloponnesus, that its name was changed from Oinône to Aigîna, owing possibly to a change from vine-culture to goat-breeding, and that Aiakos, its first ruler, was naturally called the son of Aigînâ, and like many founders of royal dynasties, the son of Zeus. In much the same way the hero eponymos of many other countries was represented as the son of Zeus and some local nymph.

If such a myth had once been started, poets were perfectly free to elaborate it and to add whatever would most please their hearers. In all such cases we must be satisfied with the main outlines of the myth, and not attempt any more minute elucidation. It is possible that Αἴακος meant originally a son of Αἶα, or the earth, a kind of γηγενής or terri-gena, but we must always remember that the poetical flights of fancy of poets five thousand years ago may have differed from our own.

5. Zeus, Kallisto, and Arkas.

Otfried Müller, without any help from Comparative Philology, has succeeded in unravelling several of these love affairs of Zeus.

There is an Arkadian legend that Zeus, after changing Kallisto, the daughter of Lykâon, and a companion of Artemis, into a bear, had from her a son of the name of Arkas. Otfried Müller sees in this legend the usual claim of a divine descent put forward by the Arkadians, as by other Greek tribes.

If the Arkadians had chosen as their ancestors Zeus Lykaios and Artemis Kallisto, everything else might be left to the imagination of Arkadian bards, though modern interpreters might possibly detect in the name of the Arkades [1] and in the change of Kallisto into a bear, traces of totemism unsuspected by Otfried Müller. Similar cases of the hero eponymos of a country being made the son of Zeus, are frequent, Akragas, Dardanos, Myrmidon, Orchomenos, Lokros, Argos, Hellen, Magnes, Lakedaimon, Makedon, all are represented as the sons of Zeus and some nymph invented ad hoc.

6. Zeus, Alkmênê, and Hêrakles.

That many ingredients in the character of Hêrakles were solar, is probably no longer denied by anybody. That Zeus should be called his father is therefore natural enough, but the meaning of the name of his mother Alkmênê is more difficult to explain, unless we are satisfied with tracing it to the root ark, to shine, from which Curtius has derived the name of her father Ἠλεκτρυών, and of Ἠλέκτωρ, an old name of the sun, used by Homer and by Empedokles [2].

7. Zeus and Semele.

It is a peculiar feature in the marriages of Zeus and of gods corresponding to him, as representing the sky or the sun, that their wives are often doomed to death, like Semele [3], and the children of

---

[1] Sk. *ṛksha*, bear, ἄρκτος, ursus, Ir. art.

[2] Empedokles, 263, ἠλέκτωρ τε χθών τε καὶ οὐρανὸς ἠδὲ θάλασσα.

[3] The original character of Semele remains doubtful. But why should she be called Hye (rain), while Zeus is called Hyes and Hyetios? Are not these names derived from the same root su

the marriage exposed or deserted. The children are often twins, and there is often a third child, generally a beautiful sister. The facts of nature which explain these legends are the short union between the sun and either the dark night or the first glimmerings of the morning light. The death of Semele before the brilliant effulgence of Zeus, is only a Greek rendering of the violence done to Ushas (dawn) by Indra, and her disappearance in consequence. The daughter of that union is sometimes the dawn again, which vanishes as soon as the sun rises above the horizon, or which remains visible for a short time, during the bright hours of the morning, nay which sometimes is recognised as returning again into the arms of the setting sun, as the twilight of the evening.

Twin Deities.

The twins have been recognised by us as representing the prominent dual aspects of the diurnal drama, that is, light and darkness, morning and evening, day and night, heaven and earth, sometimes sun and moon, summer and winter. These double aspects are represented in Sanskrit under various names, such as Asvinau, Dyu-nisau (rodasyau), Dyâvâ-prithivyau, Ushâsâ-naktâ, Ahorâtrau, also Yamau, Bhrâtarau, nay even Mitrâ-varu*n*au, Agnî-varu*n*au, &c. Every one of these names and concepts may lead to new legends, in appearance totally different from each other, and yet in their deepest roots the same.

---

which gives us Soma and Savit*ri* in the Veda? Why should another of her names be Thyône, and Thyôneus that of Dionysos, who was her son by Zeus? The Greeks took the name Semele as a dialectic variety of Θεμέλη in the sense of earth. Are all these questions disposed of by the discovery of Samlath?

8. Zeus, Antiope, Amphion and Zêthos.

The two Dioskouroi, the brothers of Helena, the sons of Lêda, are apparently very different from Amphîon and Zêthos, the twin sons of Zeus and Antiope, yet we shall see how these two couples of twins also were in their origin nearly related.

Antiope is called the daughter of Nykteus, just as the dawn is frequently represented as sprung from the night. The name of 'Ἀντιγονεία has been explained by Stephanus Byz. by προσεσπέριος, western. It is possible, therefore, though I should say no more, that the same idea was expressed in the name of Antiope, who would then be the western bride of Amphîon. And who could Amphîon be if he is the son of Zeus and Antiope, and if he is called he who moves around, like Hyperîon, he who is above, if not the daily sun? He became afterwards the husband of Niobe, and thus entered into a new mythical cycle.

If the Dioskouroi, the twin sons of Lêda, were originally day and night, what else can Amphîon and Zêthos have been in the beginning of their mythological career? And does not Euripides in the Phoenissae 609, actually call Amphîon and Zêthos the two Dioskouroi on their white horses[1]?

9. Zeus, Diône, Dia.

Other marriages of Zeus admit of similar explanation. In the same way in which Eurynome became the mother of the Charites by Zeus, Diône (Sk. *divânâ), became by him the mother of Aphrodîte, the principal Charis.

---

[1] Hesychius, s.v. Διόσκουροι, οἱ Ἑλένης ἀδελφοί, καὶ Ζῆθος καὶ Ἀμφίων, λευκόπωλοι καλούμενοι.

Dîa (Δία), another wife of Zeus, becomes through him (who had assumed the form of a horse) or through Ixîon, the mother of Peirithoos, again, he who runs round. Kuhn explained Ixîon as the solar wheel, Mannhardt takes him in the sense of a whirlwind, and Dîa in the sense of Nephele or cloud. M. Michel Bréal (Mélanges, p. 169) sees in Ixîon the Sk. word akshivan, i.e. with a wheel, and explains him as the solar wheel turning round and round every day. When this which was originally a simple physical fact ceased to be understood, it was explained as a punishment. Then came the time when the question was asked why Ixîon was punished in that way, and the answer was that he, as one of the Centaurs or cloud-heroes, had attempted to do violence to Hêre, the bright air, and the wife of Zeus. And as this seemed too great an outrage, another story arose that Zeus had created Nephele, a cloud, to take the place of his wife instead of Hêre. With these few questions and answers, M. Michel Bréal thinks that the whole myth of Ixîon can be accounted for, and I think he is right in the main, but there still remains the difficulty why Ixîon or the wheel, if a solar hero, should have been a Centaur or a Gandharva, or a cloud, and whether the cloud overcasting the air could have been taken for an insult to Hêre meditated by Ixion. Here some other motives have still to be discovered. Before we can hope to discover the root of this myth, it should be settled whether Δία is simply meant for Δîα, i.e. heavenly or divine, or whether it is an independent word. The divine could hardly have been the name of an individual deity, particularly as we have different goddesses and heroines under the same name. We declined to accept Athanatos, immortal, as the original name of Athêne, nor could we accept Theia, when wife of Hyperîon and mother of Hêlios, Selêne, and Êos, in the general sense of a goddess or divine person. She could only be devî in the sense of brilliant. There may even have been a Δίος, for the great festival of the Pandia seems to postulate the existence of a Ζεὺς Πάνδιος, but this is a question which must be left to Greek scholars to answer, while Latin scholars will have to account for their Dea dia.

10. Zeus, Protogeneia, Aethlios.

If Zeus is said to be the father of Aethlios, i.e. the race-horse, this race-horse can only be the horse that every day races across the sky, and if his mother is called Protogeneia, the first-born, her name speaks for itself as that of the dawn (Primigenia).

11. Zeus, Êlektra, Harmonia, Dardanos, and Jăsion.

On similar grounds Êlektra, the bright, can only be the dawn, and if she by Zeus became the mother of Harmonia and of Dardanos and Jăsion, we have here again the usual birth of the dawn-goddess and of the diurnal twins corresponding to Helena and the two Dioskouroi.

12. Zeus, Danae, and Perseus.

It is more difficult to discover the etymology of Dănae. Being the mother of Perseus, in many respects a second Hêrakles, she must be a representative of the morning, like Alkmêne, like Eurymede, Eurymêde or Eurynome, different names of the mother of Bellerophon, or like Aithra (Αἴθρα, clear sky), whom Bellerophon wished to marry, but who became the mother of Thêseus by Aigeus. We think first of the dawn when Danae is said to receive showers of the golden rays of the sun or the sky in her bosom, but she may also have been meant for the earth, being revived by the rays of the sun. Danae (Δανάη) may be a half-historical name, if it could be taken as the feminine of Δαναός, and we should remember that Dănae is the great-granddaughter of one of the Dānaides, Hypermnêstra. But the name has also been connected with the Vedic Dânu, which means a demon, both in the singular and plural, and is really a synonym of V*r*itra, though in one passage it seems to be the name of the mother of V*r*itra. The descendants of this Dânu, or the Dânavas, are the demons who are always the enemies of the Devas. We have seen that several of the bright deities are represented as the offspring of the dark powers, for the simple reason that the first light of the day might be said to spring from the darkness of the night. Dănae[1] would then stand for Dânavî, and her nocturnal nature would well harmonise with her being kept in a dark tower, with the name of her mother Eurydike, and likewise with that of her father Akrisios (indistinct ?). But the name is in this case of little help, while the general character of the story is such that it cannot have had any but a solar origin. It is a thoroughly solar idea, for instance, that the offspring is destined to become the murderer of his

---

[1] The shortening of the vowel in Dănae and Dănaides may be due either to the requirements of the epic hexameter, or to a recollection of the historical name of the Danaoi.

father or grandfather. This fate seems inevitable with every young sun or coming day, whose very birth implies the death of the preceding day. Thus Oidipus is the predestined murderer of his father Laios, Jâson indirectly of Pelias, and Perseus of his grandfather Akrisios. Perseus, whatever else he may be meant for, was clearly a luminous hero, χρυσόπατρος, the son of a golden father.

Whatever may be said against this or that name, is it likely that in this cluster of the wives of Zeus the same idea should suggest itself again and again without a cause? No doubt if we read of Aithra being taken captive by Kastor and Polydeukes and sent to Troy as the slave of Helena, again if we read how her grandson Dêmophon claimed her from Agamemnon, and how Agamemnon at last obtained her freedom from Helena, we perceive little of the clear sky in her or of the birth of the morning in Thêseus. This physical background lies far beyond the beginning of what we possess of Greek mythical poetry, but it existed nevertheless as surely as the coarse Xoana existed before the statues of Phidias, as surely as even in the French word Journal there hides the name of Dyaus. And is it not strange that even in her legendary character Aithra should be the captive of the Dioskouroi and the slave of Helena, all of them, as we saw, matutinal deities, all of them children of Zeus, the bright sky, and of some nymph or goddess representing the many-sided and many-named Dawn? Surely these broad facts cannot be put aside for the sake of some phonetic irregularities, supposing they existed, or because to our modern mind many of these ancient fancies seem far-fetched or monotonous or monstrous. It is easy to cavil at this or that equation, but to treat the whole mass as a farrago of mere unmeaning coincidences is more, I hope, than even the most determined Euhemerist would venture to attempt.

Vedic and other Aryan Mythologies.

It is true the lesson of the origin of the Aryan gods is learnt more easily from the Veda than from any other source, but when once learnt we cannot hesitate to apply it to other mythologies also. That we shall ever gain perfect certainty in our interpretations is out of the question, and that we shall ever convince those who do not wish to be convinced, and who shut their eyes to the dangerous charms of Vedic literature, is extremely doubtful. But that should never discourage serious inquiry, particularly when some of the most interesting and most important questions in the early development of the human race are at stake. We know that it was impossible to convince the most learned cardinals of the movement of the earth. We are better off than Galilei, for at all events we are not forced to recant, whatever anathema popular journalists may hurl at our heads. We are convinced in our hearts, and truth, we know, is in no hurry.

Indian Myths.

The case of Zeus = Dyaus will show us most clearly what we ought to expect in comparing Greek and Vedic mythology, and likewise what we ought not to expect. There are many legends in India which are exclusively Indian, and of which we can watch the growth on Indian soil, such as the stories of Siva, Vishnu, and Brahman. It is true that even

these have antecedents that may go back to a
far more distant antiquity than we imagine; still
the form in which they have reached us is so
peculiarly Indian that no one would think of a comparison between them and Greek or Roman legends
on genealogical principles. Unfortunately these
were the very myths on which Sir William Jones
and his contemporaries exercised their ingenuity so
that *S*iva was equated with Ζεύς, Ga*n*esa with
Janus, and an opinion was expressed 'that Egyptian
priests had come from the Nile to the Gangâ and
Yamunâ to visit the *S*armans of India as the Greeks
visited them at a later time, rather to acquire than
to impart knowledge[1].' These premature attempts
at Comparative Mythology roused a feeling among
scholars which is not yet extinct, and which has been
strengthened of late by Professor Gruppe's attempt
to explain the similarities between all the religions
and mythologies of the world by means of actual
exportation from India, and not as the result of
a common development like that of the language
of the Âryas in Asia and Europe. If others have
again and again expressed their conviction that it
was impossible that the ancient Âryas should have
elaborated so many of their oldest myths from the
same solar materials, all we can say is that by
a study of the Veda they should try to learn what
is real, before they attempt to prove what is
impossible. That people who know the Veda should
ever doubt the prevalence of solar ideas in the Vedic
hymns, and the survival of some of them in the
mythologies of other Aryan speakers, I consider

---

[1] Chips, iv, p. 209.

simply impossible. However ready some of us may be to listen to what Maoris and Hottentots have to tell us, nothing will shake our conviction that the substance of the Vedic and most of the Aryan gods is physical. One thing is certain, and not denied even by the most determined doubters, namely, that the common background of Zeus, Jupiter, and Dyaus has been discovered in the Vedic hymns. Nay, even those who are fond of scoffing at the labours of such men as Kuhn, Bréal, Darmesteter and others, fall down before Zeus = Jupiter = Dyaus. They believe in the father of the devas, but not in his sons and daughters. Now it is quite true that the idea of a divine family under the patriarchal authority of a father of gods and men is much less prominent in the Veda than in Homer, yet it exists, and the thought that the principal gods are the sons of Dyaus, as they are of Zeus, meets us clearly in scattered passages of the Veda. We know that Athêne, Apollon, Artemis, Ares, Eileithyia, Hermes, Hêphaistos, Dionŷsos, Persephone, Hêbe, and Aphrodite, besides minor deities, such as the Charites, the Muses, the Horae, the Dioskouroi, and Helena, and many other heroines, are all represented in Greece as the children of Zeus. The family of Dyaus is not so large, still the name of Divas putra, Divo duhitâ, or Divo napât is assigned to many gods in the Veda also. Ushas is constantly called Divo duhitâ, the daughter of Dyaus, and is the prototype, as we have seen, of ever so many of the daughters of Zeus. The Asvins are always the Divo napâtâ, the two descendants, or Divo narâ, the two men of Dyaus. The Maruts are the sons of Dyaus, or his men (nara*h*). Even Agni (III, 25, 1) and Indra

(IV, 17, 4) appear in some places as his sons, and the same applies to Par*g*anya (VII, 102, 1), Sûrya (X, 37, 1), Âpa*h*, the waters or clouds (III, 1, 6, yahví*h*), nay even to the Oshadhîs or plants (VII, 70, 3)[1]. But though this large assembly of the children of Zeus in Greece and of Dyaus in the Veda exhibits the common background of Greek and Vedic mythology in the clearest light, we see at the same time the characteristic difference between these creations of the Greek and of the Indian genius. The Greek, to whom everything divine had become human, postulated for each child of Zeus a mother, and thus a number of goddesses and heroines were called into being, and drawn into the net of more or less exciting intrigues. There is little or nothing of this in the Veda. The sons, no doubt, presuppose a father, and that father is decidedly Dyaus as a masculine. But no further question was asked as to who in each case was their mother, nor were such stories invented as that of Zeus giving birth by himself to his daughter Athêne, the famous Divo duhitâ of the Veda, or of Hêre taking her revenge by becoming by herself the mother of Hêphaistos.

Dêmêter. Earth.

P*r*ithivî, the Earth, is the companion of Dyaus in the compound name of Dyâvâ-p*r*ithivî. By herself she has at least one hymn of three verses addressed to her in the Rig-veda, V, 84. But she is much more fully celebrated in the Atharva-veda. Here in XII, 1 she stands before us as a full-grown goddess like Dêmêter in Greece, like Tellus in Italy, like

---

[1] Cf. Ludwig, iii, p. 313.

Nerthus in Germany. In India this Prithvî is invoked as the mother of men (7, 10). All mortals are said to be born of her and to be supported by her (v. 15). Her name Prithivî for Prithvî seems at first very unmeaning. It corresponds to the Greek πλατεῖα, and means no more than broad. But that this broad goddess had been recognised at a very early time we learn from finding a similar word used in Icelandic and likewise as a name of the earth. It is Fold in Icelandic, folde in Anglo-Saxon, Feld in German. In the Edda (Hymis kwidha, 24) we read :—

> Rocks crashed, gulfs howled,
> The old earth (fold öll) trembled sighing.

The Vedic poet calls himself the son of the Earth, and he speaks of Parganya (rain-cloud) as his father (vv. 12, 42). In another verse of the same hymn, however, Indra is said to be her husband, nay Agni (vv. 6, 19) and Dyu also (v. 63) are mentioned as in close connection with her. This shows again the as yet pliant character of the Vedic gods. Though they have assumed a few definite features, they all seem to rise from an undefined background in which they lose their definite outlines and are mingled with other deities. Thus Indra, though different from Parganya, may in several of his activities, particularly in the giving of rain, be actually replaced by him, just as Dyu[1], the god of the sky, may be merged in Agni, as the god of light, or be absorbed by Indra as the god of the thunderstorm. Nay Vivasvat, Tvashtri, Gandharva[2], all

---

[1] Cf. Rv. X, 10, 4.
[2] Rv. X, 10, 4 : Gandharváḥ apsú ápyà ka yóshà sā naḥ nâbhiḥ

occur as names of Dyu. This allelotheistic tendency, though perfectly intelligible, led to very perplexing complications when some of these names and phrases were worked up into a complete story where father and son, mother and wife, could no longer be kept apart, though they were quite apart in the minds of those who gave them their first names and their original functions.

The best known instance is that of the Sun and the Dawn, the Sun, under his various names and disguises, being called the father of the Dawn, and at the same time her follower or lover (Rv. I, 92, 11), her husband (VII, 75, 5), nay sometimes her destroyer also (II, 15, 6). These are facts, not fancies. From very early times, and before this mythology was finished, the people of India had begun to be shocked themselves at what seemed to them a case of incest, sanctioned by the gods. Some of their theologians were able to account for these apparent horrors, and to clear their gods from this terrible charge, but even during the mythopœic age a legend sprang up that the gods were so incensed against Pra*g*âpati or whatever name the solar deity then bore, that they had him punished by an arrow discharged at the culprit. The same story might have been told against Agni, for of him too our poet (Rv. X, 3, 3) says that he followed his sister from behind, svásâram *g*âráh abhí eti pas*k*ât, the same that was said of Sûrya, I, 115, 2, Sûrya*h* devím ushásam ró*k*amânâm máryah ná yóshâm abhí eti pas*k*ât, 'The Sun goes from behind after the brilliant shining Dawn, as a man follows a woman.'

---

paramám *g*âmí tát nau, 'The Gandharva in the waters and the water-woman, that is our origin, that is our highest kindred.'

That such things should have offended the Mrs. Grundy's of four thousand years ago is intelligible, but that mythologists, hardened by long intercourse with savages, should express themselves unspeakably shocked at the Chronique scandaleuse of the Vedic gods, seems strange. What would they say of Egyptian mythology where Osiris is the father, the brother, the husband, and son of Isis, nay the son of their child Horus? (Le Page Renouf, Hibbert Lectures, p. 85.)

Gaia and Dêmêter.

If now we turn our eyes from India where we found Prithivî, the Earth, as the companion of Dyaus, to Greece, we see the Earth represented there not only by one, but two great goddesses, by Gaia and Dêmêter, the former representing the earth in her purely elementary character, the latter as the field cultivated by the hand of man. Homer knows of Gaia as a great goddess invoked by people in taking an oath. Hesiod places her in the very centre of his theogony, as the first born after Chaos, as the mother of Ouranos, of mountains and sea. From her union with Ouranos sprang, we are told, the Titans, Kronos, Themis, Rheia, Ôkeanos, Koios, Krios, Hyperion, Japetos, Theia, Mnêmosyne, Phoibe, Têthys, the Kyklôpes, Brontes, Steropes, Arges, Kottos, Briareus, and Gyges. Some of these names speak for themselves, and are clearly representative of physical powers, others are as yet quite unexplained etymologically, and those who bear them act hardly any definite part in the mythological drama of Greece, so far as it is known to us. The most important among them is Kronos, who was instigated by his mother to mutilate his father with an adamantine sickle. Drops of blood falling on Gaia became the Erinyes, the Gigantes and the Melian nymphs, also Aphrodite. Many more children of Gaia are mentioned, for she was indeed a mater omniparens et alma. By the marriage of two of her children, Kronos and Rheia, a new divine dynasty was ushered in. Their children, Hestia, Dêmêter, Hêre, Plouton, and Poseidon, after having been swallowed by Kronos, were delivered by the youngest child Zeus, with the assistance of his mother Rheia, and of Mêtis, the daughter of Ôkeanos. Then followed the ten years' war between the Kronidai and the old Titans, which ended in the defeat of the Titans, and the permanent supremacy of Zeus and the Olympian gods.

Of all this we find no trace in the Veda, a further proof that this theogony of Hesiod, though it may contain ancient elements, is really the outcome of a later period, and possibly the work of an ancient Greek philosopher, rather than a mere chronicle of local traditions. As to the story of the gods being swallowed and brought up again, though we cannot match it exactly, we saw before that its fundamental thought was most likely that of the bright gods or Devas being swallowed by the Night and brought back again by the Morning, although possibly Winter and Spring also might act the part of Night and Morning. When we find in Greek and in Sanskrit such general coincidences as that the Earth is called mother, supporter, wide-spread (whether uruvya$k$as or εὐρύστερνος), the firm seat (ἕδος ἀσφαλὲς αἰεί or dhruvám sádaḥ), we cannot see in them more than the natural coincidences of human thought. We should probably find the same in every country and in every language which has a name for earth as an abstract being, or as a goddess. We are told that in Greek Dêmêter stands for Gê-mêter, and meant originally Earth-mother, that is Earth as mother, as Ζεὺς πατήρ meant Sky as father. Phonetic consciences might rebel against the change in the name of Dêmêter of g into d, but so far as the ancient Greeks are concerned there can be no doubt that they had accepted Dêmêter as Gê-mêter or Mother Earth [1]. It is certainly strange that Gê, so common in Greek, should in the name of the goddess have been changed to Dê. There is really no excuse for it (Ahrens, Dial. Dor. 80), and strict phoneticians would say that it was impossible. Still as the irregularity occurs in a proper name it has to be accepted, the material evidence being too strong in favour of Dêmêter being an earth-goddess. We have only to look at her epithets, which are generally very useful indications of the true character of gods and goddesses, to see what she was to the Greeks. She is called αὐξιθαλής, giving increase, χλοηφόρος, bringing green sprouts, also χλοόκαρπος, or simply Chloe. Other epithets of the same character are καρποποιός, fruit-maker, σταχυηφόρος and φερέσταχυς, bearing ears, σιτοφόρος and Σιτώ, πυροφόρος, wheat-bearing, ὡρηφόρος, bringing the seasons or the fruits of the seasons, ἀναξιδώρα and ἀνησιδώρα, who brings up gifts, ἁλωάς, belonging to the threshing-floor, ἱμαλίς, abundant, ἰουλώ, goddess

---

[1] Paus. x, 12, 10, Γᾶ καρποὺς ἀνίει, διὸ κλῄζετε ματέρα Γαῖαν.

of sheaves. The goddess who can bear all these names and many more of the same kind can only be the goddess of the ploughed field, and many of them she shares in common with Gaia, the earth.

Homer does not tell us much about Dêmêter, except in the hymn addressed to her; still he knows of the marriage between her and Jăsion, on a thrice-ploughed field, and of their son Ploutos. Whatever Iăson, Iasion, Iasos, or Iasios (not Iâson) may be meant for, whether sunlight or rain, there can be little doubt that Ploutos, their offspring, was meant for the wealth that springs from the thrice-ploughed field. Hence she is also called πλουτο-δότειρα, wealth-giving.

Triptolemos, the young friend of Dêmêter, who is represented as the inventor of the plough and as spreading agriculture everywhere, is evidently named from this threefold ploughing (πολεῖν γῆν, polare agros). The meaning of all this is so clear that it might be called an allegory rather than a myth. And the same applies, as we saw, to the story of Kore, as the daughter of Dêmêter. She is meant for the annual vegetation springing from the earth, but carried off every winter by Aidôneus, or the unseen power of the lower world. The return of Kore, or as she is also called, Persephone [1], represents

---

[1] The name of Persephone, Περσεφόνη (Περσεφόνεια and Φερσε-φόνεια), seems to have been a modification of Φερσεφόνη in the sense of death-bringing. She brought death every year when she disappeared, and it is important to observe that her mother, Dêo, was called Φερέσβιος, life-bringing. The ear of corn of Dêmêter, the στάχυς Δημήτρος, is likewise called life-giving. Proserpina is a curious imitation of Persephone, and evidently intended to convey the idea of proserpens, the forthcoming

the return of spring, while the condition that in
future she is to remain two seasons with her mother,
the Earth, and one with her husband, the lord of
the lower world, clearly refers to the great law
of nature which causes the three seasons, spring,
summer, and winter, to succeed each other without fail, which causes the descent (κάθοδος) and
the ascent (ἄνοδος) of Kore, the daughter of the
Earth, and the representative of the ever-returning
vegetation of nature. Owing to the localisation of the
principal events of the story at Eleusis, and the celebration of the Eleusinian mysteries, this simple myth
has been surrounded by a large number of details
which defy explanation as much as the Eleusinian
mysteries themselves. The original story, however,
and this alone is of interest to the Comparative
Mythologist, is very transparent, and would be
utterly meaningless unless in this myth at least we
took Dêmêter in the sense of Earth-mother.

Dêo. Erinys.

But while this part of the story told about
Dêmêter is quite intelligible, there is another which
it seems impossible to bring into harmony with a
deity of the earth. We are told that at Phygalia
in Arkadia there was a sanctuary of Dêmêter or
Dêo—the two names are supposed to be one—
consisting of a cave with a coarse idol in it, that
this idol was destroyed by fire and replaced by a
bronze statue by Onatas, representing the goddess

---

seed. If there was a Roman goddess Proserpina, representing
the forthcoming vegetation, it is clear that the Romans must
have discovered in Persephone a similar meaning, and hence
identified her with their own Proserpina.

with a female body but with the head and mane of a horse, and surrounded by serpents. Here we see that Greek art shared in its beginnings the failings of other arts, whether Egyptian, Babylonian, or Indian. It is quite true that statues must be used with great caution by the Comparative Mythologist. They hardly ever can help us to discover the true character of a god or goddess, because the artist was often influenced by his own poetical fancy more even than by fortuitous local traditions. But in our case, where we have evidently to deal with an ancient and half-barbarous work of art, and where neither the character of the Earth-mother nor the usual symbols of the earth could have suggested these equine attributes, we are justified, it would seem, in taking them as indications of an ancient myth. And not only was the goddess represented in this strange and monstrous manner, but a story was told that in order to escape from Poseidon, she had changed herself into a mare, and had been overpowered by Poseidon, who had likewise assumed an equine form, and that she had given birth to a horse, viz. to Arcion (Ἀρείων)¹, and to a daughter known by the name of Despoina (mistress). We might accept the equine form of Poseidon, for he is known as ἵππιος, ἱππηγέτης, ἵππαρχος, &c., but the metamorphosis of the Earth-goddess into a mare is more startling. Even if we accepted the explanation given by Decharme that horse was often meant for spring, and that a spring might well have been called the child of the earth and of the god of the sea, there would still remain the difficulty about the

---

¹ Paus. viii, 15, 7; 42, 7.

change of the earth into a mare. We must also remember that Dêmêter, as the mother of these two children, was called not only Dêo, but likewise Erinys, as the Greeks thought, from ἐρινύειν, to be angry, whereas ἐρινύειν can only be a denominative verb derived from ἐρινύς, and meaning originally to behave like Erinys[1].

The sister of Areion, called Despoina, was identified with Persephone, who, however, was really the daughter of Zeus and Dêmêter. Here then we have in Greece a goddess called Dêo, also Erinys, who in order to escape from Poseidon is changed into a mare, and we have a god who likewise is changed into a horse, and begets two children, called Areion and Despoina.

If we look about for analogies, we find nothing, as far as I know, corresponding to the well-marked features of this barbarous myth among any of the uncivilised tribes of the earth. If we did, how we should rejoice! Why then should we not rejoice when we find in the Rig-veda, X, 17, an allusion to a story which must have been well known before a poet could allude to it in such few words? Literally translated the text says:—

'Tvash*tri* makes a wedding for his daughter, thereupon the whole world comes together; the mother of Yama having been wedded, she, who is the wife of the great Vivasvat, vanished.'

'They hid the immortal one from the mortals, having made one like her they gave her to Vivasvat; when that had taken place, she bore the two A*s*vins, and Sara*n*yû left behind the two twin-couples.'

---

[1] K. Z., v, 454, ἐρινύειν θυμῷ χρῆσθαι.

This would of course be quite unintelligible by itself, but Yâska, in order to explain these verses, tells us in so many words that Sara*n*yû, the daughter of Tvash*tri*, had twins from Vivasvat, the Âditya (sun), the well-known twins, the offspring of the sun. She, substituting another like unto her, assumed the form of a mare and ran away. Then Vivasvat, the Âditya, assuming likewise an equine form, came together with her, and hence the two Asvins were born, but Manu was born from the substitute.

The facts therefore are much the same in Indian and Greek mythology. A god persecutes a goddess. The goddess runs away and assumes the form of a mare. Upon this the god also assumes the form of a horse, and after they have come together a couple of twins are born. But though the analogy is very marked, still, as I have often said, such analogies would not help us very far, except when the names of the principal actors give us a clue to their original meaning.

Now in our case there is a strong coincidence in the names. For the goddess that is called Sara*n*yû in the Veda is called Erînys in Greek. Is this mere accident? Few people would be bold enough to say so, but they might rightly ask the question, why both Sara*n*yû and Erînys should have been believed to have been changed into horses. But here, too, Yâska and his commentaries come to our help. In explanation of the story of Sara*n*yû Yâska adds a few words :—

'Night is the wife of Âditya, she vanishes at sunrise.' He therefore takes Sara*n*yû for the night, and I think he is right, only we must not take Sara*n*yû as standing for the whole night, or for the darkest time of the night, but rather as the moment when night and morning meet and part, that is the end of the night, the beginning of the day, or the first dawn. Yâska makes this clear by saying that the time of the Asvins, the sons of Saranyû, is after midnight; that, after the approach of light, the dark part is Madhyama¹ (Asvin), and the light part is Âditya (Asvin), but that though one Asvin abides in mid-air and the other in the sky, they are inseparably united, and always perform the same acts. They are in fact darkness and light, the one diminishing while the other is increasing, and vice versâ.

Hence we can understand why they were identified with Dyâvâ-prithivyau, Heaven and Earth, with Ahorâtrau, Day and Night, with Sûryâ-*K*andramasau, Sun and Moon. All these identifications, if properly understood, are more or less right, nay others might be added, such as Mitra and Varu*n*a, Indra and Agni, &c.

If then Sara*n*yû was the mother of these twins, it is clear that like Erînys she must have represented, originally, the grey dawn as manifested in the first streaks of glimmering light, creeping along the darkness of the sky.

When married to Vivasvat Âditya, the sun, Sara*n*yû might be said to give birth to the Yamau, the twins, originally day and night, Ahorâtrau, afterwards also represented by Yama and a sister called Yamî, the two being taken by a very natural misunderstanding for the first mortals. After a time, we are told that Sara*n*yû is

---

¹ 'When darkness prevails over light, that is Madhyama; when light prevails over darkness, that is Aditya.'

hidden, that is, the dawn disappears and the sun rises. But Sara*n*yû is followed by her husband Vivasvat, and she gives birth to the A*s*vins, the descendants of A*s*vâ the mare, again representatives of darkness and light. (Vâsatya = nocturnus, Nâsatya = νόστιος, redux.) The image or substitute of Sara*n*yû, or the early dawn, given to Vivasvat, may have been meant for the gloaming, and Manu for the moon, rising when the sun has set in the west. Lastly, as Sara*n*yû or Erînys Dêmêter was the wife of Vivasvat, the husband or favourite of Dêmêter was, as we saw, Jăson, i. e. Vivasvân (FιFασFων).

There still remains the question why in Sanskrit Sara*n*yû should have been represented as changed into a mare, and her husband the sun into a horse, and why in Greece Onatas should have represented Dêo with an equine head. This seems simply to have been due to the fact that, quite apart from this myth, the sun had, in India at least, often been conceived as a horse, cf. Rv. II, 35, 6, á*s*vasya átra *g*ánima asyá *k*a svá*h*, 'the birth of the horse was there, and his was the sun;' and because in the same manner the dawn had been likened to a mare, see Rv. IV, 52, 2, so that in the Mahâbhârata, I, 66, 25, she is without any explanation spoken of as va*d*avâ, the mare, the wife of Savit*ri*, another name of the sun, and as the mother of the A*s*vins. If after that one of the many names of day and night was A*s*vinau, this, as we saw, need never have meant the horsemen at all, but simply the connections or descendants of the A*s*va and A*s*vâ, as the descendants of K*ri*sâ*s*va are called the K*ri*sâ*s*vins, Pâ*n*. IV, 2, 66.

It must not be supposed that such a myth as that

of Sara*n*yû and the Sun-god springs into life, full and complete. In our case it probably began with such popular, half-metaphorical expressions as yamau, the twins, being meant for day and night, yamasû*h*, the twin-mother, i.e. the dawn; asva, the horse, i.e. the sun; va*d*avâ, the mare, i.e. the dawn; asvinau, the horse-children, i.e. day and night. Given these expressions, some of which were very likely to lose their original meaning, we can understand the formation of such phrases as 'Sara*n*yû is wedded to Vivasvat,' or Erînys to Jăson, i.e. the grey dawn is embraced by the sun. Other phrases would be 'Sara*n*yû has left her twins,' i.e. the dawn has gone; 'Vivasvat takes his second wife,' i.e. the sun is setting in the gloaming; 'the horse runs after the mare,' i.e. the sun has set. If lastly all these sayings are thrown together and arranged as parts of one story, we have what we find in the mythology both of Vedic India and of Greece. It follows from the nature of the case that the reconstruction of the original myth, as given above, can be hypothetical only, for we cannot expect positive certainty in a synthesis of thoughts that passed through the minds of people long before the age of the Veda, long, it may be, before the Aryan Separation. Still two such words as Sara*n*yû and Erînys, like Vivasvân and Jăson, stand before us like two inscriptions that have to be deciphered somehow, and I at least cannot bring myself to believe that such coincidences can be put aside as mere accident. That Sara*n*yû was originally a name of the dawn, the daughter of the night, has, I think, been fully proved [1]. That the Erînys or the Erînyes

---

[1] Science of Language, ii, 693.

would find out all hidden crimes meant therefore originally no more than that the dawn would bring to light every crime committed under cover of the night. The same dawn, as the end of the dark night, when united with the sun, might well be called the mother of day and night (or in another form, of the first pair of mortals), and as she had been spoken of as a mare, just as the sun had been called a horse racing across the sky, she would readily be accepted as the mother of the two Aśvins, who are but a repetition of the dual or correlative deities that divide between them light and darkness, day and night, heaven and earth, nay life and death.

So far the Vedic myth would be intelligible, but as the chief actors in it are night and day, it would be quite impossible to understand how the myth that was true of Erînys, the earliest dawn, could have been told of an Earth-goddess, such as Dêmêter had certainly become in Greece. Schwartz and others have often expressed their doubts as to Dêmêter being originally the earth, and I myself have formerly suggested that Dê-mêter was originally Dêô-mêter, Dawn-mother, something like Dyâvâ mâtâ, Dawn as mother, corresponding to Dyaush-pitâ, Sky-father. But that would carry us too far beyond the very beginnings of Greek language and Greek mythology. In early Greek mythology Dêmêter is the Earth-goddess and nothing else. Her epithets leave no doubt about this. When she is seen by Zeus embraced by Jāsion she is clearly the goddess of the field [1].

---

[1] Odyss. v, 125:—ὡς δ' ὁπότ' Ἰασίωνι ἐϋπλόκαμος Δημήτηρ,
ᾧ θυμῷ εἴξασα, μίγη φιλότητι καὶ εὐνῇ
νειῷ ἔνι τριπόλῳ.

If then we are certain that Dêmêter with the Greeks was the Earth-goddess, what remains but to admit that the story of the horse was told originally of another goddess, whether Erinys or Dêo, and that this name of Dêo or Dyâvâ was mixed up with a hypokoristic form of Dêmêter, Dêo, and thus led to the transference of her story to Dêmêter? I know this will sound very unlikely to Greek scholars, yet I see no other way out of our difficulties.

That *Dyâvâ, as a feminine of Dyu, could be represented by Δηώ can hardly be doubted. We should perhaps expect Ζηώ, but as we have Δεύς[1] dialectically by the side of Ζεύς, we may accept Δηώ also instead of Ζηώ. We should then have to admit two streams of myth, one starting from Dêmêter, Earth-mother, the wife of Zeus, and also of Jāson, and the mother of Kore, the child, the other starting from Dêo = Dyâvâ, the Dawn, the wife of Vivasvat, Jāson, the mother of the twins, the Asvins, and called by her own name Saranyû or Erinys. When their names became identical, Dêmêter being changed both to Dêmo and Dêo, some of their legends also would become mixed. Her daughter being called Dêôis and Dêôine shows at all events how old the name of Dêo must have been.

Varuna.

Next to Dyaus I look upon Varuna as one of the oldest names of gods in the Veda, for in spite of all

---

Here, as in Triptolemos, the thrice-ploughed field refers to the γῆ τρὶς πεπολημένη, namely to the ἄροτος χειμερινός, θερινός and the τρίτος ὁ μεταξὺ τούτων. See Mannhardt, Mythol. Forschungen, p. 239.

[1] Ahrens, Dial. Aeol., p. 175, Dial. Dor., p. 95; Curtius, Grundzüge, p. 620.

the shaking of heads and shrugging of shoulders there can be no doubt whatever that Varuna was the prototype of Οὐρανός. Whatever may have been said and repeated as to the equation of Ouranos = Varuna being phonetically untenable, I hope I have shown that no solid phonetic objection can consistently be urged against it. But if Οὐρανός sprang from the same source as Varuna, it follows, or, at all events, it is extremely likely, that Varuna meant at one time the same as Οὐρανός, namely sky, though more particularly the dark, the covering or the evening sky.

But the equation Varuna = Οὐρανός has been assailed, not on phonetic grounds only. These purely phonetic objections have been removed[1] before, and it seems almost a nemesis that the very form which, according to Ludwig, Ouranos ought to have in Sanskrit, i. e. Varana, has now been found, just as another postulated form, bharanyati, as the postulated etymon of Phoróneus, has been discovered by the side of bhuranyati. Into these questions, therefore, I need not enter again. But new objections have been raised. It has been contended that Varuna was a recent and extraneous god, even in the Veda. Now first of all, the same might be said of Ouranos. Ouranos has no ancient history in Greek mythology. He has been represented as a mere postulate, as a conclusion drawn from the Οὐρανίωνες or Οὐρανίδαι, just as Kronos may have been a god postulated on the strength of the Κρονίωνες or Κρονίδαι, literally the eternal beings. Still even in that case Ouranos must have been

---

[1] See p. 501 seq.

meant for the sky in Greek mythology as in the classical Greek language it means sky. But Ouranos has certain antecedents in Greek mythology which look like something more than mere mythological postulates. That he should have been dethroned by the Ouraniones, his children, might be accepted as a mere theory, but that the drops of his blood gave birth to the Erînyes, the Gigantes, and the Mělian nymphs, nay, even to Aphrodite, leaves the impression of real mythology on our mind.

Is there any evidence then in support of a theory, that Varuṇa in the Veda was a god of recent introduction, nay that, as Oldenberg suggests, he was borrowed from a Semitic source? It is true that the same was said many years ago by Dr. Pyl of Mitra, the constant companion of Varuṇa, but I am not aware that it has found favour with any Vedic scholar. We have seen that Varuṇa as a companion of Mitra was certainly known before the separation of the Indian and Iranian branches of the Aryan family, and that though his name is unknown in the Avesta, he is known in fact under the name of Asura, in Zend Ahura. This, as it seems to me, has been fully proved by the common Vedic compound, Mitrâ-Varuṇau, being represented in the Avesta by Mitra + Ahura. The etymological meaning of Mitra may be doubtful. Some derive it from mith, so that it should mean confederate or ally[1]; others from mid, as if it had been meant for a lover. But whatever the true etymology may be, it is quite clear that in the actual language of the Veda Mitra

---

[1] In the Avesta promises and treaties are under the protection of Mithra.

means friend, and that its application to the sun as the friend of all living has become so well established that even in the latest Sanskrit mitrodaya is a well-known word for sunrise. These two gods, Mitra and Varuna, have always been so closely connected that what applies to one applies to the other. There was even a special priest for the two, called Maitrâvaruna, and a sacrificial offering called Maitrâvaruniya. Besides there was a well-known tradition that Vasishtha, the famous Rishi of the seventh Mandala, was the offspring of Mitrâ-Varunau. He is actually called Maitrâvaruna in Rv. VII, 33, 11. We read :—

'And thou art Maitrâvaruna (son of Mitrâ-Varunau), O Vasishtha, born of their love for Urvasî, O Brahman ; as a drop spilled by heavenly fervour, all the gods received thee in a lotus blossom (or in a sacrificial vessel).'

This verse presupposes a legend of which Yâska gives the outlines (Nir. V, 14), and which is vouched for by the Brihaddevatâ also.

When Mitrâ-Varunau saw the beautiful Urvasî, retas kaskanda. It fell into the sacrificial vessel, called Vâsatîvara, and from it were produced the two Rishis, Agastya, also called Mânya, and Vasishtha, the Maitrâvaruna.

Here then we have in the Rig-veda not only the gods Mitra and Varuna, but even their offspring, perfectly well known ; and yet we are told that one of these gods, Varuna, was borrowed from a Semitic source ! At what time then could such a loan have been effected ? Was the companion of Varuna, Mitra, likewise borrowed from the same source ? Mitra and Varuna are so inseparable that in the Brâhma*n*as they are called the inbreathing and upbreathing (Satap.-brâh. IX, 5, 1, 56). Yet Mitra's name was well known before the Âryas of Persia separated from the Âryas of India. Besides, if Varu*n*a was borrowed from a Semitic source, what particular source was it, and what Semitic deity was there, that could have suggested such a being as Varu*n*a is in the Veda? Lastly, is there any case where a foreign god has been borrowed, and yet has found his natural place in the national pantheon as Varu*n*a has in the Veda?

If we see in the retas skannam of Varu*n*a that gave birth to Vasish*th*a, the very bright one, a myth analogous to that of the λευκὸς ἀφρός of the μήδεα of Ouranos that gave birth to the brightest of Greek goddesses, Aphrodite or Philommedeia, we might vindicate to Varu*n*a a date previous even to the Aryan Separation. But without insisting on this, let us remember that even in the hymns of the Rig-veda Varu*n*a is sometimes represented as even above Dyaus, if we may translate Rv. V, 63, 3, Dyâm varshayatha*h* Âsurasya mâyâyâ, 'You cause Dyaus to rain by the power of the Asura.' The name of Divaspati also, the two lords of Dyaus or the sky, may imply a similar supremacy of the two. Mitra even by himself is said to overcome the sky of Dyaus and the earth (Rv. III, 59, 7). All this shows at all events the high position always maintained by Varu*n*a and Mitra in Vedic mythology. Is it possible then to take Varu*n*a out of the Vedic pantheon without upsetting the whole structure? It is quite true that Varu*n*a's character, as an ethical deity, the preserver of law and order, and the punisher of sin, differs considerably from that of the purely physical deities of the Veda. But that does not prove that he had not, like other gods, a physical basis. In fact his physical germs seem to me still perfectly visible. Mitra and Varuna, in the hymns of the Rig-veda, are represented as dwelling in the highest heaven and looking down upon the world. They mount their chariot in the morning and cause the sun to shine. In other places the sun is called the eye of Mitrâ-Varunau, or sun and moon are represented as Varuna's two eyes. Varuna is addressed as wearing golden armour, and as sitting down surrounded by his spies who behold both worlds. He is the king of all the worlds, and the old title of deity, asura, is more frequently applied to him than to any other Vedic god. This may account for his appearing under the name of Ahura in the Avesta. Everything is known to Varuna, everybody is to obey his commands. But if on account of his sublime character it were supposed that Varuna must have had an origin different from that of the other Vedic gods surely he does not stand so entirely alone with his high moral attributes. Other gods also preserve the law and order of the world and are called *r*itaspati, lord of right, *r*ita*k*id, *r*ita*g*ña, *r*itadhîta, *r*itapâ, *r*itâvan, *r*itasp*r*is, &c. They punish all an*r*ita, unrighteousness [1], and are invoked as father and mother to be near their worshippers with their favours. And as we see in Greece that Zeus retains the traces of his physical origin, though at the same time he has risen to the height of a divine ideal, why should not the same have happened to Varuna?

---

[1] See Bergaigne, vol. iii, p. 299 seq.

I find it simply impossible to understand why Varuṇa should have been treated as an alien god, though he clings so firmly with all his roots to Vedic soil. The only reason I can surmise is his being the head of the seven Âdityas. But even these Âdityas and their number as seven occur in the Rig-veda, IX, 114, 3, deváḥ âdityáḥ yé saptá.

They are called the sons of Aditi, and in X, 72, 8 even an eighth (Mârtâṇḍâ) is mentioned, who had been discarded. They form a class of gods (devagaṇa) like the Vasus, Rudras, or Maruts (Rv. VIII, 35, 14) and others. Of that class Varuṇa became the head just as Agni did of the Vasus, and Indra of the Rudras[1]. All this looks systematic, and in consequence late, but there is authority for it in the hymns of the Rig-veda, or in the Brâhmaṇas, and the Âdityas have as much right to Varuṇa as their chief, as the Vasus to Agni or the Maruts to Indra. Who the seven Âdityas were originally we know as little as who the eight Vasus or the eleven Maruts were. The names vary, and it looks very much as if the system had been drawn out first, including even the numbers of each class of gods, and had then been filled with such names as seemed most appropriate. That the seven Âdityas should represent sun and moon and five planets is extremely unlikely, because the planets were never noticed by the ancient Ṛishis, still less had they been classed in the same category with sun and moon. When the number of the Âdityas was raised from seven to twelve, we can hardly doubt that they were meant for the twelve months, that is, for the suns of each

---

[1] Khând.-Up. III, 8, 1.

month, and it seems therefore to have been the consequence rather than the cause that the *Ga*gatî [1] metre, consisting of twelve syllables, was assigned to the Âdityas.

Considering how little we know about the seven Âdityas, with the exception of Varu*n*a, Mitra, and Aryaman, it would be very hazardous to connect them historically, as Professor Oldenberg suggests, with the seven Amesha-spentas or Amshaspands of the Avesta. No doubt the Amesha-spentas are seven, but many things are seven in ancient religion. Ahura may be called the lord of the Amesha-spentas, and Varu*n*a the head of the Âdityas. But Ahura existed independently of the Amesha-spentas, just as Varu*n*a of the Âdityas. Varu*n*a, however, who is so closely united with the second of the Âdityas, Mitra, has no such companion among the Amesha-spentas, for the Avestic Mithra himself has no place among them [2].

These powers are supposed to have been created by Ahura, and they represent, as we should say, divine qualities only, such as Vohu Mano = Good Thought (vasu manas), Asha Vahi*s*ta = Perfect Righteousness (*R*ita Vasish*th*a), Khshathra Vairya = Good Royalty (kshatra-vîrya). Spenta-Ârmaiti = Pious Modesty (Aramati). Haurvatât = Health (sarvatâti), Ameretât = Immortality (am*r*itatva). What similarity is there between these and the Âdityas, such as Varu*n*a, Mitra, Aryaman? And did not

---

[1] Oldenberg, Religion des Veda, p. 186 n.
[2] Oldenberg, l. c., p. 192, seems to imagine that Mithra, the Sun-god, was one of the Amesha-spentas, but Mithra is not even mentioned in the Gâthas.

Darmesteter's theory deserve to be at least mentioned that Vohu Mano is but a copy of the Alexandrian Λόγος θεῖος? This would bring the seven Amesha-spentas down to the third century B.C, rather too recent a date for the Vedic Âdityas. We know far more of the character of the Ameshaspentas than of the Âdityas. Âditya means the sun, and the Âdityas seem to have been intended originally for certain manifestations of the sun, whether in the course of the day or in the course of the year. There is no indication whatsoever that they were meant for the five planets, or in fact that the idea of five planets was known at so early a time. And how should we account for the fact that the five conspicuous planets (if the Âdityas, Aryaman, Bhaga, Amsa, &c., were ever names of the planets) should have been changed into such abstract beings as Vohu Mano, Good Thought, &c.? Can we connect any idea with such a change, or can we point out any analogy in the whole history of astronomy? And if Varuna was the first of the Âdityas, would he not have been the sun rather than the moon? And how should we be able to explain the absence of Mitra, the sun, from the seven Amesha-spentas?

So far therefore from looking upon Varuna either as a modern or as a borrowed god, or as a representative of the moon, I take him as one of the oldest Vedic deities, Indo-European because identical in name with Οὐρανός, and thoroughly Vedic because inseparable from other Vedic gods, such as Mitra, Agni, Indra, and Soma. We find hymns addressed to Mitrâ-Varunau, to Agnî-Varunau (IV, 1, 2–5), to Indrâ-Varunau (I, 17), to Soma and Varuna (V, 75,

18). Why should we tear Varuṇa away from all these companions?

Varuṇa as Moon.

There is no doubt some truth in the statement supported by Hillebrandt, Hardy, and Oldenberg (p. 193) that Varuṇa has something to do with the moon. The question is only, in what sense? The Vedic gods, as I have tried to show, are never the physical objects in which their activity was primarily discerned. Their character, as clearly seen by Yâska, is much larger and comprehends a wide sphere of activity. The god of fire is seen wherever light and warmth are perceived. The god of the thunderstorm (Indra) overcomes darkness in every form; the Aśvins are present in every kind of dualism manifested in nature. Hence, to restrict Varuṇa to the moon, would be as misleading as to identify the Aśvins with the morning and evening stars, Indra with the rain, Agni with the fire on the hearth. Varuṇa, as representing the covering or dark sky, may certainly be nearly related to the moon also[1], just as, in Greek mythology, Phoibe (the moon) is the daughter, and Asteria (the star-goddess) the granddaughter of Ouranos (sky). But to confine Varuṇa to the narrow sphere of the moon would be unnatural, and could never be brought into harmony with the magnificent descriptions of Varuṇa in the Vedic hymns. Does he not spread himself out like a cloak over all the world (VIII, 41, 7)? Does he not enclose the nights and establish the mornings, being visible everywhere (VIII, 41, 3)? Does he not change the black coverings into white

---

[1] Sun and moon are sometimes called the two Âdityas.

ones (VIII, 41, 10)? Is not the sun his eye as well as the moon[1]? Does he not dwell at the sources of the rivers (VIII, 41, 2), and is he not in the Veda already called the dark ocean (VIII, 41, 8), a prelude to his later character as god of the ocean and the Western quarter[2]? All this is surely not a description of the moon, nay, it is curious that though the moon is certainly within his domain, so very little should have been said about the moon in hymns addressed to Varuna.

It used to be maintained that there was a complete breach between the Varuna of the Mahâbhârata when he is the god of the waters, and that of the Veda. But traces of his connection with the waters can be discovered in the Veda also, and the passages quoted above from the forty-first hymn of the eighth Mandala would be sufficient to prove it, even if we took the ocean and the rivers for the waters of the atmosphere or the clouds. Varuna is often in the Veda asked to send rain; he is addressed as the lord of rivers, and in I, 161, 14, his proper domain is said to be the water (adbhíh yâti samudraíh), though not necessarily the sea.

Âdityas.

But though Varuna as the dark and Mitra as the bright god are clear and intelligible, their name as Âdityas remains obscure. Âditya came to mean the sun, but originally it can have meant son of the

---

[1] In the language of the Dayaks of Borneo the sun is called betuch anuh, from betuch, eye, and anuh, day. In Malagassi also the sun is maso andro, i. e. eye of day.

[2] Rv. VIII, 41, 8, Sáh samudráh apíkyàh turáh dyâm iva rohati.

mother Aditi only (cf. Rv. I, 72, 9), or belonging to Aditi. Oldenberg's opinion (p. 203) that the Âdityas gave rise to Aditi, as the Kronidai to Kronos, is plausible, but requires fuller proof.

Aditi.

This Aditi is a goddess who has given rise to very different explanations. Etymologically Aditi means unbound, free, and I have always taken her as the first, though as yet very material conception of the Beyond. If the horizon, if sunrise and sunset marked the limits of human perception, then what was postulated by the very idea of horizon or limit, was the Beyond, the Unbound, i. e. the Unlimited, or what in later philosophy was called the Infinite. I see the difficulties, but I see no other bridge from the etymological to the mythological meaning of Aditi. To derive Aditi from ad, to eat, in the sense of the Devourer, is possible, but no more, nor would the fact that Agni is called Aditi (I, 94, 15) help us to prove this derivation. If the Vedic poets postulated a third heaven and a heaven beyond, why not an Aditi beyond the world of sense, beyond the sun, beyond the dawn. From that goddess, sun, moon, and other luminous manifestations might well be supposed to have risen, and hence be called Âdityas. The dawn is actually called the face of Aditi (aditeḥ anîkam); why then should not the sun have been called the son of Aditi? If the Vedic Indians had been familiar with the five planets, I do not deny that these also might have been called the sons of Aditi. But even with the Greeks the discovery of travelling by the side of fixed stars belongs to a comparatively late age, and though the names of the Âdityas are obscure and probably therefore very ancient, they do in no wise point to the planets. They may represent phases of the sun in his various manifestations, but even this cannot be proved. What then can be the meaning of such statements as that the Amesha-spentas are the Âdityas, and what shall we say if we are told that the existence of seven planets was known in the Vedic age, though probably borrowed from a Semitic source? The consequences of such a statement would be far-reaching indeed, and would, if fully proved, revolutionise the whole history of astronomy.

I know well that the conception of Aditi as the Beyond may seem too modern, too metaphysical for the physical pantheon of the Veda, too abstract for poets who are supposed to have been no better than naked savages. But let scholars read the Rev. W. Gill's papers on Polynesian folklore, and they will be surprised to see with what airy abstractions even these naked thinkers were able to deal. Anyhow I cannot for the present find any truer explanation of Aditi and Âditya, and I cannot say that anything better has as yet been suggested. Oldenberg's idea that Aditi may have meant freedom is not very different from my own, only he seems to me to narrow her sphere of action too much by confining it to moral freedom, or freedom from sin (anâgâstvám). Aditi takes sometimes the place of the wife of Tvash*tri*, instead of B*ri*haddivâ, and would in that character be the mother of Sara*n*yû, and therefore as yet thoroughly physical. The Veda keeps true to its character, all its gods, even Varu*n*a, are children of nature, and if Mitra represents from the first the bright day, Varu*n*a is and remains in the Veda the representative of the dark, yet brilliant, sky, of the night and all that is connected with it[1].

Asvinau and other Dual Gods and Heroes.

I may seem very pertinacious, but in spite of all that has been written since I attempted the first explanation of the Asvinau in my Lectures on the Science of Language in 1863 (p. 606 seq.), I still hold to what I then wrote about the dual gods. I then pointed out that in the most general sense the Asvinau were the male representatives of light and darkness, the two Ahans, as they are called, i. e. day and night, and that they exhibit the eternal dualism of nature which has found expression in ever so many mythological names and stories. The Asvins are in fact the principal actors in the diurnal drama which forms the ever recurring theme of Aryan mythology. In Greek and Roman mythology the two are generally either brothers or twins, often separated by an irresistible fate, great benefactors or rulers of men, founders of cities, and generally more or less closely related to some beautiful woman, whether their mother, their sister, their friend, or their wife.

The Relations of the Asvins.

To begin with the Asvins, we learnt before, when examining the myth of Sara*n*yû = Erînys, that

---

[1] I have since read Prof. Oldenberg's defence, 'Varu*n*a und die Âdityas,' but I have nothing to alter in what I had written before I received it. I can discover nothing new in support of a postulated Semitic origin of Varu*n*a.

Tvash*tri* made a wedding feast for his daughter Sara*n*yû, and that she, the wife of the great Vivasvat, having been wedded and become the mother of Yama, disappeared. The immortal (Sara*n*yû) was hidden from the mortals, and a likeness of her was made and given to Vivasvat. She, Sara*n*yû, then bore the two A*s*vins and left the two couples behind.

This outline of an old and clearly physical myth was filled out by tradition in various ways, and we are told that Vivasvat when married to Sara*n*yû, became the father not of Yama only, but of twins, called Yama and Yamî, afterwards of Manu, as the son of the woman who had been made to serve as a substitute for Sara*n*yû, and lastly of the two A*s*vins. According to another half-forgotten myth, it was not Vivasvat, but her own father Tvash*tri* who was the progenitor of all these children, or, according to still another account, of Vâstoshpati, fire, and A*s*va, the horse.

Names and Legends of the A*s*vins.

This is not, however, the only account given of the A*s*vins in the Veda. In Rv. I, 116, 17, the daughter of Sûrya mounts the chariot of the A*s*vins; in I, 117, 5, it is distinctly said that she chose them as her husbands. In other places, again, they act as varas, or groomsmen only. Soma is the bridegroom, while Agni acts as herald at the marriage procession (Ath. XIV, 8-9). In trying to unravel this myth in its various forms as contained, for instance, in the Rv. X, 17, we must remember that the A*s*vins are constantly called the grandsons of Dyaus, Divó nápâtâ, and I believe we may take that name in its literal sense, not simply as the sons or offspring of Dyaus, but literally as his grandchildren. It would follow thence that Tvash*tri*, their grandfather, the father of Sara*n*yû, their mother, is in this case but another name for Dyaus, that is, Dyaus in his character of shaper of the world. In the Veda, as we possess it, the supremacy of Dyaus among the gods has come to an end, and his place has in many respects been taken by Indra, his son. In order to confirm the often neglected identity of Dyaus and Tvash*tri* it is important to observe that the same Indra, who is called the son of Dyaus, is likewise represented as the son of Tvash*tri*[1]. We also saw that Tvash*tri* is called b*ri*haddiva*h* (X, 64, 10), and his wife B*ri*haddivâ, i.e. the wide-shining dawn[2]. We must not, however, attempt to define too much, but be satisfied with taking Tvash*tri* like Dyaus as simply an old god of former times, the maker, the father, and in our case the parent of Sara*n*yû, the goddess of the dawn, who becomes the wife of Vivasvat, the shining sky, and the mother of Yama, the twin. Who this twin was, we shall have to consider afterwards.

As to Vivasvat there can be little doubt about the meaning of his name. In the Veda, vivasvat is still used as an adjective and means brilliant. Ushas, the dawn, is called vivasvatî (Rv. III, 30, 13). As a substantive Vivasvat has been translated by sun, and it certainly has that meaning in later Sanskrit also. In the Veda, however, its meaning is not yet narrowed down to sun, but Vivasvat may stand for

---

[1] Rv. III, 48, 2 and IV, 18, 3.
[2] Rv. V, 41, 19; 42, 12.

the bright sky, the bright day, the early morning, and it is in that character that Vivasvat appears as the husband of Sara*n*yû. The meaning of Sara*n*yû can hardly be doubtful if we remember that she is the daughter of Dyaus, Duhitâ Diva*h*. This, as we know, is first of all the dawn; nor can there be a more appropriate wife for Vivasvat, the morning sun, than Sara*n*yû, the dawn. Thus we read, Rv. X, 39, 12 :—

Yásya yóge duhitā́ *g*ā́gate divā́*h*
Ubhé áhanî sudíne Vivásvata*h*.

'O A*s*vins, when your chariot is harnessed, the daughter of Dyaus is born, and the two bright Ahans (day and night) of Vivasvat.'

Every new addition to the family circle of Vivasvat renders its general character more clearly perceptible. Sara*n*yû is said to be born when the chariot of the A*s*vins is being harnessed. This surely means that the dawn appears when the chariot of the A*s*vins is ready for their daily journey. That the same dawn is the mother of the A*s*vins must not perplex us, for in the Veda the physical meaning of the gods is constantly breaking through their mythological disguises. The gods are said to be born and die with their daily appearance and disappearance in nature, but they are called immortal gods for all that, as if they were beyond the reach of birth and death. In our case the daughter of the sky is born (*g*âyate, i. e. appears), while her own twin sons are waiting for their chariot. And when the poet continues that the two Ahans of Vivasvat are born, these two Ahans are clearly meant for day and night, the twins, and the very prototypes of the A*s*vins themselves.

The Dawn as the Mother of Twins.

The idea that the dawn gives birth to twins had evidently become so familiar with the poets of the Veda, that they were able to speak of her as simply Yamasû*h*, i.e. twin-mother. One pair of twins consisted of the two A*s*vins. But we must now face a new and very serious difficulty, namely that in the Vedic hymn quoted above (X, 17), it is said that when first married to Vivasvat, Sara*n*yû gave birth to a Yama, lit. the twin.

Yama, the Twin.

What can be meant by a single twin? Tradition seems to have supplied the answer, by adding Yamî as the sister of Yama. This pair of twins was likewise known in Vedic times, though Yamî is evidently a later creation, and mentioned in one hymn of the Rig-veda only (X, 10), and this clearly a comparatively late composition. In this hymn, which is a dialogue between Yama and his sister Yamî, the sister invites her twin-brother to become her husband, while the brother expresses his horror at so unnatural a marriage.

This Yama and Yamî are supposed by some scholars to have been, like Adam and Eve, the progenitors of the human race [1]. They had evidently forgotten that, according to the Rig-veda, Yama and Yamî were never married, and never became progenitors. There is besides this difficulty, that the poet in X, 17 calls Sara*n*yû the mother of Yama in the singular, though he afterwards speaks of dvâ

---

[1] Cf. E. H. Meyer, Gandharvas, p. 229 seq.

mithunâ, two couples of children, that is, as it would seem, four children belonging to Sara*n*yû. Dvâ mithunâ can hardly be meant simply for two children. We shall have to admit, I think, that this Yama in the singular was really meant for the sun, but in order to explain why the sun could be called the twin by himself, we should be obliged to look upon the sun, when represented by Yama, as a double sun, the sun of the day and the sun of the night, conceived as one and yet as two inseparable beings [1]. This seems, no doubt, a very strange idea, but it is difficult to account for our Yama in any other way, and in studying the ancient poetry of the Veda, we must accustom ourselves to ideas which to us may seem strange and illogical, but which were not so to people in their first endeavours to comprehend and name the daily marvels of nature.

Sun and Dawn as Horse and Mare.

To us it may sound strange to call the sun simply the horse, or the dawn the mare. Yet these were quite familiar names to the Vedic poets. At first the sun was spoken of as quick (âsu) like a horse (asva), but very soon the like was taken as understood, and the horse or the white horse was accepted by everybody

---

[1] As Mannhardt remarks, l. c., p. 232 seq.: 'the twilight of the morning and of the evening, the dawn and the gloaming, are often taken as one and the same phenomenon,' and on p. 306 he writes: 'Further research has shown that the apparently double apparition as evening and morning star was sometimes taken as single and called the God-son, and at other times led to the admission of two God-sons, who often, whether in the evening or the morning, are conceived as acting together.'

as a name of the sun. In Rv. IV, 52, 2, the dawn is still spoken of as brilliant like a mare, ásvâ iva, in the Mahâbhârata (Âdip. 2599) va*d*avâ, mare, is used as the very name of the dawn. When the twin sons of the dawn are called A*s*vin, this has generally been translated by horsemen, and there is no doubt that in later times these gods were conceived as riding on horseback[1]. Originally, however, this riding on horseback is by no means a distinguishing feature of the A*s*vins, and I much prefer therefore to take A*s*vin as a patronymic meaning sons or descendants of the famous A*s*va or A*s*vâ[2], i. e. the sun and the dawn.

Sara*n*yû as the Dawn.

If we render Sara*n*yû by the dawn, it should be understood that the ancients distinguished among several dawns, or among several agents of the dawn. There was the first, which was still the night rather than the day, the earliest glimmer of light, and this was Sara*n*yû, the retreating night and the returning light.

In a Swedish song the Sun (fem.) is represented as sitting on a bare stone, and spinning three hours before the sun rises. (Mannhardt, l. c., p. 218.) It was she who was the true mother of the A*s*vins, the representatives of morning and evening, who were ready even before the chariot of the sun had been harnessed, nay before their own mother was born. This dawn, this Morgengrauen, might truly be called

---

[1] Riding on horseback was supposed to have been altogether unknown in the Veda, but I think I have produced evidence to show that it was not.

[2] Like K*ri*sâsvin from K*ri*sâsva; see above.

not only the mother of the Asvins, but their friend also, their sister, and even their wife. All these phenomena of the morning are so variable and so apt to run into each other, that Yâska showed a wise discretion in defining the character of the two Asvins by saying no more than that the one represented light gaining on darkness and the other darkness gaining on light. It would be equally difficult to define the exact domain of the dawn and of her sister, the night, sometimes called the black sister. As soon as the one leaves, the other steps into her place (Rv. I, 113, 1. 2; 16; 124, 8). As soon as Saranyû, the flying night, became the wife of the bright sky, the new sun of the day was born of her, and she for a time was the far-shining Ushas. As the clouds of the sky were often called the waters, we can understand why the dawn was also called ápyâ yóshâ, as in X, 10, 4, where Yama reminds his sister that their common mother is this waterwoman, ápyâ yóshâ, and their common father the Gandharva in the waters, another name, as we saw, of Vivasvat and indirectly of Dyaus. We can also understand why the Asvins should sometimes be called sindhu-mâtarâ, the children of Sindhu, the sea, a name shared by the Maruts and by Soma.

Meaning of the Old Myth.

So far the old myth of the Asvins seems intelligible. Vivasvat, the bright sky, was united with Saranyû, the absconding night or the returning light; and from their union arose Yama, the twin, that is the inseparable couple of day and night, the Nychthêmeron, or, as we should say, the Nychthêmeros. But there was another couple to be accommodated. If day and night had been spoken of as the sons of the mare, as A*s*vinau, and if they also were looked upon as sprung from the bright morning, the Vivasvat, it was necessary to invent a metamorphosis of the dawn or Sara*n*yû into a mare, and of Vivasvat, her husband, into a horse. As soon as that was done, there followed the whole story, so often told by Vedic folklorists, that Sara*n*yû, the dawn, had vanished for a time, alluding probably to the disappearance of the dawn after the rise of the sun, and that her husband had followed her, till from their union a new couple was called into life, only under a different mythological name and disguise, namely the couple of day and night. This is what frequently happens in ancient mythology. The same thing is called by two or three different names, and these names have afterwards to be accommodated as brothers and sisters, as fathers and sons, thus causing confusion which is enough to break up the best regulated families in heaven or on earth. Yama, the twin, though he afterwards received a sister of the name of Yami, was originally, only in a very wide sense, the ditto of the A*s*vins, and we saw how the two couples of twins had finally to be sheltered under the same roof.

Yama.

We have still to follow the later history of Yama. Originally he was, as we saw, the daily sun, and I see as yet no other way of accounting for his name except by taking him to represent the twins, morning and evening, taken as one.

Yama as Agni.

We must now remember that the sun was often

treated in the Veda as one of the many manifestations of Agni, the god of light and warmth, and that this Agni is said to have entered the sun [1], nay to be the sun, just as he was said to be Tvashtri [2], Indra, Vishnu, Mitra and Varuna, in fact everything that is bright. Thus we read, Ath. XIII, 3, 23, 'Thou, O Agni, hast shone as the sun enkindled;' and of Rohita, another name of the sun, it is said that he is Varuna and Agni at evening, rising in the morning he is Mitra, moving through the air he is Savitri, and as warming the sky in the middle he is Indra [3] (Ath. XIII, 3, 13). We saw how Agni, fire, being the sine quâ non of the beginning of any civilised life, was often represented under different names as the founder of towns, as the ancestor of royal families, nay as the ancestor of mankind at large (Phorôneus, Promêtheus, &c.). Let us then take into account a very general idea that the life of nature and of man begins every morning with sunrise, and comes to an end every evening with the setting or dying sun. This is no more than what we still say ourselves when we speak of a man whose sun has set, i.e. whose life on earth has ended.

---

[1] Ait.-br. VIII, 5, 28 : Âdityo vâ astam yan agnim anupravisati, agner vâ âdityo gâyate. 'Âditya, the sun, when setting, enters into Agni ; from Agni, Âditya, the sun, is born.' More frequently still is Agni identified with the sun in the Brâhmanas, for instance, Sat.-br. IX, 2, 3, 12 : Sûryarasmir harikesah purastât Savitâ gyotir udayân agasram ity asau va âditya esho gnih. 'When it is said that Savitri, with sunny rays and golden hair, brought forth in front the eternal light, it is indeed yonder sun, it is this Agni' (Rv. X, 139, 1).

[2] Rv. II, 1, 5.

[3] See also Victor Henry, Vedica, p. 15.

Yama as the Firstborn and the first to die.

We have only to continue these two ideas in order to understand what is so often said of Agni, that he was the firstborn, Rv. X, 5, 7, Agní*h* ha na*h* prathama*g*á*h* ritâsya, 'Agni was the firstborn of Rita or order for us;' or that he was our eldest brother, Rv. X, 11, 2, Bhrâtâ na*h* *g*yesh*tháh* prathamá*h* ví vo*k*ati, 'May our eldest brother speak first[1].' But if Agni, as the twin, or as one of the twins, is the first who was born, Agni, as the other twin, as Yama, was also the first who died. 'Yama,' as Kuhn remarked long ago (Herabkunft, p. 235), 'the god, having descended on earth, fallen under the lot of mortals, becomes mortal and the first of mortals, and Yama, who is but another Agni, is expressly called so in one of the Vedic hymns.' In this I agree with Kuhn except that I see no evidence of Yama having been a god who descended on earth. Yama was simply the twin, the daily sun, more particularly in his character as the setting sun or the evening, and in this character he was conceived as the first instance of death, as the forerunner or path-finder of all who departed from this life after him, after the first of days.

All this is mythologically intelligible. Unfortunately a passage from the Atharva-veda has been appealed to by Kuhn and others to prove that Yama was not a mythological being at all, but was really a human being and the first of mortals. In the Ath.-veda, XVIII, 3, 13, we read: Yó mamára prathamó mártyânâm, yá*h* preyáya prathamó lokám

---

[1] Mr. Griffith thinks that Varu*n*a is here meant.

etam Vaivasvatâm sangámanam *g*ânânâm yamâm râ*g*ânam havíshâ saparyata.

'Serve with offering the king Yama, the Vaivasvata, the gatherer of men[1], who died the first of mortals, who went forward the first to that world.'

This verse is comparatively modern[2], still it is perfectly intelligible if we take Yama, the son of Vivasvat, here called a king, as the type of mankind, and if we try to understand how this type was borrowed from Yama, as the diurnal twin, who every day is born and dies, and may in that sense be called the first of those who were born, and likewise the first of those who died. But if we took Yama here as a real king, or as the first human being who lived and died, the nerve of the whole myth would be cut, and we should ask in vain why he was called Vaivasvata, the son of the bright sky, why he should have been born, and why it should be said that he was the first to die.

Was Yama = Adam?

It is easy to say that Yama was with the Vedic poets what Adam was to the Jews. In the Bible the whole human race is derived from one couple, Adam and Eve, the first man and the first mother. Such a couple is postulated in many mythologies and religions, but it is supplied under very different forms in different countries. Adam and Eve are not much more than simple ancestors. At a later time, however, the Jews themselves, at least those who had embraced Christianity, and under-

---

[1] In other places sa*m*yamana.
[2] The word Lokâ, world, is always a sign of a late origin.

stood Neo-Platonic philosophy, when they had to give an account of Adam, called him the son of God. But such was not the Aryan idea of the beginning of the human race.

Many of the Âryas believed in Autochthones, men sprung from their native soil. In that case the Earth became naturally their mother, and the god of the sky or some other great deity their father.

How Agni also, as fire, became the ancestor of one race, and then of all races of men, we saw before, and we have only to remember how in the Veda Agni, fire, and the sun are one and the same in order to understand the mythological saying that Yama, the solar twin, was the first of those who died. And if this is once clearly understood, the next step follows almost of necessity. Yama, the twin, the first who died, became the king and ruler of the dead, the gatherer of men, the lord of the other world, nay the god of death. He is himself called death already in the Rv. X, 165, 4: Tásmai Yamáya námo astu Mrityáve; and still more clearly in the Atharvaveda, VI, 28, 3: Yá/ prathamá/ pravátam â sasáda, bahúbhya/ pánthâm anupaspasâná/, Yo‹syáse dvipádo yás katúshpadas, tásmai Yamáya námo astu Mrityave, 'Let there be reverence to Yama, to Death, who first approached the precipice, finding out the path for many, who rules over bipeds and quadrupeds' (cf. Rv. X, 14, 1). Could this be said of a being such as Adam was conceived to have been, or of the first of mortal men? In the Rig-veda Yama, as the son of Vivasvat (X, 14, 5), and Varuna are both represented as drinking with the gods in the other world, sitting under a tree. Two dogs also are mentioned in their company. These are the same as the dogs of Saramâ, the Sârameyau, which the departed are told to avoid on their way to Yama's abode (Rv. X, 14, 10–11). If it is said that they are the messengers of Yama (here, of death), and we can recognise in them once more a remote repetition of the twins, that is, of day and night, the true messengers of death, for they are indeed asu-tripau, they feast every day on the vital breath of men, and, like all the other twins, are the offspring of the dawn, here introduced under the name of Saramâ. This Yama, however, as the ruler of the departed, or even as Death, though best known to us from the later literature, has his first beginnings in the Vedic conception of light and darkness, day and night, morning and evening personified as inseparable twins, the sons of the sun and of Saranyû, the dawn. Here we have the simplest original outlines of a myth, first suggested by nature, but afterwards elaborated with poetical freedom by the ancient story-tellers of India and Greece.

It takes, however, a long time before an idea once started and fitting in well with any favourite system, is given up again. When, in answer to Kuhn (Roth's Nirukta, XIII, 3, 13), I pointed out that there was no Vedic authority for taking Yama as a human being, I ought no doubt to have said Rig-vedic. But this might have been understood, nor would it have been safe to trust to the Atharva in such a matter. If Yama had really been the Vedic Adam, is it likely that he should never have been mentioned as such in the Rig-veda?

The first question to be answered would have been whether we are to take Yama as a real person, as the first mortal who died, or simply as a postulate to satisfy our logical instincts. In either case we should be called upon to conceive Yama as a man who, after his death, was raised to the rank of a god, and of a lord of the departed.

Now, I ask, is there any other case in the Veda where a man, real or postulated, has been changed into a god? There are many cases in which gods have sunk down to the level of mortals (even Agni), but I know of none where a man has become a real deva.

The next question would be, whether any man, real or imaginary, was ever in Rig-vedic times honoured with sacrificial offerings (Rv. X, 14, 1, Yamám rágânam havíshâ duvasya). It would also be important to see in whose company Yama is mentioned : Noscitur a sociis. It is well known that in later times Yama became one of the four or eight Lokapâlas. These are all gods, why then should Yama alone have been chosen from among mortal beings? Yama cannot even be considered as one of the Pit*r*is or fathers, for we read that the Pit*r*is go to him in the highest heaven and rejoice in his company. And if Yama had been originally a real man, would not his two dogs also have to be taken as real dogs? But these messengers of Yama who roam about among the people, who are supposed to be able to restore to man his vital breath, are the children of Saramâ, and no one has yet maintained that she also was originally a human being.

Prof. Hillebrandt has pointed out that even in the Atharva-veda Yama is not called a man (manushya or *g*ana), but only a mortal, and it is well known that the gods also are in the Veda conceived as subject to birth and death. When Yama is called the collector of men (saṅgamano *ganânâm*), we can clearly see the distinction between him, the gods, and the fathers, i.e. the departed.

The myth of Yama is perfectly intelligible if we trace its roots back to the sun of the evening, while the admission of an apotheosis of Yama, which is not even postulated by the passage in the Atharva-veda, would completely isolate him from his mythological surroundings.

We saw how the tragedies in the solar family begin already in the Veda. There is incest between Tvash*tri* and Sara*n*yû, there is threatened incest between Yama and Yamî, and the fact that Sara*n*yû is both the mother and the friend of the A*s*vins contains the seeds of further complications. Nor must we forget that there is another story, running parallel with the wedding of the daughter of Tvash*tri*, namely the wedding of Sûryâ, the daughter of Sûrya or Savit*ri*, with Soma, when the A*s*vins acted as best men, and Agni was the leader of the hymeneal procession. Here Sûryâ, the daughter of Savit*ri*, the sun, that is the dawn, has again to act a very doubtful part, for though her intended husband is said to be Soma, the moon, she evidently is in love with the A*s*vins, chooses them as her husbands, and is carried off by them on their golden chariot. Nay, another god, Vâyu, the wind, who is often confounded with Indra, is likewise called the son-in-law of Tvash*tri*, and hence, it must be supposed, the husband of Sara*n*yû (Rv. VIII, 26, 21).

That the tragedies of Aeschylus and Sophocles should have sprung from these distant physical myths seems at first incredible, quite as incredible as that a magnificent oak-tree should have sprung from a small decaying acorn, but the one lesson is as important to learn as the other. This whole subject has been very fully treated by Dr. Ehni in his 'Der Vedische Mythus des Yama' (1890). I agree with him in all he says to prove that Yama was the sun and could never have sprung into being as the first of men; but I do not see the necessity of his elaborate arguments to show how Yama could have become the first of those who died, and afterwards the lord of the departed, nay the god of death. All these ideas seem to me to arise most simply and naturally from a contemplation of the setting sun. Here, if anywhere, we may consult the thoughts of other nations, even of savage races, to find out what the Vedic poets could have meant when they made Yama the first who died, the first who went over to the other world and became there the king and ruler of the departed. To us, brought up on Semitic ideas, this postulated Adam may seem a very natural thought. But if we want to know what thoughts were really natural on such a subject, why not consult the traditions of the real Naturvölker, on points where they might safely be consulted?

I pointed out long ago [1] how the Hervey Islanders speak of old age as a mountain-top yellow with the rays of the setting sun. Now with them to die a natural death is called 'to follow in the track of the sun,' while if a man recovers from a serious illness, they say 'that he has come back to the region of sunrise.'

The Maoris also express their desire 'to go down with the sun,' and one of their songs says, 'Wait, wait awhile, O sun, and we will go down together.'

---

[1] Science of Language, ii, p. 635.

And did not a German poet also sing: 'Ich möchte hingehn wie das Abendroth'? Why should such ideas, which came quite naturally to these savages, which are perfectly intelligible even to us, have been absent from the thoughts of the Vedic people when they said that Yama (the setting sun) had been the first to find the way that leads to the world beyond, to the home of the departed, afterwards called the realm of Yama and Varuna, and that we are but following his guidance?

Bergaigne (ii, 98; 506), faithful to his own peculiar system of interpreting the thoughts of the Vedic poets, explains our myth by taking Vivasvat as the sacrificial fire, and Yamî as prayer. Such a view seems to me to destroy the whole physical foundation of Vedic mythology, and to derive no support either from the utterances of the Vedic poets or from the statements of their ancient commentators. When Yâska says that Yama is a name of Agni, he probably knew what he meant, and felt himself supported by the authority of ancient tradition. We also can with some little effort connect a definite meaning with his words. For though it may be true, as Roth says, that Yama never occurs in the Veda as a name of Agni, we must remember that with Yâska Agni was more than the terrestrial fire, and that the presence of Agni was perceived by him whenever there was light or heat. In that sense, therefore, Agni might well be called Yama, and vice versâ.

We saw before that Agni and Indra together were actually called the two Yamas or twins. I say once more that in a case like this, where we have to deal with human nature in its most general character, we may safely consult the eschatological ideas of the so-called Naturvölker, and not attempt a philosophical interpretation of Yama, such as has been attempted by Prof. Oldenberg and others. I can understand that Vedic interpreters should have admitted two Yamas, a Yamá and a Yamî, but if, like Prof. Oldenberg, we admit but one original Yama, how could that being, if meant for the first man, be said to have given the horse which Trita harnessed, and which Indra was the first to mount (X, 163, 2), a horse which is identified with Âditya, the sun? How could he have mentioned the same Yama in I, 164, 46, as between Agni and Mâtari*s*van, or in X, 64, 3, in the company of sun and moon, of Trita, Vâta, the wind, the dawn, Aktu (night), and the A*s*vins, all mythological beings, among whom a mere mortal would seem to be entirely out of place? Dr. Ehni has also clearly pointed out how in a myth, alluded to in Rv. X, 61, Tvash*tri* became the husband of his own daughter, Sara*n*yû, and their children were Vâstoshpati (i. e. Agni) and A*s*va, the horse, i. e. the sun; and, if so, how could we find a place here for the first man?

When Dr. Ehni tries to prove that Yama, in order to be called twin, must have had a twin, and that this twin was Yamî, meaning the moon, I cannot follow him. No doubt it seems to stand to reason that a twin presupposes another twin, but mythology and reason are two very different things. In the Taitt. S. III, 3, 8, 3, where Yama is explained as Agni, Yamî is explained as the earth. I prefer to think, strange as it sounds, that the daily sun by himself was called Yama on account of his double nature, being both day and night, both bright and dark, both Mitra and Varuṇa; while I take Yamî, his sister, to have been an afterthought, possibly as intended for the night. I readily admit, however, that on this point the evidence is far too scanty to enable us to speak with any confidence, a lesson which is impressed on us more and more when we try to restore from the scanty ruins preserved in the Veda the old temple in which the Vedic Âryas celebrated their Devas.

Greek and Roman Twins.

If now we look once more into Greek or Roman mythology, we find many legends which remind us of the myth of the Asvins, only we must not expect to find more than the groundwork of the Vedic myth often hidden beneath the marvellous stories which Greek imagination has erected on it. We shall easily discover the general outlines, as described before, namely, two brothers and a beautiful sister or wife or friend, all of them the children of one of the great gods, all of them mixed up in strange adventures, and in the end admitted to the company of the gods, but we must not expect to be able to account for all the details of these Greek stories from Vedic sources. These details may have been historical and local, and though in some of them we may recognise mythological elements, we ought not to attempt too much. We must learn to be satisfied if we can show that the principal actors in the tragic stories of Thebes, Sparta, and Argos are a pair of brothers and a beautiful sister or friend, in order to feel convinced that the distant background of these stories in their various localities was the same in Greece as in India. Or, can we bring ourselves to believe that it is a mere accident if we find in Greece the same three actors, 'the two with the one,' as in India, only under different names? as for instance, as—

1. Kastor, Polydeukes, and Helena in Lakedaimon (parents, Zeus [Tyndareus] and Lêda).
2. Amphîon, Zêthos, and Antiope in Thebes (parents, Zeus [Epôpeus] and Antiope).
3. Dardanos, Jāsion, and Harmonia in Arkadia (parents, Zeus [Korytos] and Êlektra).
4. Pelias, Nêleus, in Pylos (parents, Poseidon [Krêtheus] and Tyro).
5. Hêrakles, Îphikles, and Alkmêne in Thebes (parents, Zeus [Amphitryon] and Alkmêne).

There are some unmistakable lines of agreement running through all these stories. Hêrakles and Îphikles have the same mother, but different fathers, one divine (Zeus), the other human (Amphitryon); so have Kastor and Polydeukes (Zeus and Tyndareus); and so have Dardanos and Jāsion (Zeus and Korytos), and, to a certain extent, Pelias and Nêleus; Poseidon (Enîpeus and Krêtheus) and Amphîon and Zêthos (Zeus and Epôpeus). The children are considered dangerous to their parents or grandparents, and are therefore either exposed or persecuted. Sometimes, in order to make them innocuous, they are sent out on desperate errands, such as to fetch the golden fleece, or to perform the twelve labours. Some of them, such as Kastor and Polydeukes, Amphîon and Zêthos, are actually called Διόσκουροι, and white-horsed, λευκόπωλοι, λεύκιπποι.

It would be useless to attempt to trace in the stories of these couples more than a very vague memory of their original character, or to discover any solar elements in them beyond the twinhood of day and night, their descent from the sky or the sun, their relationship with the beautiful dawn, and their supposed dangerous character arising from the necessary destruction of the preceding day or season or year by each succeeding one. But on the other hand we can hardly believe that this fundamental theme—Rv. VIII, 29, 8, Dvā́ k̇arataḣ ékayā sahā́, 'The two move along together with the one'—which appears in all its natural simplicity in the Veda, should occur again and again in Greek and other Aryan myths, unless there was something more in it than mere accident, or unless we believe that our common human nature is really sufficient to account for all such coincidences. Of course our common human nature, and likewise the common physical nature by which we are surrounded, have something to do with all mythology, but whereas if we had to deal with Zulus or Mincoupies we should probably have to be satisfied with this appeal to our common humanity, it seems to me that we have here a little more. We have something that has grown and become named and fixed; we have something in a certain sense historical, and yet so prehistoric that it must have existed before the Aryan Separation, and have been carried off in its undeveloped stage by the different branches of the Aryan family.

Other Names of the Asvins.

And this is to a certain extent confirmed by the names also of some of these mythological characters. Those names, if they stood alone, might perhaps be put aside as uncertain or as the result of mere accident, but as additional fulcra they are of real importance.

The Aśvins, as we saw, were called Divo napâtâ, grandchildren of Dyaus, while their mother bore the name of Duhitâ Diva*h*, the daughter of Dyaus. In Greece, not only the sons of Lêda, but the sons of Antiope also, were called Διόσκουροι, i. e. the sons of Zeus. The Aśvins have brilliant or white horses (su*k*aya*h*), the sun itself is called the white horse, and the Dioskouroi also are supposed to ride on white horses (λευκόπωλοι, λεύκιπποι). And be it remembered that this epithet λευκόπωλος is in Greek an epithet of Hêmera also, or the daybreak.

Dasra is often used as the name of one or both of the Aśvins. Their mother who, as we saw, was called Yamasû*h*, mother of the twins, was in later times called Dasrasû*h* also, the mother of the Dasras. Sâya*n*a explains dasra by destroyer of enemies, Roth by wonder-working. It may possibly be connected with das in the sense of hunting (cf. abhidâs), which may have been further developed in δηριάομαι, to wrestle, and δῆρις, fight (cf. vas, vasar, vasra, ἔαρ, ἦρ), unless we connect δῆρις with δέρω, remembering that one of the Dioskouroi, Polydeukes, is always conceived as πύκτης, the pugilist.

Nâsatyâ.

Nâsatyâ also is used whether of one or of both the Aśvins. They are called Nâsatyau in the dual, according to a very common Vedic custom which sanctions Mitrâ for Mitrâ-Varu*n*au, Naktâ and Ushasâ for Naktoshasâ, Dyâvâ and P*r*ithivî for Dyâvâ-P*r*ithivî. But Nâsatya occurs in the singular also, Rv. IV, 3, 6, nâsatyâya párigmane, and we have the compound Indra-Nâsatyâ, Rv. VIII, 26, 8. What is more perplexing is the use in Latin of Castores in the plural, meant for the dual, for Castor and Pollux (Plin. H. N. 10, 43), and according to some, even of Polluces, as comprehending both the Dioskouroi. How did the Romans evolve this use which is not sanctioned in Greek, and how did they change Polydeukes into Pollux? It is a very useful lesson on the changeableness of mythological names, but it is difficult to explain the exact process. In Greek Dioskouroi never occurs in the singular except in grammars.

Nâsatya is a troublesome name. It is explained by Sâya*n*a as na-asatya, not untruthful, by others as na-satya, very truthful, nay even as nâsatya, nasutus (Bergaigne). I doubt whether any one of these explanations has proved acceptable. My own derivation from nas is difficult, but not impossible. The root nas, meaning to come towards something, has, particularly in Greek, taken the meaning of returning. This is shown in νόστος, return, from νέομαι (Goth. nisan). An important portion of Greek mythology consisted, as is well known, in the Νόστοι or the returns of the Greek heroes. The Odyssey was in fact the Nostos of Odysseus. The heroes who return or who are saved were called νόστιμοι, and in their first beginning, long before the rise of epic mythology, these terms seem to point back to the return of all the heavenly bodies, whether at the end of the night, or at the end of the winter. The Asvins are most prominently the ever-returning heroes, and nâsa-tya like νόστι-μος would therefore have been by no means an inappropriate term for one of them, if we derived it from nâsa, return, and the local suffix tya. This is no more than a guess which would carry little weight by itself, but may claim consideration as throwing light on the most distant background of Aryan mythology, and as indicating once more the physical origin of this whole cluster of myths.

On some points in the character of the Asvins the language of the Veda allows of no doubt. If it is said that Sûryâ, the daughter of Sûryâ, was given to the Asvins to be their wife, or that they won her in a race against all the gods, no one would doubt that Sûryâ, sometimes called the daughter of Sûrya, was the sun in her female character, or the morning sun, the dawn, together with whom the Asvins drive along on their chariot which is said to strike the ends of the sky (VII, 69, 3). Sometimes they are actually called Sûryâvasû, brilliant with Sûryâ (VII, 68, 3), sometimes, as we saw, Sûryâ is said to have chosen them for herself (VII, 69, 4). The Asvins are the sons of Vivasvat, and they are supposed, in their independent character, to dwell with him, I, 46, 13, vâvasânâ Vivásvati [1]. Anyhow, if any gods in heaven are solar, the Asvins are so, as representatives of day and night, starting every morning on their journey, and returning the next morning. They are in consequence invoked and worshipped both in the early morning and in the evening.

---

[1] There is a special development in the meaning of Vivasvat which made him a priest on earth, just as among the gods Vivasvat, like Agni, performs the office of the priest. We must remember that the sacrifice on earth is often an imitation of phenomena in the sky and vice versâ. In the plural the Vivasvats are a priestly family like the Aṅgiras, the Bhrigus, &c.

Asvins as Temporal Gods.

That everything belonging to the Asvins is golden or white would be quite consonant with their solar character, but we must not restrict their dramatic sphere to that of the sun only. They are from the beginning temporal rather than local gods, representing all that happens in the daily struggle between night and day. This temporal character of theirs accounts for their manifold and various manifestations[1], and the numerous acts ascribed to them. There are few things that cannot be considered as the acts of Day and Night. Hence in the morning the Asvins may be said to bring light or to deliver the light from the fangs of the night. They also may be praised for delivering the world from darkness, and, one may add, from all the miseries which Hesiod describes[2] as the brood of the night.

During the day they may be asked to assist both the labourers and the warriors, and at the end of the day to grant victory, peace, and rest. There are few things therefore from birth to death for which different poets may not have invoked or praised the Asvins, and hence the many legends alluded to in the hymns of the Rig-veda, and taken as generally known, in which the Asvins appear as benefactors or deliverers.

Achievements of the Asvins.

The persons whom they delivered may in some

---

[1] Rv. I, 117, 9, purū́ várpāṃsi Asvinā dádhānā.
[2] Theogony, vv. 211–232.

cases have been real persons of whom of course we can know nothing. In other cases, however, those who were delivered by them were clearly, like their deliverers, mythological characters[1]. The stories are very much alike, and this by itself would indicate their mythological character. There is great similarity in the misfortunes that befall their favourites, and in the manner in which they were delivered by the A*s*vins. The stories themselves are often so uninteresting that, unless they had rested on a mythological foundation, they would hardly have been recorded at all. Thus we read that a quail, Vartikâ, had been swallowed by a wolf, but was delivered by the A*s*vins from his jaws. Even if we took Vartikâ as the name of a real woman, her being saved from the jaws of a wolf would hardly have been of sufficient importance to inspire various Vedic poets, nor is it clear how the A*s*vins could have saved her from being swallowed, unless, with the Aitihâsikas, we took them for two ancient kings.

Vartikâ.

Vartikâ[2] in Sanskrit means quail[3], and corresponds to Greek ὄρτυξ. The etymological meaning is the returning bird, like Vertumnus, the returning or revolving year. If then the A*s*vins had rescued a real quail or a real woman from the jaws of a wolf,

---

[1] See Myriantheus, Die Açvins oder Arischen Dioskuren, 1876.
[2] Science of Language, ii, p. 626.
[3] In Greek χελιδών, the swallow, signifies the return of the year, see Bergk, p. 1034, ἦλθ', ἦλθε χελιδών, καλὰς ὥρας ἄγουσα, καλοὺς ἐνιαυτούς.

would that have been an event to be immortalised in Vedic mythology? Surely we must look somewhere else to account for our Vartikâ myth. Vartikâ, the returning, might well have represented the return, either of the day or of the spring. If she represented the return of the day, i.e. the dawn, she was indeed rescued by the Asvins from the jaws of the night; if she represented the return of the year, she might have been the spring rescued from the prison of the winter. It should also be remembered that Hêrakles, clearly a solar hero, was once revived by an Ortyx (Gerhard, Griech. Myth., § 355, 2). We have seen how these two ideas, the matutinal and the vernal, are constantly running together in ancient mythology[1]. If then we find that Lêto was delivered of her two children, Apollon and Artemis, in the island of Ortygia, the quail-island, we can hardly look upon this as an accidental coincidence, but have to recognise here too a very slightly altered repetition of the old story that the solar god was delivered at the return of the morning, or at the beginning of the spring. We can then understand why Apollon was called Lykoktonos, the killer of the wolf, and why his sister Artemis was called Ortygia. That island, Ortygia, which was originally a mythological postulate rather than a geographical reality, is best known by the name of Dêlos, and this again means the bright island or the morning island, that is the Eastern sky. The complete legend of Lêto giving

---

[1] Sonne, K. Z., x, p. 121. In Germany the stork was looked upon as the ἄγγελος ἔαρος, and there is a modern epigram by Olearius: 'Ver laetum rediit, rediitque ciconia grata.' Cf. Grimm, Mythologie, p. 723.

birth to Apollon and Artemis was afterwards variously elaborated by poets and story-tellers, but the original elements of the legend need not have been more than a few proverbial sayings such as, 'The wolf has swallowed the quail,' i. e. it is night; 'The quail has been delivered from the jaws of the wolf,' i. e. it is morning. 'The night has brought forth her twins,' i. e. a new day (day and night) has begun. Such popular sayings are all that we have a right to expect in the as yet indifferentiated state of Aryan mythology; still if the occurrence of two such words as vartikâ in Sanskrit, and ὄρτυξ (= *vartukâ) in Greek, proves that the quail was known to the Âryas before their separation, the occurrence of Vartikâ as saved by the Asvins from the mouth of the wolf, and the birth of Ortygia (Artemis) and of Apollon Lykoktonos in the island of Ortygia, prove that the first germs of the much deprecated Solar Myth had begun to break forth when the ancestors of Greeks and Hindus were still living in close contact together. It is easier, no doubt, to say that the quail may have been a totem or a fetish, it is quite possible also that the Âryas never ate quails, in which case we should be told that we need not look further or trouble ourselves with doubtful etymologies.

I think on the contrary that the story of the Vartikâ ought to be a lesson to us, and that we should learn in how many fragments an old myth may have been shattered before it reaches us. There seems at first little reason why the story of a quail being rescued from the jaws of a wolf should have had anything in common with the story of Apollon and Artemis being born in the island of Délos. But when we see that Artemis is called Ortygia, and that the same name is given to the island of Délos, while in the Veda the person delivered from the wolf is called Vartikâ, we begin to feel that there must be some reason for it, and that if we but admit that in the most distant Aryan past, Vartikâ meant both quail and dawn, we can understand how the old story of the delivery of the ever returning dawn from the darkness of the night or the jaws of the wolf might have assumed these different disguises in the course of centuries, nay, of thousands of years that passed between the first origin of these early sayings and the days of the Vedic *R*ishis or the Greek rhapsodes. Anyhow, we may learn the lesson that if in this case the beings delivered by the A*s*vins from the wolf were the dawn and the rising sun, other beings also, delivered by the A*s*vins, may have had a similar origin, and that if the Vartikâ represented the returning light, the wolf, killed by the Lykoktonos, could hardly have been meant for anything but the retreating darkness.

*K*yavâna.

We read in the Vedic hymns that the A*s*vins restored *K*yavâna to youth, delivered him of his decrepit body, and made him acceptable once more to his wife. We can see in this case how early these old stories were amplified and diversified, for while the hymns presuppose nothing more, we read in the *S*atapatha-brâhma*n*a IV, 1, 5 a much fuller account. We are told there that the wife of *K*yavâna was called Sukanyâ (good girl), and that she was given to the old and decrepit *R*ishi *K*yavâna[1]

---

[1] *K*yavāna instead of *K*yavâna is the later form.

by king Saryâta, to make up for an insult offered him by the king's people. Then the Asvins came and tried to tempt her away, but she would not leave her old husband, and even derided the Asvins. When the Asvins wished to know why she derided them, she promised to tell them if they would make her husband young again. Upon this the Asvins made *K*yavana step into a pool, promising that he should come out of it at whatever age he should desire. When this had been done, *K*yavana told the Asvins that they were derided because they had formerly been excluded by the gods from a solemn sacrifice. This story may have existed when the hymn was composed, for it contains some mythological elements known in other Aryan mythologies also. There is a spring produced by Hades near the place where the earth opened to receive him and Persephone, and where Hêrakles is supposed to have founded a great annual festival. This spring is called Kyane. The pool, called *saisava*, youth, seems the type of the German Jungbrunnen, O. H. G. quickprunno, Grimm, D. M., p. 554, while Sukanyâ, as the wife of the old man, will remind many of the story of Êos and Tithônos[1].

As to the name of *K*yavâna, afterwards *K*yavăna, it is derived from *k*yu, and *k*yu has been identified with σεύω, as expressing any violent movement, not only that of driving or pushing, but also that of falling down, e. g. târâ ambarâ*k k*yavante, 'stars fall from the sky, or set' (Râm. V, 13, 31), or svargâ*k k*yavate lokât, 'he falls from the Svarga

---

[1] Myriantheus, l. c., p. 94. His identification of Sukanyâ with Mêdeia seems very doubtful.

world.' It may therefore have been used for the set or the setting sun, of which it might well be said that it had fallen into the fiery or dark abyss of the West, the very abyss from whence the A*s*vins were born, Rv. III, 39, 3, tápusha*h* budhné á itâ, and that it rose again rejuvenated by the A*s*vins in the morning. The idea also that the A*s*vins removed *K*yavâna's body like an old cloak would find an explanation in the clouds surrounding and hiding the sun at its setting[1].

Atri.

Much the same story is told of Atri. He is supposed to have been thrown into a fiery pit, sometimes called *ri*bîsa[2], an oven, another metaphor, it would seem, for a flaming sunset. The A*s*vins protected him from the heat and from the darkness, and restored him also to youth and strength. In this case the name of Atri is less clear than that of *K*yavâna, yet it may have been connected with Avestic âtar, traces of which are preserved in Lat. atrium, and in Sk. athar-van, fire-priest. Others explain Atri as ad-t*ri*, devourer, a common name for enemies of the gods (O. N. jötunn)[3]. In cases like this we can do no more than suggest; we

---

[1] I find the same explanation in V. Henry's Mythes Naturalistes, p. 12. The same scholar derives the name of Sisyphus also from the root *k*yu, in the sense of pushing, and I think he is right.

[2] If *ri*bisa means oven, it would be the old oven, a hole dug in the earth, in which meat was cooked or baked by means of hot stones, a kind of oven that was used by savage tribes. Cf. Tylor, Early History, p. 260; Klemm, Kulturgeschichte, iii, 222.

[3] Mannhardt, Germ. Mythen, p. 168.

cannot undertake to prove the origin of every ancient proper name with mathematical certainty.

Vandana.

But it is important to observe that almost the same story as told of Atri, is told once more of Vandana. When the old and decrepit Vandana had been thrown into a pit and buried alive, the Asvins rescued him that he might see the light again. It would be difficult to achieve this even with the help of the Asvins. The idea, however, that Atri or his body had been dug in (nikhâta), occurs again, as we shall see, though in a somewhat different form, when it is said that the Asvins brought up gold that had been dug in or hidden (Rv. I, 117, 12, &c.). It does not seem very bold to take this gold for the golden body of the sun (hira*n*yagarbha), and to recognise in Atri another mythological representative of the sun.

I pointed out many years ago how sometimes the Vedic *R*ishis betray the secret of their myths by using the very comparison from which certain myths originally sprang. Thus Urvasi, the dawn, says to Purûravas that she is gone away like the first of the dawns[1], while Purûravas calls himself Vasish*th*a, which may be translated by the brightest, but also by the greatest of the Vasus, that is, the sun. In the same way we read in Rv. I, 117, 5, that the Asvins dug up for Vandana some bright buried gold for new splendour, 'like one asleep in the lap of Nir*r*iti'[2] (death), 'like the sun dwelling in darkness.'

---

[1] Chips, vol. iv, p. 111.
[2] The same expression here used of the sun, or of Vandana, nir*r*iteh upâsthe, occurs in X, 95, 14 with regard to Purûravas. Is all this mere accident? On Nir*r*iti, see Chips, vol. iv, p. 304.

Possibly sushupvâmsam (like one asleep) refers likewise to the sun, or to some of its many representatives.

Bhu*g*yu Taugrya.

Bhu*g*yu, another worshipper, who is supposed to have been rescued by the A*s*vins after his friends had deserted him on the sea, may be a name of the flying (bhu*g*, φεύγειν, φύξιος) sun, drowned in the sea. If he is called *g*ahita, forsaken or drowned, it should be remembered that we have from the same root *G*âhusha, who is another hero saved by the A*s*vins. This *g*ah-usha agrees in its radical elements with ζόφος and Ζέφυρος, the West or evening wind. (Cf. M. M. in Techmer's Internat. Zeitschrift für Allgem. Sprachwissenschaft, vol. i, p. 215.) Buttmann already, Lexilogus, i, 616, derived Ζέφυρος from ζόφος.

V*ri*ka.

Of V*ri*ka, who was likewise rescued by the A*s*vins, we know little except that the word means wolf. This is generally used as a type of darkness and mischief rather than of light or a friend of light. Hence Apollon was called λυκοκτόνος or wolf-killer. It is only if we take darkness as the antecedent, the origin, the parent of light, that we can account for the A*s*vins extending their help to a V*ri*ka.

Kali.

Kali, whose youth the A*s*vins are said to have renewed, can hardly be meant for the sun; Kali was originally a name of the last quarter of the moon, afterwards of the fourth or last Yuga also, and likewise of the lowest among the dice[1]. Of that Kali, the waning moon, it might well have been said that day and night or the two Asvins restored the moon's youthful strength, and this would be further confirmed, if we are right in our interpretation of Vispalâ.

Vispalâ.

Of Vispalâ it is said that her leg, which she had lost in battle, was replaced by the Asvins by an iron leg. As vis+patnî[2] is an epithet of Sinîvâlî, the goddess of the first day of the new moon, we can hardly be wrong in looking on the restored iron leg as the first quarter or pâda of the new moon, called iron on account of its darkness as compared with the golden colour of the full moon. Pâda meant both foot and the fourth part of anything.

We see therefore that the Asvins, though originally diurnal in their character, and therefore saviours of the morning light, gradually assumed the more general character of helpers, helping the moon in her distress, and possibly the annual sun also in his weakness, in his exile and his return at the time of the winter solstice.

Nor do I deny that after the Asvins had once assumed this character of helpers, they may have been praised for helping real persons also in their distress. Thus if we read that Vishnâpû was restored by them to Visvaka, that he might see him, it is quite possible that these two persons may have lived in India, though others might possibly detect some relationship between Vishnâpû and Vishnu.

But when we are told that the Asvins restored

---

[1] M. M., Hist. A. S. L., p. 412.   [2] Rv. II, 32, 7.

his eyes to *Rigrâsva*, i. e. Red-horse (cf. Rohidasva, i. e. Agni, Haryasva, i. e. Indra), who can this person with reddish horses be, who was cured of blindness by the Asvins? Is not blindness very commonly ascribed to the night and to the winter? Dem Winter die Augen ausstechen or ausblasen means to kill the winter (Grimm, D. M., p. 725). If therefore the Asvins are said to have restored his eyes to *Rigrâsva*, this may refer to the work of the Asvins both as bringing about the return of the year or of the day, of the yearly or of the daily sun. But the rest of the myth remains dark for the present. We are told that *Rigrâsva* slaughtered 100 or 101 sheep and gave them to V*ri*kî, the wolf, and that on that account his own father, being angry, deprived him of his sight. The sheep may be the stars, which in other mythologies also are called sheep, and may have been said to have been surrendered in the morning or even to have been slaughtered by the rising sun [1]. If for this misdeed the diurnal sun was punished at first with blindness before sunrise, the Asvins, the two Ahans, day and night, might well have been praised for having restored his sight to Red-horse in the morning.

Parâv*ri*g.

Another friend of the Asvins, Parâv*ri*g, who was equally blind and lame, can hardly be separated from *K*yavâna and *Rigrâ*sva. The sun after sunset, or near the winter solstice, is blind and lame. And if he becomes again bright and brisk in the morning, or vigorous and triumphant in spring, to whom would this daily or yearly miracle be ascribed with

---

[1] Cf. Myriantheus, l. c., p. 80.

greater truth than to the Asvins? Parâv*ri*g means outcast, prav*ri*kta is used of Rebha, in whom we may recognise the winter sun. I can find, however, no name in other Aryan mythologies corresponding to Parâv*ri*g.

Rebha.

Of Rebha it is said that he was bound and overwhelmed in the waters and left there till he was nearly drowned. Here we find that the Lets also (Mannhardt, l.c., p. 206) tell of the God-sons as saving the golden boat or the Sun-daughter in her boat from drowning. Nay in New Zealand it seems a common saying that the setting sun has been thrown out of a boat into the water. In the case of Rebha one important item is added in the Vedic myth, namely that he remained bound in the water for ten nights and nine days. This is about the time, as Benfey has pointed out, assigned to the winter solstice, the so-called twelve-tide, the time when the sun seems bound and to stand still till he jumps up and turns back (Sonnenwende). Whether this time lasted for ten or twelve nights would have been difficult to settle even for more experienced astronomers than Vedic *Ri*shis. In Rome the time for the Saturnalia, the festa calendarum, was from the 24th (or 17th) of December to the 7th of January.

And these ten days of the lameness, the blindness, the binding or drowning of the sun, may help to confirm our explanation of the gold or the golden treasure or the pot of gold dug into the earth (nikhâta) like Vandana's body. For in Rv. I, 116, 11, we read that the Asvins had thrown up something like a pot of gold (nidhím iva ápa-gû*lh*am) on the tenth day, which is surely the same thing as the sun dwelling in darkness (I, 117, 5) and dug up for the sake of Vandana.

Vimada.

Of Vimada to whom the Asvins brought the daughter or the wife of Purumitra we know nothing, nor can we make anything for the present of her name Kamadyû. We may be dealing here with a stratum of mythology which has absorbed real or historical events. The same may apply, though no one would venture to speak positively, to several more of the protégés of the Asvins. But if the Asvins are always the same, the objects of their favour also shared most likely the same character. If then in some cases the persons whom they rescued were representatives of light, the chances are that they were so in other cases also.

Vadhrimatî.

If it is said that the Asvins gave to Vadhrimatî a son called Hiranyahasta, we can easily see that Hiranyahasta, 'Gold-hand,' is the morning sun, and that Vadhrimatî therefore must be the dawn. But why should she be called 'the wife of the eunuch'? This may be explained by another story which tells us that the Asvins delivered Atri Saptavadhri, and opened and shut for him the tree[1], that is the wooden case in which he had been imprisoned. If this tree or this wooden case is meant for the night, then by being kept shut up in it he was separated from his wife, he was to her like a vadhri, and in the morn-

---

[1] Is this the Wundereiche so famous in the Finnish and Estonian mythology? Cf. Mannhardt, l. c., p. 285.

ing only, when delivered by the Asvins, he became once more the husband of the Dawn¹.

But though we may understand why during the night the sun should be called not only lame and blind, but also a eunuch, so that his wife, possibly the night, might be called Vadhrimatî, married to a eunuch, it would be difficult to explain why Atri, in his character of the nocturnal sun, should be called not only a vadhri, but Saptavadhri, a Seven-eunuch. This Saptavadhri has been derived from vadhri, a leathern strap, so that Atri would represent the sun as caught in a net, as it was by Maui caught in six nooses². But if vadhrî occurs only as a feminine (see P. D.), it would be difficult to derive saptavadhri from it. Sâyana, however, has the masculine form, and explains vadhrinâ by pâsena (Rv. X, 102, 12). The name of the husband of Vadhrimatî is not mentioned in the Veda.

Ghoshâ.

Of Ghoshâ also to whom when she was old the Asvins are supposed to have given a husband, we know no more. Ghoshâ means sound, which tells us nothing; all we can say is that, as a friend of the Asvins, she belongs to the same class of beings as Vadhrimatî.

---

¹ Cognate ideas exist in other mythologies. Mannhardt, l. c., p. 242, writes: 'Es ist wahrscheinlich, dass das aegyptische Märchen ein uralter verdunkelter Sonnenmythus war, ein Mythus, die Geschicke des Sonnengottes darstellend, vom Abend, wann er sich das Zeugungsglied abschneidet, bis zur Nacht, wann er ... stirbt und in den Amenti geht ... und endlich zum Morgen ... als das neue Tagessonnenkind emporsteigt.' 'Das Schamglied des von Typhon zerstückelten Osiris geht dann verloren.'

² W. W. Gill, Myths and Songs from the South Pacific, p. 62.

Sayu.

Nor can we say much more about Sayu, whose cow, we are told, after she had left off bearing, the Asvins filled once more with milk. Cow, as we saw, is a regular name of the morning, and each morning in its change from grey to bright, may be said to have been reinvigorated by the Asvins, the powers presiding over day and night. Sayu, derived from si, to lie down, would be an appropriate name for the nocturnal sun who, as we saw, was said to be sleeping in the darkness, and to be brought forth by the Asvins for the sake of Vandana (Rv. I, 117, 5). We might possibly think of Κοῖος, the father of Asteria and Lêto, and grandfather therefore of Hekate, the moon, but we know too little of his character and antecedents to enable us to compare the two.

Pedu and the Horse Paidva.

If another favourite of the Asvins, Pedu, receives from them a swift white horse, we must rest satisfied that here also, as in all the other achievements of the Asvins, some matutinal event is referred to. We know that the white horse, so well known from the λευκόπωλος ἡμέρα, the κόροι λεύκιπποι, or the λεύκιππος Ἀώς of Theocritus, is always meant for the light of the sun. The idea that the Asvins gave such a horse to Pedu, or that they themselves possessed such a horse, occurs again and again. And when in Rv. I, 116, 6, they are praised for having given a white horse to Aghâsva, 'the rider of a bad horse,' this white horse is sometimes called Paidva, the horse of Pedu, and, like the horse of the Asvins themselves, it is represented as ahi-han or serpent-killing. These ahis or serpents therefore cannot be taken as real serpents; they can only be meant for the dangerous brood of the dark night or the black clouds.

It should be borne in mind that whenever these three classes of serpents[1] are mentioned, those of the air, those of the sky, and those of the earth, the last, the terrestrial serpents, may indeed have been meant for real serpents, but those in the air and the sky and in all the quarters can be meant for demons only, for V*r*itras or enemies of light. Thus only can we understand that they should be trodden under foot by the white horse of Pedu, sometimes called U*kk*ai*hs*ravas (with pricked-up ears, or with glory on high), or killed by young Hêrakles, who was a *Svârâsravas, in his cradle. If Dr. Winternitz is right in classing every white horse in the mythologies of the Aryan nations, and of other nations also, as the sun, the enemies crushed by the horse's hoofs must necessarily be the powers of night and darkness, whether we call them demons or goblins or any other unmeaning name.

Serpent-worship in the Veda.

Many years ago it was strongly denied by Fergusson and others that a belief in and worship of serpents was ever of Aryan origin. They were right if by serpent-worship they meant that of African savages. But there can be no doubt that a belief in serpents had its origin in the Veda, though the serpents meant there were at first the serpents of the dark night or the black clouds, the enemies of the solar deities, such as the A*s*vins, and not yet the poisonous snakes of the earth. The later

---

[1] Cf. Winternitz, Sarpabali, p. 27.

development of these serpents and the idea of pacifying them by sacrificial offerings is likewise, as has been well shown by Dr. Winternitz, thoroughly Aryan, nor is there any necessity for adopting that laziest of all expedients, that of ascribing all that seems barbarous in Indian religion to the influence of the aboriginal inhabitants of the country of whom we know next to nothing. If people will only read what Dr. Winternitz has collected in his Sarpabali[1], we shall probably hear no more of the Non-Aryan character of Tree and Serpent-worship. The Lituanians kept, fed, or, if you like, worshipped their house-serpent (gyvāte) till very recent times, and the Vedic people were not so different from other races that they would not have identified their old mythological serpents of the air and the sky with the real serpents in which their country abounded, or that the fear and hatred which they felt for them should not have suggested to them also the idea of pacifying their old enemies by kind words and kind deeds. Wherever there are serpents in any part of the world, we find something like serpent-worship, if only for propitiating them, and there is no reason whatever for supposing that the Vedic people alone had to borrow a feeling of fear and awe for these mysterious creatures from their Non-Aryan neighbours. We should not be justified in saying that the serpent-worship of Africa and America also must have been preceded, as in the Veda, by a belief in evil spirits or serpents of the air and the sky. That would be repeating the same mistake which ethnological mythologists are so apt to commit in their comparisons between Aryan

---

[1] L. c., p. 41, note.

and Non-Aryan mythologies. There are certainly striking similarities between the two, but we know nothing, and shall probably never know anything of the antecedents of African and American serpent-worship; and until we know the antecedents or causes or intentions of any custom or belief, all comparisons or even juxtapositions are vain, and may become even mischievous. We find cromlechs in Cornwall and in the Dekhan, but unless it can be proved that they had the same object, or were actually built by the same builders, as Fergusson supposed, is it not wrong to call them by the same name? People in Italy venerate the bones of saints as sacred relics, some negroes in Africa have a bone as their fetish, but would anybody call the bones worshipped in Italian churches fetishes, considering how different was their origin, their purpose, and their whole character? Comparing is one thing, confusing another. Again, because my friend Abeken (small ape) had an ape in his coat of arms, should we call the ape his totem? It is true I never saw him eating an ape, but I feel certain this was not from any regard for his supposed ancestor or totem, but was with him a mere matter of taste.

The true and undefined character of the Asvins.

If we consider the evidence hitherto examined, it is not surprising that Sanskrit scholars when they first become acquainted with the Asvinau should at once have declared that they are the same as the Greek Dioskouroi, only they should have stated clearly what they meant by the same. If Professor Pischel declares with equal confidence that they are not the Dioskouroi, this may sound startling, still more, when I venture to say that both opinions seem to me perfectly tenable. I believe that this would have been seen by others also, if the defenders of these opposite opinions had only clearly stated what they meant by their assertion and by their negation.

Whoever was the first to say that the Asvins were the Dioskouroi could not possibly have meant that they were the same persons or the same mythological creations, and that the two horsemen of the Veda had galloped from India to Greece, or had been brought from one country to another like the Palladium or like Anchises on the shoulders of Aeneas. We must never forget that the Asvins, like all other divine or heroic personalities, were not made of flesh and blood, but represented simply objects of poetic fancy. These fancies sprang no doubt from something real and visible, but their further development depended entirely on the brains and hearts of their worshippers. It seems strange that it should be necessary to say this, but, considering some of the criticisms addressed to me, it was absolutely necessary to do so. If therefore Benfey, or any one else, said that the Asvins were the Dioskouroi[1], he, as a reasonable being, could not have meant more than that the first impulse given to these two mythological creations was one and the same, just as the first impulse to such a word as deva, bright, was the same, though, as early as the Avesta, it came to mean devil in Media, while in the Veda it continued to mean god. The only thing therefore on which Benfey might differ from Prof. Pischel would be the exact point reached in the growth of the original concept of these 'heavenly twins,' before those who at first held that concept in

---

[1] Myriantheus, Die Asvins, p. 49.

common were completely separated in language and mythology. Whenever that separation between the ancestors of Hindus and Greeks took place, the common concept would flow on afterwards in two independent channels, and those who maintained that the mythological ice carried down by the two rivers was the same would be as right and as wrong as those who asserted that it was not the same. It may be safely said that the Asvins were not the Dioskouroi, as little as India was Greece, and yet in analysing their character we may discover by the side of much that is decidedly Greek or decidedly Vedic, some elements common to both, the presence of which cannot be accounted for by mere chance. That the Asvins should be twins, that they should have a beautiful sister or friend, that they should be represented as possessed of white horses, that they should bring back light and safety whenever they appear, all this shows a common background for the mythology of Greece and India. It cannot be mere accident as little as the fact that they have the name of Divó nápâtâ in the Veda and of Διόσκοροι in Greek. All this leaves on my mind the impression of something real, and almost historical, something that was thought or done, once for all, something that must date from before the Aryan Separation. When we read how the Dioskouroi waged war against Thêseus, who long before Paris had carried off their sister Helena, or against Idas and Lynkeus, the sons of Aphareus, to whom Thêseus had promised to give Helena in custody at Aphidnai[1], and when we hear of the brave twins

---

[1] Aphidnai has been explained as Ahidanâ, formed like Echidna; but this is very doubtful.

bringing back their truant sister with Aithra, the mother of Thêseus, in triumph to Athens, we feel that we are moving on Greek soil. While when we read of *K*yavâna as an old saint having been pelted and insulted by the sons of *S*aryâta, and then pacified by the gift of the beautiful Sukanyâ, who became his devoted wife and resisted the temptations even of the divine A*s*vins, we perceive clearly that we are moving in a late Vedic atmosphere. But this does not prevent us from discovering behind both these stories a common though far distant past. In this way the views put forward by different scholars of the original character of the A*s*vins may well be brought into harmony, and we may learn once more how right Yâska was when he defined the A*s*vins by simply assigning to them their place and their time. They bide in the sky, he said, and they appear after midnight, when light encroaches slowly on darkness. The same idea is expressed Rv. X, 61, 4, 'I invoke you, O A*s*vins, when the black cow (night) sits among the red cows,' that is in the morning, when the night is surrounded by the red clouds in the East. As they are twins, two, yet inseparable, they must have represented something that corresponds to that character, and this can only have been the Nychthêmeron (Dyuni*s*am), night and day, conceived as one, and yet being in character two. Hence the A*s*vins are invoked not only in the morning, but in the evening also, cf. Rv. X, 40, 4, Yuvā́m—doshā́ vā́stor havíshā ní hvayāmahe, 'We invoke you with offering by night and by day.' See also Rv. X, 40, 2. If we once admit an agent or two agents behind these visible phenomena of Day and Night, then the agents behind them may be accepted as really possessing every one of the characters ascribed to the Asvins by different scholars, whether native or European. They may have been the agents 'behind the rays of light preceding the dawn' (Lassen), they may have been 'the morning and evening stars' (Benfey), 'the first messengers of light' (Roth), 'the twilight' (Myriantheus), nay even the double star of the Dioskouroi (Weber). Every one of these phenomena may now and then be brought under the influence of the Asvinau, though, no doubt, some of them less naturally than others. In one sense we saw that even Indra and Agni, sometimes called yamau or twins, may be identified with the Asvinau[1]; nay Mitra and Varuna may now and then seem to exercise the functions peculiar to the Asvins[2]. This may be called a vague, but it is for that very reason a much truer explanation of mythology than that which would restrict the activity of mythological characters to one small sphere, to one special birthplace. True, all Devas must have started from one small nest, but they soon took wings and soared away, far and wide.

Mitra may have been in its origin a name of the sun only, but in the Veda he is far more than a mere representative of the sun. He surpasses heaven in greatness, he surpasses the earth in abundance of food; he sustains all the gods. (Rv. III, 59.) Apollon had no doubt the same solar origin, but even in Homer's time he was no longer a mere solar god, and what a difference is there between him and Hêlios, whose very name always

---

[1] Rv. I, 109, 4.   [2] Rv. V, 25, 5; Ath. III, 4, 4.

kept him within much narrower limits. Indra, as connected with indu, must certainly at first have been a god who sent rain, but he soon became the strong, fighting god, who did everything that required strength, who opened the rock or the stable of the night to free the cows of the morning, who brought out the streams of water (or light) from the rocks of heaven, i.e. the clouds, who slew all the demons of darkness when they kept back the light or the rain, who lighted up the dawn and lighted up the sun, who at the head of the Maruts conquered all enemies, and drenched the parched earth with rain. How different from Par*g*anya who again, owing chiefly to the clear meaning of his name, remained in the minds of many of the Vedic poets the simple agent behind the rain-cloud.

Rudra and the Rudras.

Sometimes we can see how the same name, that is, the same god, retains in one form his original character, while in another he has assumed larger dimensions and a wider meaning. The Maruts are clearly the storm-gods. So are the Rudras, the two names being often exchangeable. But while we have no Marut in the singular (that would be Indra), we have a Rudra, and this god has assumed quite an independent character. The Rudras are awful: so is Rudra. The Rudras tear the rocks, the clouds (cloud is clod, i.e. rock) to pieces, Rudra rules in the mountains, becomes the mountain-god, and after, in later times, assuming the name of Siva, he has for his wife Pârvatî, the rock-goddess. That the storm is supposed to carry off the souls of the departed, we know from German and other mythologies. The soul had been conceived and named wind (spiritus); hence the souls might be conceived as in the wind, and the lord of the winds might thus become the leader of the departed (ψυχοπομπός). Hence there is nothing unusual in the Maruts and Rudras being connected with the souls of the departed. All Rudra's qualities, both the terrible and the beneficent, seem to me to spring naturally from the character of the Maruts and Rudras, though local worship may have impressed the stamp of more savage tribes upon him. The Vedic Hindus were not all Vasishthas, and even Vasishtha knew how to utter savage curses. There is an element in human nature which requires a terrible god, and this craving was fully satisfied by the worship of Rudra or Siva.

Rudra as Siva.

The horrible worship of Siva and his wife must not be treated as a purely modern invention, though there is no trace of it in Vedic ceremonial. At the time, for instance, when Hiouen-thsang travelled peacefully from China to his Holy Land, and describes India as if it had been ruled by saints and philosophers, and absorbed in the metaphysics of religion, in the seventh century A. D., Vâkpati, the author of the Gaudavaho, gives us a very different picture. He tells us what the worship of Pârvatî, the consort of Siva or Rudra, really was even at that time:—

'The door of her temple was covered with stains of blood of the sacrifices offered. She had a necklace of human skulls. The flesh of human beings was exposed at night about her temple for sale to those who wished to offer it to her. It was visited by jackals in search of flesh and blood lying about the temple. When a human sacrifice was offered, the women of the Kolis hurried up to obtain a sight of the victim, as he was being slaughtered. Victims were slaughtered daily before the goddess, and streams of blood poured through the temple gates[1].'

This is what had become of the Vedic Rudra and his consort Rodasî, the lightning, with which she was still clearly identified in Vâkpati's time.

The lightning of Rudra is not unknown in the Veda. Few only of the hymns addressed to him have been preserved to us, and these are all translated in the S. B. E., vol. xxxii. There we read, Rv. VII, 46, 3: 'May that thunderbolt of thine, which, sent from heaven, traverses the earth, pass us by.' His character as storm-god could not have been more clearly expressed than in the words of v. 4: 'Do not strike us, O Rudra ... may we not be in thy way when thou rushest forth furiously.' He is actually called the red boar of the sky, the bright tawny bull, the father of the Maruts, bearing like his sons, the Rudras, bow and arrows.

But it is extremely interesting to see how in other hymns all that is left of the storm-god Rudra, is his strength, his purifying character, for the storm in tropical countries is a purifier, and connected with this, his healing power. As in the case of Apollon, the god who sends pestilence can also send healing, and this healing power of Rudra has become so prominent that it is actually said of him, Rv. II, 33, 7, that his softly stroking hand cures and relieves, and that, like Soma and the Asvins, he is a physician, nay the best of physicians; able to remove even the evil

---

[1] Gaûdavaho, ed. Pandurang, p. ciii.

that man may have committed (VI, 74, 3). We have only to remember the sayings of modern physicians, that mountain air is the best medicine, or that what cannot be cured by water, cannot be cured at all, in order to understand why Rudra, who is the storm-god and with the Maruts the bringer of rain, was praised as the best of physicians by the Vedic *Ri*shis.

Yâska's Mythology.

If we remember all this, we shall have to admit that Yâska has really shown great judgment as a mythologist by being satisfied with defining the ποῦ and πότε of the Vedic gods, admitting the rest to have been left to the fancy of the poets. In the case of the Asvins, all that he adds to his local and temporal account of them, is that the one gives dew and moisture, the other light, that the one dwells in the air, the other in the sky, that one represents the increase of light over darkness, the other the increase of darkness over light, that one is madhya, the middle or Indra, while the other is the highest or Âditya. He quotes a passage from an unknown hymn: Vā́sâtya[1] anyá u*k*yate usha*h* putrás tavấn-ya*h*, 'One is called Vâsâtya (nocturnal), the other, O Ushas, thy son.'

I believe that this so-called unscientific method of Yâska will prove in the end the truly scientific one, and that the less we attempt to specialise the origin and to circumscribe the spheres of activity of the ancient Vedic gods and heroes, the nearer we

---

[1] Vâsâtya, formed to match nâsatya, occurs here only, and is derived from vasâti, night. Being absent in the Dictionary of B. and R., it is absent in all the other dictionaries.

shall approach to an understanding of the unfettered imaginations of the ancient world, gathered up in what we call their mythology and their sacred books.

Differences and Similarities.

When we attempt to compare Vedic with Greek gods, the Vedic Aśvins with the Greek Dioskouroi, we must, of course, be prepared to find differences as well as similarities. We can never expect to find the same gods in Greece and India.

In the Sanskrit and Greek names for the dawn, Ushas and Êos, one letter only is the same, and yet to the eye of the grammarian the two are simply identical. If then we find instead of the Vedic Saranyû the Greek Erinys, we must not expect a complete likeness in their respective personal characters in Greece and India. That the names were originally the same, in spite of small differences, will hardly be denied, except by those who imagine that it is more scholarlike to point out phonetic irregularities than to show how they can be accounted for. Homer still knows the name of one Erinys only, though he also speaks of many. This Erinys lives in Erebos, just as Saranyû appears at the end of the dark night. No word could better depict the character of Saranyû than the epithet of Greek Erinys, ἠεροφοῖτις, moving in the dark mist. If Epimenides described the Erinyes as daughters of Kronos and Eurynome, we should learn with how much freedom the ancient myths could be handled by poets and philosophers. We may indeed recognise in Kronos the old postulated god, a fitting substitute for Tvashtri or even for Dyaus, while in Eurynome we have a name corresponding in meaning to B*r*ihaddivâ, the wife or daughter of Tvash*tr*i in the Veda, and represented in Greece as the mother or the prototype of the Charites. Even Aphrodite, it should not be forgotten, is called the sister of the Erînyes; Aeschylus speaks of them as daughters of the Night, Sophocles as children of Skotos or darkness.

If it be asked why the Erînys should have become in Greek mythology the discoverer and avenger of all crimes, the answer is surely easy enough. If she represented the first rays of the dawn, these rays might well be said to discover and disclose any dark deeds performed unbeknown during the night. That the night was the mother of every kind of crime was well known to Hesiod and other Greek poets; why then should not the early dawn have been conceived as the revealer and ipso facto as the avenger of all misdeeds?

If the Vedic people hardly knew why the grey dawn was called Sara*n*yû, still less could the Greeks have guessed the original meaning of their Erînys. In the Veda, however, we have cognate words such as sara*n*y*ŭ* and sara*n*yati, and they, clearly connected with the root sar, to move, express the idea of rapid movement or flying. Sara*n*yû seems therefore to have been conceived at first as the running dawn, hastening away when her time was over, and when the light came to fill the place from which she had been driven forth. All this growth of meaning from the physical to the purely ethical, may, nay must have taken place in very remote and distant periods of time; but it would require courage to say that it never took place, and that whatever similarities may be pointed out between the characters and the names of Sara*n*yû and Erînys are the result of mere chance, the great deity of ignorance and indifference.

One other though rather vague indication of the nature of the Erînyes may be mentioned. They were born from the drops of blood that fell from Ouranos into the lap of the earth. We saw that the same or a very similar birth was ascribed to Aphrodite, and again to Urvasî, a dawn-goddess, sprung from the seed of Mitra and Varu*n*a. The circumstances may be different, but the common idea seems to have been the same, that when the nocturnal Heaven (Varu*n*a or Ouranos) had been vanquished, some drops of blood, or of seminal light, were received by the earth, and sprang up in the light of goddesses in whom we cannot but recognise representatives of the dawn.

At all events we have gained in the equation of Sara*n*yû = Erînys the first evidence to show that the name and concept of Erînys were common Aryan property, and must have been elaborated in their general outline before the Aryan Separation took place. I am afraid to go much further, and to see in the horse's head given to Erînys on ancient gems, a remnant of the equine form assigned to Sara*n*yû. This kind of evidence may become stronger in time, for the present we must leave aside all artistic representations in trying to trace the character of ancient gods and goddesses[1]. They belong clearly to an exclusively Greek soil, and there is no trace of them in that period of Vedic mythology which

---

[1] Milchhöfer, Anfänge der Kunst in Griechenland, and E. H. Meyer, Gandharven, p. 109.

alone concerns us. We must be satisfied with broad similarities of character, and with more or less accurate similarities of names; we cannot expect similarity in plastic representation.

The Children of Sara*n*yû.

We have now to consider the offspring of Sara*n*yû, 'the twins and their friend,' 'the two with the one,' and try to discover whether any of the couples of brothers or twins in Greek mythology betray some traces of their common origin with the offspring of Sára*n*yû.

Hêrakles and Îphikles.

That Hêrakles was in his origin and his character a solar hero, is hardly denied any longer except by those who hold that mythology had no origin at all. This Hêrakles had a brother, only one night younger than himself. His father was Amphitryon, the legitimate husband of Alkmêne, while the father of Hêrakles was Zeus. The serpents sent to kill the brothers in their cradle—we know what these serpents are—were strangled by Hêrakles, while his brother Îphikles was frightened by them. We know little of Îphikles, except that he accompanied his brother on some of his expeditions, and was killed long before his brother. His name also tells us nothing, and his only value for mythological purposes is that he supplies that twin or uterine brother whom we have a right to expect in the story of heroes such as Hêrakles. The name of Hêrakles is perplexing when we try to see in it any indication of his relation to Hêre, for she was the life-long enemy of the hero. It is only by admitting a continuance of the original meaning of $ἥρη$, namely *svârâ, from svar, the sun and the sky, that we might possibly discover some intention in the name of Ἡρακλῆς, as a hero of the sky or a solar hero. In Alkmêne for Arkmône we have a right to recognise a derivative of the root ἀλκ = Sk. ark, to shine[1]. Her father Êlektryon has a name derived from the same root, from which Curtius has correctly derived ἠλέκ-τωρ, a name of the sun, and ἤλεκτρον, bright metal and amber. We must not go beyond, and try to account mythologically for the death of the father of Alkmêne by the hand of his son-in-law Amphitryon. There are elements in that story which have a mythological ring, such as the promise exacted from Amphitryon not to approach Alkmêne till Pterelâos and the Taphians[2] had been punished for the murder of her brothers. The story also that the Taphians, though punished by Amphitryon, could not be entirely vanquished so long as Pterelâos was alive, who had one golden hair given him by Poseidon in order to render him immortal, and that one of the daughters of Pterelâos, Komaitho, from love for Amphitryon, cut off this golden hair (generally explained as the last ray of the sun), is clearly mythological rather than historical. With these details, however, we have no concern at present, as they do not seem to influence the story of Hêrakles, beyond the fact that they explain how he was the firstborn of Alkmône's children, his father being Zeus under the disguise of Amphitryon,

---

[1] According to some authorities her brother was called Alkmaion, generally derived from ἀλκή, strength.
[2] The island of Taphos may derive its name from the same root Dah which we discovered in Daphne, and which exists likewise in θάπτω, ἔταφον, &c., to burn, to bury.

while Îphikles was his junior by one night, and the son of Amphitryon himself, after his return from the war against the Taphians.

Amphitryon.

The name of Amphitryon yields a meaning analogous to that of parigman, applied to the Asvins (Rv. I, 46, 14), and other solar deities, who move around the sky or round the earth [1]. Amphi would express around, the root would be tru, a modification of tar, meaning to rub, to bore, and to turn. Thus while τέρετρον means a borer, and τόρος a chisel, τόρνος is a circle. Amphitryon might therefore have been one of the many minor names of Zeus, just as parigman is an epithet of the sky or of Dyaus (Rv. I, 127, 2, párigmânam iva dyā́m). When the epithet became an independent name, Amphitryon would take the place of Zeus, or Zeus of Amphitryon, as we see in their common attachment to Alkmêne, the bright one. Such possibilities would carry little weight, if they stood alone, but they possess some importance when they come in in support of what we expect. Suppose the drama of the twins were not in its origin solar, would it not be more than surprising that the names of several of the actors even in these much later and purely Greek developments of the twin myth should have preserved names that so easily lend themselves to a solar interpretation? We have no right to expect more, and we should not therefore undervalue what we do find. If all these stories were really history, slightly disguised by poetry, the occurrence of these intentional names would be impossible to account for.

---

[1] IV, 45, 1, ráthaḥ párigmā diváḥ.

And that they require some account is admitted even by those who hold that Hêrakles was simply a prince of Thebes, a young man of great physical strength, and hence called the son of Alkmênê and the grandson of Alkaios, both names supposed to be derived from ἀλκή, strength. But though the general outlines of Hêrakles disclose his real nature clearly enough, no one would think of denying that there may be historical and local elements mixed up in the numerous stories about this half-divine hero. But we have only to compare the principal events in the life of Hêrakles with those of other solar heroes to see that all these pictures are embroidered on the same canvas, though with different colours.

Perseus.

Let us take Perseus who, according to some accounts, was the grandfather both of Amphitryon and Alkmêne—and there is more atavism in mythology than anywhere else—and we see that Perseus like Hêrakles is the son of Zeus and a princess of Argos, Danae. Everything was done to prevent the birth of Perseus as of Hêrakles, which simply reflects the idea that the birth of the sun is preceded by a struggle between darkness and light, between night and day, which may be witnessed by any one who has eyes to see. Both Perseus and Hêrakles were for a time in bondage, Perseus to Polydektes, Hêrakles to Eurysthenes, Polydektes being a name of the much-embracing Hades, and Hades originally a name of the no longer visible sun, the sun that has set in the West, and has become, like Yama, the ruler of the invisible world, the lord of the departed.

Perseus who came from the East, or from the mountain Dikte on the eastern side of Krête, was sent to the West to fetch the head of Medousa; Hêrakles was sent westward to fetch the golden apples. Perseus delivered Andromeda from a monster and married her, Hêrakles conquered his wife Dêianeira after a fierce fight with Achelôos, who had assumed the shape of a wild bull.

Such coincidences can be neither historical nor accidental, they can be due to that common store only from which the authors of Greek mythology took their materials to work them up into popular poetry for the amusement of the people. Hence we find similar stories not only in Greece but in India also.

Karna, son of Prithâ.

In the Mahâbhârata one of the great heroes is Karna. His mother was fabled to have been Prithâ (Πέρση?), the daughter of king Kuntibhoga. His father was the sun-god. The child when born was hidden and thrown into a river, whence it was rescued, as Perseus was by Diktys, and brought up by a servant and his wife. The mother who had in no way suffered from having given birth to this child of the sun-god, became afterwards the legitimate wife of king Pându, and as there were no children of that marriage, she once more became the mother of the three great heroes of the Indian epic, Dharma, Bhîmasena, and Arjuna, being respectively the sons of the three gods Dharma, Vâta, and Indra.

We see here the free use which epic poetry has made of mythological traditions. And we find a similar case in the myth of Perseus. For while the ancient Greek story tells us of Perseus and his mother Danae being rescued in the island of Seriphos, Roman poets relate how the case which held her and her son was driven toward the Italian coast, where Pilumnus married her. A third legend speaks of her arrival in Italy with two sons, Argos and Argeus, the children of Phîneus, and of her settlement on the spot where afterwards Rome was founded. What happened in Italy and in India may have happened in the earliest home of the Âryas also.

If Prithâ could be taken as a parallel form of Prithivî, or Prithvî, a name of the earth as the broad, this might possibly explain the name of Perse or Persêis (cf. $\pi\epsilon\rho\theta\omega$ and $\pi\epsilon\rho\sigma\iota\varsigma$), who was likewise the wife of the sun-god, Hêlios, and of Perses her son, frequently called Perseus, though different from the son of Danae. What Persĕ can be in Persephone, Persephoneia, or Persephassa is more difficult to say.

If the solar character of Hêrakles is less pronounced in his relations to his various wives and slaves, Alkmêne being his mother, we have in his case the advantage of knowing a great deal more of his adventures in later life which leave little doubt as to the character of the man we have to deal with. Only we must be prepared to find by the side of some of his labours which admit of a mythological explanation, others which refuse to answer to any mythological tests, and which, for the present at least, must be left as either historical or purely imaginative.

Labours of Hêrakles.

If we examine the so-called labours of Hêrakles, whatever their number may originally have been—for

I do not think that in the beginning they had much to do with the twelve signs of the Zodiac—no doubt can remain as to the solar nature of that hero [1]. His birth seems the very image of the birth of Apollon, only somewhat lowered. Both are the sons of Zeus and of a human heroine, Lêto in the case of Apollon, Alkmênê in the case of Hêrakles. Hêre is jealous of both of them, even before their birth, nay tries to prevent the birth of Apollon, while she tries to retard at least the birth of Hêrakles. Immediately after their birth, she sends monsters to kill the one and the other, Pŷthon against Apollon, and serpents against Hêrakles. It is important also to observe that as Apollon slays Linos who dares to be his rival, Hêrakles kills Linos, who was his master in music. When Hêrakles, in order to expiate the murder of his children whom he had killed in a fit of madness, becomes the bondman of Eurystheus [2], he shares again the fate of Apollon, who for a time was bondman to Admêtos [3]. This servitude of solar heroes is a very general feature in ancient mythology. We find the elements of it in the story of the Peruvian Inca, who declined to worship the sun, because it was not free, but had to perform its appointed course from day to day and from year to year [4]. We find the same idea mythologised in the story of Perseus serving Polydektes, and of Bellerophon serving the king of Lydia, and still more obscured in the case of Siegfried, when he had to act

---

[1] This has been fully worked out by Decharme in his excellent Mythologie de la Grèce, p. 480.
[2] Or Eurysthenes, like Polydektes, a name of Hades.
[3] Cf. Adamastos, name of Hades.
[4] Natural Religion, p. 345.

as bondman to Gunther, the king of the Burgundians. This shows at once how variously the same idea may be worked out, how easily it may be connected with local circumstances, and even, as in the case of Siegfried, with real historical events. It warns us at the same time against trying to explain everything. We must be satisfied with discovering the fundamental ideas, and tracing the general outlines of a myth, and in the case of Hêrakles this fundamental idea is clearly the fight of light, represented by a hero, against darkness and all that is connected with darkness, such as dragons and other monsters, wild beasts, noxious vapours, storm and rain, clouds and deluge. When this fight is represented as taking place in certain parts of Greece, whether in Argos, Arkadia, Elis, Thrace, or near the Black Sea, we must be prepared for local elements, and these, of course, defy all mythological analysis.

I. Looking first of all at the enemies whom Hêrakles has to conquer, we find the Nemean Lion, located in the Eastern part of the Peloponnêsos. He is the offspring of Typhâon, or of Orthros and Echidna, and belongs therefore to the kith and kin of the powers of darkness. As lions were unknown in the Peloponnêsos, my conjecture that the Nemean lion owes its origin to a misinterpretation of the old name of Leóphontes, i.e. Deóphontes = Sk. Dâsahantâ, proposed so long ago as 1855, will probably retain the approval of those who are familiar with the origin of mythological names and persons.

II. The second enemy is the Hydra of Lerna, located again in the Peloponnêsos, not far from Argos. She also was a daughter of Typhâon and

Echidna, a sister therefore of Orthros and Kerberos, all of nocturnal origin.

III. The third monster is the Boar of Erymanthos in Arkadia. The boar is often a symbol of the thunderstorm. In the Veda Rudra, the father of the Maruts, is called Varâha, the boar. This fight against the boar led to another fight against the Kentaurs, who were vanquished by Hêrakles. These Kentaurs ($\phi\hat{\eta}\rho\epsilon\varsigma$ ὀρεσκῷοι λαχνήεντες) were the sons of Nephele, the cloud, and Ixîon. The names of some of these Kentaurs are sufficient to declare their character, for instance Imbreus (rainer), Melanchaites (black-haired), Bromos (thundering), Eurytion (name of the shepherd of Gêryon also), Petraios, Phlegraios, Pyretos, &c. In Greek mythology therefore, whatever has happened to them afterwards, the Kentaurs were at first conceived as cloud and storm-gods.

IV. The Stymphalides or birds of the lake near Stymphâlos in Arkadia are called the offspring of Ares. Their destruction by Hêrakles seems to have had a purely local origin.

V. The doe of the mountain of Keryneia in Arkadia, though under the protection of Artemis and Apollon, was slain by Hêrakles. Its character is difficult to understand mythologically, unless we see in it the fragments of a lunar myth, localised and revived in Arkadia.

VI. The stable of Augeias or Augĕas was in Elis. Augeias was the son of Hêlios, and one of his oxen was actually called Phaethon, which throws light on their original character. If we remember that in Vedic mythology every day, as carried off by the power of night and darkness, was conceived as a cow, kept by Vritra in the dark stable, and rescued from it by various representatives of light, it is possible that the same stable was meant by the Augean stable, burst open by a solar hero in his matutinal or vernal capacity. But it is possible also, though we can say no more, that the dirt and filth of the stable may have been suggested by the state of fields and forests at the end of the year which everybody who has eyes to see can see, before the vernal winds sweep away the dead leaves, and the sun beautifies once more the meadows and the hedges.

VII. The Krêtan Bull had been given to Mînos of Krête by Poseidon. Hêrakles brought the wild animal, which is said to have vomited fire, to Mykênai and then set it free.

VIII. The mares of Diomêdes, the son of Ares, had been fed on human flesh. After Hêrakles had brought them to Thrace to Eurystheus, he set them free. They fled to Mount Olympos and were torn to pieces by wild beasts.

IX. Hippolyta, who had received a golden girdle from Ares, was one of the Amazons. Their names such as Aella (gale), and Kelaino (black), reveal once more one side at least of their character. In his fight against them, and in the conquest of the girdle, Hêrakles was assisted by his double, Thêseus; and it was after this victory, that he was fabled to have gone to Troy.

X. The last fight of Hêrakles took place near the Black Sea. His labours now took Hêrakles beyond the regions known to the ancients, and thus betray at once their mythological character. The isle of Erytheia, though afterwards identified with Gadeira, was originally a name of the Far West, the red setting of the sun. Here Gêryones, a son of Chrŷsâor and Kallisto, possessed a large herd of red oxen protected by a shepherd Eurytion, and guarded by the dog Orthros. Eurytion is called the son of Ares and Erytheia. Hêrakles had to march through Europe and Libya, where he erected his two famous columns. After an encounter with Hêlios, he received from him a golden goblet in which he crossed the Ôkeanos and landed in Erytheia. Attacked by Eurytion, he slew him and his dog Orthros (two-headed). Gêryones (three-headed), on being informed of this by Menoitios, another shepherd who guarded the oxen of Hades, pursued Hêrakles, but was killed by his arrows near the river Anthemos. After that, Hêrakles returned with his booty in the golden goblet, and after slaying Alebion or Albion, and Derkynos who wished to carry off the oxen, he reached, though not without various adventures, the Hellespont and finally Mykênai, where Eurystheus sacrificed the oxen to Hêre.

XI. In eight years Hêrakles had finished these ten labours, but on some excuse Eurystheus required two more, namely, to bring him the golden apples of the Hesperides, and the dog Kerberos. The golden apples were to be found on Mount Atlas in the country of the Hyperboreans, beyond the limits of the known world. These apples, once given by Gê to Hêre, were guarded by a dragon, again a son of Typhon or Typhâon and Echidna. The Hesperides themselves were called the daughters of Night and of Erebos. On his way thither Hêrakles killed Kyknos, a son of Ares, Antaios, a son of Poseidon, Bousîris and his son Amphidamas in Egypt, Êmathion, a son of Tithônos in Arabia, and lastly the eagle who was feeding on the liver of Promêtheus. After freeing Promêtheus, he took himself for a time the place of Atlas, while he sent Atlas to fetch the apples. When Hêrakles had brought the apples to Eurystheus, the king restored them to Hêrakles, who gave them to Athêne, to be returned to their former place in Hesperia.

The last labour, the conquest of Kerberos, was preceded by a descent into Hades. Here Hêrakles had to fight once more with a Menoitios, whom he strikes down, and delivers to Persephone. He succeeds at last in dragging Kerberos to the light near Troizên, releasing him afterwards to return to his own place in Hades.

Difficult, nay impossible as it would be to discover the meaning of all these labours, no one acquainted with the spirit of ancient mythology can doubt that throughout them all Hêrakles represents a solar hero, a power of light and warmth, fighting against darkness, whether of the night or of the storm-clouds, and becoming in the end the embodiment of valour and goodness, a destroyer of evil in every shape (ἀλεξίκακος), like Apollon or Zeus, a bringer of light, and an establisher of order and law. This is enough, and we have no right to expect more.

And who were his enemies? Noscitur ab inimicis is a good rule for the Comparative Mythologist to follow.

The Adversaries of Hêrakles.

His enemies are Hêre, Ares, Poseidon, and their offspring; his friends are Athêne and Apollon. Typhon, Echidna, Orthros, Kerberos, Eurytion, Menoitios, Nephele, Nyx and Erebos, and even

Eurystheus, all show traces of a nocturnal or an infernal origin. But the modifications of the original mythological elements brought together to form the labours of Hêrakles have been very considerable. We saw that the lion of Nemea may have owed its origin to a misunderstanding, and the same has been maintained even by ancient authorities with regard to the apples of the Hesperides. The Greek μῆλα meaning both apples and herds, it was supposed that, as in the case of the herds of Gêryones and of Augeias, Hêrakles [1] had to rescue the herds of the West also, herds which were originally the same as the cows so constantly mentioned in the Veda, viz. either the days carried off by the night, or the rain-clouds held captive by V*r*itra, the Pa*n*is, and other powers of darkness, to be rescued by Indra and other well-known gods of light. This would be a case of what has been called a disease of language, but in the narrowest sense of the word, and not in the sense in which I ventured to call the whole of mythology an affection or pathos of language and thought.

The Golden Apple.

There is, however, another explanation of the golden apples which has been suggested by Mannhardt in his Lettische Sonnenmythen, where he shows that the sun, after setting, was spoken of as a golden apple that had fallen from a tree. To bring back this apple would originally have meant to bring back the sun from the West where it had vanished, to the East where it was to rise again, a work which could be performed by a solar hero only, that is, by a half-human representative of the sun. (Mann-

---

[1] Hêrakles himself is called Mêlon and Mêlios.

hardt, Lettische Sonnenmythen, pp. 103, 234.) We must not attempt to be too positive in our reading of the riddles of mythology. The general character, however, of the labours of Hêrakles, as just explained, seems to me beyond the reach of scientific doubt, while with regard to smaller details we must never forget that the license of the ancient story-tellers was as great as that of the authors of our modern historical novels.

The Hind of Keryneia.

We can well understand why the killing of lions, of giants and robbers, should have been ascribed to a son of Zeus, even though it had been performed by a local hero, but the killing of a hind hardly seems to require the intervention of a Hêrakles. Yet one of his great achievements, the fifth, is said to have been the catching of a hind. It is true that it was a peculiar hind, just as the eland was, the catching of which proved the most difficult task for Lemminkäinen, before he could win the maid of Pohjola[1]. It was a hind with golden horns and brazen feet, and scientific people, beginning with Aristotle (Poetics, xxv, 5), have been at great pains to point out the ignorance of Pindar (Ol. iii, 31), in speaking of a hind with horns. They ought to have remembered, however, that though real hinds may have no horns, least of all, golden horns, a myth is free to speak of golden horns, and has as much right to that poetical license as it has to the brazen feet which are ascribed to the same hind. Even in our time learned zoologists have actually wasted their time in trying to prove that there is one species of

---

[1] Kalewala, rune B, v. 29.

the cervine race in which the female has antlers, viz. the reindeer of the North of Europe and Asia. Now as Hêrakles is supposed to have gone to the North in his chase of the Keryneian hind, the fact of these antlered reindeer hinds has been supposed to prove the reality of the exploit ascribed to Hêrakles. Others have tried to show that we need not suppose that Hêrakles actually went as far as Norway or Iceland in search of his hind, because antlers of the reindeer have been discovered in the lake-dwellings in Switzerland, or as Dr. Nestlé points out (Academy, Dec. 1st, 1894), near the spring of the Schussen (a little river flowing into the lake of Constance), some twenty kilomètres from the nearest point of the Danube or Ister, the shady sources of which Hêrakles is said to have reached in his journey in search of the golden-horned hind.

All this shows how myths ought not to be treated. Surely we are no longer in that stage of mythological science when people tried to discover the cradle of Jupiter in Krête, or the palace of Priamos in Hissarlik, or the bones of Arthur in the island of Avalon. Was Hêrakles really no more than a mighty hunter before the Lord, a Grant or Speke who went out to shoot lions and steenboks, more particularly steenboks with brazen feet and golden horns! The essential points in the hind-myth are that the hind is never tired, that Hêrakles has to follow her for a whole year, that the animal, when tired at last, returns to Arkadia on the same road on which it had fled, and takes refuge in a sanctuary of Artemis. Hêrakles, however, catches it on the bank of the river Lâdon, and is on the point of killing it when Apollon and his sister intercede for it, and save its life. No one accustomed to the true ring of mythology can suppose that this hind was a real hind, though it may be difficult to determine with certainty what object it represents. Preller (Griech. Myth. ii, 196) took it for the moon chased by the sun and caught at last by its golden horns, the cornua lunae. But the hind is also a name of the dawn in the Veda. In the Rv. X, 3, 2, we read: Kr*i*shn*â*m yát éni[1] abhí várpasâ bh*û*t, 'When the bright (hind) overcame the dark one (night) with her apparition.' It is true that enî, as the feminine of eta, is expressive of bright colour only, but it soon became the regular name for hind, and this is the very process by which mythology arises. People say one thing, but they are understood as meaning another. If then the dawn was called enî, and if that word meant at the same time hind, what was more natural than that a hero, representing the sun, should have been conceived as chasing or following the dawn (enî), and as catching her at last, though not destroying her altogether, but letting her live for another day at the instance of Apollon and Artemis? The stories of the moon and the dawn often run together, and we need not attempt to separate what probably, in the earliest periods of mythological speech, was not always sharply separated[2].

Kerberos.

One of the most famous monsters overcome by Hêrakles was Kerberos, of the same kith and kin as Typhâon, Echidna, Orthros, Eurytion, Gêryones,

---

[1] Read éni instead of énim.
[2] In the Lettish songs we meet with a wether with golden horns (p. 243), meant for the sun.

Menoitios, &c. They are all powers of darkness, nocturnal and infernal powers that have to be fought again and again by the representatives of light. That Kerberos was a representative of the night, and that his name is connected with the name of night, sârvarî, was one of my earliest identifications of Greek and Sanskrit mythologies. It was at once adopted by Weber, Benfey, Aufrecht and others. I had not said that Kerberos was sabala, though sabala was connected with sarvara. The loss of r is startling, but I pointed out the analogous cases of savara and sarvarîka, both meaning barbarian, of sârvara, dark, mischievous, and sâvara, low, vile. I also pointed to passages where it is said of the Dawn that by her light she makes all things that had been coloured by nocturnal darkness (tamasâ sârvarena digdhâni) to appear as if they had been washed. That sarvarî was understood in India as a name of the night is shown by such names of the moon as Sarvarîpati or Sarvarîsa, which continued to be used in later Sanskrit. Much new evidence has since accumulated to confirm my conjecture, as I pointed out in a paper on 'Prof. Bloomfield's Contributions to the Interpretation of the Veda,' in the Academy, Aug. 13, 1892. Thus in the Kâ*th*aka-samhitâ XVII, 14, it is simply stated that the two dogs of Yama were day and night. And in the Kâ*th*.-brâhmana we read: 'Sabala, the speckled, is the day, Syâma, the dark, is the night.' Here we must remember what I often pointed out before, that the divine representatives of any physical phenomena represent these phenomena in a very general way. Thus sabala, the speckled day, instead of being always the day in all its solar brightness, may stand for the beginning of the day, or for the first peep of the morning, that is the Kerberos or Sarvara whom Hêrakles just drags up to the light and then lets slip again into Hades. The same applies to Orthros or Vritra. Sometimes these two dogs represent not only day and night, but even sun and moon. Thus while in Greek mythology the representative of the dim twilight survived in Kerberos, in India the dog who represented the morning and the morning sun assumed far greater prominence, and it is clear from passages collected by Professor Bloomfield in his Contributions that Divyah svâ, i.e. the heavenly dog, became afterwards simply the sun. Thus we read in Ath.-veda VI, 80 :—

'He (the sun) flies through the air, looking down upon all beings, we desire to do homage with havis to thee (who art) the majesty of the heavenly dog,' or, more literally, 'That which is the majesty of the heavenly dog, under that form we worship thee.'

'In the waters is thy origin, in heaven thy abode, in the midst of the sea and upon the earth thy greatness. That which is the majesty of the heavenly dog, under that form we worship thee with this havis.'

But the moon also was called the heavenly dog. In Sat.-br. XI, 1, 5, 1, we read : 'He (the moon) is the heavenly dog; he watches the animals of the sacrifice.' If then sun and moon, day and night, are called the heavenly dogs, the dogs of Yama, the god of death, that thought was evidently suggested by the fact that day and night, or sun and moon, go on for ever looking out for men, and at last hunting them down, like dogs seeking for prey.

If we once knew that the two dogs of Yama were sun and moon, day and night, called also, as we saw,

Sabala (speckled) and Syâma (black), we can understand what is said in the *Kh*ândogya-Upanishad, VIII, 13, where the journey of the soul after death is described, and where we read: 'From the black (syâma) I come to the spotted (sabala), from the spotted to the black, that is from the sun to the moon, from the moon to the sun.' Sun and moon, or day and night, in their regular succession are of course the cause of death. Not only is the sun called death, Sat.-br. II, 3, 3, 7, and the year called death because it destroys life by means of day and night, but we read in Kâ*th*.-br. II, 9: 'Day and night are the two arms of death.'

What then is more natural than that in Greek Kerberos should be the dog of Hades, or the dog of death, and if he is called Kerberos = Sarvara, can we doubt that Kerberos meant originally speckled and grey, and that Kerberos and Sarvara started from the same source.

If a single letter in the equation Sarvara-Kerberos is wrong, let us have the phonetic rule which it contravenes. But if Dr. Gruppe has his doubts, and if Professor Rhode (Psyche, p. 281) declares that the equation is badly supported, what shall we say? All that Professor Erwin Rhode says about Kerberos being without a name in Homer and named for the first time by Hesiod, I had fully explained myself, but when the same objections are raised again and again, and the fact that they have been answered is passed over in silence, what are we to do? Iteration is no argument, but neither is silence. Again, how does the fact that even Greek poets looked upon Kerberos as a kind-hearted and tame dog, prove that others did not look upon him as dangerous. Hêrakles at all events did not look upon him as a friendly beast, and in the Κερβεροκίνδυνος Τάρταρος he was evidently looked upon as dangerous. All these matters require careful study and a certain knowledge, not only of Greek but of Sanskrit also. Whoever possesses that, will have little doubt that Kerberos was originally one of the many personifications of the dark night, while those who in the Veda and in later Sanskrit read of the two dogs who spy about among men and carry off the victims of death, will easily discover the common background from which Sarvara in the Veda and Kerberos in Greek emerged.

If it be asked what could be the meaning of the fight of Hêrakles with Kerberos, and of his dragging him forth from Hades if only for a short time, that is a question difficult to answer in any case. But there is no reason why it should not have arisen from some proverbial saying that the rising sun had grappled with the darkness of the night and let it fall back into the abyss the very moment he himself had risen to the sky victorious.

Many other exploits ascribed to Hêrakles, beyond his famous twelve labours, confirm, I think, the view which we have taken of him. He is supposed to have joined in the Argonautic expedition, in the Kalydonian chase, nay he is reported to have besieged the old Troy, long before the famous siege described in the Iliad. This alone should suffice to show to what class of sieges the siege of Troy belongs, and who were the warriors engaged in it, in the Argonautic expedition, and in the Kalydonian chase. That the siege of Troy by Agamemnon was not an historical event is surely proved, if any proof were required, by the siege being ascribed to other heroes, such as Hêrakles (Il. v, 641), while Helena also was carried off by more than one lover, for instance by Thêseus, even before she had become the wife of Menelâos. Whoever believes in Helena as historical, must also believe, as I said before, in her brothers and in the egg of Lêda, for in these matters we cannot pick and choose. This, however, by no means excludes the possibility of some historical siege of Troy, which has been lighted up by the rays of another siege beyond the reach of any spade and shovel, but belonging to the heavenly drama that forms the background of so much mythology and so many epic songs in Greece and elsewhere.

In treating of mythological cycles, like that of which Hêrakles forms the centre, it must never be forgotten that identical names in Greek and Vedic mythology are by no means requisite in order to enable us to see what was the real background of Aryan mythology. We should know it even if the gods and heroes had no names at all. But for all that the name is a great help, and gives to the analyser of myths a ποῦ στῶ which nothing else could supply. In our case the name of Hêrakles unfortunately does not tell us much, but points only in the most general way to Hêre, by no means a friend, but rather the declared enemy of Hêrakles. Still, if Hêre corresponds to a possible *Svârâ, a feminine of Svar = sol, she would represent the bright sky or atmosphere conceived as a feminine like Sûryâ, while Hêrakles might have been meant from the first for the glory or the hero of the bright sky, in some respects even as a human reflection of his divine father Zeus. Hence we can understand why the two, Zeus and Hêrakles, share several epithets in common, such as Alexikakos, Olympios, Idaios, &c.; they are in fact, in several cases, simply different actors, one divine, the other human, of the same acts. But though this is true with regard to the general character of the god and the hero, we must not expect that we can find a mythological solution of all the exploits assigned to the one or the other. We know from other mythologies that local, historical, and purely fanciful additions were constantly mixed up with ancient and truly mythological lore. It is the unwillingness to recognise these natural limits of mythological interpretation which has caused so many failures in etymological analysis and mythological interpretation by tempting scholars to explain what by its very nature defies interpretation.

The Two with the One.

In looking further for parallels to the old story of the 'Two with the one,' we have to examine next some more of the legends of the Greek Dioskouroi, properly so called, Kastor and Polydeukes. We find their history localised in the Peloponnêsos where Tyndareôs or -reos was supposed to have ruled. This Tyndareôs, like all kings, had of course to be provided with a genealogy. He was represented as the son of Periêres and Gorgophone, and as the brother of Aphareus, Leukippos, Îkarios (father of Pênelopeia), and Arêne. Periêres was the son of Kynortas (or of Aiolos and Enarete); Kynortas, the son of Amyklas; Amyklas, the son of Lakedaimon and Sparte; Lakedaimon, the son of Zeus and Taygete. Thus the great object was obtained, and the family of the Tyndarides was proved to have descended from Zeus and to rule by the grace of God. These genealogies vary considerably according to different authorities, and they betray their true character in almost every name. The Greeks believed that these royal ancestors had given their names to the localities in which they ruled. It may be so, but more likely the names of these localities, of towns, mountains, and rivers, such as Amyklai, Lakedaimon, Sparte, Eurôtas, and Taygete, existed before their time, and were changed, as even now in Scotland, into names of persons, and lastly arranged into real pedigrees. At the head of them we generally have Zeus, or some hero eponymos of a whole race, as, for instance, Lelex, the father of Eurôtas, who represents the ancient race of the Leleges in Lakonia, formerly called Lelegia.

After Tyndareôs had thus been provided with a divine pedigree, he was represented as the husband of Lêda, and as the father of Helena, Klytaimnêstra, Kastor and Polydeukes. Here again there are various versions, the oldest being that in the ninth book of the Odyssey, where Lêda appears as the wife of Tyndareôs, and the mother of Kastor and Polydeukes. The Dioskouroi are there supposed to have died, but to enjoy, for all that, the privilege of being ἑτερήμεροι, i.e. being dead one day and alive the next. Some traditions represent the Dioskouroi and Helena as children of Zeus and Lêda, and as being born together, all three from the same egg, or Helena from one egg, the Dioskouroi from another; others make Helena and Polydeukes only children of Zeus, Kastor and Klytaimnêstra children of Tyndareôs. Pindar represents Lêda as becoming the mother of Kastor and Polydeukes in the same night, Kastor being the son of Tyndareôs, Polydeukes of Zeus. Hence Polydeukes only was immortal, but Kastor mortal till Polydeukes exchanged half of his immortality with his brother. Why Zeus should have been fabled to have assumed the form of a swan as the father of the Dioskouroi, is more difficult to explain from a purely Greek point of view. But we know that Vedic poets speak of the sun as patañga, the bird, or as aruṇaḥ suparṇaḥ (Sat.-brâhm. IX, 2, 3, 18), the red bird, and even as haṁsa, goose or swan, and that in other mythologies also the sun is spoken of as a falcon, a vulture, a red flamingo, &c. In Greece we have at least the poetical expression of Aeschylus, who speaks of the sun as Ζηνὸς ὄρνις[1]. It is quite possible, however, that the swan was really suggested by the egg, and the conception of the sun as an egg is not only natural, but attested in various mythologies, both ancient and modern. The mundane egg is mentioned in the Vedic Brâhmaṇas; a duck who lays a golden egg in the morning, and a silver egg in the evening (sun and moon), is mentioned in the Russian Märchen collected by Afanasief, while Mannhardt (l. c., p. 226) tells us of a Milanese riddle that is to be solved in the same way:—

  Pjöv, pjöv,
  La gaijina fa l' oeuv.
  'It rains, it rains,
  The hen lays an egg,'

---

[1] Cf. Mannhardt, l. c., p. 233, note.

that is, the sun will shine when the rain is over. If then we saw that in the Veda the mother of the twins, Sara*n*yû, was meant for the moment between the retreat of the night and the return of the morning, Lêda too, while laying the swan's egg, may have sprung from the same conception. In that case her twins could only be what the twins of Sara*n*yû were, day and night (Ahanî), Kastor and Polydeukes, and her beautiful daughter, the bright dawn. As the twins of Sara*n*yû, the Asvins were represented as the suitors of Sûryâ, the sun, fem., who carried her off against all the other gods. The carrying off of Phoibe and Hilaeira, the beautiful Leukippides, by the Dioskouroi may therefore be accepted as a very close counterpart of the Vedic legend.

If there could be any doubt as to the character of their father Leukippos, 'White-horse,' the fact that Leukippos like Phoibos was believed to have been the lover of Daphne also (Paus. viii, 20, 2) would be sufficient to remove it, and to prove in return the meaning assigned to Daphne as *Dahanâ, i.e. Ahanâ, dawn.

It is very tempting, no doubt, to see in Kastor and Polydeukes representatives of sun and moon, as M. Decharme has done. But did the Greeks ever look on the moon as a brother of the sun, and could it be said that the moon always died when the sun appeared? The relations of the moon to the sun are so uncertain and irregular that they do not easily lend themselves to mythological expression. Is it not far more likely that the two Dioskouroi were really what the two Asvins were, day and night, light and darkness, or the two sides of the sun in his daily course from morning to evening, from this world to the next, one twin being invisible in the lower world, while the other was ruling in the sky, and the two (yamau) forming in reality but one person, the day of twenty-four hours, sometimes, it would seem, called collectively Yama, the Twin?

There is another pair of brothers, represented as the cousins of the Dioskouroi, the sons of Aphareus, the brother of Tyndareôs, known as Îdas and Lynkeus, both expressing sharp-sightedness or brilliancy. Their rivalry with their cousins is explained in different ways; the principal reason seems to have been that they had been betrothed to the Leukippides, and that Kastor and Polydeukes had carried these off as their intended wives. In the conflict Kastor was slain by Îdas, Lynkeus by Polydeukes. What is said both of Îdas (the seeing) and of Lynkeus (the lynx), is that they could see through everything. But while their own names agree to this, the name of their father Aphareus gives us no help. It may be, as some have suggested, that the two Apharides were but a local Messenian repetition of the Lakonian Dioskouroi, and hence their conflict about the Leukippides, whom they both claimed as their own. But this is only a guess, and under the circumstances cannot be more.

A more important adventure of the Dioskouroi is their fight against Thêseus, who had carried off their beautiful sister Helena, and given her to his mother Aithra, to be guarded by her at Aphidnai. Here we see the physical outlines more clearly through the mist of local legend. Helena is certainly a Dawn-goddess, who, as we saw, was loved by and in love with ever so many solar heroes, carried off by them for a time, but reconquered after the twins, Day and Night, had performed their daily task, and reappearing the next day in her old home, the brilliant East. That her name agrees with her character as the dawn we shall see afterwards, nor should it be forgotten that the names of two other heroines, carried off by Thêseus, Aigle and Phaidra, are both names most appropriate to the brilliant Dawn, the latter being the daughter of Pàsiphae (Aphrodite), and herself called Pâsiphaêia, all-shining. The name of the mother of Thêseus too, with whom Helena abides at Aphidnai, and who afterwards follows her as her slave to Troy, is not inappropriate. For Aithra can only be a feminine form of Aither, the serene sky, from which sun and stars are supposed to have risen, and who might well have been fabled to have been for a time the guardian of the dawn. We must never forget that these names and the adventures of the Dioskouroi which have been preserved to us, are but like isolated rocks rising from a large field covered with snow, and that this snow, i.e. the accumulated folk-lore of centuries, hides and always will hide from our eyes large tracts of the surrounding country. What the real mythological landscape of ancient Greece may have been, we shall never know completely. We may guess at it here and there from the view offered to us in the Veda, where the snow does not yet lie so deep as in other Aryan countries. Some people think that they know of mythological landscapes free as yet from all snow, such as Tasmania or the Andaman Islands. It may be so, but we must wait patiently till by careful labour scholars have discovered the same stratum in the homes of these so-called primordial sons of nature which we meet with in the homes of the Âryas. Rich finds of gold have been promised us for many years, but I am not aware that a single nugget has as yet reached our mint, to be assayed and turned into current coin.

We saw why the Asvins were believed to have acted as benefactors and saviours. We saw why in the Veda they were supposed to have rescued certain persons from drowning and shipwreck. This reputation must have clung to them, for in Greece also they were believed to have saved the Argo, and even in historical times we often hear of their help being invoked with prayers and sacrifices by crews when tossed about by violent gales. Their presence was supposed to be indicated by phosphorescent light after a storm.

This may possibly explain the supposed relation between the Dioskouroi and the Kabeiroi as worshipped chiefly in Samothrace. They were both called Ἄνακες and Μεγάλοι Θεοί, and may have shared more than one feature in common. Unfortunately the origin of the Kabeiroi themselves seems to me so mysterious and so uncertain that I can derive no help from them in deciphering the adventures of the Dioskouroi. Their name has been derived from every possible and impossible language, from Hebrew, Syriac, Persian, Egyptian, Sanskrit, and Greek. I shall not add a new etymology, nor any hypothesis about their origin. Their worship is localised in so many places, in Lemnos, in Samothrace, Boeotia, Egypt, Phenicia, Pergamos, Macedonia, and Etruria, that one feels inclined to admit a real propaganda of Kabeiric mysteries even in historical times, though where it started from at first, and where it ended, I should not venture to determine. The name is applied not only to gods, such as Zeus and Dionysos, and to heroes, such as Dardanos and Jasion, but also to the priests and servants of these gods.

We are on firmer ground when we examine the relation of the Dioskouroi to Helena. I cannot but look on her name as a reproduction of the Vedic Saramâ[1], and I see in Saramâ one of the many names of the dawn. Our ideas of Helena are so entirely derived from the Iliad, that we find it very difficult to believe that she was originally a goddess. But it is a fact that in historical times she was still[2] worshipped as a goddess by the Lakonians. Besides, her divine character is fully attested not only by her being the daughter of Zeus, but by another pair of parents ascribed to her by Hesiod[3], Thetis and Ôkeanos. Aphrodite also is called her mother, and she is even represented as the child of Hêlios and Lêda. Another mother assigned to her is Nemesis[4]. The story told of Zeus assuming different animal forms in pursuit of her, and of her becoming at last by him the mother of Helena is but the repetition of the tale of Saranyû as pursued by Vivasvat in the form of a horse. In

---

[1] See pp. 108, 516.
[2] Isokrates, Helenae Encomium, 13.
[3] Schol. Pind. Nem. x, 150; Decharme, p. 611, n.
[4] The close connection of Aphrodite and Nemesis is indicated by the story of Agorakritos changing his statue of Aphrodite into that of Nemesis by a mere change of attributes. Plin. H. N. 36, 4, 4.

this Nemesis, however, we must recognise not simply the later ethical goddess, but her physical prototype, Saranyû. Hence she is called the daughter of the Night, or of Erebos, and is joined with the Erînyes in punishing all dark deeds and righting whatever seemed wrong in the world. How closely Nemesis is connected with Lêda and with Helena is shown by another legend which tells of Nemesis, the beloved of Zeus, laying an egg which was found by Lêda and from which were produced the Dioskouroi and Helena. The very variety of these legends shows that behind all of them there was one and the same original theme of the Dawn, and of Day and Night, being produced from the golden egg laid by the disappearing Night when caught by the Sun. Can all this be the result of mere accident? Is there any one left to maintain that Helena was originally a beautiful princess, tempted away from her husband Menelâos by Paris, a prince of Troy, and that all that reminds us in her of her auroral character from her birth to her death is pure imagination? For we must not forget that even after her death Helena retains traces of her divine origin. She is carried off by Apollon to Olympos, to live together with such beings as Hêre and Hêrakles. Others relate that in the isles of the Blessed or in the island of Leuke (light) she became the wife of Achilles, and we know from historical records that her worship continued in Lakonia till quite recent times.

To my mind there is no chapter in mythology in which we can so clearly read the transition of an auroral myth of the Veda into an epic legend of Greece as in the chapter of Saranyû (or Saramâ) and the Aśvins, ending in the chapter of Helena and her brothers, the Διόσκοροι λευκόπωλοι.

Antiope.

We have now to proceed from Sparta to Boeotia and see what form our twin story has assumed in Thebes, a town which generally claims the Phenician Kadmos as its founder, but which, according to the Odyssey, had been founded and fortified by the twins Amphion and Zethos long before the arrival of the Phenician colonists. The fact that they also were called Dioskouroi and represented as riding on white horses sufficiently indicates their origin. Their father was Zeus, who requires no explanation, their mother was Antiope. This name does not tell us much, except that in Anti we may see a reference to the evening or the West[1]. Stephanus Byzantinus explains Antigoneia by προσεσπέριος. Her father is called Nykteus which means nocturnal, and can hardly be put aside as a merely accidental name. This Antiope, daughter of the West, possibly an evening goddess, or goddess of the gloaming, became by Zeus the mother of twins. She had to fly from Thebes to escape from the fury of her father, and when arrived at Sikyon she was married there to Epôpeus. Nykteus killed himself, but ordered his brother Lykos to take vengeance on Antiope and Epôpeus. This was done, and Antiope (like Helena) was brought back by Lykos to Thebes. There is much discrepancy about her relation to Lykos. She is sometimes called his wife, and is said to have been rejected by him, after she had been seduced by Epôpeus, and it was related that it was after her

---

[1] In Sanskrit pratyak is used in the sense of West.

seduction by Epôpeus and her rejection by Lykos that on her way back to Thebes she gave birth to the twins, who claimed Zeus as their father. Like most of these twins, the children of Zeus, these sons of Antiope also were exposed by their mother, found and brought up by a cowherd, and recognised at last by their mother. Next follows the well-known tragedy.

Antiope escaped from the prison in which Lykos and his second wife Dirke had kept her, her twin sons took up her cause, marched against Thebes, killed Lykos and tied Dirke to a bull till she was killed, a scene so powerfully represented by the famous Farnese Bull at Naples. Her body was thrown into a spring at Thebes bearing her name. It is told of Amphion that when he and his brother were building the walls of Thebes, he was able, like Orpheus, to move the heaviest stones by the music of his lyre which had been given to him by Hermes or Apollon. Zêthos is afterwards married to Aêdôn (nightingale) or to Thêbe, while Amphion marries Niobe, the daughter of Tantalos. Aêdôn, envious of Niobe, the mother of six sons and six daughters, intends to kill her eldest son, and by mistake kills her own son Itylos. There are several varieties of this myth.

It is impossible to follow the myth of the twins Zêthos and Amphion without seeing that here also we are not dealing with historical facts but with physical events put into mythological language. Certain names in the story are clear, such as Nykteus, night, Epôpeus, the looker-on, the sun, Amphion, $ἀμφίων$, the round-going (parigman), the diurnal sun, and Antiope, the opposite, the West or gloaming.

This Antiope, the gloaming, the daughter of the night, after escaping from Epôpeus, the sun of the previous day, might well be said, when united with Zeus, the bright sky of the next morning, to bring forth the twins, a new day and night, and these children might be supposed to have killed Lykos, the wolf, well known in mythology as the representative of darkness. But in treating of these details there must always be much uncertainty. The old myth-makers and poets took a few names and a few sayings that were floating in the air, but in weaving them into their stories they did not allow themselves to be hampered, but thought only of what their hearers might like to hear. Were we to attempt to discover in all these details some exactly corresponding physical events, we should attempt what from the nature of the case is impossible. Many such attempts have been made. Preller sees in Antiope the moon which disappears in winter and returns in spring with Lykos, the light. But does the moon disappear in winter? Sir G. Cox thinks that Lykos, the light, brings back Antiope, the dawn, after she had been carried off by Epôpeus, the sun. Such divergent interpretations have often been made use of to show that a belief in a physical background of Aryan mythology is altogether a mistake, while in reality they ought to convey a very different lesson to all true scholars, by teaching them that the ancient myths, before they reach us even in Homer, have been so freely and fancifully handled, that we must be satisfied if we can discover what can at best be compared to a few Roman bricks only, imbedded in a magnificent Norman wall. As the presence of such bricks is sufficient to prove that there were Romans in England before the Norman conquest, such names as Dioskouroi, Leukippos, Erînys, &c., justify us in admitting the existence of an earlier stratum of mythological language on which Greek, Roman, and Vedic mythology have all been built up. What is important is the establishment of rational antecedents for irrational mythology. If that is granted, and I believe that by this time it is, we have gained the same as what geologists gained by proving that many strata which seemed to be unstratified or irrational, are really stratified or rational. If it is once admitted that behind the many twin stories in Greek and other Aryan mythologies, there is the old myth of the twins, Day and Night, we have reconquered a very important period of human thought, we have strengthened our conviction that in the growth of the human mind, as in the growth and development of nature in general, there is no break, and that behind all apparent unreason there is and there always has been reason, or cause and effect.

Harmonia.

The next twin story is that of Dardanos, Jăsion or Îăsion, and Harmonia. Their mother is Êlektra, married to Korythos, but their father is Zeus; or, as in other similar cases, the father of Dardanos and Harmonia is Zeus, the father of Jasion is Korythos. The name of Êlektra, as we saw before, is clear, and it should be added that Eustathios actually calls her Hêmera, day. She therefore was originally intended for the Morning, and the children of the Morning by Zeus are the diurnal twins. Their history has, however, been so much mixed up with historical or local details, that there are but few indications left of their physical origin. Still two such names as Êlektra and Hêmera would be sufficient to indicate who these children were supposed to have been. Dardanos has been localised in Korythos (Cortona) in Italy, and he is supposed to have emigrated to Phrygia and to have founded there the Dardanian kingdom, while his brother became settled in Samothrace. The name of the other brother Îasion, varies between Îāsion, Îāsios, Îāsos, and Iâson. These names seem to have had the same origin, but the persons bearing them have been separated in Greek mythology. Two certainly have to be distinguished, Iâson, the son of Aison of Iolkos, and Iāsion, the son of Zeus and Êlektra (Hêmera), the beloved of Dêmêter. But there are besides Îasos of Argos, son of Phorôneus, or the son of Argos, or the son of Îo, and several more. I distinguish the son of Zeus and Êlektra by a short ă, the son of Aison and Polymêde by a long â, leaving the suffixes undetermined. Îāsion, the son of Zeus and Êlektra, was the favourite of Dêmêter; Iâson, the son of Aison and Polymêde, was the husband of Mêdeia. The name of Iâson or Îāsion corresponds strictly to Vivasvân, the sun, ϜιϜασϜων, Ἰάσων, or Ἰασίων; and this, as we saw, might account for his marriage with Dêmêter on the thrice-ploughed field, and for the birth of Ploutos (wealth) as their child. The migrations of Îāsion, like those of his brother Dardanos from Italy or Krête to Samothrace, seem to point to events outside the pale of mythology, and may possibly be connected with the spreading of the mysteries of Dêmêter or the goddess of agriculture. As to Harmonia, we could hardly derive her name from ἁρμόζω or ἀραρίσκω, in the sense of harmony; rather, I think, from the same root that yielded the names of Saramâ, Helena, and Hermes[1], in the sense of morning. She is represented not only as the daughter of Zeus and Êlektra, but likewise of Ares and Aphrodite, nay sometimes, as if to leave no doubt as to her character, she is herself called Êlektra, while Êlektra, as we saw, varies with Hêmera. Her marriage with Kadmos was celebrated by gods and men. She received a peplos embroidered by Athêne, and the famous necklace wrought by Hêphaistos, while Dêmêter presented her with corn, and Hermes with a lyre. All this shows that she was not an ordinary mortal, a Miss Harmony, as Mr. Herbert Spencer would say, but a goddess, the well-known goddess of splendour and beauty. After their death both Kadmos and Harmonia were, like Helena, transferred to Êlysion. Her daughters by Kadmos were Semele, the mother of Dionŷsos; Ino, the mother of Melikertes; Autonoe, mother of Aktaion; Agaue, mother of Pentheus, and Polydôros, the father of Labdakos.

It has been a very generally received opinion that in the names of Kadmos as well as of some of his descendants we have indications of Phenician immigration, and that his name and that of his grandson Melikertes suffice to prove this. This may be so, though I must still say that the only tangible evidence of Phenician influence in the Kadmean kingdom are the Kadmean or Phenician letters.

Here we see the traces of Phenician schoolmasters, better than either in the ancient architecture of Thebes, or in the legends of the Kadmean family.

---

[1] Harmonia = sarmanyâ, Hermeias = sàrameya.

The last things, we should always remember, that are affected by strangers are religion and mythology in ancient as well as in modern times. The mere possibility of personal contact between strangers, whether simple travellers, missionaries, or even more numerous colonists, can prove nothing as to an actual grafting of foreign ideas on the native mind. Such ideas, even when they can be proved by historical evidence, remain always isolated, unless there is a complete conquest of one nation by another, a systematic extirpation of an old and a planting of a new religion. The influence of Phenician on Greek religion and mythology has always been a postulate rather than a fully proved fact, except in some isolated cases where Phenician idols were in later times identified with Greek ideals in a way that admits of no doubt.

Hitherto the father of the brothers or twins has been Zeus. But other gods also act the same part, as for instance Poseidon, who falling in love with Tŷro, the wife of Krêtheus, begot in the disguise of Enîpeus, a river-god in Thessaly, the two brothers Pelias and Nêleus, while the other children of Tŷro, Aison, Pheres, and Amythaon were the children of Krêtheus. Her children by Poseidon were, as usual in these stories, exposed and rescued by a shepherd. Pelias was kicked by a mare, Nêleus was suckled by a bitch. These sons when grown up revenged their mother by killing her mother Sidêro, who (like Dirke) had been cruel to her unfortunate daughter.

After the death of Krêtheus, Pelias seized the sceptre and expelled both his brother Nêleus and his half-brother Aison from Jolkos. Afraid of

Aison's son, Jâson, he made him join the Argonautic expedition, but was murdered, that is, cut up and boiled in order to be rejuvenated by Mêdeia, the wife of Jâson, after their victorious return from Kolchis. There are many varieties in this story, but the original character of Jâson [1] is indicated in different ways, as when Hêre is said to have been in love with him and to have been carried by him across the river Anauros, Enîpeus, or Euênos.

Several more cases belonging to the same class might be mentioned from Greek mythology. Most of these have been carefully collected by Hahn in his Sagwissenschaftliche Studien, a work far too much neglected by students of mythology. He quotes another parallel story of Lykastos and Parrhasios from Plut. Par. min. c. 36 :—

'Phylonome, the daughter of Nyktimos and Arkadia, when on the chase with Artemis, was carried off by Ares in the disguise of a shepherd. She gave birth to twins, and being afraid of her father, threw them into the Erymanthos. When they were driven on shore in a hollow tree, a she-wolf threw her own young into the river and suckled the twins. Afterwards a shepherd, Tyliphos by name, saw them and brought them up like his own children, calling one Lykastos, the other Parrhasios, who afterwards succeeded as kings of the Arkadians.'

As the authority of this story Zopyros Byzantios is cited, but the story itself is so common that it hardly required any authority.

---

[1] Jâson, by being connected with ἰᾶσθαι, to heal, and ἰατρός, was supposed, like Mêdeia, to have derived his name from his knowledge of medicines and poisons. Iâtros was a name of Apollon. It would be better to treat the initial always as a vowel.

Hahn's Sagwissenschaft.

Hahn has tabulated a number of these stories, and has shown how the points on which all or most of them agree are :—(1) the illegitimate birth of the hero; (2) the mother a native princess; (3) the father a god or a stranger; (4) warning signs given to relations; (5) the hero exposed; (6) suckled by animals; (7) brought up by (childless) shepherds; (8) pride of the boy; (9) servitude; (10) victorious return and departure for new enterprises; (11) fall of his persecutors, restoration of the kingdom, the mother revenged; (12) foundation of city; (13) peculiar death or apotheosis.

The instances chosen by him to illustrate these points in the history of mythological heroes are taken from (1) Argos (Perseus); (2) Argos—Thebes (Hérakles, Oidipous); (3) Thebes (Amphîon and Zêthos); (4) Mynian Thessaly (Pelias and Nêleus); (5) Arkadia (Lykastos and Parrhasios); (6) Rome (Romulus and Remus); (7) Attika (Thêseus); (8) Thidrek story (Wittich, Siegfried); (9) Wolfdietrich story (Wolfdietrich); (10) Persia (Kyros); (11) Baktria (Kay Chrosrew); (12) India (Karna, Krishna).

Of course it is open to all Euhemerists to say that, for all we know, these events may have actually happened, and for ethnologists to collect similar stories from savage tribes. But unless we can discover the origin of these savage stories, they leave us exactly where we were, while by means of an etymological analysis of some at least of the principal mythological names of the Âryas we may catch the thoughts which suggested these names, and discover the phenomena of nature which suggested the thoughts. That these stories have often attracted and absorbed historical recollections cannot be doubted, nor do I wish to deny that some of the prominent names may have been wrongly interpreted. But even thus enough will always remain to show that there was originally a purpose in the names and in the stories, and that is what is of the highest importance to the student of history and psychology. If we take the last mentioned Arkadian legend, to say that the occurrence of such names as Nyktimos (night) and Lykastos (light) are due to chance only, is more than could reasonably be conceded.

Mundilföri.

It would be desirable, no doubt, if we could always discover names as clear as some that occur in the Edda. Here we read that a man of the name of Mundilföri had two children, fair and beautiful, the boy called Máni, the girl Sól, married to Glenr. The gods from envy placed them in the sky, where Sól has to lead the horses of the sun's chariot, while Máni conducts the moon. In the poetical Edda also we read of Mundilföri as the father of Máni and Sól, who every day make the round of the sky and mark the times of the year.

When we know that máni and sól are names of moon and sun, we can have little doubt that Mundilföri, i.e. the axe-mover, is meant for the god who makes the world move round its axe. In Greece this simple phase of mythological language is past, but enough remains to show that it formerly existed, though it was afterwards overlaid by poetical fancy or what we should call romantic inventions.

Hêlios.

The sun under its ordinary name of Sûrya or Hêlios has not become so much as we should have expected the centre of attraction for the floating elements of mythology. Under various more or less intelligible names the sun has played, no doubt, an important part in the traditions of the past. But the name of Sûrya or Hêlios seems to have been too clear and too intelligible to admit of much mythological metamorphosis. While Greek poets have much to tell us of Apollon and Hêrakles and other divine or heroic representatives of the sun, they have little to say of Hêlios beyond his being the son of Hyperion, the one on high, and Theia, the bright[1]. Who Theia was we can easily guess from her substitute, Euryphaessa. We can hardly call it as yet mythology when Hêlios appears as the brother of Èos, the dawn, and Selêne, the moon. That Hêlios rises from the ocean, traverses the sky, and enters into the ocean through the gates of the West is no more than what our own poets might say of the sun, and if ancient poets fabled of a palace of Hêlios in the East and another in the West, and of a stable for his horses, modern poets would not hesitate to follow their example. How Hêlios after diving in the West, appears again in the East, was a problem which Homer and Hesiod left untouched, but which was solved by other poets, either by giving him a golden boat or a golden bed,

---

[1] This name of Theia can hardly be translated by godlike or divine, but shows rather that the people who gave that name were still aware of the original meaning of theos and its connection with deva.

on which he floats every night round half of the earth and then appears again every morning in the East. The story of Hêrakles shooting an arrow at Hêlios till he gave him a golden boat in which he could cross the ocean and return to Erytheia, shows the close relationship between the god and the hero. All this however is hardly as yet mythology, while the few myths told of Hêlios that he possessed chariots and horses, and that he owed seven herds of oxen, each consisting of fifty, and never more nor less, require hardly any explanation.

Sûrya.

The same, as we shall see, applies to Sûrya in the Veda. There are several hymns addressed to him, but whatever they tell of him is clear and transparent, while when the same things are told of solar gods such as Savit*ri*, Mitra, Vish*n*u and others, the mist of mythology rises at once and often renders the features of the god difficult to recognise. In the Veda the father of Sûrya is Dyaus (sky), his wife is Ushas (dawn), but the Ushas in the plural are likewise and very naturally said to have given birth to him. Whether the chariot assigned to Sûrya in India as well as in Greece should be accepted as part of the common Aryan inheritance, or as invented independently in India and Greece, is difficult to say, because the idea itself is so very natural. The idea that Sûrya himself was a white horse, led forward by the Dawn (*s*vetam nayantî sud*ri*sikam a*s*vam, Rv. VII, 77, 3), may be called Vedic, though there are allusions to it in the Greek Leukippides; but the seven ruddy horses, the Haritas, that draw his chariot show us by their name that they were known before the first parting of the Aryan tribes. These horses, the Haritas, are feminine in the Veda and called ghṛitâkî, nay they are already spoken of as sisters, such as we see them in Greece as the Charites. There is a long hymn addressed to Sûrya, Rv. X, 37, but from beginning to end we can hardly find one idea that can be called strictly mythological.

Sûrya is called the eye of Mitra and Varuṇa, and is said to see far away, though the floods of rain sent by the Maruts are sometimes said to dim his eye (Rv. V, 49, 5). He is the son of Dyaus, like many of the Vedic gods. He is called irresistible when he once has started on his daily journey. He is called upon to shine and to drive away disease and sleeplessness, also to grant a long and happy life. He is called golden-haired (harikesa), and asked to bestow riches on his friends. But he is also invoked to remove sin, and to cast all guilt on the enemies who distress his worshippers. In VI, 70, Sûrya is called man-eyed or man-seeing, beholding the good and evil acts of men. He drives with his seven Haritas from their stable across the world, but sometimes he is said to be drawn like a ship through the water (Rv. V, 45, 10). Eclipses of the sun are mentioned and the demon who attacks Sûrya is Svar-bhânu (not yet Râhu), who is in the end destroyed by Sûrya, after the sun had been discovered and set free again by Atri (V, 40, 8). In a more poetical passage (IV, 13, 4) we read: 'Thou movest along with thy quickest horses spreading thy web and undoing the dark cloth; the rays of the trembling Sûrya hide the darkness, like a skin, in the waters.'

There is a slight attempt at mythology when in I, 115, 2, we are told that Sûrya follows the Dawn as a youth follows a maiden, and that as soon as he unyokes his horses, the Night spreads out her garment over the whole world.

In I, 50, 4, Sûrya is called taraṇiḥ, he who crosses, which becomes afterwards an ordinary name of the sun, and gives us, as we shall see, the key to another name of the sun, Tritaḥ, he who has crossed. In the Atharva-veda much is said about Sûrya, but again hardly anything that would seem to require mythological analysis. Sûrya is said to survey the sky, the earth, and the waters. He is called the single eye of all that is (XIII, 45). When the two Dawns are called Sûrya's wives (Ath. VIII, 9, 12) we know what this means. His burning and fatal rays are mentioned in VII, 11, 1, while from VI, 106, 5, we learn that the light of Sûrya was believed to impart intelligence, thus explaining how Ahanâ, the dawn, became Athênê, the goddess of wisdom.

Rohita.

In the Atharva-veda we meet with a new name of a representative of the sun, Rohita, which does not occur in the Rig-veda. In the Rig-veda rohita means the horse of Agni, who is himself called Rohidasva, possessor of a red horse. In the Atharva-veda, however, Rohita is a god by himself, clearly showing traces both of sun and fire, but raised to the highest position above all gods by some of his panegyrists. This Rohita is said to have produced heaven and earth (XIII, 1, 6), to have made firm heaven and earth (ver. 7), and to have established the light and the firmament. He created all that has breath through rain (XIII, 1, 52), nay it was through him that the gods obtained immortality (ver. 7). That he was conceived as the sun we learn from his being described as ascending the heaven, as filling the heaven, and standing high on the firmament, a sage, begetting all forms.

As Agni dwells in the sun, Rohita often represents certain sides of Agni also, and is distinctly said to shine as Agni and to be the mouth of the sacrifice, that is, Agni. That Rohita should also be said to surpass Agni and Sûrya (ver. 25) need not surprise us. Does not Indra surpass his father Dyaus, and is not nearly every god praised occasionally as supreme?

It stands to reason that all that is new in Rohita and special to him, cannot be expected to exist in Greek or other Aryan mythologies. Still the general characteristics of the solar god are there, and we need not be surprised if some of these meet us again among the solar gods of Greece.

Threefold Character of Sûrya and Agni.

One of the most prominent features in the character of Sûrya, the sun, as well as of Agni, as dwelling in the sun [1], consists in their triple character, according as they represent the rising, the culminating, and the setting of the sun. The birth of the sun is from the waters, his glory in the highest heaven, the zenith, his rest in the waters again and what is beyond the waters.

In the Atharva-veda, XIII, 3, 21, we read even of three settings (nimru*k*), three risings (vyush), of

---

[1] Ath. XIII, 3, 23, 'Thou, Agni, when kindled, hast shone as the sun in heaven.' Tvam agne . . . arka*h* samiddha udaro-*k*athâ divi.

three welkins (ra*g*as), and three heavens (div), and of three birthplaces of Agni. Generally these three birthplaces of Agni are explained as heaven, earth (altar), and the waters (clouds), (Rv. X, 45, 1), and again Rv. I, 95, 3, as the sea, heaven and the waters.

We find a similar division in Greece where the whole world is divided into three realms, the highest sky belonging to Zeus, the sea to Poseidon, and the lower world to Hades, these three sons of Kronos being originally three personifications of the same Zeus. The three brothers were all called Kroniônes, Ouraniônes, nay even Olympians. Hence we saw that while Zeus is called Ζεὺς Ὀλύμπιος, Hades was actually called Ζεὺς ἄλλος or καταχθόνιος, and Poseidon Ζηνοποσειδῶν.

Olympos.

Olympos, as the home of Zeus and the abode (δώματα) of most of the members of his family, was originally no doubt the name of the mountains on the northern frontier of Thessaly (about 6,000 feet high), though afterwards it was often used as synonymous with οὐρανός, sky. It is unfortunate that no etymology has yet been found of Ὄλυμπος. The derivation of Curtius from λάμπειν, to shine, is not convincing. Curtius was always better as a critic than as an inventor of etymologies [1]. But for whatever reason Olympos received its name, it was

---

[1] Phonetically Ὄλυμπος or Οὔλυμπος might be identified with the Vedic Uloka, Weitblick, u = o as in ululo = ὀλολύζω, lu nasalised = lum, as in λύγξ, and k = p. But the etymology of Uloka itself is uncertain (Journ. Am. Or. Soc. Proceed., vol. xvi, p. xxxv). If we adopted *urvañk, the nasalisation might be explained. As to the meaning, compare Balder's home Breida blik.

due to its sublimity and impenetrability that it was supposed to be the seat of Zeus and the Olympian gods, while other mountains in Mysia, Lakonia, Elis, Lykia, and Kypros were probably called Olympos in imitation of the Thracian mountain.

If from his abode on Olympos Zeus was called Olympios, he was called Îdaios from another mountain, Îda, the wooded mountain range in the Troad, though there is also an Îda in Krête, where Zeus was supposed to have been born. But we know from the Iliad how Zeus, in order to be nearer to the battlefield, went from Olympos to Îda, and his altar on Gargaron, the highest peak of Îda, was widely known. But though Zeus was called Îdaios, this name was never applied to his brothers, Poseidon and Hades.

Poseidon.

Îda, from which Îdaios is derived, has retained its appellative meaning of wood, and we may therefore take Îda also to have meant originally wooded land or terra firma. Let us remember then that the old name of Poseidon was Potidan, and that several names of this god express the idea that he was always at war against the land, held the land (γαιήοχος), moved the land (γαίης κινητήρ), or shook the land (ἐνοσίχθων, ἐννοσίγαιος), &c. He is also called προσκλύστιος, he who washes (the shore) with his waves. If then the god of the sea impressed the Greeks with his constant fight against the land, with his encroachments on the land, as seen in many parts of Greece and particularly on the coast of the Troad [1], everywhere hollowed out by the sea,

---

[1] On the cult of Poseidon in the Troad, in the neighbourhood of Îda, see Gerhard, Griech. Mythologie, § 234, 2 a.

might not his name Potîdas, Potîdân, Potîdâon, be explained as a dialectic form of Poti + îdaios, he who is near or against the wooded land, or against Îda, formed like προσάρκτιος, προσάντης, &c.? This name would come very near to πρόσγειος and ποτίγειος, near the land, without necessarily conveying a hostile meaning. We actually have Poseidon's old name Potîdaios, preserved in the name of the town of Potîdaia, afterwards Kassandra, but now called again Potîdaia, on the neck of the peninsula of Pallêne, called so, it would seem, from its being altogether at the mercy of Poseidon. That Poseidon is a later form of Potîdân, not vice versâ, cannot be doubted, as various inscriptions confirm this name, as well as the geographical name of Potîdaia. To derive the name from *ποσ-ειδ, to swell towards, might be supported by προσκλύστιος, but this would hardly explain Potîdân. There is another epithet of Poseidon, namely ἐννοσίδας, which by the side of ἐννοσίγαιος might suggest δᾶς as a representative of γᾶς, so that his name of Potîdas might mean the same as ἀμφίγαιος. But this etymology would leave the long i and ei unexplained. I therefore see in Potîdaios a name of the sea that constantly moves against the land, or against Îda.

If then we see in Zeus, Poseidon, and Hades three expressions of the same god, the Zeus of the sky, the Zeus of the sea, and the Zeus of the lower world, it must not be supposed that these three gods are simply the sky, in three different manifestations, or the sun in its three stages as rising from beneath the water and the earth and culminating in the sky, and as setting again in the waters of the West. Difficult as it is to revive the long-forgotten thoughts that led to the creation of the gods and of the myths about the gods, we ought always to remember that Dyaus was no longer the mere sky in the Veda, nor Hêlios the mere sun when the gods were systematised in Greece, and each had his own peculiar place assigned to him. Zeus had long become the agent of the sky, and therefore the author of all the important influences of the sky on the earth or on man, before he was called Kronios or Kronides, the eternal, before he had a father Kronos, or a grandfather Ouranos, or a great-grandfather Akmon, assigned to him, before he was looked upon as one of three brothers, and before one of the three realms of nature was assigned to each of them. No doubt this influence of Zeus on man and nature was most powerfully manifested through the sun, and in that sense some of the most prominent acts assigned to Zeus may be called acts of the sun, but whoever it was that divided the kingdom of the world between Zeus the wielder of the thunderbolt, Poseidon the wielder of the trident, and Hades the invisible in his helmet (tarnkappe), he had learnt to think of Zeus and his brothers as agents, as persons, as independent gods. To say that the three Kronides were the sky under three aspects, or the sun in his three stages, would therefore be an anachronism; but that their deepest roots sprang from thoughts suggested by the workings of the sky, or the manifestations of the sun, is the conviction shared by all who have thought on the growth of language, mythology, and religion, and studied its nascent traces whether in India, Greece, or in Africa and Melanesia, among the highest of the high, or among the lowest of the low.

Trita and Trita.

As in many hymns of the Rig-veda Agni is the alter ego of Sûrya, the sun, we can understand why he, like the sun, should so often be represented in a threefold character. The three steps of the sun, best known from the myth of Vish*n*u[1], are very prominent in the hymns addressed to Agni. But by the side of the three steps, that is the sunrise in the East, the point of culmination, and the sunset in the West, there is in his case another threefold division, according as the solar light is looked upon as dwelling on earth, chiefly as the fire kept up on the hearth and worshipped as Agni on the altar, secondly in the firmament as the sun, sometimes as the lightning, and thirdly as descending into the sea and dwelling in the unseen abyss of the waters.

This threefold character of Agni or Sûrya must have been fully recognised before the close of the Mantra period, for we find numerous passages in the hymns alluding to it. Thus in Rv. III, 26, 7, Agni, speaking of himself, says arká*h* tri-dhấtu*h*—asmi, 'I am the threefold splendour.' Again in X, 45, 1, we read: 'Agni was born first in heaven, secondly from us (from among men on earth), thirdly in the waters (clouds of the sky, or waters of the sea).' A spring also is mentioned from which Agni was supposed to have arisen, and this can only be meant for the place beyond the horizon from whence the light of the sun seems to spring every morning, the same place which, if we are right, the ancient *R*ishis assigned to Aditi, the infinite goddess.

---

[1] Rv. I, 154.

We thus find three lights, according as Agni, fire, appears (1) on earth as the actual fire, kindled by rubbing with fire-sticks; (2) as the fire in the sky, the dawn, the sun, and during a thunderstorm, the lightning; and (3) as the fire beyond the sky, the sun after it has set in the water and descended into the invisible world.

This last light of the sun, when it had finished its course and had passed beyond the ends of the sky, was called Tr*i*ta (not yet Trita), literally passed, gone, set, from the root tar, later tr*i*, to pass, which could be rendered by transitus. Soon, however, this tr*i*ta (whether more or less regular than the later tîr*n*a[1]), and meaning originally gone beyond, was taken for tr*i*ta or tr*i*tîya, in the sense of third, and then irregularly changed to Trita, in analogy with tri, three. By the side of this ungrammatical Trita, the Third, another deity of the name of Dvita, the Second, was invented, who occurs already in the Rig-veda. Later on the Brâhma*n*as added even an Ekata, the First, a flagrant solecism. Little is known of these fanciful beings Dvita and Ekata, but much is said about Trita in the Rig-veda, which may throw light on Greek mythology.

When it is asked why the sun should have been called Tr*i*ta, i.e. gone, passed away, we should remember that tara*n*i, going beyond, originally an adjective, has afterwards become a well-known name of the sun. Tarîyân means passing through or over, and the wanderer would seem as good a name of the sun as Muni, the hermit. The night even has been called a parivrâ*g*aka. Thus we read, Rv. V, 41, 12, that Agni (ûr*g*ấm pátih, pári-

---

[1] On the form of roots like tr*i*, see de Saussure, § 14.

gmâ) traverses the sky quickly, nábhaḥ târîyân. We read in Rv. VII, 63, 4: Diváḥ rukmáḥ urukákshâḥ út eti dûré-arthaḥ taránịḥ bhrā́gamânaḥ, 'The jewel of the sky, the wide-seeing and far-reaching one, rises, passing onward, resplendent.'

We saw before how the disappearance of the sun was metamorphosed in the Veda, and frequently represented as a falling into a pit of certain heroes who represented the setting sun, and who were rescued by the Aśvins, the representatives of day and night. In the same way it is said of Trita that he fell into a pit (Rv. I, 105, 17), and that he was rescued by Bṛihaspati or by Agni (Rv. X, 8, 7).

That the Vedic Trita represented a far-off deity, the most remote known to the poets of the Veda, may be seen from passages such as Rv. VIII, 47, 16: 'O Ushas, carry sleeplessness to Trita and Dvita,' which means, of course, Carry it far away. Again, Rv. VIII, 47, 17: 'We bring all sleeplessness to Âptya,' where Âptya stands for Trita Âptya, i.e. the Trita who abides in the waters. This we see still more clearly in Rv. VIII, 47, 13: 'O gods, whatever sin is open or hid, put all this away from us on Trita Âptya.' This would seem to be a sufficient explanation of how Trita became what Prof. Bloomfield called the scapegoat of the gods [1].

What waters were meant as the abode of Trita we learn when we read that he dwells with Yama, the god of the departed, or with Manu, the son of Vivasvat, the companion of Yama, or when he is mentioned immediately after Ahi Budhnya and Aga ekapâd (Rv. II, 31, 6).

---

[1] Am. Or. Soc. Proceed., March, 1894, p. cxx.

I am fully aware that this interpretation of Trita as the setting or set sun differs from all interpretations hitherto proposed. These interpretations differ very much from each other, but what they all agree in is that Trita must have been the name of a very remote deity. Some have explained Trita as the wind of whom we know not whence it cometh, and this is confirmed by his supposed dwelling in company with the Maruts or storm-gods; others have taken him for the highest sky, for he dwells with Vishnu, others for the sea, because the samudra is said to be his abode. He has also been identified with lightning[1], with Agni, Vâyu, Soma, and Indra. The truth in these explanations is that Trita was a god dwelling in the most distant region, the sunset; their mistake consists in their neglecting to pay any attention to the various reading of Trita, and in trying to confine the sphere of his activity too narrowly. Trita differs from other gods in that he does not represent a visible object, for the set or invisible sun can hardly be called a visible object. He is not, however, like Brihaspati or Tvashtri or Aditi a purely abstract deity, for though he cannot be pointed at, he was nevertheless in his beginning a Sûrya or an Agni. If we keep in mind the natural sphere of his activity in the Far West, and in the waters beyond, and again his return in the morning in the East, it can easily be understood that his activity may often happen to be the same as that of other gods like Indra, Sûrya, or Agni, when overcome by darkness and when issuing into light after a victory over their enemies.

---

[1] See a valuable paper by Prof. Macdonell in the J. R. A. S., vol. xxv, p. 419 seq.

Agni more particularly may occupy the place of Trita or vice versâ, when he is said to be hiding in the waters and to emerge from them as the Apâm napât (Rv. V, 41, 10). Thus we read, Ath. I, 25, 1: Yád agníh ápah ádahat pravísya . . . tátra ta áhuh paramám ganítram, 'Where Agni blazed, having entered the waters, there, they say, is thy highest birthplace.'

But though I believe that this view of Trita would harmonise with most passages in which his name occurs, there is this difficulty, why his name in the Rig-veda should have been changed to Trita and mean the third. Trita never means the third in Sanskrit. How early, however, Trita was taken as Trita in the sense of the third, we see from the fact that two other names were formed in accordance with Trita, viz. Dvita and Ekata. And more than that, we find a derivation Traitana, which presupposes Trita, not Trita, to say nothing of the German Thridi (S. B. E., vol. xxxii, p. 305).

But old as this acceptation of the original Trita may be,—and we may safely ascribe it to a period before the separation of the Vedic and Avestic Âryas,—it would seem extraordinary that the postulated form of Trita, of which no trace occurs in the Rig-veda, should turn up in the Atharva-veda which by common assent is regarded as of later origin, unless we remember that the Atharva-veda, though containing many modern elements, has now and then preserved very ancient remnants also. Certain it is that instead of Trita we find in the Atharva-veda throughout Trita, transitor, a fact that cannot be safely ignored.

We have seen that Trita, whatever else he might be, was certainly a distant deity, far removed from men and from the other gods. If then we find that his name of T*r*ita, as preserved in the Atharva-veda, would have meant departed, gone, distant, we can hardly look upon this as a modern invention, particularly if we consider that the other meaning assigned to Trita as the third Agni, would be opposed to grammar, and would require the invention of a second, if not a first Agni, of a Dvita and Ekata, both grammatical monsters.

Trita is clearly a representative of Agni, as Agni is of Sûrya, while in some of his acts he takes the place of Indra. Like Agni, Trita has to fight V*r*itra and is assisted in his battle by the Maruts, who are known as the constant helpers of Indra in the same battle. Trita, like Indra, is said to have cleft the defences of Vala. When hidden in the waters, Trita was said to have been inside the vavra, the very name given elsewhere to the hiding-place of the cows, the cows of Tvâsh*t*ra (Vi*s*varûpa), which Trita had to rescue (Rv. X, 8, 8), or which Indra rescued for him (Rv. X, 48, 2). Here we see again how easily the Vedic gods exchange places, and how they perform the same work, only under different names. The hiding-place of Trita, the vavra, is really the same as the anârambha*n*am tamas, the endless darkness from which the light and some of its legendary representatives such as Atri, Vandana and others emerge every day. Sometimes vavra occurs in the plural as the endless hiding-places (vavrân̐ anantân̐, Rv. VII, 104, 17) into which evil spirits are to fall. Trita's home and character appear very clearly when it is explained (Rv. I, 163, 2) how the gods made a horse out of the sun, that is, represented the sun as a horse. At that time Yama, it is said, the most distant deity, gave the horse; the next in place, Trita, harnessed it, and Indra was the first to bestride it. Sometimes this solar horse is actually identified with Yama and Trita (Rv. I, 163, 3); or it is said that Trita, standing, as it were, behind the rising sun, blows like a smith with his bellows upon the rising Agni (Rv. V, 9, 5). It is said of the same Agni that he was found by Trita (i. e. in the far distance) before he, Agni, whether fire or sun, became by his light the friend of all householders (Rv. X, 46, 3).

The difficult part of the Trita myth is his fight with Tvâsh*t*ra Vi*s*varûpa. Before we can attempt to explain this we must remember that Trita before his fight drinks Soma, and likewise provides Soma to impart strength to Indra for his daily fight. The underlying idea seems to have been that Tvash*tri*, who was the father of Sara*n*yû, the earliest dawn, was also the father of the moon, called tri*s*iras, three-headed (the waxing, the full, and the waning moon), saptara*s*mi, seven-rayed (the sennight), and sha*d*aksha, six-eyed (seasons?)[1]. This demon was slain by Indra as well as by Trita, and thus the Soma or Am*r*ita in the moon was set free. That Tvâsh*t*ra, the son of Tvash*tri*, was meant for the moon is indicated by the epithet vi*s*varûpa, assuming all forms, i. e. constantly changing, and as such a proper epithet of the constantly changing moon. Rv. VI, 41, 3 : Eshâ*h* drapsâ*h* v*r*ishabhâ*h* visvárûpa*h* índrâya v*r*íshne sám akâri sóma*h*, ' The strong multi-

---

[1] The seasons are sometimes called the brothers of Soma, cf. Hillebrandt, p. 298.

form drop, Soma, was prepared for the strong Indra.' Tvash*tri* himself also is called vis*v*árûpa (Rv. III, 55, 19), and he is said to have created all forms and all things.

If, therefore, the moon or Visvarûpa held the Soma, the rain or the refreshing dew of the night[1], it was but natural that Trita or any other solar deity should, in order to gain the invigorating Soma, fight him or cut off his three heads. In this way we gain some kind of meaning in the destruction of Tri*s*iras Vi*s*varûpa, the son of Tvash*tri*, by Trita or by Indra. Whether this is the exact meaning which was in the minds of the poets of the Rig-veda or the writers of the Brâhma*n*as, I should not venture to assert positively, but it is at all events the meaning at which another scholar, Prof. Hillebrandt, arrived independently in his Vedische Mythologie, p. 53 seq. No better interpretation has as yet been suggested, and till that is done, it may be allowed to stand.

If, then, we saw in Trita a derivative of one root tar, to go through, older than t*ri*, and if that conception of the transit of the heavenly bodies from East to West found constant expression in the Veda, the question is whether it has left some traces in Greek mythology also.

Trita in Greek Mythology.

We saw that Trita was supposed to dwell in the most distant region from whence rose the sun, or the solar horse. This is to all intents and purposes the place which the Greeks meant by Tartaros. Tartaros, however, was originally, like Hades, not

---

[1] Yad ârdram tat saumyam, râtri*h* saumyâ. Taitt. Sa*mh*. I, 6, 3, 23. Hillebrandt, p. 459.

the name of a place, but of a person, the son of Aither and Gê, himself father of Typhôeus, Echidna, and the Gigantes. Homer always uses Hades as a personal, not yet as a local name. We can watch the same transition in the case of Trita, for though originally clearly a person, we can see how in certain passages Trita also assumes a local character. In Rv. IX, 37, 4, we read: Sáh Tritásya ádhi sấnavi, '(he lighted up the sun) on the top of Trita.'

Tartara would be a reduplicated form of the same root that yielded Trita, or rather Trĭta, for which we expect in Greek ταρτος, and would originally have meant he who constantly goes beyond or sets in the sea or in the place where the nocturnal sun after its setting was supposed to dwell, the place of Yama, himself originally the setting sun, sometimes spoken of as the first of those who died.

Benfey has shown[1], that Tartaros is a parallel form of Talâtala, which means the lower world in Sanskrit, but he takes it in the general sense of what is below, the descent, or the bottom (tala). He has removed all formal objections to the equation τάρταρος = talâtala, but he did not perceive the mythological connection between Trita and τάρ-ταρ-ος. The intensive of tri is tâtarîti and tâtarti.

Having now cleared up the meaning of Trita and his close relation with the lower world in the waters (samudre) or under the waters, I feel more inclined than formerly to accept the equation Trĭta (Âptya) = Trîton. Of course the Greek i in Trîton is long, and therefore the equation is irregular, but so is Trĭta from trĭ, and Trita from tri, three, and yet both

---

[1] Hermes, Minos und Tartaros, 1877.

are real forms. If the irregularity in Sanskrit is due to an attempt to supply a clearer meaning to Trita, could not the length in Greek Trîton be due to the length of the î in Tritogeneia? This was a very common and popular name, and if the i had once been lengthened in it, in order to make the name possible in epic poetry, it would become almost a necessity to speak of Trîton, a double perversion of Trita. The change of Trita into Trita would then seem to be previous not only to the Indo-Iranian, but even to the Aryan Separation. The derivative suffix in Trîton differs as that of Ploutos and Ploutôn, but if Trîtôn is a son of Poseidon and Amphitrîte (or Kelaino), if he with the other Tritons lives with his father on the bottom of the sea, this would agree with the true Trĭta, nay it would help us to understand why the same name occurs in different places in Greece, that is, wherever the sun seemed to descend, and dark surroundings had suggested an entrance into the lower regions of the earth. The names of Athêne, as Tritogeneia, Trîto, Trîtônia, and Trîtônis, might thus receive new light, for if the sun was supposed in the Veda to rise from the top of Trita, the goddess of the dawn could not claim a truer birthplace.

We need hardly refer to the old derivations of Tritogeneia from the Krêtan word τριτώ which is said to have meant head, or from the Boeotian river Trîton, which falls into the Lake of Kôpais, near the Pelasgian city of Athênai. Both derivations would give to the name of Tritogeneia too local and too narrow a character, and they both leave the impression of being scholastic interpretations of a name that had become unintelligible. In later times wherever there was a river Triton, the people naturally claimed Tritonia or Tritogeneia as their goddess.

One more step remains. We saw that Manu Vaivasvata was mentioned in conjunction with Trita (Rv. VIII, 52, 1) and with Yama, the lord of the departed. That Manu is the Sanskrit form to which Mînos corresponds in Greek can no longer be doubted after the explanation given by Kuhn and afterwards by Benfey[1]. We thus arrive at an important conclusion, namely that before the Aryan Separation took place, not only had a belief grown up in an underworld, but one person at least had been named whose duty it was to represent it, Manu among the ancestors of the Indians, Mînos among the ancestors of the Greeks.

I suggested some time ago that the idea of a third god, a Trita, had been reached before the Teutonic and Indian branches separated. I thought this could be admitted on the strength of the Old Norse Thridi, a name of Ódinn, as the mate of Hár, and Jafnhár. Grimm's Tweggi[2], however, is very doubtful, and could not represent Dvita. If we accept Trita in Sanskrit as a misapprehension of T*r*ita, we should have to admit that this misapprehension took place before the Aryan Separation. But the admission of three characters as the representatives of the sun as morning, noon, and night, is so natural that we cannot deny the possibility of its having arisen independently among different branches of the Aryan family. On the other hand, we can hardly doubt that the misapprehension took place before the

---

[1] Hermes, Minos und Tartaros, pp. 11-14.
[2] Germ. Mythol., p. 149.

Separation of the Âryas of India and Persia, for the Avestic form Thraêtaona presupposes a form derived from Trita, such as Traitana (Rv. I, 158, 5), not from Trita. Besides, in the Avesta Thrita is constantly spoken of as the third of Soma-priests, as the most beneficial of the Sâmas, the third mortal who prepared Soma for the mortal world, &c.

It was probably the most brilliant discovery ever made in Comparative Mythology that the name of the great hero of the Persian epic, the Shâhnâmeh, Feridun, is a lineal descendant of the Sk. Trita and Traitana, that the Vedic Trita Âptya appears in the Avesta as Thraêtaona, son of Âthwya. It is extraordinary that this discovery of Burnouf's should again and again have been ascribed to Roth, who, I believe, would have been the first to protest against it. The identity of Vivasvat and Vivanhvat was discovered by Bopp, but it was Burnouf who traced the Persian Feridun back to Thraêtaona, and the Persian Gershâsb, the Avestic Keresâspa, back to the Vedic Krisâsva. It was from 1840 to 1846 that Burnouf published in the Journal Asiatique his 'Études sur la Langue et les Textes Zends,' and showed for the first time how the three epic heroes of Persia, Jemshîd, Feridun, and Gershâsb descended from Yima Kshaêta, Thraêtaona, and Keresâspa, the Avestic representatives of the three earliest generations of mankind, whose more distant prototypes again can be discovered in the Vedic Yama, Trita, and Krisâsva. He showed further that as Vivasvat was the father of Yama in the Veda, Vivanhvat was the father of Yima in the Avesta, and that as Trita is called Âptya in the Veda, Thraêtaona in Persia is the son of Âthwya. Zohâk, the Persian tyrant who was slain by Ferîdun, was likewise traced back to the Avestic Azhi dahâka, the serpent, the Ahi of the Veda. These brilliant discoveries were important, not only as showing the intimate relation between the Veda, the Avesta, and the Shâhnâmeh (1000 A.D.), but as a palpable illustration of the transition of ancient mythology into epic poetry, and lastly into so-called history, a transition which has been so lightly set aside as incredible, when it was attempted to prove that the siege of Troy was a mythological and not a historical event in the strict sense of the word.

Hermes and Apollon.

If we accept Zeus as representing the god of the sky in his highest glory, as the ὕψιστος μέγιστος of the gods, and if we leave the earth, the common realm of the three Kronidai, as represented chiefly by Dêmêter, Kore, Hestia, and other female agents, we have still to analyse some other gods, representing the sun at his rising and setting, or as the morning and evening sky, viz. Hermes and Apollon.

We have already examined several names of the Dawn; but there is one more of great importance, not so much for the sake of the Dawn herself as for that of her son.

Hermes. Saramâ.

We have seen already that Saramâ like Saranyû was originally meant for the Dawn, the names meaning the swift runner. This may seem a very unmeaning name for the Dawn. But we know by this time that nearly all names were in their beginning very general and, in that sense, unmeaning. It could not be otherwise. Thus from the root sar, to go, we

have not only Saramâ, the swift goer, but likewise
sarâ, waterfall, sara*t*a, wind, saras, water, sarit, river,
sarayu, wind, air, sari, spring, sarma, motion. All
these words were general in the beginning, but
they were narrowed down and made special by
constant usage.

The name of Hermes, however, was not derived
direct from the root sar, but from a derivative of
that root, namely from Saramâ. We saw, when
examining the many stories of 'the Two with the
One,' that her name had been carried along on the
stream of mythology as that of the sister of the
Dioskouroi, and afterwards as Helen of Troy. We
must not imagine that Saramâ in the Veda and
Helena in Homer are one and the same person.
There would be no sense in that. All we have a
right to say is that they both started from Saramâ,
used in the Veda as a name of the Dawn, or from
something older still. But afterwards, when
numerous stories came to be told of the Dawn, the
ways of Greeks and Hindus parted once for all.
Saramâ, though she became the cause of war between
Indra and the Panis, never became the beautiful
woman of whom Homer tells. Helena, after she had
once been changed into the daughter of Zeus and
Lêda, the wife of Menelâos and the cause of the
Trojan war, showed no longer any traces of her auroral
or of her canine origin. In Greece we have more than
one Helena, for she can hardly be called the same
mythological person when carried off by Thêseus and
when carried off by Paris. All these stories, and
probably many more, were told by the people of
Argos, and what they had in common was no more
than the far distant physical background of the

Dawn being loved and carried off by ever so many suitors, and being reconquered after a long fight between the powers of the East and the West, of Light and Darkness.

Saramâ in the Veda is spoken of as a dog (not as a totem, however), but as a swift dog running along the sky that was supposed to find out the cows that had been carried off by the Panis and hid in a cave. What is said of Ushas is said of Saramâ, that she espied the strong stable of the cows, that she discovered the cleft of the rock, and that she led the cows out. But she is represented as doing all this, not of her own free will, but as the messenger of Indra. We hear in Greek mythology of a similar dog that belonged to Êrigone, the early-born, but there is but little known of that dog, called Maira, and what she has to find is not the herd of cows, but the corpse of Êrigone's father, Ikarios, whatever that legend may have been meant for.

The Vedic story tells us of a stable beyond the half real, half mythical river Rasâ. Saramâ had to cross that river in order to reach the cows. The stable is opened at last by Indra or Brihaspati, and the cows, that is, the rays of the morning, are released. This is only the old story of the morning cows told once more under a new form, and after the various versions of it which we have had before us, it need not detain us [1] at present.

Sârameyau.

What interests us at present is that Saramâ is said to be the mother of one or two dogs, called Sârameya. It was Kuhn's merit to have discovered

---

[1] Aufrecht, in Z. D. M. G. xiii, p. 493.

the identity of the name Sârameya with the Greek Hermeias. This discovery marked a new starting-point in our studies, and it was so brilliant and so convincing that for a time it took even classical scholars by storm. Afterwards followed a reaction. Every kind of phonetic difficulty was raised, but every objection was met, and after Benfey's exhaustive paper on Hermes, Mînos, and Tartaros, the phonetic objectors were finally silenced. That the Greek Hermes is a character very different from Sârameya was never denied. It seemed to have been forgotten that Comparative Mythology must be satisfied with a comparison of mythological germs, and that we can never hope to explain what is secondary and peculiarly Greek in the character of Hermes from Vedic sources. Etymology takes us back to the cradle of a god, but seldom to his later manhood. Otfried Müller knew very well what he meant by saying that 'name and myth are coeval'— but for that very reason the name cannot tell us all that happened to a god in his later career. Kuhn's discovery would, I believe, never have been challenged if no attempts had been made to compare too minutely the details of the myth of Sârameya with those of the myth of Hermeias. We know very little about Sârameya. As a couple the two Sârameyas are described as broad-nosed, four-eyed, grey, guarding the path to the realm of Yama, also as moving about to find those who are to die and accompanying them to the abode of the dead. In the singular Sârameya seems to be a more or less mythical watch-dog who is implored not to hurt the worshipper of Indra [1].

---

[1] Aufrecht, Ind. Stud. iv, 337.

What is important is that in Rv. VII, 55, 2, one Sârameya is called ar*g*una, bright, while the other is called pisanga, reddish brown, a sufficient indication that the two dogs were originally meant for day and night, and therefore distinguished as ar*g*una, white, and pisanga, brown or tawny. In other places, however, they are called syâma-sabalau, black and brindled. That the name of one of these dogs is found again in the Greek Κέρβερος we saw before. It would seem difficult to construct out of such poor fragments[1] a mythological story. We must be satisfied to take the two Sârameyas as the sons of the dawn, that is as day and night, as 'the Two with the One,' i.e. with their mother Saramâ. It is quite different with Hermes. Greek poetry has built up a complete character in which the traces of the Sârameya dogs have almost, if not altogether, vanished, or are at all events not easy to discover. All we ought to do is to try and understand how out of the poor seeds which are presented to us in the Veda, so magnificent a plant as Hermes could have grown up in Greece. The mistake that has been made consisted, here as elsewhere, in trying to prove too much, while the real task of the comparative mythologist is simply to show, that, granted that the two names are phonetically one, it is possible to account for the differences between Hermes and Sârameya in their later careers in Greece and India. It may seem that in trying to discover the original character of Hermes different scholars have arrived at very different conclusions. But the difference is not so great as it seems. Roscher sees in Hermes a representative of the wind, so does Cox. Menand

---

[1] Science of Language, ii, 594.

takes him for the twilight, so does Ploix, and Mehlis sees in him a general solar deity. Instead of trying to understand why these scholars differ from each other, their divergence has been represented as the surest proof of their incompetence. Still Darwin and Agassiz were allowed to differ without being called hard names, nor was Comparative Physiology tabooed because it was progressive.

The divergence between these scholars was chiefly due to their attempting to circumscribe too narrowly the activity of the ancient gods. Hermes, as the son of Saramâ, belongs certainly to the dawn and the twilight, but the morning wind belongs by right to the same domain, and as the twilight of morning and evening was frequently conceived as one, the god of the morning may well finish his course as god of the evening. In this way the various characters of Hermes, as messenger of the gods, as winged, as the robber of the cows, and as musician, may all be traced back to one and the same original concept.

Nor does the view of Mehlis [1] interfere at all with the other explanations of Hermes, for Hermes as the son of the dawn may well be called a solar deity, only not of a solar deity in general, but as one of many agents discovered in the morning sun. If we take this more comprehensive and at the same time more natural view of Hermes, we shall see how nearly all his epithets harmonise with his original character. I quote the epithets from the valuable essay of Dr. Mehlis. Hermes as the rising sun is called φαιδρός, bright, λευκός, white, εὔσκοπος, far-seeing, χαρμόφρων, joyous, ἡγεμὼν Χαρίτων, leader of the Charites (the dawn-goddesses), ἀέριος = *ἤριος

---

[1] Die Grundidee des Hermes, 1875, 1877.

ἦρι, early, the morning wind, Διὸς τρόχις, the runner of Zeus. His oldest names were Διάκτορος, the huntsman, and Ἀργεϊφόντης, the slayer of Argos, often used together as Διάκτορος Ἀργεϊφόντης. Mehlis' derivation of Διάκτορος from a root διᾱκ = διῶκ is doubtful, still more the comparison with German jac in jagôn¹ (praya*gy*u). But nothing better has yet been suggested, and the meaning of 'storming forward' would at all events have been appropriate to the god of the rising sun. Dr. Mehlis' etymology of Argeiphontes also is somewhat doubtful. The ancients explained it as the slayer of Argos, undisturbed by the ει for o; or as he who makes everything to become bright, ἀπὸ τοῦ ἀργῶς πάντα φαίνειν καὶ σαφηνίζειν. Preller accepts the former, Welcker the latter explanation. Mehlis takes ἀργει for an adverbial form like ἀμαχεί, πανδημεί, &c., in the sense of white (cf. Sk. arg-una, ἀργ-εννός), and φοντης for φαντης, shining, not in the sense of slaying. If the original meaning of Argeiphontes was 'the white illuminator,' the myth of the slaying of Argos would take its place among the numerous myths which owe their origin to a disease of language, in the narrowest sense of that term, that is to a mere misunderstanding. This is confirmed by the fact that neither Homer nor Hesiod knows of the slaying of Argos by Hermes, not even the author of the hymn to Hermes. The story of Argos grew, however, most rapidly. Argos, a giant with a thousand eyes, became the keeper of Ἰώ, after she had been changed into a cow by Hêre. Hermes being sent by Zeus to deliver Ἰώ, killed Argos (as Argeiphontes). Aeschylus (Prom. 568) is

---

[1] On praya*gy*u, see Vedic Hymns, S. B. E. xxxii, p. 335.

the first who mentions it. He also calls Argos panoptes, all-seeing, but the story itself may of course have been much older, like many myths not mentioned by Homer.

Dr. Mehlis has given us an exhaustive treatment of the whole mythology of Hermes, and has traced his numerous epithets back to what was discovered as his original character.

As Hermes, or Sârameya, the son of Saramâ, shared in the double nature of his mother, both the morning and the evening twilight, such epithets as νύχιος, nocturnal, νυκτὸς ὀπωπητήρ, the seer of the night, and προσέληνος, before the moon, speak for themselves. Like Saramâ, her son too came from the East and opened the brilliant gates of the sky, but he also descended in the West, and as the setting of the sun and of other heavenly bodies was looked upon as a descent under the earth, the name of χθόνιος, in the sense of below the earth, would naturally lead to the conception of Hermes as conductor of the dead to their subterraneous abode.

Almost all the blessings, which, as we saw before, were referred to the Dawn, as bringing light, life, happiness, and wealth to her worshippers, could be ascribed indirectly to her son also, to Hermes, who appears as δώτωρ ἐάων, giver of all good things, one of the oldest names as we saw of the beneficent gods of the Âryas (dâtâ vasûnâm, Zend, dâta vanhvâm), or ἐριούνιος, the ready helper or luck-bringer, which became in the end a proper name of the god himself.

Cognate Gods.

There is a very useful way of testing the accuracy and truth of our comparisons of mythological names, namely by finding out whether gods that start from some special point of nature, and extend their activity over a definite domain, are afterwards brought into contact, whether friendly or hostile, with other gods that are supposed to have had the same origin, and to rule over the same domain.

Apollon.

Every one would admit the solar character of Apollon. That, like Hermes, he was more particularly a representative of the rising sun and the opener of the heavenly gates, is indicated by his Latin name of Aperta, preserved to us by Festus, and by such Greek epithets as προθύραιος and προπύλαιος in Greek. Their being thus contiguous in their origin, would account for Hermes and Apollon being brought together again and again in Greek mythology. Hermes was supposed to have stolen some of Apollon's cows, that is, two out of the fifty. It has been imagined that there is an astronomical meaning in these numbers, the two killed cows being supposed to stand for the two intercalary months which, added to the forty-eight, would complete the period of four years or the Olympiad. It may be so, but Apollon, like Hêlios, has always had his herd of cows, and if Hermes wished to establish his reputation among the gods,

ὃς τάχ' ἔμελλεν
ἀμφανέειν κλυτὰ ἔργα μετ' ἀθανάτοισι θεοῖσιν,

nothing was more natural than that he should try to show himself cleverer than Apollon, who nevertheless remained his friend and brother.

The really important point is the brotherhood and the common activity of Apollon and Hermes. They share some attributes in common, such as the lyra and the staff, and their antagonism is more apparent than real. Even in their worship they remained united, often sharing the same altars. Several epithets belong to the one as well as to the other. Apollon is perhaps more clearly the brilliant, far-shining god, but in other respects, and even in their best-known statues, it is often difficult to tell the one from the other.

Aphrodite.

If Aphrodite was originally the principal of the Charites, and the Charites were the Haritas, the bright rays of the morning sun, embodied in female form, we can understand again why Hermes should have been called the leader of the Charites, ἡγεμὼν Χαρίτων. The names of ἀναδυομένη and ἀργυννίς leave no doubt as to the conception of Aphrodite as the bright sun rising from the waves of the sea, where the Charites bathed her and anointed her with immortal oil (Od. viii, 364).

Athêne.

And if, as I hold, Athêne also was a name of the Dawn, we can account for the statue of Hermes being placed in the temple of Athêne Polias at Athens, and for the cock being sacred to her as well as to Hermes.

If Herse or Erse, the Dew, was the beloved of Hermes, who can Hermes have been if not the rising sun?

If Daphnis is the son of Hermes, must not his mother have been a nymph like Daphne, the beloved of Phoibos Apollon?

Most extraordinary is the myth that Penelope [1],

---

[1] In hexameters Πηνελόπη and Πηνελόπεια.

the very type of a faithful wife in Homer, should be represented as the beloved of Hermes, and by him the mother of Pân. This can only be an old tradition, older than the Odyssey, and which therefore could not easily be suppressed. Pân, however, is represented also as the son of Penelope and Odysseus, and there are, no doubt, many points of similarity between the πολύτροπος Odysseus and the Hermes δόλιος, κερδῷος, &c. Whether we may go as far as Dr. Mehlis, and look upon the myth of Odysseus and Penelope as a heroic variation of the same physical theme of which we have the divine version in Hermes, is a question that must be left to future research. The weaving and unweaving of the dawn is alluded to in Rv. III, 61, 4, if I am right in translating—Áva syűma iva kinvatî maghónî ushâh, 'The mighty dawn as if unweaving her handiwork.' I derive syûman from siv, to sow, from which suo, κασσύω, &c. Sowing and weaving were not so different from each other in ancient as in modern times, and even if, as Mr. Griffith proposes, we were to translate syûman by reins, a meaning which it seems to have in syûmagabhasti, we could hardly render avakinvatî by dropping. It is curious that the name of Pênelopeia has long been explained as weaver, from πῆνος, woof. If so, it might be possible to see in lopeia a derivative of the root rap, λέπω (also rup, lup), to tear off, so that the meaning of her name might have been from the beginning, 'she who tears or undoes the woof.' If we adopt that view, 'Οδυσσεύς would have to be explained as δυσσευς, the setting sun, from δύω, δυσμή, the setting sun being likewise the returning sun (νόστιμος) of which we spoke before.

Mehlis recognises in Odysseus a representative of the sun who in the morning has to forsake his wife, and after travelling over the whole world and descending even into the lower regions, returns again to deliver her from her suitors and to kill them with the arrows shot from his bow which no one else could bend.

Zeus and Maia.

We have still to consider the parents of Hermes, Zeus and Maia. His mother Maîa is called the daughter of Atlas and Plêione, the oldest of the Pleiades, whom Zeus met in a cave on the Arkadian mountain Kyllêne. Her name, which the Greeks took in the sense of old mother, has been traced back by Benfey, Kuhn, and Grassmann to the Vedic Mahî. Mahî for *Mahyâ is difficult, but the omission of the h can be paralleled in Latin, where she is called Maja, by major for mahior; in Greek we could only appeal to such words as ἥ, νέω, &c. Mahî means great and grand, and is often used of goddesses, more particularly of the Dawn and the Earth. The Dawn is called mahî, Rv. I, 48, 14; 16; VII, 81, 4; VIII, 9, 17; IV, 14, 3; Agni is called the friend of the mighty Dawn, Rv. VIII, 19, 31, tvám mahinâm ushásâm asi priyá*h*.

The Earth also is called mahî, Rv. I, 131, 1; and more particularly mahî´ mâtấ, Magna Mater. Rv. I, 164, 33: Dyaú*h* me pitấ *g*anitấ nấbhi*h* átra, Bándhu*h* me mâtấ p*r*ithivî´ mahî´ iyám, 'Dyaus is my father and begetter, my birth is there, my kin and mother is the earth, this great one.'

The question then arises whether we should take Maia, the mother of Hermes, as the Earth or as the Dawn. In Sanskrit mahî has retained the meaning of earth to the present day. The Romans also held that Maja was Tellus, and likewise Bona Dea and Fauna; and as in the Veda also mahî prithivî occurs frequently, and is mentioned as the wife of Dyaus and the mother of Ushas, the Greek Maia also may, it seems to me, be safely taken in that sense. It should be remembered that Earth and Dawn are closely connected whenever there is a question of the sun as springing from the eastern quarter of the earth or from the East in the sky. Thus Lêto, the mother of Apollon, though she may be the night, may likewise be the earth at night, and this would explain why Lêto is called both νυχία [1], nocturnal, and μυχία, embayed.

Apollon.

In analysing the antecedents of Hermes we have several times come across the traces of Apollon. But though the two gods are similar, though they share some epithets in common, such as νόμιος, κουροτρόφος, ἀγήτωρ, ἀλεξίκακος, ἐπιμήλιος, though they actually exchange some of their offices, Apollon taking the lyre which had been discovered by Hermes, and Hermes accepting his wand of gold from Apollon, it is easy to see that in the thoughts of Greek poets Apollon occupied a far more exalted place than Hermes. The first and most important question, however, is, what was the first conception, the origin and meaning of Apollon, for no one who knows Vedic and Homeric poetry would expect to find the full-grown Apollon in the Veda. Apollon is certainly a difficult name to analyse, and that its true etymological meaning was lost long before we

---

[1] Hermes also is called νύχιος.

know anything of Greek literature, is shown by the vain attempts made by the Greeks themselves to discover any etymological meaning in it.

I referred before to a Latin name of Apollon, namely Aperta, -ae. This is evidently an old Latin name of a Latin deity, worshipped in Italy before the name of Apollon was known there. But just as Coelus, Sol, and Luna were known in Italy before Ouranos, Hêlios, and Selêne were grafted on them, Aperta also was a deity representing the opener of the morning sky; nay it may possibly have been an epithet of Janus. About the meaning of Aperta there could never have been a doubt among the people, though the learned explained it by 'quia patente cortina responsa ab eo darentur.' But if the people transferred this name of Aperta to Apollon, the reason can only have been that they had discovered in the Greek god the character of Aperta, the opener. If they called him Apollo, that was probably no more than an adaptation of Apollon, while Aperta must have been an old and truly Italian name.

As we look further among the Greek epithets of Apollon, we find a considerable number alluding to his connection with the gates. As Janus was connected with janua, Apollon was called θυραῖος, προπύλαιος, προστατήριος, all expressing the same idea of a god who presides over the doors, or who opens the gates. What these gates were really meant for we can best learn from his epithet Ἐῷος, auroral.

There has always been great unwillingness on the part of classical scholars to admit the solar character of Apollon, nor can it be denied that Apollon, as conceived by Homer, displays but little of his solar origin. Some scholars[1] have therefore gone so far as to say that in the Homeric poems Apollon was not yet a solar deity, which seems a curious inversion of the growth of Aryan mythology. It would have been far more correct to say that in Homer Apollon was no longer a solar deity. And the same might be said of most of the Homeric gods. They are no longer what they were in the beginning, they have left their physical stage behind, and have become half human, half divine.

In the eyes of the poet of the Iliad and Odyssey, Apollon was the son, and the beloved son of Zeus, always carrying out his father's behests. He was distinguished by manly beauty, famous for his gift of song and poetry, endowed with wisdom and prophetic powers. Still there are traces left of his former physical nature. He carries bow and arrows, the usual attributes of solar deities all over the world. In obedience to his father Zeus he punishes the Greeks by sending pestilential arrows into their camp. He is φοῖβος, pure and radiant, like his sister φοίβη, Artemis, the moon ; he is Λυκηγενής (Il. iv, 101), light-born. This was afterwards explained as born in Lykia, because λύκη had ceased to be understood in Greek as meaning light. But the generally accepted birthplace of Apollon was Dêlos, the bright island, and had nothing to do with the real Lykia, nor with the island afterwards called Dêlos and Ortygia. It was, however, as an old representative of the sun, and not as the god of poetry and wisdom, that Apollon sprang first into life. Even in Homeric times he was still sup-

---

[1] Friedreich, Realien in der Iliade und Odyssee, p. 696.

posed to be the frequent author of death. As sun and moon were in ancient mythology considered as the givers of life, they consequently became the givers of death also. Hence both Apollon and his sister Artemis send death with their rays, either suddenly or gently [1].

As to the name and the first conception of Apollon, many conjectures have been started. The latest is that of Dr. von Schroeder in Kuhn's Zeitschrift, xxix, p. 193. He derives Apollon from the Vedic Saparyenya, worshipful, an epithet of Agni, fire or light. I quite agree with Dr. von Schroeder in his tracing many of the features of Apollon back to the character of the Vedic Agni (Sûrya), and some of his parallels seem to me irrefutable. But the etymology proposed by him would be difficult. First of all, the meaning of saparyenya is far too abstract for an original name of a deity. All the gods might have been called saparyenyas, not one so clearly standing out from all the rest as Apollon. For such a god we want a more individual name, if it were only Phoibos. But Phoibos and Apollon start from independent beginnings, and were united in later times only.

Secondly, 'Απόλλων, -ωνος, could only be Saparyan, and that would mean worshipping, not worshipped. But as Dr. von Schroeder says himself, p. 229, note, his equation of Apollon and Agni would remain unaffected, even if his etymology proved untenable, and though I venture to propose a different genesis of the god's character, I fully accept the general outline of it as traced by Dr. von Schroeder.

---

[1] See Schwartz, Prähistor. Studien, pp. 328 seq. and 412.

If now we turn to Greek mythology, no one, I suppose, would dissent if we called Hêlios the sun, or the god of the sun, or a solar deity. But if we say the same of Apollon, there will be an outcry in the whole classical camp. And yet Apollon, as we shall see, is as much a solar deity as Mithra or Savitri. The ancients derived 'Απόλλων from ἀπόλλ-υμι in the sense of destroyer, and when Kassandra in Aesch. Agamemnon, 1081, exclaims, Ἄπολλον, ἀγυιεῦ τ' ἀπόλλων ἐμός, 'Apollon, my leader and destroyer,' she clearly had this etymology in her mind. Phonetically, there is nothing to be said against it, for by the side of verbal stems in u or nu there were often stems in a or ya. Ὄλλυμι stands of course for *ὀλ-νυμι, but οὐλόμενος presupposes οὔλομαι for *ὀλ-λομαι, and from a stem such as ὄλλο, 'Απόλλων, if not 'Απέλλων, might well have been derived. So much for the form. But we cannot decide on an etymology by means of phonetic laws only. The meaning also has a right to be considered. Now we have no right to say that from the beginning Apollon was a destructive god. It is quite true, and cannot be too often repeated, that the earliest information within our reach as to the original character of the Aryan gods, is always what is involved in their names. But that information, though highly important, is by its very nature very limited. And after the etymological phase there generally follows a gap which may be of a hundred or a thousand years. When we meet with a Greek Apollon he is a work of poetic, if not yet of a plastic art, and he shows the lines of a long growth. He holds a silver bow, and 'Αργυρότοξος has become one of his recognised names. He has arrows which never fail, he is called Ἑκατηβόλος, Ἑκάεργος, and Ἕκατος, all implying his power to hit from a distance. These arrows are no doubt generally pernicious, but he is by no means an evil spirit. When discharging his arrows he may often be meant as a punisher and revenger, but he is likewise the protector and healer, ἀλεξίκακος, ἀποτρόπαιος, ἀκέστωρ, and σωτήρ. He is the god of wisdom, of music, of prophecy. All these ideas require time to grow, but they certainly could not spring from the germ of Apollon, if that name had from the beginning been meant for a noxious spirit.

The Greek verbal stem ολ or ορ may represent not only the root AR, to injure, but likewise the root VAR, or Fορ in its various meanings. Var in Sanskrit, if preceded by apa, means to uncover, to open, and this var with apa or vi, in the sense of uncovering, revealing, opening, is constantly applied in Vedic Sanskrit to solar deities who appear in the morning, uncovering the darkness of the clouds, revealing the light and opening the sky for the birth of the day.

For instance:—

Rv. I, 68, 1: Srîmán úpa sthât dívam bhuranyúh sthâtúh karátham aktűn ví úrṇot, 'The quick one with his heat has approached the sky; he has revealed the night, and all that stands and moves.'

Rv. I, 132, 4: Yát ángirobhyah ávriṇoh ápa vragám, 'That thou openedst the stable (of the night) for the Aṅgiras.'

Rv. I, 51, 3: Tvám gotrám áṅgirobhyah avriṇoh ápa . . ., 'Thou openedst the cow stable for the Aṅgiras.'

The same is said of Soma, IX, 86, 23, and of Indra.

Rv. I, 51, 4: Tvám apấm apidhấnâ avriṇoh ápa,

'Thou (Indra) uncoveredst the coverings of the waters (the clouds).'

Rv. II, 11, 18: Ápa avrinoh gyótih áryâya, 'Thou (Indra) revealedst the light to the Árya.'

Rv. II, 34, 12: Ushấh ná râmíh arunaíh ápa úrnute. 'Like the dawn they uncover the nights with the red rays (úrnute = úrnuvate).'

Rv. X, 81, 2: Ví dyấm aúrnot mahinấ visvákakshâh, 'Visvakarman, the all-seeing, uncovered the sky by his might.'

Rv. III, 34, 3: Índrah vritrám avrinot, 'Indra (un)covered Vritra (the demon of darkness).'

Rv. X, 88, 12: Ã́ yáh tatấna ushásah vibhâtíh ápo úrnoti támas arkíshâ yán, 'He who spreads out the shining dawns, uncovers the darkness, moving in light.'

In Rv. X, 40, 8, the two Asvins are said to open the stable (vragá saptásya) of the night. This stable is called gávya úrváh in VII, 90, 4, and the waters are said to flow out, when it has been opened.

In Rv. VIII, 40, 5, Indra and Agni uncover the arnavá, the sea (saptábudhna) of the firmament.

In Rv. III, 31, 21, we read: Dúrah ka vísváh avrinot ápa svấh, 'He opened all his doors:' cf. X, 120, 8.

In Rv. X, 139, 6: Ápa avrinot dúrah ásmavragânâm, 'Savitri opened the doors of the stone-stables.'

The cows in these stables are likewise said to have been discovered by the bright gods. Thus Rv. VIII, 63, 3: Sáh vidvấn ángirobhyah Índrah gâh avrinot ápa, 'He, the wise Indra, opened or discovered the cows for the Angiras,' while in Rv. II, 34, 1, we see the same act performed by the Maruts. Sometimes two doors are mentioned in the dual which Agni opens when he brings light and wealth to his worshippers. Generally, however, they appear in the plural as the doors of wealth (I, 68, 5), as the doors (dvârau) of Rita, also as the doors of darkness (III, 5, 1). These doors, called by various names, are the eternal heavenly gates through which the representatives of the light of day come and go. What was on this side of the heavenly gates, was the home of man, what was on the other side, was the home of the gods. They assumed afterwards a kind of mythological personality, and under the name of Devîr Dvârah, the heavenly gates, we saw that they had a definite place assigned to them in the Âprî hymns. Thus we read again and again (V, 5, 5): 'Heavenly Gates move asunder, easy of access, for our protection, fill the sacrifice more and more.'

If then, phonetically, there is no possible objection to the derivation of 'Ἀπόλλων from a Sanskrit form *Apa-var-yan, or *Apa-val-yan [1], and if the opening of the heavenly gates was a characteristic feature of several of the solar or luminous deities in the Veda, the question arises whether in the myths about Apollon also some traces of this character of door-opener or porter of the sky may be discovered. We have mentioned already some of the epithets of Apollon, clearly referring to the opening of gates, such as that of 'Ἀπόλλων θυραῖος [2]. This is Apollon of the door, a name which, like Propylaios, was in later times explained as he whose statue stood at the door, but which long before the invention of statues had a very different meaning, as opening the gate of

---

[1] The Cypric form 'Ἀπειλων stands for 'Ἀπέλγων = Apavaryan.
[2] Gerhard, Griech. Mythologie, § 308, 6.

the sky, and as stepping forth from the door of the morning, as Ἐκβάσιος and Ἐμβάσιος. Besides having the epithet of Ἑῷος, he is actually called Ἀβέλιος, which was the Krêtan name of Hêlios, the sun, and has sometimes been considered as the true etymon of Hêlios. Artemis, his sister, born with him at Dêlos, is likewise called Propylaia. A nymph who by Apollon became the mother of Kyknos, was called Thyria, while another, called Thêro, bore him a son called Chairon. These names are generally explained as derived from localities where Apollon was worshipped, but the question is whether here, as in other cases, the localities were not originally called after Apollon and his friends. Thyrion was the place of a temple of Apollon near Chairôneia [1], and in Italy Thurium or Thurii, the modern Sybaris, was famous as a place of worship of Apollon. It is quite possible, therefore, though I shall say no more, that the nymphs who were united with Apollon received their names originally for the same reason for which he himself had been called Thyraios.

I write all this being well aware of the objections which have been raised against explaining the name of Apollon or Apellon as meaning originally the opener of the heavenly gates. Greek scholars, however, should not forget that we actually have in the Aiolic dialect ἀπέλλω in the sense of ἀποκλείω, to shut off, and that the act of shutting off the darkness implies the act of bringing out the light. If mathematical proof is required of Ἀπέλλων having been Apavaryan (Abwehrer), I confess I cannot produce it. It is easy to say that a mere opener, a janitore, or even a herald of the day could never

---

[1] Gerhard, l. c., p. 321.

have grown into the glorious personality of the Greek Apollon. But we must not be so positive in our negative criticism. Just as the most perfect Greek statues were the last outcome of a movement that began with crude stones and hideous idols, just as the Hermes of Praxiteles is the direct descendant of the old images of the god which consisted of two stones on each side and a third placed across [1], the mythological and religious conceptions also of Aeschylus and Sophocles presuppose a continuous growth beginning with the simplest and crudest conceptions of the agents or powers of nature. Far from looking on the Vedic hymns or on the Homeric poems as representing the primeval beginnings of mythological and religious thought among the Âryas, I have pointed out again and again that we can perceive rings within rings in their language, rings within rings in their mythology, and that the antecedents which we have to postulate require to be measured by geological rather than by historical periods. We may find it difficult to understand why a god of light, of wisdom, of prophecy, and of healing should originally have been called the Opener, or Revealer, *Apavaryan or Apollon; why his enemies, the powers of darkness, whether of the dark night or of the dark clouds, should have been called Coverers (V*r*itra), and why at last this v*r*itra should come to mean enemy in general, so that v*r*itraghna, lit. V*r*itra-killer, became the genius of victory, and the later Persian Bahrâm, the name of the fire that is kept burning to the present day to secure protection and victory to its worshippers.

---

[1] Casanowics, Relig. Ceremonies in the Talmud, Proceedings of Am. Orient. Society, March, 1894, p. lxxix.

If V*r*itra, from var, was the coverer or the genius of darkness, Apa-v*r*itra, Apa-v*ri*nvan, or Apa-varyan would have been the most appropriate names of the uncoverer or the genius of light, one of those fundamental conceptions which was personified in Agni, in Indra, and in ever so many Aryan gods.

This might suffice to show that the name of Apollon or Apellon was originally meant for the god who shuts off the darkness of the night or the darkness of the clouds,—both, as we saw, constantly running together,—and who thus opens or reveals the light. In matters like these we must learn to be satisfied with what is possible or probable. we cannot, nay we ought not to clamour for mathematical certainty.

As I derive Apollon not from apa + ar, or ἀπόλλυμι, but from apa-var, it might be objected that the Greek form ορ or ερ would have had an initial Digamma, and this ought to have asserted its former presence by preventing contraction with the final vowel of the preposition. Thus we have ἀποέργω, ἀποείκω, ἀποειπεῖν, &c. But by the side of ἀποειπεῖν we find ἀπειπεῖν in classical Greek, so that *ἀπολλειν for *ἀπο-ολλειν would rest on very strong analogy. There is besides the Lesbian ἀπέλλω in which ἔλλω, Dor. Ϝήλω, Hom. εἴλω, certainly begins with the Digamma, and in which the final ο of the preposition is omitted just as it is in Ἀπέλλων, the Doric form of Ἀπόλλων[1].

If, then, etymology teaches us that Apollon was in the beginning conceived as a revealer of light, if his epithets teach us that his original home was in

---

[1] Brugmann, Grundriss, § 611.

Dêlos, or in the East, that he was Phoibos, brilliant, having for his sister Phoibe, the moon, that he was Lykeios, illuminating, gold-haired, and with blonde locks, is it not clear that nearly all the stories told of him confirm his original character or at all events are never in conflict with it? We saw already that the name of his mother, Lêto, meant the night or, it may be, the earth during the darkness of the night. It is quite true that Lêto cannot be derived directly from λαθεῖν, but that does not prevent us from taking λαθεῖν and latere as parallel roots. A comparison of Lêto with Râtî for Râtrî, night, is tempting, but hardly necessary. Dêlos like Asteria meant originally the bright place where Heaven and Earth seemed to meet, and whence sprang the golden light of the young sun, who was hence called Dêlios, the brilliant. If one myth tells us that Lêto was in travail for nine days, that may refer to the vernal sun who, before beginning his northward course, was supposed, at the summer solstice, to remain stationary for nine or even twelve days.

In that case Apollon, though the daily sun, would have been looked upon as beginning his victorious vernal career at the time of the Northern solstice. In that case even the preceding travels of Lêto all over the earth might find an explanation. Her laying hold of a palm-tree reminds one of similar cases, particularly that of Buddha's mother, Mâyâ[1].

Ilithyia or Eileithyia.

As to Ilithyia (Εἰλείθυια), who was kept away by Hêre, but brought at last by Îris to assist at the

---

[1] It seems to me impossible to see in this act an allusion to the fire-sticks, as v. Schroeder suggests.

birth of Apollon, her name is difficult to explain. It must be remembered that she, like the Dawn in the Veda, was originally represented as more than one, the Ilithyias, but that, after the time of Homer, she is spoken of as one goddess, and not only as assisting others at childbirth, but as herself giving birth to a child. She was called Auge (Αὐγὴ ἐν γόνασι), and as Auge was a name of the dawn, it was supposed that she received that name because she presided over the dawn of life. In Latin too she is called Lucina or Juno Lucina, which points to light as her original character. If she was called older than Kronos, that again was interpreted as implying that generation began at the beginning of all things. Sometimes Hêre, who watches over marriage (γαμήλιος), and who is called the mother of Ilithyia, is identified with her daughter, nay Artemis and Diana even (possibly, like Lucina, representing the moon) are supposed to have performed her functions.

The name is given as Εἰλείθυια, ion. Εἰλήθυια, Ἐλεύθυια, and also Ἐλευθώ, and it seems to me that Eleutho, instead of being an abbreviation, is possibly the simple parallel form of Eleuthyia and Eileithyia. She would then have been called the comer, or, if we take into account the Krêtan ἐλεύθω, to bring, the Bringer, a meaning that would be welcomed by all who see in Fors primigenia the Bringer of good things. Krête was the home of Eleutho, she herself was born there in the Amnisian cave. The same root ἐλυθ (ruh) might supply a key to the name of Ἠλύσιον, that which is to come, l'avenir, as the name of the Elysian fields in the West, the home of the blessed.

We now return to Apollon, who after the advent of the coming goddess Eileithyia[1] was born at Dêlos, i.e. in the East, also called Ortygia (vartikâ) for reasons explained before, and Asteria.

Apollon's early love for Daphne also has long been accounted for as referring to the Dawn. That his fight with Pŷthon (Ahir budhnya) should be his first heroic achievement, may possibly be explained by the fact that at his first appearance above the horizon he had only just escaped from the powers of the lower regions (budhna), the serpents who were killed by the first rays or arrows of the young god. It is known, however, that other authorities defer this fight against Pŷthon to a later time and to a different locality. This shows the freedom with which mythology was handled in its origin, and shows how fully justified we are in claiming a similar freedom in our analysis of mythology. That the original idea of the fight of Apollon against Pŷthon was that of the struggle of the light of the morning against the darkness below the horizon or of the vanishing night admits of little doubt. But it is perfectly conceivable that when Apollon's sanctuary was established at Delphi, the same myth should have been localised there. Prof. Forchhammer, who had explored the neighbourhood of Delphi most carefully, gives us an explanation of the battle between Apollon and Pŷthon, which deserves more attention than it has hitherto received. I quite follow the opinion expressed by M. Decharme in his valuable Mythologie de la Grèce, p. 100.

---

[1] Θυια, if it occurs at the end of other mythological names, would seem to mean wind, cf. θύελλα, so that 'Ορείθυια would be the mountain wind.

'M. Forchhammer,' he writes, 'a Danish scholar (no, German), after having carefully explored the nature of the soil at Delphi, takes the dragon Python as the symbol of the torrent which at the beginning of spring descends from the slopes of Parnassus, forms a waterfall between the two rocks, Nauplia and Hyampeia, bounds along the successive terraces of the Delphic amphitheatre, and precipitates itself into the valley of the Pleistos. This torrent, swollen by the rains of winter and the melting of the snow on the hills, as it carries along and destroys everything in its impetuous fury, moving along tortuously like a serpent, might well have been compared by the people of Delphi to a formidable dragon, devastating the country and terrifying the people and their flocks. But in summer the water flows off, falls and evaporates, and the hot rays of the sun dry the bed of the torrent. The monster has been pierced by the arrows of the god. His body begins to putrify and he receives henceforth the name of Python, that is, the putrid.'

I cannot say that I feel quite convinced, but that these secondary myths spring up sometimes from a mere wish to explain unintelligible names, we saw in such cases as that of Argeiphontes, and if this explanation offered itself to Forchhammer while exploring that neighbourhood, it is quite possible that it may have occurred to the ancient Greeks also, when establishing the new and permanent sanctuary for Apollon at Delphi.

What is the meaning of the servitude imposed on Apollon under Admêtos, I have shown before by a reference to the Mexican Inca who though a worshipper of the sun, nay worshipped himself as a descendant of the sun, declined to recognise the sun as the Supreme God on account of

The chains
That bind thee to the path that God ordains
That thou shouldst trace[1].

This servitude has been painted in different ways, but the original thought is always the same. And as the solar god was represented as possessing herds of 350 oxen or sheep, it was natural that as a slave also he should be employed, as Apollon was by Laomedon, to watch his cattle.

Again when the annual travels of the sun had led him far away to the north, where he remained during the long winter, Apollon himself was supposed to enjoy among the Hyperboreans a happier time than the raw winter in Greece.

There can hardly be any doubt that the journey to and the stay of Apollon with the Hyperboreans reflect the annual movements of the sun from South to North, and from North to South. We have only to read Plutarch, who tells us that from spring to autumn Delphi resounds with hymns of praise and paeans to Apollon, while in winter the paean was silent and nothing was heard but the dithyrambos and songs on the sufferings of Dionysos, in order to understand the character of the Greek Hyperboreans and of Apollon's relation to them. The date of the return of Apollon from the Hyperboreans to Greece varies from spring to the middle of summer. His departure was the ἀποδημία, his return the ἐπιδημία. If, however, any doubt could still remain as to the solar origin of Apollon, his intimate relations with the Charites would settle it, as in the case of Hermes. Sometimes these Charites are called the daughters of Hêlios and Aiglê, names which speak for them-

---
[1] Chips, iv, p. 122.

selves; nor are their own names, Aglaia, Euphrosyne, Thalia, Pâsiphae, Klêta, or Phaenna, less significant. The epithet κουροτρόφοι they share in common with Apollon. Apollon was represented as carrying the three Charites on his hand, which is the same idea as when the sun-god in the Veda is represented on his golden chariot drawn by his Haritas. They are called Lampos and Phaëthon, or Pyroeis, Eôos, Aithon or Phlegon in Greece, names that are very outspoken, while in India these horses of the sun are simply called Haritas, i.e. the red or bright ones. Though Apollon was originally a light-giving, joy-giving, and gracious god, we can easily understand that the more terrible aspects of the sun also should have been reflected in him. The sun helps vegetation, but the same sun may destroy the harvest, may send pestilence and kill the very people who worshipped him. In the Veda also the solar powers assume from time to time a terrible character; and Apollon as the angry god, as moving along νυκτὶ ἐοικώς, like unto night, as οὔλιος, baneful, as ἀπόλλων, supposed to mean destroyer, comes so near to the Vedic Rudra that Rudra rather than Agni in his character of Sûrya, has been looked upon as the prototype of Apollon[1]. And curious enough, as Apollon was conceived not only as sending pestilence and death, but likewise as the physician and healer of illness, not only as οὔλιος, baneful, but also as οὔλιος, healthful, Rudra, the terrible, also was supposed to be possessed of all medicines. Hence Asklêpios, the physician of the gods, was fabled to be the son of Apollon, while the other healing god,

---

[1] K. Z., xxix, 225.

Paiêon or Paian (Παιήων, Παιάν), was actually identified with Apollon. That he became likewise the physician of the soul, the purifier and deliverer from sin (σωτήρ), these are characteristics which we must not hope to find in the Vedic gods, though they are not entirely absent, as we may see in the prayers for forgiveness of sin addressed to Varuna and others. Neither can we look in the Veda for a god representative of music and of prophecy as Apollon was in Greece. These are the reflexions of Greek life, and though they may have been assigned to Apollon without contravening his original physical character, they are of Greek, not of Aryan growth.

In all these respects, the case of Apollon allows us to see very clearly what we may and what we may not expect in a comparison of Vedic and Greek or any other Aryan mythology. There are some scholars who deny the very existence of a Pan-Aryan mythology. With them, after all that has been written, I suppose I need not argue. But these are the very writers who in the absence of all arguments try to throw discredit on mythological researches by pointing the finger of scorn at the want of agreement in the comparison of Aryan deities and in the interpretation of Aryan myths. It is well known that Kuhn has tried to identify Apollon with Rudra, von Schroeder with Agni, and I myself with neither of them, or rather with both. I have openly stated the case so as to give our adversaries a splendid opportunity. And yet to those who have followed me up to this point my answer cannot be doubtful. I hold that it is a fundamental mistake to expect coincidences in the names and achievements of Aryan gods after they have once entered into their national phase.

If such coincidences occur, they are exceptions, and have to be accounted for, just as we have to find excuses if we identify the English 'to have' with Latin 'habere.' When Aryan words have entered on their national development, when the common Aryan language has once become Latin or French, Gothic or English, we must not look for close resemblances between Gothic and Latin, English and French. We must remember first of all what is peculiarly Latin or peculiarly Gothic, and then strip the words of these later crusts before we try to discover their original form. If we come across such apparent coincidences as 'to call' and καλεῖν, 'to care' and cura, we should know at once that they cannot be real, because English and Greek and English and Latin have no right to agree so minutely, or if they do, as in the case of 'to have' and 'habere,' such exceptional agreements have to be very carefully justified.

It is much the same in mythology. If we are told, for instance, as Kuhn has pointed out, that Rudra's hair is represented as braided and tied up in a knot (kapardin), and that Apollon's hair was represented as arranged in the same manner (ἀκερσεκόμης), this is, first of all, not quite correct, and secondly, it would prove too much [1].

All that we are justified and all, I believe, that Kuhn really meant was that a god represented as moving rapidly through the air, like Apollon, would naturally be conceived as having his hair flowing freely about his head, and this is how he is represented in the oldest statues, while in the case of

---

[1] K. Z., iii, 335; and von Schroeder, K. Z., xxix, 227.

Rudra his kaparda or top-knot, formed like a shell, may be no more than a repetition of the hair-knot affected by his worshippers as, later on, by the worshippers of Siva [1].

If Kuhn compared the epithet of Apollon, Loxias, oblique, with the epithet of Rudra, vaṅku, athwart, he could hardly have taken Loxias in the sense of λοξός, crooked, as alluding to the crooked or deceitful meaning of Apollon's oracles. This interpretation of Loxias had been rejected long ago by Otfried Müller, who showed that Apollon's sister, Artemis, was likewise called Loxo, though she never was accused of having uttered oracles, whether straight or crooked. What Kuhn really meant was that vaṅku, as applied to Rudra, was probably intended for rushing violently athwart the air, and that Loxias had the same physical meaning when originally applied to Apollon. But many gods are represented as moving or rushing, without being therefore identical, nor is vaṅku an epithet exclusively belonging to Rudra.

The same may be said about Kuhn's remark that Apollon played the lyre and that there was a musical instrument called rudrî, possibly the same word as λύρα. Rudrî is a very late word and little authenticated in Sanskrit literature. The musical character of Apollon as leader of the Muses is far too peculiarly Greek to allow of comparison with Rudra, whose music, if any, was more like the whistling and howling of the storm than the strains of the lyre. Still, if Kuhn wanted only to refer to the physical character of Rudra, he might have

---

[1] M. M., S. B. E., vol. xxxii, p. 424.

strengthened his case by a reference to the Rudras, plur., that is the Maruts, storm-winds, who in the Veda are constantly represented as singers (arkin) [1]. It is true that both Apollon and Rudra have bow and arrows, but so have other gods both in Vedic and Greek mythology. Agni constantly shoots his arrows, Artemis, Hêrakles, and Odysseus were famous as archers, though with the ancient Greeks the use of the bow was not considered so honourable as sword or lance.

That both Apollon and 'Rudra are represented as the best of physicians is certainly startling, and shows that, as we shall see, there was some truth in Kuhn's theory that Rudra and Apollon were cognate gods. What Kuhn omitted to consider were the many points of difference between Apollon and Rudra, which are equally important for our purpose.

We now turn to examine von Schroeder's view that there was a deity, Apollon-Agni, that is to say, that what the Vedic poets called Agni the Greeks called Apollon. This view contains undoubtedly a certain amount of truth, if only Agni is taken, as he so often appears in the Veda, not simply as the fire, the ordinary ignis, but as the heavenly fire or the heavenly light. How close the connection between these two manifestations of light on the hearth and in the East is, has been shown again and again. If therefore v. Schroeder would take Agni not in the ordinary sense of fire, but as the fiery sun, more particularly the rising sun, I should feel in full agreement with him. Both Rudra and Agni, as presented to us in the Veda, are too far developed to

---

[1] M. M., Vedic Hymns, S. B. E., vol. xxxii, p. 95.

lend themselves to a comparison with so thoroughly Greek a deity as Phoibos Apollon. We must go behind the Vedic gods before we can hope to find the roots of the ideas which on Greek soil produced Apollon, on Indian soil Agni. The constant use of apa-var with reference to the daily revelation wrought by the rising sun, shows that behind Apollon and behind the various personalities of the rising sun, there lay the common idea of a revealing or morning deity, the germ also of the Devîr Dvâra*h*, or the Everlasting Gates of the psalmist. If from this central idea there sprang secondary thoughts connected with the name of Apollon in Greece, or with the name of Agni, Sûrya, or Rudra in Sanskrit, all coincidences, even the most minute and apparently unmeaning, will be welcome as showing that the mythological growth which began in Pre-Vedic times followed the same natural course in India and in Greece, presenting many similarities, but not preventing dissimilarities also between the gods of Greece and the gods of India. Apollon cannot be Rudra, nor Agni, as little as the Greek Archon is the Buddhist Arhan, or even Latin rex the Sk. râ*g*.

Rudra was originally a storm-god, whatever may be said to the contrary. If the Maruts were storm-gods, and even in modern Sanskrit marut means wind, we must not forget that the Maruts are called not only the sons of Rudra, but Rudras themselves.

When we read that Rudra is the most beautiful among the gods, that he holds bow and arrow, that he is the lord of songs (gâtha-pati), and that he is the best of physicians and able also to remove the evil that man has committed (VI, 74, 3), we seem to have a god before us who certainly reminds us of

Apollon, but when Rudra is called the fierce god with strong limbs, who attacks like a wild beast, when he is called the red boar, when in the Atharva-veda his belly is said to be blue, and his back red, we can no longer recognise in him the features of Apollon even in his most terrible moods. Still less would it be possible to identify Rudra and the Rudras with mere Fauns and Satyrs, with spirits of the forest and the hills[1], for Rudra is a majestic god, he shines like the bright sun (I, 43, 5), he is the lord of this wide world, and divine power will never depart from him (II, 33, 9).

Greek and Italian Gods.

If it is impossible, nay irrational, to attempt to identify Vedic and Greek gods after they have assumed a definite individuality in India or Greece, it is equally so with gods that have assumed a definite character in Greece and in Italy. What Comparative Mythology can do is to try to go behind such gods, and to discover, if possible, their common background far away from Italy and Greece; but we cannot, and we should not attempt to trace what is specifically Greek in Italian mythology.

I have always admired Roscher's essay on Apollon and Mars, published many years ago in 1873. It is full of profound learning and clear discernment, and has been followed up by other works worthy of that brilliant beginning. Nor do I deny even now that there are many things which these two gods share in common, but I cannot believe that they started from one and the same germ. Apollon was certainly, as Roscher has fully shown, a god of light, a Φοῖβος,

---

[1] Oldenberg, Rel. des Veda, p. 223.

ἀ Λύκειος, Λυκηγενής, Αἰγλήτης, Ἑῷος, and Ἔναυρος, he was likewise a god of the year, that is, a solar god, he was more particularly a god of spring and summer, he was a fighting-god, and, like most gods, a reputed ancestor of families, of clans, and of whole tribes, a patron of cities, a leader of colonies. All this springs naturally from his solar character. He was an apa-varyan, but he had not become individualised in any of the individual deities of the Veda, as we know it. If, therefore, we supposed with Roscher that for a certain time this as yet undefined Apavaryan was carried on in the same bed of mythological thought as an Italian god, who came to be called, or actually was called Mars, we should have to grant a long-continued unseparated existence of what is called, and, I believe, wrongly called, the Graeco-Italic branch of the Aryan family, and a development of a Graeco-Italic mythology different in its peculiar character from all other branches of Aryan mythology. And while this was going on, we should be called upon to believe that the name of one of these cognate Graeco-Italic deities became Apollon in Greece, but Mars in Italy, that the name changed, but that the substance remained the same. I do not deny that gods may be the same in substance, though different in name, but I doubt the possibility of the existence of any Aryan deities without a name. We saw a clear instance in the case of Varuna and Ahura Mazda, and Professor Roscher has mentioned several similar cases, such as the Erinyes, the Eumenides, Arae and Semnae; Plouton, Hades, Klymenos; Hebe and Ganymedes; Aphrodite, Kypris, and Kythereia; Persephone, Kore, and Phersephatta. But these cases are not all to the point. We must distinguish between cases where a divine individuality receives a number of names, and where one or the other of them becomes in time an independent name. If Aphrodite or Aphrogeneia was called Kythereia and Kypris, because she received special worship in these islands, and if afterwards she seemed under these names, whether they had been mere epithets or independent names, to become a new deity, we can clearly see that what may be called her substance remained the same, though her name was changed. But this is not what Prof. Roscher supposes to have been the case with Apollon and Mars. He does not hold, if I understand him right, that Apollon ever received the epithet of Mars, or Mars that of Apollon, but rather that the same as yet anonymous deity received the name of Apollon in Greece, and of Mars in Italy, that Mars and Apollon were in fact dialectic synonyms. Here we must before all things try to think the matter out clearly. We saw that every deity begins its existence with its name. I hold that even the sun and moon did not exist— for men as thinking beings—till they had been named; but at all events Hêlios and Selêne could have had no existence till they had been created by the ὀνοματοθέτης.

There never was a Hêlios or an Apollon except in the mind of him who gathered up certain sensuous impressions, comprehended or conceived them and named them from one of their prominent characteristics, and thus called a revealing god, an Apollon, into existence. After that, two things may happen. Apollon may receive a number of epithets, and some of them, such as Hekatos, far-reaching, or

Hekatêbolos, the Far-darter, or Dêlios, bright or born in Dêlos, may assume a kind of mythological independence ; or secondly the same impressions which called forth the name of Apollon may, without any reference to that name, call forth another name and another god so near to Apollon that the two could not be kept apart, and after a time became one. In this way Phoibos, the brilliant, was so clearly meant for the same concept as Apollon, that the two were joined as Phoibos Apollon, and Phoibos ceased to be a separate deity and was afterwards accepted as a mere epithet of Apollon, like Hekatos, though really produced by an independent process.

If then we ask what was the relation of the Graeco-Italic Apollon to the Graeco-Italic Mars, we cannot possibly accept one as the epithet of the other, but we can only hold that the same concept which received the name of Apollon received likewise the name of Mars. Can that be proved?

Apollon and Mars.

Professor Roscher seems not to have been aware that the identity of Apollon and Mars has been maintained by the Greeks themselves. Plutarch (Fragm. p. 15) argues that if two goddesses are represented as mothers of the same child there must have been a common element in both. Lêto, therefore, he thinks, cannot be different from Hêre, because Lêto is the mother of Artemis, and Artemis, when called Eileithyia, is the daughter of Hêre. He then goes on to argue that as Ares and Apollon have the same character ($\delta \acute{u} \nu a \mu \iota s$), the one being the son of Hêre, the other of Lêto, it follows once more that Lêto and Hêre must be taken as the same goddess.

But this would hardly satisfy Professor Roscher, for although the Romans were led to identify their Mars with the Greek Ares, he has rightly pointed out (p. 14) that this may have been done at a later time and under a mistaken view, and that these two gods had become different in character long before they met again at Rome. The question therefore is, whether the real Roman Mars shows evidence of a solar origin and of a former identity with Apollon, so that we should have to take the Greek Apollon and the Latin Mars as mere synonyms, meant from the beginning for the same object.

That Mars was one of the bright, light-bringing gods is shown by his having been worshipped as Leuc-etius, or Louc-etius, while Apollon's epithets were Λυκαῖος, Λύκειος, Λυκηγενής, &c.

But though this epithet would certainly prove that Mars belonged to the bright gods, the devas, it would only prove that he was one of the devas, a bright being, not that he was a solar god or identical with Apollon. Lucetius, as an epithet, belongs as much to Jupiter as to Mars, if not more. Festus said, 'Lucetium Jovem appellabant quod eum lucis esse causam credebant,' and according to Macrobius it was this very Jupiter Lucetius whom the Salii celebrated in their song, and not Mars[1]. The wife of this Jupiter Lucetius was called Lucetia and Lucina, while the wife of Mars was Neria.

But though we have to surrender the strongest argument for the identity of Mars and Apollon,

---

[1] Hartung, Die Religion der Römer, ii, 9.

namely his name of Lucetius, we may retain nevertheless the fact that Mars belonged to the Devas, and that he was supposed to bring light and, as we shall see, the warmth of spring also. His was therefore the month Martius, or March, the beginning of spring in Italy. He was in fact a thoroughly Italian deity, and in all his features a god of Italian peasants. To begin with his name, I still hold, for reasons explained in my Introduction to the Vedic Hymns, vol. xxxii, p. xxiv, that Mars, Martis, corresponds to Marut, the storm-wind, and meant originally the smasher or pounder, like Pilumnus with his pilum, and Picumnus, connected with the Picus Martius (the woodpecker). The old derivation of Marut from mar, to be brilliant, labours under great disadvantages. If such a root is Aryan at all, it certainly has left no offspring in Sanskrit, not even mariki. The derivation from mar also in the sense of dying is untenable in Sanskrit, because there is no allusion in the hymns addressed to the Maruts to their representing the spirits of the departed, and hardly any as to their conducting these spirits to their last resting-place. We seldom find so striking a coincidence as between the Vedic sardha mâruta, the troop of the Maruts, and the Umbrian çerfo Martio, which really ought to have settled the question of the connection between Mars and Marut. That the wind or the hurricane should be raised to the rank of a supreme god is very natural among peasants and shepherds, and the same process can be watched not only in the case of Hurakan [1], but likewise in that of Wuotan [2]. That the winds possess all the

---

[1] M. M., Natural Religion, p. 453.
[2] L. c. p. 324. Physical Religion, pp. 314, 324.

qualities which appear in the warlike character of Mars, that the Maruts are in fact represented in the Veda as fighting-men in full armour, can easily be seen in the volume[1] which gives a translation of all the hymns addressed to the Maruts which we possess. But that Mars as the representative of the winds should have been regarded as beneficent to fields and meadows and forests is more difficult to explain. Our idea of March winds is taken only from what is painful in them. But in southern climates the March winds mark the return of the sun and of sunny weather. The winds themselves are felt to be necessary for sweeping the fields, for driving away whatever remains of fallen leaves or snow or dust, for drying the damp soil and purifying the air, for cleaning in fact the stable of Augeias. Hence Deverra, the sweeper, was a fit companion of Pilumnus, while Picus or Picumnus was credited with the introduction of manuring, both being friends and companions, sometimes the very deputies of Mars.

The son of Picus and father of Latinus and the tutelary deity of agriculture was Faunus. Faunus and the Fauni were afterwards identified with the Greek Pàn and Pânes. Their name is generally derived from favere, to protect, but as there is a class of beings called Dhuni in the Veda, which means shakers or shouters, Fau-nus is more likely a derivative of dhu or dhev, from which θύελλα as well as fumus, than of the unmeaning favere, to be propitious. The form Mavors by the side of Mars is difficult to explain. Maurs occurs in inscriptions, and is taken by Mommsen as representing Mars, the

---

[1] S. B. E., vol. xxxii.

murderer. Ritschl takes it as representing Mavors; but what is Mavors? Unless it could be taken as a mere elongation of Maurs (like Favonius of Faunus), I see no possibility of explaining it. Corssen explains it as a contraction of mag-vors, and takes mag as a possible Latin form of μάχη. This would give the meaning of battle-turner, like τροπαῖος in Greek. A similar idea must have been entertained by Latin writers, who take Mavors to be qui magna vertit. But all this is extremely doubtful, if not impossible, on phonetic grounds.

Mamurius.

Another perplexing name is Mamurius, which is evidently derived from the same root mar, but in the sense of dying, and has, I believe, nothing whatever to do with Mars. The idea that this Mamurius is Mars has created great confusion. Mamurius has, I believe, no more to do with Mars than that in the month of Mars when the new year begins the old dying year Veturius Mamurius dies and has to be buried.

The birth of the new year and the death of the old were still celebrated in Germany when I was a boy. They probably continue to be celebrated in outlying villages even now, though those who celebrate them are hardly aware whether these festivities are of Christian or pre-Christian origin. But while such customs are rapidly dying out in the towns of Germany before the approach of elementary schools, railways, and telegraphs, they seem to continue to form the chief staple of public festivities among many of the Slavonic tribes in the east of Europe. To them the birth of the vernal sun, his fight against the army of winter, his final victory, his summer sway, his autumnal decline, and at last his death, are the great events of the year; and even when these popular rejoicings and mournings have been changed into Christian festivals, the old heathen features can often be recognised behind their new ecclesiastical veil [1].

To us the expression that 'the year has died' is common enough, but when using that phrase we hardly think of more than that the year is gone. Our year dies with the civil year on the last day of December, Sylvester-day, and the burying of St. Sylvester [2] on that day, together with many other not quite Christian customs, prove that this period was once observed as a pagan festival. In many places it is neither Christmas, nor the Sylvester-night, but the Epiphany which is considered as the real beginning of the Christian new year. But with the ancient people the fight of the sun against the old year, or against the might of winter continued till the first signs of spring, of new light and new warmth appeared. The ancient Romans began their year with the month of March, the Slaves with the return of spring. At that time, about the vernal equinox, it is still the custom in many parts of Europe to 'carry out the year,' that is, to bury it. To carry out was meant originally for carrying the dead body out of the village to burn or bury it, the Latin efferre, or condere [3]. In the Voigtland (in Saxony) the children were seen some thirty years ago, and possibly may still be

---

[1] See Hanusch, Wissenschaft der Slavischen Mythen, p. 140; Grimm, Deutsche Mythologie, p. 730; Usener, Italische Mythen, p. 189.

[2] Usener, l. c., pp. 195–196.   [3] See Usener, l. c.

seen on the Sunday of Laetare (March), marching through the streets and singing—

> 'Wir alle, wir alle kommen 'raus,
> Und tragen heut den Tod 'naus.
> Komm, Frühling, wieder mit uns in das Dorf,
> Willkommen, lieber Frühling.'
> 'We all, we all are coming forth,
> And carry out Death to-day.
> Come, Spring, with us again into the village,
> Welcome, dear Spring.'

Here Death is clearly meant for Winter, the death of nature, and opposed to Spring, as the new year and the new life.

These customs and traditions change according as Winter or the dying year is conceived as an old man or as an old woman. Their time also varies slightly according as the seasons vary, and as the real periods of the vernal and autumnal equinox are modified by civil or ecclesiastical holidays. Besides the days already mentioned, the Sunday of Laetare (Mid-Lent), Good Friday, the day of St. Gregory, the day of St. Rupertus (27 March), or the Monday after the vernal equinox, the first of April, even the first of May, have all been chosen in different parts of Europe for 'carrying out Death or Winter.' But the four great events in the annual career of the sun remained everywhere the four great events in the life of a family or of a village, and produced sayings, riddles, and legends which still pervade, though hardly understood, the phraseology of our modern life.

I shall give a few extracts from the collections made by Hanusch, Grimm, and Usener (Italische Mythen), and though the repetition of the same stories may seem tedious, it is after all only by an accumulation of evidence that the incredulity of those who doubt the existence of solar customs and solar myths and of all that is connected with solar worship, can be effectually removed.

The Slaves, wherever we meet them in their village life, tell of an old woman who about the time of the vernal equinox (sometimes on the Sunday of Laetare, sometimes on Palm-Sunday) is carried out and either burnt, or buried, or drowned, or cut, or sawed to pieces. In Moravia she is called Mařena, in Poland and Silesia Marzana, in Bohemia Smrt, among the Wends Smerć, elsewhere Muriena or Mamurienda (cf. Mamurius).

All these words seem to have meant originally Death and Winter, while the new year which is sometimes brought into the village when the old year has been carried out, is in Bohemian songs called Nové leto[1], the new summer.

The Masures, another Slavonic tribe, relate that on the 12th of March, the day of St. Gregory, Zima (the winter) goes to sea. Generally the Winter or the Old Year is represented by a figure made of straw, and is rendered hideous by a white mask and other paraphernalia. Sometimes it is not considered enough either to burn or to drown that figure, but it is beaten, dragged about, nailed against a tree, and finally burnt, while the ashes are scattered over the fields or thrown into the water. Among both northern and southern Slaves[2]

[1] 'The Slavonic leto corresponds to our Lent; in Bohemia it is used for year; while jaro, the German year, means in Bohemian spring.' Usener, l. c., p. 194.

[2] Usener, p. 191.

this Maŕena is sawed in two, and the children are made to believe that an old woman has actually been taken out of the village and killed with a saw. Exactly the same custom and the same belief, what the Slaves call bábu řezati, 'to saw the old woman,' must have existed among the Romanic nations also, for segare la vecchia, 'to saw the old woman,' is the name given to a popular [1] amusement at Barcelona, where on the same Sunday of Laetare boys may be seen running through the streets, carrying saws, and asking for the oldest woman that they may carry her out of the town and saw her in pieces.

In Italy, again, at the same time, a hideous doll is taken through the streets, and under fearful shoutings sawed in two. In Venice this custom is called siegàr la vechia, near Roveredo and Triest segar la veccia, in Tuscany segare la monaca [2]. These are striking and startling coincidences, more so than the mere burning or drowning of the figure would have been. In Parma a doll that is burnt on Mid-Lent is called la veccia da brusar, while in Tuscany the usual expression is fare il giorgio [3].

While these popular amusements embody the recollection of the death of the old year about the time of the vernal solstice, similar customs

---

[1] Grimm, Deutsche Mythologie, p. 742.

[2] P. Fanfani, Vocabolario dell' uso toscano, p. 805, s. v. scampanata ; Boerio, Dizionario del dialetto venoziano, p. 660 ; Giamb. Azzolini, Vocabolario vernacolo-italiano, p. 408 ; G. Patriarchi, Vocabolario veneziano e padovano, p. 179; A. Robiola, Dizion. univers. della lingua ital. (1835), 4, 429; quoted by Usener, l. c., p. 192.

[3] Usener explains this expression as borrowed from St. George (April 23), who killed the dragon and delivered the maid, possibly (horribile dictu) again a solar myth or custom.

have gathered round the Feast of the Epiphany, the first manifestation of Christ to the Gentiles. The doll which is carried about and destroyed at that time is called the Befana or Befania, which is accepted as a corruption of Epiphania. This certainly sounds strange, because it seems that the Epiphany itself would more naturally have been identified with customs celebrating the return of light, and of the new year, whether natural or civil, and not with the expulsion of the old year. This requires some explanation. But the two events hang together, and the fact remains that on the day of the Epiphany or on the day before it, the same custom with outbursts of popular hilarity can be witnessed in Italy and in Switzerland, a figure representing some detested or dangerous character being carried about under hideous noises, and finally disposed of. Different from this is the carrying off or burying of the Carnival, which seems to have little to do with any prominent epoch of the natural year, and to signify no more than a bidding farewell to the amusements of the season[1]. If the burying of the Carnival is called in some places bruciare la vecchia,—and this is doubtful,—it could only be so because the original meaning of bruciare la vecchia was completely forgotten.

These extracts may suffice to show how many of our still existing popular customs and festivals owe their origin to the observation of the influence of the sun on nature and on man, and how many stories and legends that are now told of La Vecchia, of Muriena, or Befana of Mamurienda or Mamurius.

---

[1] See, however, Usener, l. c., pp. 199, 202.

had at first a purely solar meaning. In ancient times both customs and legends were naturally far more transparent and intelligible than they are at present.

That the lustrum at Rome represented a quinquennial solar cycle, has never been doubted, but that lustrum facere meant originally a burying of the cycle, as the burying of La Vecchia meant the burying of the old year, is an ingenious guess of Usener, which deserves serious consideration [1].

Each year was inaugurated at Rome by the festival of Anna Perenna on the Ides of March. People drank as many draughts of wine as they wished to live years, and the result may not have been very different from what happens in modern Rome on the Sunday of Laetare.

Anna, the year, wrongfully identified with Anna, the sister of Dido, was supposed to have been drowned in the river Numicius, and this seems to have been all that remained of the drowning of the old year [2].

Besides this festival of Anna Perenna at the time of the vernal equinox, there was another, shortly before the time of the summer solstice, dedicated to Anna, and another legend was told of her as an old woman, who had once during a famine fed the plebs with cakes. This may refer to Anna as the goddess of the year, in the sense of harvest, for we have an ancient sacrificial formula, preserved by Varro [3], 'Te

---

[1] Usener, l. c., pp. 204, 206. Liv. i, 44, 'ibi instructum exercitum omnem suovetaurilibus lustravit, idque conditum lustrum appellatum, quia in censendo finis factus est.'

[2] Corssen, in K. Z., ii, 34; Usener, l. c., p. 208.

[3] Varro, Fragm. ed. Buecheler, p. 219; Usener, l. c., p. 209.

Anna ac Peranna¹, Panda Cela, te Pales,' in which she is invoked together with goddesses of a similar character.

Even in the legend told of Anna, the old woman, who, when asked by Mars to procure him the love of Minerva (originally of Neria), disguised herself as a young woman, the spring, and then laughed at Mars, we can still recognise the old year and the young year, and survivals of customs once very prevalent among the Aryan nations². Besides this female representative of the year, Anna and Peranna, we find in ancient Rome a masculine representative also of the old year. We saw that in Germany, where the names for winter and death are masculine, the old year was often represented as an old man, not, as among the Slavonic tribes, as an old woman. The figure to be beaten or burned at the end of the year is called the Straw-man, the Death-man, or the Old Jew. In the same way the Romans celebrated their Mamuralia about the time of the vernal equinox, part of their rejoicings consisting in carrying about a man, clothed in skins, and beating him unmercifully till he was driven out of the town. This man was Mamurius, and was supposed to have made the new ancilia, when the old shields, which were believed to have originally fallen down from the sky, had been lost during the reign of Numa.

Usener identifies this festival of Mamurius with the Feriae Martis. Certain it is that the Salii, who carried the twelve shields (ancilia) in procession,

---

¹ Peranna is the oldest authentic form instead of Perenna, and perannare is used in the sense of living one year. Perennis was originally perennis, like sollemnis.

² See Usener, l. c., p. 224.

invoked Mamurius Veturius at the end of their carmen saliare, according to some traditions, as a reward for the service rendered by the clever old smith Mamurius in making eleven new ancilia after the pattern of the only old ancile which remained; but far more likely as the representative of the old or dying year. But although Mars was the god of the Salii, there seems no excuse whatever for identifying Mamurius with Mars. Marmar and Mamers can be understood as names of Mars, derived from the same root as Marut, though independent in their formation, but Mamurius was from the first meant for something not only different from Mars, but in one sense the very opposite of him, the dying year as opposed to the new year introduced by Mars. If Mamurius represented the old year, its death would take place about the same time when the new vernal god, Mars, asserted his universal sway. I venture to go even further and to suggest that the eleven ancilia which were lost and were replaced by the smith Mamurius Veturius, a kind of R*i*bhu, and which were carried about by the twelve [1] Salii, were intended originally for the eleven months of the old year which were lost, but forged again after the pattern of the last month by the old smith or the old year. No doubt, all this was forgotten at Rome, yet some recollections seem to have survived. For what can Varro have meant when he wrote (L. L. 6, 45, p. 226), 'Itaque Salii quod cantant Mamuri Veturi, significant veterem memoriam'? What can be the meaning of a passage in the Liber glossarum (cod. Vat. Palat. lat. 1773, f. 40 r),

---

[1] Usener, l. c., p. 226.

'Ancilia, scuta anni unius'[1]? Professor Usener, though like Corssen he identifies Mamurius[2] with Mars, is evidently of opinion that these names and the legends connected with them refer to the old and the new year. He also accepts the ancile which fell from the sky on the first of March, the natalis Martis, as the first month of the new year. If then we have recognised in Veturius Mamurius the dying year and in Mars the god of the month of March, as the beginning of the new year, we can well understand why Mars, as Prof. Roscher has so well shown, should, like Apollon, though for different reasons, have been looked upon as the god of the year, the seasons, and the months. With Apollon this was due to his solar nature, with Mars to his representing the season of the March winds (the Marutas), the return of spring, and the beginning of the new year. Hence we naturally find several points of coincidence between Apollon returning from his winter ἀποδημία, and Mars driving out the old and bringing in the new year. But the reasons are different. Mars is never supposed to have been absent among Hyperboreans, or in Aithiopia, or in hiberna Lycia; his existence begins every year in March, and nothing is said about his whereabouts in winter. It may be admitted that Apollon and Mars had the same birthday, but their very birth had a different meaning. Apollon was born once, and the spring, though it may be called his birth, was really looked upon as his return only from a distant land. In the case of Mars, we hear of no birth in Dêlos or anywhere,

---

[1] Corssen, in K. Z., ii, 55; Usener, l. c., p. 213.

[2] Formed like Mercurius, a purely Latin name derived from merc, in merx, mercis, but see p. 725.

and it is extremely doubtful whether his so-called birthday in March was ever looked upon as his return from a far country.

There is hardly anything told of Apollon that cannot be explained by his solar character, by his opening the heavenly gates, while in the case of Mars, though there are some solar traces, they are restricted to his representing the spring and all that at Rome was connected with the spring, the festivities of the Salii, warlike expeditions and emigrations, such as the ver sacrum, &c. As the father of Romulus and the patron of the people of Rome, Mars could hardly avoid becoming a warlike deity, a Mars Gradivus rather than a Mars Silvanus, and the later identification of Mars with the Greek Ares may have helped to accentuate his warlike feature more strongly, and to give him as his companions Pallor and Pavor, like Δεῖμος and Φόβος in Greek. That the Greek Ares was ever genetically connected with Mars seems to me far more doubtful now than formerly, though Prof. Decharme has certainly brought out a number of striking coincidences between Ares and the Maruts which had escaped me when writing my Lectures on the Science of Language. Ares, however, was a Thracian rather than a Greek god, and the loss of an initial m in his name, though possible, would be very exceptional. We must leave the successful analysis of Ares to future researches. Neither his being chained during thirteen months by the Aloadai, nor his being chained by Hêphaistos, allows us to see any clear physical background behind the veil of mythology. After all, the Greeks were at no time restrained from indulging in poetical fancies about their gods, and a song of Demodokos, however risqué, was sure to find an appreciative audience.

If Mars was originally a god of the storm, and had his name in common with the Maruts, the name of Mercurius, if like Hermes, originally a wind-god, might be a variety of Merturius, by a change analogous to that of Marcus, Marcellus, and Martellus.

There were local stories at Athens about Ares as a more peaceful deity, but these too have hitherto resisted successful interpretation.

Athêne.

No goddess has caused so much controversy as Athêne. She is so well known from the Homeric poems, and she has gained so many friends and admirers, that any attempt to trace her glorious features back to a more humble origin has been resisted as if it were an outrage, or even a sacrilege. But are we to make an exception in favour of the beloved daughter of Zeus, if Zeus himself and Apollon and Hermes have been made to disclose their physical antecedents? Even if she springs full armed from the head of Zeus, is not that 'head of Zeus' the Vedic mûrdhâ divah, the forehead or the head of the sky, that is, the East? The sun also is said in the Veda to have been born from the head (sîrshatâh gâtám, X, 88, 16). And what goddess springs from the East, if not the Dawn, the Koryphasia of Messene, the Akria of Argos, the Agryâ of the Veda, and the Capita of Rome?

It is quite true that Homer does not relate her more miraculous birth from the head of Zeus, when laid open by the axe of Hêphaistos, or of Promêtheus, or of Hermes. But that does not prove that he or his contemporaries did not know of it, that it was in fact a post-Homeric creation. At all events he knows of no mother of Athêne, and he says in Il. v, 875, σὺ γὰρ τέκες ἄφρονα κούρην, 'for thou hast begotten the demented maid,' and again, Il. v, 880, αὐτὸς ἐγείναο παῖδ' ἀΐδηλον, as if wishing to throw the whole responsibility for Athêne on the shoulders of Zeus. She is called ὀβριμοπάτρη, the daughter of a mighty father, and she is throughout the daughter of Zeus, just as Ushas, the Dawn, is the duhitâ Divah. If there was no other evidence, this would suffice in the eyes of any comparative mythologist to show that the prototype of Athêne, however distant from the horizon of Homer, was the Dawn, born from the forehead of the sky.

Name of Athêne.

But let us see once more what is the origin of her name? It is mere accident that there should only be one passage in the Rig-veda where the name of the Dawn that corresponds to Athêne has been preserved. That name is Ahanâ, and in the only passage in which it occurs it means dawn. I have tried to show in the chapter on phonetics that the equation of Ahanâ = Athêne is phonetically irreproachable, and I hope that I need not return again to this point. We possess fragments only of Vedic poetry as it was four thousand years ago, fragments only of Greek mythology as it was during the Homeric period. We must not demand more than we have any right to demand, and be grateful for the unexpected emergence of Ahanâ from the deluge that has buried so many words and so many thoughts of those who lived before Agamemnon and before Vasish*tha*. If anybody expected to find Athêne, the goddess of wisdom, the protectress of every Greek art, and of all the ἔργα ’Αθηναίης, among the half-fledged goddesses of the Veda, he will be disappointed.

Athêne having long been the protectress of Athens, naturally reflected the character of the Athenians, and not of Vedic *R*ishis. She became Βουλαία, presiding over the Senate, ’Αγοραία, watching over the popular assemblies, ’Εργάνη and μηχανῖτις, the work-woman; but after the victories of the Athenians, and after the erection of her statue by Phidias, seen from afar by travellers and sailors, every Athenian thought of her chiefly as the fighting-goddess, as πολιοῦχος, protectress of the town, as νικηφόρος, victorious, as Νίκη ἄπτερος, Victory without wings, that is, never flying away from Athens.

Whether all this could have grown out of a goddess of lightning, as Decharme seems inclined to suppose, is a difficult question. Lightning, no doubt, is a light-bringer, but it seems far too momentary a phenomenon to serve as the support of an immortal goddess. It is different with the Dawn who returns regularly every morning, who is represented not only as lighting up the whole of nature, but as waking men to a new life, as imparting to all beings the blessing of new intelligence. To be awake and to be intelligent are often expressed by the same word, and hence the rays of the morning have been compared to the bright thoughts of the mind. Why should not the same metaphor have occurred to the ancient Âryas who saw so much more in nature than we are able to discover. Even the stories of Athêne's relations with Hêlios, Hêphaistos, and Hêrakles, conflicting as they are with her later character of the παρθένος or the virgin, would hardly have survived if, during her purely physical stage, she had not been in close contact with these solar gods and heroes. Such incongruities are sometimes very instructive. As they run counter to the later and established character of certain gods, they may be supposed to be of an early date, and to allow us an insight into what these gods were or were considered to be before they had taken their place in the well-organised pantheon of Homer or Hesiod.

Aphrodite = Charis.

If the change of the Dawn into a goddess such as Athêne requires careful proof, the metamorphosis of the same natural apparition into the goddess of beauty and love, under her numerous names, has been accepted without much demur. The old question has of course been asked, How is it possible? How can that charming being whom the Greeks worshipped as Aphroditê have been the red blush of the morning? And how can the same apparition be called the horse (asvâ or harit), the dog (saramâ), the cow (go), the bird (patanga), &c.?

All we can answer is that we have to deal with facts that may be ignored, but cannot be annihilated, and that all that the historian of the human mind can do is to accept facts and to try to understand them. When the Vedic poet says (I, 163, 2), 'Ye Vasus, you have made a horse out of the sun,' language could hardly be clearer. That the Dawn was spoken of as a cow was clearly shown before from passages of the Veda and from verses of Estonian peasants. That the red horses, the Haritas, were meant for the Dawns as companions of the sun, is no longer called in question, and that Saramâ, who finds the entrance of the black stable of the night, is represented as a swift dog belonging to Indra, any one who can read the text or a translation of the hymns of the Rig-veda, may see for himself. One verse will suffice to describe what the Vedic poets saw or imagined they saw every morning. 'B*r*ihaspati drove out the cows, he split the cave by his word, he hid darkness, and made the sun to be seen.' (Rv. II, 24, 3.) Are these cows to be called Kuhfetische? (Oldenb., Rel. des Veda, p. 207.) Or in less metaphorical language, Rv. I, 157, 1: 'Agni awoke, the sun rises from the earth, the bright, mighty Dawn opens with her splendour, the Asvins have yoked their chariot for their course, Savit*ri* (sun) has brought forth every living thing.'

And what should we gain by calling the Dawn a Kuhfetisch? In the Veda, the Dawn has already become a woman, a beautiful woman, arrayed in beautiful garments, dancing and displaying her charms. She appears in golden splendour, drawn by red horses, and followed by the Sun, as by a lover. I ventured many years ago to explain the name of Charis (Aphrodite) as the Greek equivalent of Harit, plur. Haritas, and I have shown again and again that phonetically no objection can be raised. But how, it has been asked again and again, could Harit, the name of the red horses of the sun, have become the name of Aphrodite? It did not become, no Sanskrit word ever becomes a Greek word. But both Charis and Harit were derived by the same suffix from the same root Har, to shine.

The seven horses or far-shining rays of the sun were called harit, the splendour of the dawn was likewise called harit. Splendour and brilliancy came to mean beauty and grace, χάρις, and to be bright (χαίρειν) came to mean to be glad, to rejoice. Where is there any difficulty? Even in the Veda the seven red horses are sometimes, when the work assigned to them is more appropriate for women, replaced by the seven sisters, 'the seven maidens, who nursed the white one, when born, the red one when growing [1].' But immediately afterwards the poet continues, 'the mares came near as to a foal when born, the gods admired Agni at his birth.' Sometimes these seven sisters are called gâmi, relations, as when we read in IX, 37, 4, that Soma has brightened up the sun together with the sisters.

We must not judge Vedic poets by our own standards of taste, and we must remember that when they called the quickly-spreading splendours of the Dawn, red horses, beautiful maidens, or bright cows, these were metaphors that came natural to peasants, however strange they may sound to modern poets, and as their Dawn had not as yet assumed the sharp and settled outline of a woman like Aphrodite, they did not jar on Vedic as they would have jarred on Greek ears. Homer calls Aphrodite the Charis [2], and as such the wife of Hephaistos. This

---

[1] See also Rv. X, 5, 5 ; 8, 3 (svásri*h* árushí*h*).

[2] The close connection of Aphrodite and the Charites is vouchsafed by inscriptions found near the Theseion, where an altar was dedicated Ἀφροδίτῃ ἡγεμόνῃ τοῦ δήμου καὶ Χάρισιν. See Gruppe, Jahresbericht, p. 70.

marriage is supposed to express the union of the crude handicraft of the smith Hêphaistos with the charms of the goddess of beauty and art. It may be so, but if this allegory should seem too modern for Homer, the marriage of Hêphaistos and Charis might possibly be traced back to the union in nature of the fire of the morning Sun emerging from the dark smithy of the night, with the splendour and charm of the Dawn. But we must not attempt to explain too much. It is enough for us to know that Charis was Harit (morning-splendour) just as she was Argynnis, the Sk. argunî, the bright, a name of the Dawn in the Veda, and just as arguna is the epithet given to the child (vatsa) born of the dark night (Ath. XIII, 3, 26). Why this Dawn-Charis should have been called Enalia and Pontia becomes clear when we remember the beauty of the sunrise on the coasts and the islands of Greece, though originally it is quite possible that the sea from which she rises may have been intended for the clouds that looked like a sea in the sky from which both Sun and Dawn were daily seen to rise. The Dawn is often called Apyâ yoshâ, the Water-woman, and 'the daughter of Dyaus,' duhitâ Diva*h*, all floating mythological molecules which assumed shape and beauty in the hands of the Greeks till the finished goddess stands before us as Aphrogeneia, the cloud-born (abhra is cloud in Sanskrit), Aphrodite[1], the foam-born, Anadyomene, rising from the sea, and Ourania, the heavenly, the daughter, as she was

---

[1] Though δίτη has not yet been explained, it must have corresponded in meaning to duhitâ or -γενεια. Professor Victor Henry explains Aphrodite as abhra-ditâ, celle qui vole dans le nuage, l. c., p. 7, and Rv. I, 180, 1.

called at Elis, of Ouranos and Hêmera, of sky and morning.

That at the time when the Greeks came in contact with Semitic nations, they should have recognised their Aphrodite in the foreign goddesses of love and beauty, whether Mylitta or Astarte, is intelligible, but it would not be intelligible were we to suppose that it was only by the help of these hideous idols that the Greeks formed the first conception of their Charis, or their Aphrodîte [1].

Artemis.

The last of the great Greek goddesses whom we have to consider is Artemis. Her name, we shall see, has received many interpretations, but none that can be considered as well established, none that, even if it were so, would help us much in disentangling the many myths told about her. Easy to understand as her character seems when we confine our attention to Homer, it becomes extremely complicated when we take into account the numerous local forms of worship of which she was the object.

We have here a good opportunity of comparing the interpretations put forward by those who think that a study of the myths and customs of uncivilised tribes can help us towards an understanding of Greek deities, and the views advocated by classical scholars who draw their information, first of all, from Greek sources, and afterwards only from a comparison of the myths and customs of cognate races, more particularly from what is preserved to us in ancient Vedic literature, before they plunge into the

---

[1] The common background of Athéne and Aphrodite has been pointed out, as I see, by Schwartz, but he does not mention the title of the book where his evidence has been given.

whirlpool of ill-defined and unintelligible Kafir folklore. The former undertake to explain Artemis by showing us the progress of human intelligence from the coarsest spontaneous and primitive ideas to the most beautiful and brilliant conception of poets and sculptors. They point out traces of hideous cruelties amounting almost to cannibalism, and of a savage cult of beasts in the earlier history of the goddess, who was celebrated by dances of young girls disguised as bears or imitating the movements of bears, &c. She was represented as πολύμαστος, and this idea, we are told, was borrowed from the East, which is a large term. We are told that her most ancient history is to be studied in Arkadia, where we can see the goddess still closely connected with the worship of animals, a characteristic feature of the lowest stage of religious worship among the lowest races of mankind. We are then told the old story of Lykâon, the king of Arkadia, who had a beautiful daughter called Kallisto. As Zeus fell in love with her, Hêre from jealousy changed her into a bear, and Artemis killed her with one of her arrows. Her child, however, was saved by Hermes, at the command of Zeus, and while Kallisto was changed to the constellation of the Ursa, her son Arkas became the ancestor of the Arkadians. Here, we are told, we have a clear instance of men being the descendants of animals, and of women being changed into wild beasts and stars, beliefs well known among the Cahrocs and the Kamilarois.

Otfried Müller in 1825 treated the same myth without availing himself of the light now to be derived from the Cahrocs and the Kamilarois. He quoted Pausanias as stating that the tumulus of

Kallisto was near the sanctuary of Artemis Kallistê, and he simply took Kallisto for an epithet of Artemis which, as in many other cases, had been taken for a separate personality. He also pointed out that at Brauron in Attika Artemis was worshipped by young maidens called ἄρκτοι, but he concluded no more from this than that the bear was an animal sacred to Artemis. He did not go so far as some modern mythologists who want us to believe that originally the animal, the she-bear, was the goddess, and that a later worship had replaced the ancient worship of the animal pur et simple. We are told now, though without any reference to Pausanias or any other Greek writers, that the young maidens, the ἄρκτοι, when dancing round Artemis, were clad in ancient times in bear-skins, and that this is a pretty common custom in the dances of totemic races. In support of this, however, we are not referred to really totemic races who

> —painted on the grave-posts,
> On the graves yet unforgotten,
> Each his own ancestral totem,
> Each the symbol of his household,
> Figures of the bear, the reindeer,
> Of the turtle, crane, and beaver,

but to the Hirpi of Italy, and to the Διὸς κώδων in Egypt. The fact that the goddess was originally a she-bear is, we are told, probably the most archaic element in the whole character of Artemis. Fortunately, however, this phase in her mystic and religious evolution is almost inperceptible, and such questions as how the complex nature of Artemis arose, how it was developed, at what exact time it freed itself from savage beliefs, and by what process the image of the Greek goddess formed itself from such elements, will probably never be answered, though we are referred to analogies in the particular relation between the gods of Samoa and the different totems (pace Dr. Codrington) in which they are supposed to manifest themselves.

Let us now see what classical scholars deprived of the light to be derived from totems and fetishes have made of the legends of Artemis[1]. That her worship contains traces of savage rites, possibly of human sacrifices, has long been known, and that both the Greeks and the neighbours of the Greeks in the North and in the West had not always been like the Greeks of Phidias and Perikles has never been doubted. What is most interesting in the worship of Artemis is that we can still discover the substitution of animal for human victims, nay of the mere drawing of blood by flagellation or some other process for real immolation. The Greeks themselves were perfectly aware of these their real savage antecedents, nay they seem to have been much less troubled by them than we should have expected.

But let us now take the classical view of Artemis, and let us try to recover what was her conception in the mind of Homer. There she is the sister of Apollon, the daughter of Zeus and Lêto. In Homer's poems she is chiefly the goddess of the chase, but to Aeschylos (fragm. 169) she was already the same as Selêne, the goddess of the moon. If Apollon, the son of Lêto, was of solar origin, what could his sister Artemis have been from the very beginning, if not

---

[1] See particularly Gerhard, Griech. Myth., pp. 336-367.

some goddess connected with the moon? She is called χρυσηλάκατος, with golden arrows, κελαδεινή, boisterous, ἐλαφηβόλος, deer-shooting, ἰοχέαιρα, pouring forth arrows; she is known as the sister of Apollon, the daughter of Zeus and Lêto (τέκνα Διὸς καὶ Λητοῦς ἠϋκόμοιο). She is conceived as a beautiful maiden, graceful in stature, a virgin in mind and body, a majestic huntress. Homer does not yet know of her as assisting women in childbirth, and this peculiar office of Artemis instead of Eileithyia, is easily accounted for whether we trace it back to her arrows which can bring death but healing also, or to her lunar character, the moon being everywhere considered as determining the birth of children.

As little, however, as Apollon was the sun, can we say that Artemis was the moon, though, as certainly as the chief characteristics of Apollon were borrowed from the sun, were those of Artemis borrowed from the moon. In that sense, but in that sense alone, may we say that Apollon was a solar, and Artemis a lunar deity, different the one from Hêlios, the other from Selêne, as much as a portrait is different from a mere photograph.

The first thing we must try to explain is, how a lunar goddess could have become what Artemis was in Homer's eyes, a huntress, the patroness of the chase, the guardian of the forests and of the beasts of the forest.

Here we must remember that the chase in olden times was not, as it is with us, the wholesale slaughtering of game by daylight. The chief art of the sportsman was to find the wild beasts, to trace them to their lairs, and then to surprise them there. And this was done in the morning twilight, nay even during the night, not at midday. Hence Artemis was not only Diktynna, so called from setting nets, but also Dâdouchos, carrying torches which served to find and to frighten the game. All this had to be done under the eye of the moon, and what was more natural therefore than that the lunar goddess should have been conceived as participating in the chase as the protectress and goddess of the chase? Hence even Homer knew that it was Artemis who had taught Skamandrios to hunt, and that it was she who in the past had sent the boar to Kalydon to avenge the neglect of her sacrifices.

When we have once got so far and recognised in Artemis the huntress and the lunar goddess, the rest of her story, at least what was of purely Hellenic growth in it, will soon become intelligible even without calling in the aid of Cahrocs and Kamilarois, or trusting to the relation in which the gods of Samoa stand to the different totems in which they are supposed to manifest themselves.

We have to deal with Arkadia, a country of wooded hills, the most excellent country for sport. We have only to admit what has never been doubted that Artemis, such as we know her, received special worship from the Arkadians. Almost every Greek race, as we saw, tried to trace its origin back to Zeus. If then the Arkas, the ancestor of Arkades, had been recognised as one of the many sons of Zeus, who could well be his mother, if not the favourite goddess of the country, that is Artemis, under one of her many names? One of her names was Kallistê, the most beautiful. But how could the virgin goddess herself be the mother of

Arkas? This being impossible, her worshippers had no great trouble in finding a way out of their difficulty, by slightly changing the name of Kallistê into Kallistô, and representing her, not as the goddess herself, but as one of her attendant companions. However, even thus Kallisto had incurred not only the jealousy of Hêre, but likewise the anger of Artemis, and as the name of Arkas reminded the Arkadians of arktos or arkos, bear, and as there was a famous arktos, the Ursa Major, as a constellation in the sky, what was more natural, I ask again, than that Kallistô should be changed into an arktos, a she-bear, slain by Artemis, and then placed by Zeus, her lover, in the sky as the bright star shining in the winter nights? The change into a she-bear was suggested probably by the custom, called ἀρκτεύειν, which meant the dedicating of the young Arkadian girls to the service of Artemis and their performing the service of the goddess in their well-known ursine disguise. See Harpocr. s. v., ἀρκτεῦσαι ... τὸ καθιερωθῆναι πρὸ γάμων τὰς παρθένους τῇ Ἀρτέμιδι τῇ Μουνυχίᾳ ἢ τῇ Βραυρωνίᾳ.

Whether the name of Arkas, Arkades was connected with the name of arktos, ursus, bear, so that Arkadia meant originally the Bear-country, is a question which cannot be answered positively. It is possible, for the t is dropped in ἄρκιλος, a young bear, and ἄρκος also occurs for ἄρκτος, while in Sk. we have ríksha, in Lat. ursus. In that case the dances of the maidens, called ἄρκτοι, would receive an easy interpretation. They were Arkades, and why not ἄρκτοι, and if ἄρκτοι, why not clad in bear-skins, and all the rest? Even in the Middle Ages we hear of the Burgundians disguising themselves as calves or stags for the festival of the New Year's Day[1]. But if anybody prefers to say that the arctos was something like a totem of the Arkadians, and that these Arkadians most likely abstained from eating the flesh of their reputed ancestor, the bear, why not? Only as in all mythological solutions we must learn not to be too positive, and be satisfied with what is nearest, even though far-fetched similarities with Cahrocs and Kamilarois may in the eyes of some of us have a charm and value of their own which escapes the student of Greek or Vedic mythology.

This must suffice as a contribution towards the solution of the riddle of Artemis, as she has grown up on purely Hellenic soil and from purely Hellenic sources, and it may serve at the same time as an illustration of the different methods adopted by the two schools of mythological science, the Genealogical and the Ethno-psychological, each useful in its way, though hardly of the same value in the eyes of scholars. But if the story of Artemis as here explained accounts for the kernel of the myth, it is not to be supposed that it also accounts for the many stories that have gathered round it. The circumstances under which purely Hellenic myths became the centre of attraction, either for the floating folklore of outlying settlements in Greece or on the borders of Greece, or for the fully developed religious myths of foreign nations, whether Phenicians, Egyptians, Babylonians, or the inhabitants of Asia Minor, have never been fully explained, and probably never will be. With the limited

---

[1] Mone, Geschichte des Heidenthums, ii, 167; Mannhardt, Germ. Mythen, p. 41.

knowledge at our disposal at present, we can only say that Greek mythology and religion, like Greek language, was by itself a fully developed organism before it came in contact with these more or less foreign elements, and began to absorb them. That in some cases it should seem as if there was nothing left of the original growth but the standard on which the foreign god was grafted is not surprising, for local fables and local worship have the growth of weeds, and their very strangeness seems to secure to them a more intense interest and a wider propagation. But as little as Zeus awaited his birth till the Greeks became acquainted with the worship of Ptah Ammon, did Charis delay her rising from the waves as Aphrogeneia or Anadyomene, till the frantic worshippers of Baaltis Astarte or of Istar had invaded the islands and the very shores of Greece. Mythology is as old as language, and older than the oldest records we possess. As little as the Greeks modified or enriched their language by the adoption of Phenician, Egyptian, and Babylonian words, except in a few well-known and quite intelligible cases, did they wait for the advent of Phenician sailors or Egyptian and Babylonian exiles before they created their gods and goddesses, their heroes and heroines. This is the only safe position from which the influence of Oriental on Greek religion and mythology can be rightly judged, and though we have little historical information on the different periods when the Greeks tried to recognise their gods and goddesses in those of Phenicia, Egypt, or Babylon, still whatever there is tends to show that the Olympian gods are as old as the gods of any other country, and as little borrowed from other nations as the gods of the Veda were from the Akkadians.

The name of Artemis, which ought to disclose the first conception of the goddess, has hitherto yielded no information. It has been derived from ἀτρεμής, not trembling, unmoved, calm, or as some render the word, fresh, virginal. But this is far too modern a conception for an ancient deity. Besides ἀτρεμής is not ἄρτεμις. Another form of her name is Ἄρταμις, and if μις could be accepted as a derivative, as in θέ-μις, θέμιδος, we should have arta derived from the root ar, which in Sanskrit has yielded derivatives expressive of order and law, as in *ri*ta, and more particularly of the order of time, as in *ri*tú, season. But -μις is a primary suffix, whereas in ἄρτα-μις we have a secondary suffix. What one would expect is a compound such as *k*andra-mas, namely *ri*ta-mas, determining the order of the time, or measuring the seasons and the months. But this is a mere pium votum, and we must for the present leave Artamis as a name belonging to far too ancient a stratum of Aryan speech to allow us to find the connecting-links between it and even the earliest remnants of the Greek language.

And even if we could prove the name of Artemis to have been originally a name of the moon as the measurer of time, we should be able to account for one side only, and perhaps not the most original, of her character. She is called very truly πολυωνυμίη (Callim. Dian. 7), and her μυρία ὀνόματα, derived from mountains, forests, and rivers, struck even the ancients.

It should be mentioned that instead of Lêto, Dêmêter and Persephone also are called her mothers,

Zeus being her father in each case; and it is important to observe that one of her epithets, προσηῴα, matutina, shows once more the close contact between goddesses of the moon and of the dawn. Daphnaia, Akria, and Propylaia also are epithets of Artemis, and may contain hints as to her original character.

Artemis was worshipped in ever so many places and with ever so many names, in Thessaly (Pheraia, Mounychia), in Thrace (Kotys, Hekate, Bendis), in Lemnos and Tauros (Taurika, Tauro, Oreiloche, Iphigeneia [1]), in Euboia (Aithopia, Proseôa), in Thebes (Eukleia), in Aitolia (Laphria), in Phokis, Krissa, Delphoi (Sibylla), in Attika (Agrotera, Chitône, Aristoboule, Selasphoros, Amarysia and Propylaia), in the Peloponnêsos (Akria, Peitho, Soteira, Lykeia, Orthia or Orthosia, Oupis, Leukophryne, Karyatis, Daphnaia), more particularly in Arkadia (Kallisto), in the island of Krête (Britomartis, Diktynna), in Samos, Aigina, Rhodos, Dêlos (Ortygia). In Asia Minor she was worshipped at Ephesos, in Lydia, Mysia, and Lykia; lastly in Magna Graecia, and Italy. But though we may thus learn how widely the name and the cult of Artemis were known, more widely, it would seem, than the name of any other Greek goddess, yet beyond her local names we have little information as to what was her peculiar character and her peculiar worship in different parts of the world. In many cases, particularly when we hear of her worship in Egypt, Kappadokia, and Persia, we can only suppose that her name was given to a native goddess who possessed some attributes in common with her,

---

[1] Hesychius says: Ἰφιγένεια Ἄρτεμις, Ὀρθία Ἄρτεμις.

whether as goddess of the moon (as Hekate, Selêne[1], Phosphoros, ἀστερωπὸν ὄμμα Λητῴας κόρης), or as goddess of the chase (Koryphaia, Akria, Oreiloche, Iocheaira, Dilonchos, Klytotoxos, Agraia and Agrotera, Mêtêr thêrôn).

To the Greeks of Athens and Delphi, however, Artemis remained throughout the sister and companion of Apollon, the daughter of Zeus and Lêto, sharing the sublime character of Apollon and even some of his epithets, such as Lykeia, Delphinia, Daphnaia. Like her brother she prophesies as Sibylla, and distributes justice as Hêmeris. Their arrows bring death, but they are likewise the givers of health, vigour, and other blessings (θεοὶ οὔλιοι). As a heroine Artemis has been recognised in Îphigeneia, and as the beloved of Endymion, the setting sun, her lunar character admits of little doubt, though the fifty sons of their marriage are more difficult to account for, unless they were meant for the fifty months of the olympiad, two of which had been stolen, as we saw, by Hermes. And who can be the parents of these months, if not the moon[2] and the sun, and who can be the aging, though never dying, lover of the moon, if not the setting sun?

Indra.

Before we can go on with our analysis of some of the great gods and goddesses of Greece, Italy, and India, we have once more to return to Indra, and to examine his friendship with or hostility to earlier deities which seem to have left traces in the mythologies of India, of Greece, and Italy. The

---

[1] Somnambulists were called Selênoblêtoi and Artemidoblêtoi.   [2] See Chips, iv, p. 87.

principle by which we are guided is the old one of Noscitur a sociis, to which we have added, Noscitur ab hostibus.

We owe to Mannhardt a very minute analysis of Indra. In a well-known article of his in the 'Germanische Mythen' he instituted a detailed comparison between Indra and the Teutonic god, Thunar or Thôrr, the god of thunder. In it he is particularly anxious to show that while Indra is identified with Thunar he has nothing in common, as Kuhn supposed, with Wôdan or Odin. On this point he might have learnt something from Yâska. Though Wôdan may be the god of the storm rather than of thunder, both Wôdan and Thunar belong to the same sphere of natural phenomena, so that it would not be easy, nor very useful, to try to separate the two. Even in the Vedic Pantheon it is sometimes difficult to keep the activity of Indra apart from that of Vâta (wind) or of Rudra and the Maruts. Even in their own home Wôdan and Thunar were not always kept apart, and the chief office of Wôdan, the leadership of the reid or the Wild Host, was in Norway, at least, assigned to Thôrr [1].

I subjoin a list of the analogies between Indra and Thunar as elaborated by Mannhardt many years ago, showing him in his true character as a Comparative Mythologist, such as he was at the beginning of his career and again at the end of it.

I.	II.
1. Indra is originally a sky-god. [Indra is always active, and does not represent the quiet blue sky, but rather the	1. Thunar or Thôrr is an old sky-god.

---

[1] Sophus Bugge, K. Z., iii, 29.

welkin with its changing phenomena of storm, rain, lightning, &c.]

2. Indra, the storm-god, milks with his lightning the clouds, represented as cows, and drinks their milk, the rain. Oxen are sacred to him.

3. Indra himself is conceived as a bull. [His name of vrishabha does not involve his animal nature and form, but strength only, or manliness.]

4. Indra is followed by Maruts and Ribhus who milk the cow and make a new cow out of the skin of one that has been killed. [Cf. Rv. I, 161, 7; Mannhardt, Germ. Myth., p. 58.]

5. The demon Vritra (the coverer) steals the cloud-cows (sometimes conceived as heavenly women, devapatnis). Indra kills him and he falls on the earth as the dragon Ahi (Agi, Oegir, Ecke).

6. Indra drinks the heavenly Soma, the waters of the clouds, in order to gain strength for the battle.

7. Indra brandishes the thunder-weapon, Vagra, whether made of gold or stone or brass, and this weapon when hurled at his enemies always returns again to his hand. It was made by Tvashtri and the Ribhus. The thunderbolt is personified as Mudgala.

8. Heaven and earth are the girdle of Indra. [?]

2. Thunar milks the cloud-cows. Their milk is rain and dew. He uses the lightning-hammer.

3. Thunar is a bull.

4. The Mâres and Elbes milk the cloud-cows, and make a new cow out of the killed cow. [The identification of Mâres and Elbes with Maruts and Ribhus is no longer tenable.]

5. The cloud-cows, represented as women, are carried off by a demon, known by the name of Agi, &c. Loki is another form of the same demon.

6. Thunar refreshes himself with the water of the clouds, hence his immoderate love of drink.

7. Thunar carries the thunder-hammer, Mjölnir, made of gold, stone, or brass, and this weapon always returns to the hand of the god. It was made by the Svartàlfars, and has also been personified.

8. Thôrr possesses a strength-girdle, Megingjardr.

9. Thunder is the voice of Indra, and the far-sounding war-cry.

10. Indra drives on his thundering chariot, drawn by lightning horses.

11. Indra wears a golden beard, and shakes it when he is angry.

12. Indra is the god of strength. His weapons increase his inborn strength, he is lord of strength, husband of strength.

13. Indra becomes furious.

14. Indra is god of life, of marriage, and a blessing to families.

15. Indra in later times phallic.

16. Indra guardian of horses, dwellings, and the fire on the hearth.

17. Indra, healing-god, delivers men especially from skin diseases and worms in the body.

18. Indra, giver of plants. Many plants called after Indra and his thunderbolt. Indra gives food.

19. Indra brings light to the sky.

20. Indra, storm-god.
21. Indra, rain-god.
22. Indra digs a path for the

9. Thunder is Thunar's Bartery. To him belongs also the Gjallar horn.

10. Thunar is the driving-god, and there are traces of his having been drawn by lightning horses.

11. Thôrr when angry shakes his beard.

12. Thôrr is the god of strength. His hammer and girdle increase his strength, he is the father of strength, the strong lord of the gods.

13. Thôrr becomes furious.

14. Thunar is god of life, of marriage, and a blessing to families.

15. Thunar phallic.

16. Thunar god of herds, guardian of the clan (husband of Sif), and of the land.

17. Thunar, healing-god, heals skin diseases, drives worms = Elbe out of the body. His way of healing is the same as Indra's.

18. Thunar causes growth of plants; herbs and trees called after him. Thunar gives food.

19. Thunar gives sunshine, fastens the shining stars to the sky as in the myths of Örvandill and Thiassis.

20. Thunar, storm-god.
21. Thunar gives rain.
22. Thunar changes the hea-

rivers, changes the heavenly milk into running rivers.

23. Indra makes the rivers fordable.

24. Indra crosses the heavenly ocean in a boat.

25. Indra, god of treasures.

26. Indra fights with demons in the East, is lord of the East.

27. Indra's adversaries are one or more demons, supposed to reside in the cloud (as a mountain), to keep the rain captive, to carry off cows and women, to cover the sun and the light of the stars, to hide the gold, the treasure of the sun, or to bring back the shades of night. Such are the Pisâkas, Druhyus, and the giant-like Râkshasas who are cannibals. At last they build the seven strongholds of autumn, and freeze the cloud during the seven winter months. Indra is the destroyer of the strongholds (puran-dara). Opposed to the gigantic Râkshasas are the dwarf-like Pa*n*is. These demons are voracious, and are killed sleeping by Indra. He fights them, lightning against lightning, pushes them with his foot into the fire of the storm, chains them, and frustrates their tricks. They dwell behind the heavenly waters,

venly milk into rivulets and digs the bed for the rivers.

23. Thunar wades through the waters (of the sky), Wato in the heroic traditions.

24. Thôrr's navigation.

25. Thunar, god of treasures.

26. Thôrr's travels to the East.

27. Thôrr's adversaries, the giants and black elbes, are old heaven-demons. The giants are called Jötnar, i. e. eaters (Sk. atrin), and Thursar, the thirsty (because they swallow the rain-water). The Thursar originally (heavenly) water-sprites, their dwellings surrounded by (heavenly) waters. They steal (cloud) oxen and (water) women. They carry off and keep the treasure. As nebular beings they are characterised by the possession of a golden ram, a golden fire, and similar valuables which are emblems of the lightning and lightning clouds. The thunder-giant Thrymr carries off the water-woman Freyja; Thôrr adopts the form of the water-woman Freyja, in order to kill the giant. Thunar and the giants fight, lightning against lightning (Âsmóðr and Jötunmóðr). The giants hurl axes.

The demons, in the form of mountains, keep the rain

and are the spirits of bad people deceased; Indra assumes the form of the water-woman, in order to destroy the demon.

captive in the cloud and cover sun and moon.

The giants as the demons of winter. The Jötun building master. Giants bring the shades of the night. Thôrr frustrates the tricks of the giants. The giants as the spirits of the dead. Cannibalism in the Hymir myth. Thiassi. Carrying off of Idun, the water-woman. Giants adopt animal forms. Geirröđr as a storm-giant. Thôrr kills the giants when asleep. The physical meaning of the giants remains vague for a time. Dragons and evil dwarfs originally the same as the giants, and adversaries of Thunar. Etymological coincidences between Indian and German demons (Ahi = Âgias (?), Rauhinâ = Raugna, Atrin = Jötun; dhvara = Zwerg (Kuhn), Druhyu = Draugar).

28. Indra, born of the waters (âptya), dies or flees after his victory over the demons. As Trita he fights the serpent with seven tails.

28. Thunar, born of the waters, fights the seven-headed dragon, and after his victory is killed.

29. Indra, protector of men, is accompanied by heroes (personifications of heavenly phenomena) on his expeditions.

29. Thunar, friend of men, has Thialfi, Röskva, and Örvandill (personification of the lightning) as his companions.

30. Indra, war-god, invoked by the clan in battle.

30. Thunar, war-god, praised by the army when marching to the battle, arranged according to clans and families.

31. Indra, young and old.

31. Thôrr, young and old.

32. Sudden appearance of Indra, when invoked.

32. Sudden appearance of Thôrr.

33. Sacrifice offered to Indra on mountains and in forests.	33. Worship of Thunar on mountains and in forests.
34. Sacrificial posts sacred to Indra.	34. Door-posts sacred to Thunar.
35. The cuckoo belongs to Indra. Indra assumes the form of a ram. The thunder of his jaws.	35. The cuckoo sacred to Thunar. His symbol the chattering ram, with gnashing jaws.
36. Indra, god of death, receives the souls of the dead.	36. Thunar, god of death, receives the souls of the dead.

This is a long list of coincidences, and though on several points Vedic scholars would probably demur to the meaning which Mannhardt has put on certain verses in the Rig-veda, still enough of his evidence will remain to show the general similarity between Indra in India, Thunar and Donar in Germany, and Thôrr in Iceland.

And here we have an important lesson to learn. As Thôrr is a mere contraction of Thunar, these two gods were, of course, originally one god, worked out of the phenomena of nature once for all, and then modified according to the different character of the people of Germany and Scandinavia. We can also learn how wrong we should be if we supposed that Thunar represented nothing but thunder. He is the god of thunder, the agent behind the thunder. But he often represents the power that is manifested in the sky, in the rain, in the stormwind, nay, he becomes, as it were, the supreme deity, the guardian of man and beast, the defender of right, the punisher of wrong, the giver of life and the god of death. If these numerous coincidences occurred between Indra and some Polynesian deity, it would be difficult to decide whether they were due to universal psychological motives, or whether they postulated a real community of language and thought between Hindus and Maoris.

Importance of Names.

Everything depends here on the names. Coincidences such as that of the hammer Mjölnir returning like a boomerang to the hand of the god, whether Indra or Thunar, would, no doubt, always be startling. But is it not equally startling as between the Âryas of India and of Norway? Even in their case we might well hesitate before declaring that the myth of Mjölnir was invented but once, and at a time before the ancestors of these two Aryan branches were separated in speech and in locality. For, after all, the idea that the thunderbolt, though hurled from the sky to the earth, was always hurled again from the arm of Thunar, might have suggested the idea that it went back by itself, particularly if ethnologists could prove that weapons like the boomerang were known in India as well as in Norway. But now suppose that we found in Sanskrit a name for the thunderbolt corresponding to Mjölnir in Norse, would not the question be solved at once? It should be remembered that a name is a work of art, and originally the work of an individual. If therefore the same name occurs in the south of India and in the north of Europe, there must have been an historical centre from which it started. In such a case we are dealing with historical facts, whatever their date, and not with mere psychological possibilities.

And here we see the importance of the labours of the linguistic and, what is the same, the genealogical school. If the name of Indra occurred but once in German, or that of Thunar or Thôrr as a proper name in Sanskrit, we should feel on terra firma, as we do feel on terra firma when we deal with Dyaush-pitar and Jupiter, Ushas and Êos, the Harits and the Charitas, Erînys and Sara*n*yû. Small irregularities in these names would have to be tolerated as they are tolerated in the local and dialectic names of many a Greek god. But the fact would remain, not only that the Âryas, before their separation, had elaborated the names of these ancient Devas, but that the different branches of the Aryan family had carried them away to their new homes, only modifying their pronunciation, each according to their own phonetic idiosyncrasies.

This does not apply to the comparison of Indra and Thunar, and if mythologists should prefer to assign an independent origin to each, we could not silence them, even though it would be easy to show that the word for thunder, corresponding to Thunar, existed as noun and adjective in the undivided Aryan speech [1]. Here we see once more the difference in the results which may be expected from the Linguistic and the Analogical Schools of Comparative Mythology. With the evidence at present before us, all we can say is that the probabilities would be strongly in favour of supposing the myth of Indra and Thunar to have existed before the Aryan Separation, but that the possibility of their independent origin cannot well be denied.

Indra in the Veda.

It is certainly very curious that the name of Indra has left no traces in any of the other Aryan languages, not even in Zend.

---

[1] Sk. tanyatu and tanayitnu, thunder, Lat. tonitru, O. H. G. donar.

This very absence of the name of Indra from the lists of Aryan deities anywhere but in India ought to convey an important lesson to comparative mythologists, because it shows most clearly that what we call the original and common Aryan mythology had long been left behind by the Vedic generation, and that there had been ample time for the growth of new deities before we get a glimpse of the Vedic Pantheon. If we look upon the naming as the real birth of a deity, the birth of Indra, that is, the naming of Indra, must therefore be referred to a time later than the Aryan Separation.

I have always looked upon Indra as in the beginning the god of rain, his name being clearly derived from the same root which yielded indu, rain-drops. In India more than in any other country rain meant life, absence of rain, famine and the most terrible death. I cannot therefore follow Prof. Oldenberg in his opinion that Indra has little to do with rain, and that his striking the parvata with the thunderbolt means that he thus called forth the great rivers of India from the Indian mountains. There is nothing in nature corresponding to this. Rivers do not gush out of rocks, even when they have been struck by lightning; their sources are mostly small and insignificant, and they do not in the least suggest the idea of a struggle between a god and a demon. When Indra strikes the parvata, parvata is the cloud, when he delivers the rivers, the rivers are the streams of rain which he has to conquer, and which are indeed, if we only think about it, the real rivers of the country of the Seven Rivers, often entirely dried up in summer like the Sarasvatî and the D*r*ishadvatî, and called back to life by the god of the rainy season.

Indra, more than any other Vedic god, is a fighting-god, and fighting always either for rain or for light. Indra's hurling the thunderbolt shows that he is the god of the thunderstorm, and a thunderstorm surely means rain. The Maruts, who are his companions in battle, are constantly praised for sending rain on the earth. The same is told of Indra also. Rv. X, 50, 3: Ké apsú svā́su urvā́rāsu paúṁsye, 'Who are they who excite thee in thy power in the waters for their fields?' Hence we may translate in the preceding verse also, V*r*itré vā́ ápsu abhí sū́ra mandase, 'Thou delightest over V*r*itra, over the waters.' In Rv. X, 49, 2, we read that the people of the sky, of the waters, and the earth have established Indra as god, and Kavandha or Kabandha, one of the demons whom Indra slew, meant originally, like kośa, the barrel, i.e. the cloud.

That the waters which Indra sets free are often meant for actual rivers is quite true, but this is so because these rivers were in the eyes of the *R*ishis the very streams of rain rushing down from the sky. The rivers of the Panjâb might well be called the streams (sindhu) that came from the clouds as from mountains. Thus we read, Rv. VII, 21, 3:—

Tvám Indra srávitavaí apā́ḥ kaḥ, páristhitā́ḥ áhinā sū́ra pūrvī́ḥ

Tvát vâvakre rathyā̀ḥ ná dhénāḥ, ré*g*ante vísvâ k*r*itrímāni bhîshā́.

'Thou, O Indra, hast caused the many waters to flow which were hemmed in by Ahi; they rolled down from thee like cows yoked to a cart, all created things tremble from fear.'

In what sense could real rivers like the Gaṅgâ and Yamunâ be said to be hemmed in or kept captive by Ahi, if they had not been connected by the poets with water poured down from the clouds? The very language, here applied to the rivers of rain, occurs in passages which clearly refer to real rivers, fed and kept alive by rain. Rivers in India often run dry, and disappear altogether, but they reappear after the season of thunderstorms, the Varshâ, or the rainy season, and all this was looked upon as the work of Indra. Hence we find that the rain waters are called sindhu, or streams where there can be no doubt that they are meant for rain, for it is said the sun had drawn them up to the clouds; for instance, Rv. VII, 47, 4: Yâh sûryah rasmíbhih âtatâna, yâbhyah índrah âradat gâtúm ûrmím, Té, sindhavah (voc.), 'The waters which the sun attracted and for which Indra made a path, those streams, té sindhavah,' &c.

Even in a hymn such as III, 33, 6, which is clearly addressed to real rivers, the rivers are introduced as saying: 'Indra holding the thunderbolt has dug us out, he struck down Vritra, who encompassed the rivers, the good-handed Savitri (sun) led us; at his command we, the streams, are moving on.'

And again in the next verse it is said that Indra killed those who surrounded (the water), and that the waters (âpas), (here clearly meant for the rivers) wishing for a path, moved along.

If then even with us the rivers which are dry in summer are swollen and flooded in the autumn, so that they cover miles of land as with a deluge, how much more was this the case with the mountain-streams of the Panjâb. Bergaigne (ii, p. 184) was perfectly right that in the actual fight between Indra and V*ri*tra, Indra was looked upon by the *Ri*shis as the conqueror of V*ri*tra, not as the direct giver or producer of rain, like Par*g*anya. For the same reason it is quite intelligible also that the verb v*ri*sh, to pour down rain, should not be used of Indra. But Indra remained for all that, ab*g*it, the conqueror of the water, it was he who broke open the stable of the cows, it was he who set the captive rivers free (IV, 19, 5). He was in fact, though indirectly, what his name declared, Indra, the moistener of the land.

I have tried to prove in another place that Soma, so intimately connected with Indra, was in one of its acceptations, if not in its original sense, the rain (su = $\check{v}$-ει) ; and that there are passages in the Veda where Soma is not only compared, but is actually identified with rain, has been shown by Professor Oldenberg, p. 459, note. Thus we read, I, 32, 12 : Á*g*aya*h* gā*h* á*g*aya*h* sûra sómam, 'Thou, hero, hast conquered the cows, thou hast conquered the Soma,' which, in this and similar passages, I should venture to translate simply by rain. The preparation of the Soma-juice at the Soma-sacrifice seems often a conscious imitation of the process by which the rain was supposed to be poured down through the clouds; nay, Soma is actually called V*ri*trahan, and implored to send rain from heaven[1].

But though Indra under this name was a more recent and peculiarly Indian god, the possibility is

---

[1] This has been fully worked out by Hillebrandt, in his Vedische Mythologie, 1891 ; see also Oldenberg, Religion des Veda, p. 459 ; Bergaigne, Religion Védique, i, p. 214 seq.

by no means excluded that some of the myths told of Indra were of earlier date, that they were told originally of some other god manifested in the sky and the storm, such as Dyaus, or Parganya, and that they gathered afterwards round this new name. We have only to accept Indra in the Veda as the conqueror of water (abgit), and everything else that is told of him can easily be accounted for as springing from this original character.

Andra.

If, as is now supposed, Andra in the Avesta was not meant for Indra, we should have to look upon Indra as later even than the separation of the Âryas of India and Persia, but the occurrence of Verethraghna as the genius of victory makes us hesitate. Verethraghna presupposes V*r*itrahan, a constant epithet of Indra in the Veda. Indra's chief duty was, as we saw, to kill V*r*itra, i. e. the coverer, a demon who keeps the rain imprisoned in the cloud, and at the same time keeps the light of the day captive. Hence V*r*itra in later Sanskrit came to be a name for cloud, as well as for enemy in general. It is important to remark that though V*r*itra, as a demon, is not mentioned in the Avesta, yet verethraghna, meaning literally, V*r*itra-killing, could not have assumed the meaning which it has in the Avesta, viz. victorious, except for the antecedents which we can see in the Veda. But for the victory of Indra over V*r*itra, darkness or clouds, as celebrated in the Veda, v*r*itraghna could never have assumed the meaning of victorious, so that we must admit a knowledge of the demon V*r*itra, and of his destroyer, though not yet under the name of Indra, in the background of Avestic mythology also. We must remember that in the Veda it is not only Indra, but Agni also, Soma, the Asvins and the host of the Maruts who are called vritrahan, or Vritra-killing, demon-killing. This is all the more important, because it justifies the occurrence of Vritra as Ὀρθρος in Greek mythology, and of Azhi = Ahi in the Avesta.

Indra, an Agent.

It should be remembered that the name of Indra expresses by its very form an agent, and not a visible object of nature. We saw before that all mythological names expressed originally agents, that even Dyaus was a name of the sky as an active power, before it was used as a name of the objective sky, that Ushas was not simply the red light of the morning, but the agent who brought the light, and was active in that light, nay that even Agni, before it became the recognised name of the material fire, meant the swift mover. Still, there is this difference that Indra, being from the first conceived as the causer of rain, was never identified with any physical object, whether rain or cloud, or light or sky, but at once grew into a dramatic character, a hero, a conqueror, a supreme ruler.

Indra Supreme.

In that capacity Indra came naturally into competition with other gods, such as Dyaus and Varuna, and even Agni. Though called the son of Dyaus, Indra is actually praised for having excelled, and in the end replaced his father [1].

---

[1] Science of Language, vol. ii, p. 543.

As to Varu*n*a, he held his own in the thoughts of his worshippers, but some rivalry between the two must have been recognised, as there is actually in the Rig-veda a dialogue between Indra and Varu*n*a, in which each asserts his supremacy, Varu*n*a trusting more, as it would seem, in his long-established character, Indra in the works which he had performed. This change in the supremacy is clearly alluded to in a hymn of the tenth Ma*n*dala, 124, 4, 'Many years I sacrificed here; choosing Indra, I leave the father (Dyaus?). Agni, Soma, Varu*n*a, these go; the kingship turns, I approach and cherish this' (i.e. Indra). Agni also was praised for performing the very acts in which Indra displayed his prowess, and it would be easy to collect passages in which every one of these gods, Dyaus, Varu*n*a, Agni, and Indra, was praised as supreme. Here we see once more this peculiar stage of thought, which seems to us almost inconceivable, but which is of the greatest importance for a proper understanding of the development of the religion of India, and for which I suggested the name of Henotheism, not as if it were a necessary phase in the growth of all religious thought, which few would admit even in the case of Fetishism or Totemism, but simply as a convenient comprehensive title for actual facts which are familiar to every Vedic scholar.

V*ri*tra, Ahi.

The enemy who is slain by Indra, whether he is called V*ri*tra or Ahi (serpent), was probably as old as, if not older, than Indra. V*ri*tra is called, I, 32, 4, prathama*g*âs ahînâm, the firstborn of serpents, and his mother also is called Ahi and Dânu, Rv. I,

32, 9. Hence though Indra's name is absent from other Aryan mythologies, we can quite understand that that of Vritra should appear as Orthros. Ahi, also the serpent, originally the throttler, the enemy of the bright gods and of all that is bright in nature, occurs under various forms in other Aryan mythologies. In the Avesta he is mentioned as Azhi, particularly as Azhi dahâka (Zohâk). In Greek Echis and Ophis would both correspond to Ahi, and we find Echi-dna as the name of a monster, the daughter of Tartaros and Gê (or of Chrysâor and Kallirrhoe), the wife of Typhon, and the mother of Chimaira, of Orthros, the dragon in Kolchis, of the Sphinx, Kerberos, Skylla, Gorgon, and other horrible creatures. She was killed by Argos Panoptes, while Typhon, Typhâon, or Typhôeus was slain by Zeus[1]. There is another derivative, Echion, the name of one of the Gigantes who fought against Zeus. Ophis, serpent, has not assumed mythological independence in Greece, but Ophion is again the name of one of the Titans and one of the Gigantes. The same being appears in Greece under such names as Drakon, dragon, or Python, the son of Gaia, whom Apollon killed at Delphoi. The name of Pyth-on seems connected with πυθμήν, bottom, Sk. budhna for budhma. The root of πύθων was *bhudh, in Greek πυθ, and this with the suffix ων gave πύθων. This name has nothing to do with πύθω, to rot, but with πυθ-μήν,

---

[1] There is some confusion between these names, Typhâon being sometimes represented as the son of Typhôeus. The general idea, however, which they expressed in the eyes of the Greeks, was the same, that of violent storms darkening the sky, also of volcanoes vomiting fire.

the lowest bottom, or, as we should say, the bottomless pit, possibly the abyss of the sea, from which in the Veda another demon, Ahir budhnya*h*, derived his name, a kind of Ἔχις πυθώνιος. The fates of Ahi in Teutonic mythology have been traced by Mannhardt in such demons as Âgî and Oegir, nay in Uoki, in Ecke, and in the faithful Eckart of mediaeval epic poetry[1]. All these evil powers were powers of darkness, whether of the night or of the black storm-clouds, and Indra, their born and sworn enemy, developed thus naturally the character of a fighting and victorious god.

Dâsas.

Nothing was more intelligible, therefore, than that the people of the Vedic age in their conflict with the black inhabitants of the country should have invoked Indra's help. That these enemies or Dâsas were originally meant for the black native races of the country whom the Âryas had to subdue, I tried to prove in my Letter to Bunsen in 1856[2]. And as the life of the gods is always the reflection of the life of man, it was but natural that the enemies of the gods also should be represented as Dâsas. As the Âryas in their conflict with the real Dâsas were chiefly fighting for cows and such like booty, being goshu-yudh, fighting among or for cows, the gods also were naturally represented in the same way, as fighting for cows, or as trying to rescue stolen cattle. It might also have happened that some of the women

---

[1] Mannhardt, Germ. Mythen, p. 93.

[2] They are called mûradeva, apavrata, anindra, anri*k*, sisnadeva, anâs, kravyâd, amânusha, tva*k* krishnâ, &c. On modern names of aboriginal inhabitants, see Kittel, Sacrifice, p. 16.

of the Âryas had been carried off, and had actually become the wives of the Dâsas (dâsapatnî); and as these were rescued by the Âryas, Indra also was invoked to rescue the waters that were kept captive, ahi-gopâḥ, guarded by Ahi, as dâsapatnîḥ, or wives of the Dâsa [1]. We must try to enter into this narrow circle of the thoughts of the Vedic Âryas if we want to understand their poetry. When they saw the dark night suddenly opened by the light, their nearest thought was their own dark stable, often a mere cave, which was shut during the night and opened again in the morning. If that conception had once been transferred to the dark night as illumined in the morning, what stepped out of this stable, the bright beams of the morning, could only be to them the cows, the red cows. It was thus that the dawn became to them naturally the red cow, or the mother of the cows. There were thus three kinds of cows, the real cows, the cows in the dark cloud (rain = milk), and the cows stepping forth from the dark stable of the night (the rays of the morning). These three are not always easy to distinguish in the Veda, nay, while we naturally try to distinguish between them, the poets themselves seem to delight in mixing them up. In the passage quoted above we saw how the captive waters were compared to cows that had been stolen by Paṇi, but what is once compared in the Veda is soon identified. As to the Dawn, she is not only compared to a cow, she is called the cow straight out [2]. Thus when we

---

[1] Rv. I, 32, 11 : Dâsápatnîḥ áhigopâḥ atishṭhan níruddhâḥ âpaḥ paṇinâ iva gâvaḥ, Apâm bilam ápihitam yát âsît vṛitrám gaghanvân ápa tát vavâra.
[2] Science of Language, vol. ii, p. 583.

read, Rv. I, 97, 2, 'These dawns have made a light, on the eastern half of the sky, they brighten their splendour, the bright cows approach, the mothers,' the cows, gávah, can only be the dawns themselves, the plural of dawn being constantly in the Veda used where we should use the singular. In Rv. I, 93, 4, we read that 'Agnishomau deprived Pani of his cows and found light for many.' Here again the cows are the dawns kept by Pani in the dark stable or cave of the night, discovered by Saramâ, and delivered every morning by the gods of light.

We read in Rv. I, 62, 3, that Brihaspati split the rock and found the cows.

Of Indra it is said, II, 19, 3, that he produced the sun and found the cows; of Brihaspati, II, 24, 3, that he drove out the cows, that he split the cave by his word, that he hid the darkness, and lighted up the sky. What can be clearer? The Maruts also, II, 34, 1, are said to uncover the cows, and Agni, V, 14, 4, is praised for killing the fiends, for having overcome darkness by light, and having found the cows, water, and the sun.

In all these passages we find no iva or na, which would indicate that the word cow was used metaphorically. The dawns or days, as they proceed from the dark stable or are rescued from evil spirits, are spoken of directly as the cows. If they are spoken of in the plural, we find the same in the case of the dawn (ushas), who is often conceived as many, as in II, 28, 2, upāyane ushásâm gómatinâm, 'at the approach of the dawns with their cows.' From that it required but a small step to speak of the one Dawn as the mother of the cows, IV, 52, 2, mâtấ gávâm.

Kuhn thought that these cows should be understood as the red clouds of the morning. But clouds are not always present at sunrise, nor can it well be said that they are carried off and kept in prison during the night by the powers of darkness.

But what is important and settles the point is the fact that these cows or oxen of the dawn or of the rising sun occur in other mythologies also and are there clearly meant for days. They are numbered as 12 × 30, that is the thirty days of the twelve lunar months. If Hêlios has 350 oxen and 350 sheep, that can only refer to the days and to the nights of the year, and would prove the knowledge of a year of 350 days before the Aryan Separation.

When in German mythology we read of the 700 gold rings of Wieland, the smith, we cannot but recognise in that number also the 700 days and nights of the year. In the Veda[1] we find the number 720 instead of 700, when we read, Rv. I, 164, 11, 'The twelve-spoked wheel of Rita rolls round the sky, never to decay, the 720 paired sons have approached.' It is clear therefore that the cows of the morning are really the 350 dawns of the year, each day representing one cow, while Dawn in the abstract or as a goddess may be represented as the mother of all the cows. The cows or oxen of Hêlios thus receive their background from the Veda, but what is told of them by Homer is by no means clear. When it is said that the companions of Odysseus consumed the oxen of Hêlios, and that they thus forfeited their return home, we can hardly take this in the modern sense of consuming or wasting their

---

[1] Kuhn, l. c., p. 140.

days, though it may be difficult to assign any other definite meaning to it. Equally puzzling is the fable alluded to in the Homeric hymn that Hermes stole the oxen of Apollon and killed two of them. The number of Apollon's oxen is given as fifty [1], which looks like the number of weeks in the lunar year, but why Hermes should be represented as carrying off the whole herd and then killing two, is difficult to guess, unless we refer it to the two additional months in a cycle of four years. We must here keep to the general fact that the cows or oxen of the dawn or the morning represent the bright days or the bright suns stepping forth from the stable of the night, that these cows come from the East but disappear in the West, carried off by the powers of darkness, the enemies of the bright gods. Beyond that we cannot go, and must make allowance for the free fancy of ancient bards and story-tellers.

Conquest of Cows.

The next idea seems to have been that these cows or 350 days had each year to be reconquered whether by a god or by a hero, who alone was able to perform this difficult task, and who, when he had performed it, under every possible difficulty, grew gradually into a character such as we see Indra in India, Hêraklês in Greece, or Siegfried in Germany. This very simple tale of bringing back the days or suns, or the lost cows, has been told again and again under ever varying forms, and has supplied one of the most popular themes of Aryan mythology. In the Veda we still see this fight in its simplest form, it is

---

[1] Others give the number as 100 cows, twelve oxen, and one bull. The number of 112 would represent sixteen weeks.

occasionally no more than a description of nature. The light drives away the night, the sun appears, the sun sets, but these set or vanished suns are not lost for ever. They are kept captive somewhere, and they have to be liberated and brought back by some god or hero, such as Indra in India, Zeus, Apollon, or Hêrakles in Greece. One of the best known of these stories is that of Hêrakles travelling to Erytheia[1], an island in the extreme West, where Gêryones kept the oxen. Gêryones, possibly vorax, a giant with three bodies (τρισώματος, tricorpor), possessed red oxen guarded by Eurytion, and by the dog Orthros, here called δικέφαλος, two-headed. Gêryones, Eurytion, and Orthros we know already as belonging to the same ill-omened kith and kin. Hêrakles kills Orthros and Eurytion; Gêryones, informed by Menoitios of what had happened, pursued Hêrakles, but was likewise killed by him. Then Hêrakles travelled home in a golden boat given him by Hêlios, and after many adventures brought the oxen to Eurystheus, who sacrificed them to Hêre. The Greeks seem to have delighted in filling this mythic frame with all the knowledge they possessed or gradually acquired of any distant country that Hêrakles might or might not have visited with his drove of oxen. In these stories we cannot expect much of real mythology, but we can easily recognise the old and ever recurrent theme, the fight for cows or for the patnîs, the wives, and the old Vedic fighting-god Indra, whether repeated as Hêrakles or as Perseus (Andromeda), Bellerophon, Jâson, &c.

---

[1] Erytheia stands for Eurytheia, uru for varu. ἐρυτήρ for varutā́.

Cacus and Hercules.

One of the best known, but at the same time most troublesome myths referring to the recovery of cows is that of Cacus and Hercules. It has been treated in a masterly manner by Professor Bréal[1], whose essay contains all the information for enabling us to form a correct judgment. First of all, the name of Hercules has nothing in common with Hêrakles, as little as we can recognise Hêre in the Latin hera. The initial h is sufficient to show this. There was, no doubt, an old Italian deity Herculus, called rusticus, domesticus, agrestis, probably, like Terminus or Horta, the protector of property, but again unconnected, for the same reason, with Herceus = Ἑρκεῖος.

The Romans, before they became acquainted with Hêrakles and with Greek mythology in general, had probably a local tale that one of their gods had a fight with Cacus, a cattle-thief, killed him, and recovered the oxen. This is the old Aryan tradition taken straight to Italy, without passing through Greece. This tale must have been very popular at Rome, for it was commemorated there, not only by the forum boarium, the cattle-market, but by the Porta trigemina, by the steps of Cacus, by the Via triumphalis, by the Ara maxima, and by another altar to Jupiter Inventor. The most solemn sacrifices were performed there every tenth day, and again once in the year with the greatest solemnity. But who was the god that was celebrated? It could not have been Hêrakles, because he was a Greek god, and did not become known at Rome much before

---

[1] Hercule et Cacus, 1863.

355 P.U.C.[1] Nor could it have been the Italian Herculus, because he never was a fighting-god. Prof. Bréal seems to me to have proved that it was the old Italian god Sancus Recaranus. Sancus was actually called the conqueror of the robber, and Festus says in so many words that Sancus and Hercules are the same name. This may have been so in later times, but originally the two were clearly distinct, and Sancus only was the fighting-god, also called Semo Dius Fidius. In his capacity of conqueror or reconqueror of the cows he was also called Recaranus, for which Varro gives Garanus (wrongly explained by Grassmann as creator). All these names vanished more and more from the memory of the Romans, and when they became acquainted with a very similar story told of Hêrakles which they had heard told of Recaranus, Garanus, or Sancus, they at once assigned it to the Greek hero, only rendering his name Hêrakles by a name very similar in sound and more familiar to them, viz. Herculus and Hercules. They did exactly the same when they recognised Persephone in their own Proserpina, Semele in Stimula, Mnêmosyne in Moneta. The story has become complete when it is told us by Virgil, Ovid and others who were acquainted both with Greek and Roman mythology. Hercules, we are told, after defeating Gêryon, arrived with his herd in Italy near the Tiber. While his oxen were grazing, a robber called Cacus, a three-headed (τρικέφαλος), fire-vomiting monster, a son of Vulcanus, carried them off and hid them in a cave. In order that the footmarks might not betray them,

---

[1] Livy, v, 13.

he dragged them in backwards. But the cows began to low, Hercules opened the cave and the cows as well as all the treasures of Cacus came to light. After Hercules had killed the giant, he erected the altar to Jupiter Inventor. So far the origin and the later complicated development of the myth have been perfectly well explained by Prof. Bréal.

It still remains to examine the name of Câcus. It has generally been taken for the Greek κακός, evil, as if in opposition to ev-ander, good man. But the quantity is against it. We have also by the side of Cacus the name Κάκιος [1], and there is a son of Vulcanus called Caeculus, who was represented at Praeneste as a robber vomiting fire. Cacus, therefore, seems to represent an original Caecus (like Saturnus for Saeturnus), and to have meant blind or blinding, as Typhon was connected with τυφλός, blind, dark, and τῦφος, smoke [2].

In this way we can compare, and we can separate. The story of Hêrakles and Gêryones is the Greek, that of Sancus and Cacus the Latin, that of Indra and Ahi the Vedic version of the common Aryan fighting myth. Hêrakles is a native of Greece, he is a stranger in Italy, though naturalised there at a later time. Behind all these, there is the simple Aryan myth, that the suns that have set, i. e. the cows that have been carried off, have been rescued, have been brought back by some luminous agent, stronger than all the powers of darkness, stronger than man, and therefore superhuman, if not divine. If now we were to say that Hêrakles or Sancus or

---

[1] Diod. Sic. iv, 21.

[2] Grassmann's identification of Cacus with the Vedic sâka, strong, would give us too abstract a name.

Perseus, or Jason was the Indra of the Veda, we should be talking at random. Every one of these heroes has grown up by himself, what they share in common is simply the old Aryan background of the fight between night and day, darkness and light, of spring also, it may be, and winter. Such a myth might have grown up anywhere, and has grown up in many places. Even the story of the cows being dragged into the cave backward, so that the marks of their hoofs might not betray them, exists in other countries. But how does that help us? What is important to us for an understanding of the myth is that there are names and other ingredients in our myth to show that the Âryas had not yet separated when the object of the fight was defined as cows or treasure, and when a number of names were fixed both for the victorious hero and for the defeated enemy. Hêrakles is Greek, Herculus Latin, Ahi and Azhi were Indo-Iranian, but Ahi and Echidna, V*r*itra and Orthros must have been named before the Aryan Separation, that is, before the North-Western and the South-Eastern branches of the Aryan family had become finally separated.

Indra, Ushas, &c.

We have now to consider Indra in his second capacity, not as the enemy of the dark night and the dark cloud, but as in contact and in conflict with the bright gods or Devas, more particularly with the Dawn. The Dawn is the daughter of Dyaus, and from one point of view, Indra may be called her brother. But if we accept Indra as driving away the dark night and as opening the gate for the cow or the cows, we have likewise to accept him as for a time following the Dawn, and, as the day advances, as driving her away or destroying her. This is clearly expressed in such passages as Rv. IV, 30, 8 : 'That strong and manly deed thou hast wrought, O Indra, that thou hast slain a woman difficult to slay, the daughter of Dyaus.'

'Thou, Indra, who art great, hast crushed the daughter of Dyaus, Ushas, who wished to be great. Ushas went away from her crushed chariot, fearing that the bull might strike her[1].' 'Her chariot lay in the Vipâs (river) broken to pieces ; she herself went far away.'

In this and other passages we may discover the first traces of the god of light following the Dawn, possibly as assaulting her and causing her to fly. In a simpler way we saw that it was said, Rv. I, 115, 2, that Sûrya, the sun, follows the Dawn, as a man follows a woman, and lastly we read, Rv. X, 189, that 'the Dawn comes near the strong one (mahisha),' and 'that she expires as soon as he begins to breathe, and the mighty one irradiates the sky[2];' that is, as soon as the sun draws his first breath every day, the Dawn draws her last, or dies in the embraces of the sun. No one, I think, can read these passages without being reminded of Daphne, followed by Phoibos or Apollon, fleeing before them and vanishing or being changed into laurel as soon as the solar god touches her[3]. That the mere name

---

[1] Chips, iv, 99.   [2] Chips, iv, 293.
[3] More of these Dawn-stories have been treated by me in Chips, iv, 293, 566, 571, and Science of Language, ii, chapter xii.

of Daphne can be equated with that of the Vedic Ahanâ, Dawn, I hope I have established in the chapter on Phonetics (p. 403).

Indra, as Deliverer of Women.

We have so far followed the postulated being that was called Indra in the Veda, Hêrakles and other names in Greece, in his various characters, (1) as opening the stables of the Dawn in the East, to bring out her flock of days, (2) as fighting against the demons of the night who had carried them off to the West, (3) as following the Dawn for a while, trying to take possession of her, threatening violence to her, and losing her in the end.

We have to look now for traces of one more achievement of Indra often described in the Veda, that of delivering the rain-waters, conceived as women, who had been carried off and kept prisoners by the Dâsas. We saw that these Dâsas were meant for the Vritras and Ahis who kept the rain-water or the rivers imprisoned in the clouds or mountains. When in prison these women were called dâsapatnî (slave-wives, or, as others propose, having slaves for their lords); when free, they go by the name of devapatnî (god-wives). As Devapatnîs, they weave a song for Indra, when he is going to kill Ahi (Rv. I, 61, 8). Their later names are given in Rv. V, 46, 8, as Indrânî, Agnâyî, Asvinî, Rodasî, Varunânî, &c.

On the contrary, when Indra and Agni shake the ninety strongholds (III, 34, 1), which are said to hold the Dâsapatnîs as prisoners, when Indra has split the stone with the lightning, and opened the cave, he is said to have rescued the waters, the Dâsapatnîs. In VIII, 96, 18, we read that Indra, when he had killed the V*ri*tras, let loose the hemmed-in Sindhus, and conquered the waters, the Dâsapatnîs. Aryapatnî also is used in the sense of devapatnî as in Rv. VII, 6, 5, yâ*h* aryápatnî*h* ushásah *k*akâra, where Agni, a more appropriate deliverer of the Dawn than even Indra, is said to have made the Dawns once more wives of the Aryas, thus showing the close connection, or rather confusion in the minds of the *R*ishis of the imprisoned Dawns with the imprisoned streams. In Rv. X, 43, 8, almost the same words are used of Indra, who is said to have made the waters wives of the Âryas, yâ*h* aryápatnî*h* ák*ri*not imâ*h* apâ*h*.

Hêraklês and his Heroines.

The question now arises whether in the names of the women set free by Hêraklês and similar heroes in Greece we can still discover some faint traces of the names applicable to the Dawn as occurring in the Veda. We easily find among the wives of Hêraklês significant names, such as Auge (sunlight), Xanthis (yellow), Chrysêis (golden), Iole (violet), Aglaia (resplendent), and Êône, which cannot be separated from Êos, dawn. There are besides, Prokris, dew (πρώξ), Panope, all-seeing, and a number of names beginning with εὐρύ, wide, an epithet much cherished with reference to the wide-spreading dawn, such as Eurybia, Euryke (urû*k*i)[1], Eurypyle, Eurytele, &c.

Are all these names, particularly those beginning with Eury, to be ascribed to accident? We saw

---

[1] See Chips, iv, 107, 570.

how the Dawn was represented in the Veda as rich in horses, nay as herself a horse, as rich in cows, nay as herself a cow. Is it not strange then to find among the wives of Hêrakles not only Hippos, but Nikippe, Klytippe, Pyrippe, Lysippe, Hippokrate, &c.?

Of cows there are fewer traces in the names of the wives of Hêrakles, unless we take Euboia in the sense of rich in cows (gomatî). In the case of Thêseus, when acting the same part as Hêrakles, we find Phaidra, the brilliant, as his wife, and she was the sister of Aria-dne (Aria-gne).

After all this, the question arises whether we are not justified in seeing in Dêianeira, who was carried off by Nessos, a similar name, a name that in Sanskrit might be represented as Dâsya-narî, meaning Dâsa-patnî, a woman, i. e. the Dawn, that has been carried off by a Dâsa, and not, as the Greeks thought, a name referring to the legend of the death of Hêrakles. If so, we should see once more how besides the common background of Aryan mythology, there are here and there small survivals from a secondary stage also, such as the peculiar nomenclature of devapatnî and dâsapatnî, applied to the Dawn and to the streams of rain, according as they are in the power of the devas, the bright gods, or the Dâsas, the demons of darkness. I know, of course, that modern Euhemerists will laugh at all this, and consider it labour lost, for why, they ask, should we not accept facts as facts? Why should not a prince of Argos called Hêrakles have had a wife called Dêianeira, and friends such as Iole (violet), Xanthis (yellow), Chrysêis (golden), Êône (dawn-like); and if the son of Dêianeira is called Hyllos (sûrya), i. e. sunlike, the son of Eurypyle, Leukippos (white horse), the son of Toxikrate, Lykios (luminous), is not the world full of such accidents? I confess that I feel quite unable to argue against this, and I doubt whether any other student of mythology would even enter on such a controversy. Whoever is accustomed to the language of mythology, knows what such names mean, he expects them, and he finds them exactly as he expects them. The mere looker-on, if he sees a number of flints, some carefully shaped, others roughly shaped, others not shaped at all, but simply crushed by pressure, will often ask how it is possible to distinguish natural from artificial flints; and when the geologist shows him the small bulge in the artificial flint caused by repeated blows of the workman, he will hardly appreciate this fact, so pregnant with enormous consequences, or accept so faint a sign as proving what in the eyes of the expert it does prove. It is the same in mythology. The occurrence of a few names with a clear intention is enough to convince the true student that he is exploring a mythological stratum, and not a Directory of the ancient towns of Argos and Mykenai, while to the outsider all this is mere nebulous fancy.

Dawn. Fors.

Having had to follow the Dawn in her various relations to Indra as the god of light, it may not be out of place to add a few words on the same goddess, as she appears in her relation to mankind. We can well understand that everything said of her in the Vedic hymns should be to her praise, for she is welcome to all except, as we saw, to evil-doers, whom in the shape of Sara*n*yû, Erinys, or the earliest Dawn, she finds out[1] and brings to light and punishment. We saw before how Ushas, the Dawn, the mother of the cows, the leader of the days[2], opens the darkness, the stable of the cows, the gates of the rock, and how the cows come forth, bringing light and gladness to the whole world. But in her more personal character Ushas, the daughter of Dyaus, the sister of Varu*n*a and Bhaga, the wife of Sûrya (VII, 75, 5), appears as a beautiful woman, dancing and smiling, waking men to do their work, giving them perception and vigour. She is supposed to be rich in golden treasure, and to show her riches to her worshippers (I, 113, 4), nay to lighten up the whole world with the eye of the sun (I, 113, 9). She is in fact rich in gifts, a real Fortuna, and far more than a mere Tyche, or chance. The Romans, of course, accepted Fors and Fortuna, as one who brings (ferre), though a moment's reflection would have shown them that ferre means auferre quite as much as afferre, so that even fûr and $\phi\omega\rho$, thief, have been traced back to it (K. Z., xxxi, p. 462). If Fors in the sense of luck had been derived from ferre, she would be one of those abstract goddesses, familiar to us in Roman mythology, such as Cuba, Cunina, Rumina[3], Statana, or again, Virtus, Victoria, Pudicitia, &c. But if we examine these Roman goddesses or genii more carefully, we shall find that

---

[1] Rv. VII, 75, 1: Ápa druhá*h* táma*h* áva*h* á*g*ush*t*am, 'She revealed the unlovely darkness of the enemy.'

[2] Rv. VII, 77, 2: Gávâm mâtâ, netrî áhnâm, 'Mother of the cows, leader of days.'

[3] Cuninae propter cunas, Ruminae propter rumam, id est prisco vocabulo mammam. Varro apud Nonium, p. 167. (See p. 151.)

many, though not all of them, were originally epithets grafted on more substantial deities. Augustinus (vii, 11) tells us that Ruminus was a name of Jupiter; why should not Rumina have been a name of Juno or even of Venus, with whom Juno shares other epithets in common, such as Victrix, Genetrix, Postvota? Fors also has such epithets as Genetrix, Victrix, Postvota, Muliebris, Mascula, and Primigenia, and has therefore a right to be considered as a substantial deity, quite as substantial as Juno or Venus, and different from such unsubstantial concepts as Ossifraga, Statana, Vaticanus, or Fabulinus.

These smaller gods and goddesses, if indeed they can be called by that name, and not rather spirits, genii or haltias, seem to be a distinguishing element of Roman mythology, but they existed in other mythologies also, though they have not been so fully preserved to us as those of the Romans. They deserve a special study as throwing light on one of the many sources of mythology, but they should all the more carefully be kept distinct from the class of Devas or Dii majorum gentium who represent another stratum of mythological thought. The question of priority is useless, for we have no means of answering it, and mere assertions would only do mischief. These smaller gods and goddesses were probably most cherished by the smaller people. It is doubtful whether they ever possessed temples or were represented by statues, but like the Lares, they probably were far better known among the servants and in the nurseries than Mars and Minerva.

If now we examine the nature of Fors more closely we shall find that she certainly was not a mere epithet, nor a mere haltia, but one of the oldest goddesses worshipped in Italy, a being of flesh and blood, not a mere abstraction, a fairy or bogie.

It has been doubted whether Ushas, the Dawn, was conceived in the Veda as a kind of Fortuna, but the passages quoted above are sufficient to show that she was supposed to possess treasures, and that these treasures were meant for her worshippers (Rv. IV, 51, 7; VII, 41, 2). This character of Ushas became still more prominent in the later literature, as we may see, for instance, in the Adbhuta-brâhmana[1] of the Sâma-veda. There we read (§ 101):—

If the Dawn (ushasî) does not rise, let him sacrifice:
May the beauty of the ordering Dawn rise up,
May the pale traveller make up his bundle and go!
May the wise Dawn who brings the manifold seasons,
Order what is to come to me!

Can we find a clearer Fortuna rising from the light of the Dawn? Can we have a better Fortuna than a Dawn who is rich in treasures, and who orders all that is to come to her worshippers? These facts at all events should not be doubted, but gratefully accepted as a thread to guide us through the labyrinth of mythology.

To those who think that the Romans must be the best judges of their gods, the popular idea that Fors is Dea quae fert, would no doubt carry great weight. We might even refer to the German 'Was sich zuträgt,' now called Zufall, in Icelandic at-burdr. But scholars who are aware of the etymological crudities of which both Greeks and Romans were guilty in their etymological explanations of the names of the gods, will no longer allow themselves to be influenced by Roman folk-etymologies. They will

---

[1] See Weber, Omina und Portenta, p. 364.

rather look to the old worship and the old customs which surrounded the myth of Fortuna. Now this goddess Fortuna was worshipped at Praeneste, not like a shadowy Rumina, but like Ushas as Divo duhitâ, the daughter of Jupiter, though at the same time as holding Jupiter and Juno on her lap and giving the breast to young Jupiter. This very incongruity at once tells that we are moving in ancient mythology, and reminds us of the Dawn who in the Veda is called not only the daughter of Dyaus, but at the same time the mother of all the gods (Rv. I, 113, 19). It should be remembered also that the Fortuna Virgo had her festival on the same day as the Mater Matuta, the mother of the morning, and that Fors was actually with Pales and Ceres one of the Roman Penates.

In an old inscription she is spoken of as Fortunai Diovos fileiai primoceniai. This Primogenia or Primigenia may again be matched by the Dawn being invoked in the Veda as the first (prathamâ) at every morning sacrifice. She is also called ʼagriyâ, the foremost goddess. Thus Eos is called ἠριγενής, possibly Apollon also. Erigone, again, seems to have been a name of the Dawn. It is curious that she should be called Alêtis, the wanderer, like Saramâ, &c., and that Alêtes should be the name of a son of Îkarios and of Aigisthos, just as Êrigene or Êrigone is the name of a daughter of Îkarios and of Aigisthos. Here, however, there remains much to be cleared up.

There are few things that are said of the Roman Fortuna that could not be matched by parallel sayings about Ushas, the Dawn [1].

---

[1] Biographies of Words, 'Fors Fortuna,' pp. 1–16.

The question therefore that has to be answered is whether Fors or Fortuna could in her origin have meant the Dawn. I may have been right or wrong in my derivation of Fors, but my arguments deserved at all events careful examination. Nothing is gained by mere assertions, even if they emanate from the highest authorities. When I said that Fors could not be derived from ferre, every scholar must have seen that what I meant was that, as a matter of fact, no case has hitherto been brought forward where any of the derivatives of the root bhar exhibit the deep-toned o, and that fordus forms no exception. That the deep-toned o was possible, has never been denied, and those who follow Noreen would probably go much further. The question was not whether such an o was possible, but whether it was real. By proving the unreality of o in the Latin derivatives of ferre[1], I thought I had done all that could be expected. Then, after I had proved not only the possibility, but the reality of the deep-toned o in derivatives of the root ghar and therefore the perfect regularity of the equation Forti = *Gharti, as a variety of Harit, the red horse of the Dawn, the question had ceased to be linguistic, and had become purely mythological. And here I certainly was not prepared to be asked whether I thought that forte evenit meant 'it happened by

---

[1] I quoted Brugmann, § 172, 3, where he shows that ĕ may in Latin be represented by ĕ and ĭ, but only under very special circumstances by ŏ. I quoted De Saussure, who says (p. 79): 'Le latin, fort chiche de ces a, en met parfois où il n'en faut point. Il a les neutres pondes de pend et foedes de feid, alors que la règle constante des thèmes en as est de garder a dans la racine.'

the intervention of the Dawn.' We might as well ask whether journalist meant 'a son of heaven or Dyaus.' We must not play with questions which to a scholar are serious. The result of this long and to me painful controversy may therefore be summed up as I summed it up in the Academy [1].

Is the derivation of Fors from GHAR etymologically correct? Is the conception of Fors as Dawn mythologically correct? Is there besides Fors any other derivative from BHAR which shows o? But the most important question of all is this, Is there any other ancient Roman deity like Fors, meaning no more than the carrier, and yet called the daughter of Jupiter, and the nurse of Jupiter and Juno? How well has Kuhn (K. Z., xvi, p. 173) expressed his appreciation of the true character of Fors Fortuna, when he writes: 'Es zeigt sich bei allem, was an den Dienst dieser Göttin geknüpft ist, eine so eigenthümlich Römische und tief angelegte Auffassung, dass sie gewiss nicht anders als aus dem eigensten Volksbewusstsein heraus erwachsen sein kann.'

These are very simple questions that can be answered in the negative or the affirmative by any scholar, and can surely be answered sine ira et studio. In trying to answer such questions as whether Fors was derived from ferre or from the same root that yielded formus, our language might surely be serious and scholarly, even if it cannot be courteous.

Agni.

Many people are still under the impression that Comparative Mythology is built up entirely on Com-

---

[1] Academy, March 3, 1888.

parative Philology, and that it appeals exclusively to etymology in support of its views. Nothing can be more mistaken. Comparative Mythology could exist and light up more or less the darkest corners of mythology in every part of the world, not only in India or Greece, but in Africa and America also, if not a single name of any god or hero had been preserved or could be analysed etymologically or could be compared with cognate names in cognate languages.

No doubt, etymology is an immense help, and a successful comparison of mythological names in Sanskrit, Zend, Greek, and Latin serves sometimes as an important indication, sometimes as an encouraging confirmation of our views on the character of mythology and on the origin of its gods and heroes. But the fundamental principles of Comparative Mythology must stand or fall by themselves.

Suppose we were doubtful as to the origin of certain ecclesiastical vestments used in Tibet which are very like those used at Rome, would not the whole controversy be settled at once, if we found any such names as dalmatic, cope, chasuble in Tibetan? This shows the value of names. Still if we knew nothing of etymology, nothing of a comparison of mythological names in Sanskrit, Greek, and Latin, the acts which in the Veda are ascribed to Agni would leave no doubt in our mind that he was in Vedic India the god of fire, recognised not only in the fire on the hearth, and in the flames of the sacrifice, but likewise in the flash of lightning, in the gleam of the dawn, in the fierce light of the midday sun, and in the glory of the sunset. We do not want etymology or comparisons to tell us who Selêne or Artemis was, who was Phoibos or even Phoibos Apollon.

The Vedic Ushas, if we knew nothing of the meaning of the word and its derivation from the root vas, to shine, is so clearly painted by the ancient *Ri*shis, that no one would hesitate for one moment to recognise in her a representative of the Dawn in its various aspects. And if Ushas is once recognised as the Dawn, many things follow by themselves. Her lover must surely stand for some heavenly phenomenon in close connection with her. If the light that follows the Dawn is called Hêlios or Hyperîon, we want but little knowledge of Greek to see that Hyperîon like Hêlios is meant for a solar being. If the Vedic Indra were etymologically unconnected with the root which appears in ind-u, rain-drop, any hymn in the Veda would tell us that he was conceived as the agent in the sky who gathered the clouds (νεφεληγερέτα), who slew the nebular demons in the dark thunderstorm, and sent the rain-drops down on the parched earth. And if we know this, we should also know that Zeus in his character of cloud-gatherer sprang from the same source as Indra, though there is no trace of that name in Greek or Latin.

When Darmesteter proved that Ahura Mazda was the same god as Varu*n*a in the Veda, he did not undertake to show that the names were the same or even derived from the same root. But he showed that the deeds and the characters of the two gods were the same, so much so that when we have in the Veda the divine couple Mitra-Varu*n*a, we have corresponding to it in the Avesta the divine couple of Mithra and Ahura.

Considering how peculiarly Asura was a name of Varuna in the Veda, are we to suppose that there was no historical connection between the compound Mitra-Varunau in the Veda and Mithra-Asura in the Avesta? While the name of Indra cannot be matched in the language and legends of any of the North-Western Âryas, Agni, though unknown as the name of a deity anywhere but in India, is well known as a name of fire in Latin and the Slavonic languages. This is one of the great advantages which Sanskrit, and more particularly Vedic-Sanskrit, offers for mythological studies. Whereas in Greek and Latin the names of gods have nearly all lost their appellative meaning, and oppose great difficulties to an etymological analysis, we find that many of the Vedic names have retained their appellative power in the later language, or admit at all events of etymological analysis. Thus Agni means fire in Sanskrit to the present day.

Dyaus, though no longer used as a masculine, means sky as a feminine in post-Vedic as well as in Vedic-Sanskrit. Prithivî continues to mean earth, anila, wind, ap, water, aranyânî, forest, aryaman, sun, âditya, sun, indu, moon, indrakâpa, rainbow, idâ, earth, ushas, dawn, ritu, month, gâtavedas, fire, tanûnapât, fire, tvashtri, carpenter, dhâtri, maker, nirriti, destruction, pathya, beneficial, parganya, rain-cloud, pitarah, fathers, pûshan, sun, prisni, ray of light, bhûmî, earth, marut, wind, mitra, sun, yama, twin, death, râtrî, night, rodasî, heaven and earth, vanaspati, tree, varuna, ocean, vâyu, wind, vaisvânara, fire, saranyu, wind, cloud, savitri, sun, sûrya, sun, soma, moon, and several more. It would be impossible to produce a similar list of intelligible names from among the gods of Greek or Roman mythology. And though it is quite true that the more recent meanings of some of these names are different from their Vedic meanings and may actually prove misleading, yet in most cases they indicate very clearly the original character of Vedic deities. In cases therefore where the later meaning differs from the Vedic, it becomes our duty to try to discover the links which connect the two; nay even in cases where such links cannot be found, we may rest convinced that they once existed.

Agni in India and Persia.

No doubt, the name of Agni existed before the Aryan Separation, yet there is no trace anywhere except in the Veda of Agni as the name of a deity. We have in Latin the same word, ignis, and in Old Slav. ogn'[1], in Lituanian ugnis, showing that the word was known to several branches of the Aryan family, the Italian, the Slavonic, nay possibly the Teutonic also, provided that Scottish ingle comes really from the same source. But we find no trace anywhere, not even in Persia, of fire being worshipped or deified under the name of Agni.

In Greece fire received divine honours under the name of Hestia, in Rome under that of Vesta. We know that in other parts of Europe also fire was worshipped before and after the introduction of Christianity, but we do not know the names of the

---

[1] The father and head of a family is still called in Russian ogniščaninŭ, ogništaninŭ, the arranger and keeper of the fire on the hearth, the fire-priest. See Krek, l. c., p. 203.

god of fire. I quote from Mannhardt, Lett. Sonn., p. 290 :—

'Dlugoss, in describing the conversion of Upper Lituania, writes : "Ignis qui per sacerdotes subjectis lignis nocte atque interdiu colebatur." Of Witold, when suppressing heathen practices in Samagithia, it is said: "Et ad praecipuum Samagitharum numen, ignem videlicet, quem sacrosanctum et perpetuum putabant, qui in montis altissimi jugo super fluvium Nyewasza sito lignorum assidua appositione a sacrorum sacerdote alebatur, accedens turrim, in qua consistebat, incendit et ignem disjicit et extinguit." Hieronymus, who came as a missionary from Prague to Samagithia : "Post hoc gentem reperit, quae sacrum colebat ignem eumque perpetuum appellabant. Sacerdotes semper materiam, ne deficeret, ministrabant."'

The Five Agnis in India and Persia.

But while the name of Agni is absent in the Avesta, several of his epithets have been preserved in it, such Apâm napât, son of the water, corresponding to the Apâm napât of the Veda, the light arising from and setting in the waters of the sea or of the sky [1].

Every one of the fires mentioned in the Veda can be matched in the Avesta. The vohufryâna, the fire or warmth of the body, is matched by the Sanskrit gâthara, fire; the urvâzista, the fire in the plants, by the Sk. aushadha; the berezisavanh, living in the earth, by the fire in the stones (asmasu); the vâzista, the fire of the lightning, by the Sk. vaidyuta. Thus we read in the Atharva-veda III, 21, 1: 'Let this offering be for the fires which are

---

[1] Rv. III, 25, 5 : Ágne apâm sâm idhyase duroṇé, 'Agni, thou art kindled in the house of the waters.'

in the waters, in the cloud, in man, in stones, and for those which have entered the plants and the trees.'

These five fires represent probably a secondary and rather systematising stage in the mythological conception of Agni, still they must have been fixed upon before the Indo-Iranian Separation. The fire in the waters seems to be meant for the solar light which sets in the clouds or in the sea, and appears again every morning, after passing the night in the waters; the fire in the cloud is the lightning, the fire in man the vital warmth or digestive heat; the fire in the stones refers to the fire hidden in flints, while that in plants and trees is most likely meant for the fire supposed to be hidden in the wood, before it is brought out by friction, or possibly for the fire kept up by fire-wood and by dry leaves piled up around the first spark that has been obtained. I doubt whether, as has been supposed by some scholars, the mere sap or life of plants could have been called the fire in the plants.

Agni in the Veda.

Thus we see that while in Greek and Latin such names as Hêphaistos, Vulcanus, Hestia, and Vesta are mere names with hardly any appellative power or etymological background, Agni in the Veda is simply a name of the fire, such as it was seen in every house and on every hearth. In some hymns we find Agni spoken of just as the ordinary fire would be. 'The priests,' we read, 'have by rubbing produced fire (agni) from the two fire-sticks. Agni rests in the double wood, as in his mother.' 'Agni is kindled by Agni,' &c. But how easily the fire on the hearth becomes something human and more than human, we can see elsewhere also, for instance, in the words addressed by a bride when she leaves her home, and says good-bye to the fire burning on her hearth. In the 'Sudauer Büchlein,' written between 1526-1530, giving a description of the North-Western corner of Samland, the bride in addressing the fire says : 'O my dear sacred little fire, Oho mey mile swente panike.' In the seventeenth century the Lituanians still called the fire szwenta Ponyke (ugnele), 'Sacred little fire.' And in the evening, when covering it up, they said : 'Sacred little fire, I shall bury thee very nicely that thou be not angry with me.' By such expressions the visible fire was imperceptibly changed into something personal, if not yet divine.

The fire might be called by many different names, and we can see in the Veda how the slightest change in the names addressed to Agni imparts to him a new active personality, a human, and even a superhuman character. He is called a messenger (I, 12, 1), a master of the house or of the clan (I, 12, 2). He destroys evil spirits (I, 12, 5), and protects his friends (I, 12, 8), he is the providence (pramati) of the singer (I, 31, 9). The gods made him lord of men (I, 31, 11); he is the friend of the gods (I, 31, 1), he is like a father to his worshippers, they are his kinsfolk (I, 31, 10). No man, no god is greater than Agni (I, 19, 2), he is immortal (I, 13, 5), and brings men to the highest immortality (I, 31, 7); he is the first maker (I, 13, 10), i.e. the carpenter (tvash*t*ar) of the world. All this is intelligible even to us. When the fire on the altar carries offerings to the gods in the form of smoke rising to the sky,

Agni is naturally called the messenger. When he burns on the hearth, the centre of the house, he is the lord of the family, and when he drives away darkness and purifies the air, he is the destroyer of evil spirits. As life in a severe winter would be almost impossible without fire, he is the protector of those who keep him, he protects even the poor who take refuge with him. As sacrifice is impossible without Agni, he may well be called the friend of the gods, and as he is never allowed to go out, or as he always comes to life again, he is called immortal. Sometimes it is said that Agni is kindled by Agni (I, 12, 6), that is, that he produces himself, fire produces fire, and it is in this sense that he was called Tanûnapât, offspring of his own body or self-born. As his light in the morning reveals heaven and earth, he may be said to have manifested or produced heaven and earth, and having once been conceived as a maker or creator, we can well understand (I, 67, 3) that he should have been represented as supporting the earth and as upholding the sky also by strong spells. This cosmogonic character of Agni has been so fully worked out by M. Senart[1], that no more need be said about it. He has clearly shown how the morning was taken as the type of creation, and as Agni, the light, was every day the revealer[2] or maker of the world, how he was likewise conceived as the original creator in the beginning of time[3]. Thus Agni, the light manifested in the

---

[1] Senart, Legende du Buddha, p. 96.

[2] Rv. IV, 3, 11 : Âví*h* svâ*h* abhavat *g*âté agnáu, 'The sky was revealed when Agni had been born.'

[3] Rv. VI, 7, 6 : Vaisvânarásya vímitâni *k*ákshasâ sânûni divâ*h*, 'The heights of heaven were created by his light.'

sun, was, like the sun, raised to the rank of a supreme deity, and every name assigned to Agni, all the divine characters in which Agni had become personified, whether Savitri, Vishnu, Virâg, Rohita, Skambha, Pragâpati, and still later Purusha and Brahman, were raised to the same rank.

We must also remember that a belief in the post hoc, propter hoc, is at the root of many ancient myths, and that in this way people brought themselves to believe, or, at least, to say, that the morning sacrifice caused Agni or the sun to rise. Thus we read, Rv. V, 6, 4: 'We kindle thee, O Agni, brilliant, O god, and undying, so that thy more glorious torch may shine in the sky,' and this idea [1] was more fully carried out in the Brâhmanas. Thus we read, Sat.-brâh. II, 3, 1–5: 'And when he offers in the morning before sunrise, he produces that (sun-child), and, having become a light, it rises shining.'

After a time Agni, though he retains his name, is no longer merely the visible fire on the altar. As soon as his chief attributes, light and warmth, had been recognised in other parts of Nature, Agni was supposed to be present everywhere. The fire that was lighted on the hearth, and was implored not to go away, was in the same verse asked to shine by day or in the sky so that men might long see the sun, i. e. might live. Ath.-veda XII, 2, 18: Sámiddho agna âhuta sá no mâbhyápakramíh, átraivá dídihi dyávi, gyók ká súryam drisé. Thus Agni was perceived in the sun, and he was supposed to have made the sun, whether rising or setting. Rv. X, 156, 4: 'Agni, thou hast lifted to the sky that unfading star,

---

[1] Cf. Bergaigne, i, p. 141; Oldenberg, Religion des Veda, p. 110.

the sun that gives light to men.' Agni was not only said to be the sun[1]; some poets call him the son of the sun, and the sun the father of Agni[2]. In one passage, Rv. I, 69, 1, the poet goes so far as to say, 'Being the son of the gods, thou hast become their father' (Bhúva*h* devánâm pitấ putrá́*h* sán). It is in this sense that later theologians maintain that the gods are itaretara-*g*anmâna*h*, as it were, 'mutually born.'

But though Agni was supposed to be everywhere, though in the Aitareya-brâhma*n*a I, 1, 1, we meet with the well-known formula, Agnir vai sarvâ devâ*h*, 'Agni is all deities, and all deities are Agni,' still a distinction is always maintained between Agni in his primary character as the house or family god, and Agni as in the sun, lighting the whole world, also as the dawn and the lightning. These latter characters were called by the Brâhmans gau*n*a, secondary, the former mukhya or primary.

Fire in other Mythologies.

In the other Aryan mythologies fire, as a purely elementary power, has never assumed the same prominence which it possessed in the Veda and Avesta. The Greek mind had once for all accustomed itself to conceive all elementary powers under a human shape, and seemed incapable of conceiving anything divine except under that form. Instead of an Agni, as the fire on the hearth, which was Hestia as a female goddess, we should have expected therefore in Greece, if there were anything at all

---

[1] Cf. Ehni, Yama, p. 66.
[2] Agne*h* sûrya*h*, sûryâd agni*h*. Nirukta, ed. Calc., vol. iii, p. 318.

corresponding to the Vedic Agni, some being in human shape connected with fire, or some more than human being who was believed to have discovered the fire, or to have brought it as a gift to man, by teaching them how to kindle it, how to keep it, and how to use it for practical purposes.

This change can be watched in its beginnings even in the Veda. Agni, besides being the fire, is also represented, though under a new name, as a workman using the fire for his own purposes. In that capacity, and generally under the name of Tvash*tri*, Agni is called su-apastama, the very clever workman, we might almost say the cunning smith. After that it required but a small step to bring us near to the Greek Hêphaistos and the Italian Vulcan.

Hêphaistos. Vulcan.

That both these gods were originally fire-gods was clear from the legends connected with them in Greek and Roman mythology. In the Iliad Hêphaistos is sometimes used in the sense of fire, as when, in Il. ii, 426; ix, 468, the Greeks hold the entrails to be roasted over Hêphaistos. This may be called a mere case of metonymy or metaphor, as when the Romans used Ceres for bread, and Bacchus for wine.

A clearer trace, however, of the elementary background of Hêphaistos can be recognised in his lameness. Why should Hêphaistos be lame or bandy-legged? In the Veda it is quite intelligible why Agni should be called apâd, without feet, because there is nothing in the movements of Agni that could suggest the idea of feet. Fire advances in a meandering and serpentine manner. As there is not much difference between feetless and lame, the god without feet might well be changed into a lame god. Others, however, have seen the cause of the lameness of Hêphaistos in the crooked descent of the lightning, and if we consider that the Greeks accounted for the god's lameness by his mother having hurled him from the sky, or by his father having thrown him down to the isle of Lemnos, much might be said for the identification of the lame god with the lightning rushing tortuously from the clouds to the earth. Only it has never been proved that the Greek Hêphaistos was meant originally for the fire of lightning, though in the Veda Agni, no doubt, having assumed the general character of light, wherever perceived, was recognised in the fire of lightning, as well as in all other manifestations of fire. Lemnos being volcanic, it is easy to understand why Hêphaistos should have been represented as banished from the Olympian gods, and dwelling in the dark caverns of the island. All these elementary thoughts, at first independent of one another, would afterwards be woven together, as we find them in Greek mythology. There was no difficulty in finding a reason why Hêphaistos, the lame god, dwelt at Lemnos, and why Zeus and Hêre, originally conceived as his parents, were angry with him. If at any time he had taken the part of his mother against his father, what was more natural than that Zeus should be represented as punishing or actually disowning his son? Then another story had to be invented of his mother having given birth to him by herself, just as Zeus was supposed to have brought forth Athênê by himself. All this was done without much difficulty, for we must always remember that there was no one to contradict the story-teller or story-singer who travelled from village to village to amuse the people. The story of Athêne being the child of Zeus alone and springing from the head of Zeus, had no doubt an independent origin and a physical background; the story of Hêre giving birth to Hêphaistos looks more like a later addition, merely suggested by the presupposed jealousy of Hêre, and her wish to give her husband tit for tat.

We must not forget, however, that Hêphaistos has himself also an active part to perform at the miraculous birth of Athêne. It is he who splits the forehead of Zeus. This forehead of Zeus, the mûrdhâ Divah, is meant for the East[1], and if Athêne was meant for the light of the dawn, Hêphaistos must on this occasion have been conceived in the same character in which we see him in the Veda as Agni, viz. the light of the sun, opening every morning the gates of heaven, another name for the forehead of Zeus. We saw that the gates of heaven were meant for the East. Scholars who take Athêne as representing the lightning, would find it difficult to account for the lightning (Hêphaistos) assisting at the birth of lightning (Athêne), or for the forehead or the head of Zeus being the birthplace of lightning, considering that lightning is seen to spring from every part of the sky, and not from the East only. Lightning is in fact too sudden, too transitory a phenomenon to be easily changed into a permanent, or everlasting deity. If, on the contrary, we take Athêne or Ahanâ for the Dawn, the Sun-maiden,

---

[1] Agni himself is sometimes called mûrdhà Divah, cf. Rv. VI, 7, 1.

springing from the forehead of the sky, Hêphaistos would then be the personified morning light, distinguished from the feminine Dawn by his masculine name, an Agnir aushasa, a kind of Pater matutinus or Janus. We should then understand also why this son of the morning, this Hêphaistos, was represented as in love with the Dawn, and why Athênê, like Daphne, should have been fabled to have fled from his amorous advances. In another shape, and under another name, it is really the Dawn that becomes in the end the wife of Hêphaistos. In the Iliad the wife of Hêphaistos is still called Charis, in the Theogony Aglaia, the brilliant, while in the Odyssey she is Aphroditê herself, all, as can easily be seen, originally names of the Dawn.

When occupying his Olympian abode, Hêphaistos is taken as the workman of the gods, the clever smith or artist. The chariot of Hêlios, the armour of Hêrakles, of Diomêdes, of Achilles, the sceptre of Zeus and his golden throne, all are his handiwork. The shield of Achilles, as described in the Iliad, shows how far art had been carried in the smithies of Homer's time. His Vedic representative, Tvash*tri* (τέκτων), is likewise fabled to have forged the thunderbolt of Indra (Rv. I, 32, 2), and to have sharpened the axe of Brahma*n*aspati (X, 53, 9). He is conceived as the workman of all things, as having made the various forms of all living beings (Rv. I, 188, 9), and finally as having created the whole world (Vâ*g*. S. XXIX, 9). He is called Vi*s*varûpa, i.e. possessing all forms, though after a time Vi*s*varûpa (often supposed to be a name of the moon) is represented as his son (Tvâsh*tr*a). There is very little of fixed relationship, as yet, as we saw, among the gods of the Veda, and we must not be surprised, therefore, if we see this Tvasht*ri*, that is, Agni, spoken of in other places as the father of Agni (Rv. X, 46, 9), nay as Dyaus himself.

So much for the general conception of Hêphaistos among the Greeks. We saw that his worship in Lemnos may have been due to two causes, partly to the volcanic character of the island, partly to the presence of forges worked in the town, which was called Hêphaistias, after the god, and elsewhere in the island. In this local character Hêphaistos has become the smith, the cunning artist, the sorcerer, slightly deformed and grimy, yet strong and powerful in his limbs. The character of those whose trade he protected was naturally reflected on him, but in spite of these somewhat homely features, we must never forget that Hêphaistos, as the god of fire, was originally one of the great Olympian deities, the child of Zeus and Hêre, and that the most beautiful of the Greek goddesses was, for some sufficient reason, given him as his wife.

It is clear even from these few coincidences between Vedic and Greek mythology that it would be a mistake to expect a whole cluster of names and myths connected with fire to be the same in India and in Greece. As in comparing the two languages we find but few compounds, still fewer phrases, the same in Greek and Sanskrit, such as εὐεστώ = sv-asti, δωτῆρες ἐάων = dátá vásûnâm, rátám astu = ratum-esto [1] ; we must not expect any more to find composite stories of gods the same in the Veda and in Homer. What we find are the floating atoms, the mythological

---

[1] K. Z., viii, p. 64.

roots or germs, growing up independently each on its own soil, so that in their later growth, as we watch it in the mythologies known to us, they are often changed beyond all recognition. A kaleidoscope well shaken seems to give the best idea of the ever-varying aspects of ancient Aryan mythology. While Agni in India gave rise to an abundant growth of mythology, we find ignis in Latin perfectly sterile mythologically. We find Agni represented as Tvash*tri* in the Veda, the clever workman, in Greek κλυτοτέχνης, πολύμητις, χαλκεύς, the smith, but likewise the maker or creator of all things, while in the Greek Sagas Hêphaistos became a well-marked legendary figure, involved in many more or less creditable adventures, but never, even in his few local sanctuaries, rising to the rank of creator and ruler of the world.

Bhura*n*yu = Phorôneus.

We have now to look at another word, which in the Veda is applied to Agni, and which has left some traces in Greek. Bhura*n*yu is an epithet of Agni in the Veda, and is, as I showed in the chapter on Phonetics, the same word as Phorôneus in Greek. It is derived from bhur, to move quickly; and, as applied to the fire, it means moving, glittering, flickering, blazing. Bhur may be a secondary form of bhar, if bhar ever had the meaning of vah, to carry, from which we have vehemens, carried along, and Sk. vahni, fire, as the name of Agni has been connected with ag-ilis in the sense of moving quickly. Bhura*n*yati occurs in the sense of bubbling, stirring, and bhura*n*yu would be a regular derivative of that verb. The Greek Φορωνεύς, if not exactly the same word, is clearly derived from the same root[1], and this is all we have any right to expect in mythological names. Phorôneus, however, in Greek mythology is no longer the name of a god, least of all of the god of fire. It is the name of a mythical king in the Peloponnêsos, who must have occupied an important place in ancient Greek mythology, but of whom we do not know much more than that he induced the people now scattered in Argos to live together, that he founded a town, and that he instituted sacrifices to Hêre. If, as Pausanias tells us, he was also supposed to have been the discoverer of fire, we can hardly hesitate to recognise in him a representative of the fire, a kind of Hêphaistos or Promêtheus, only lost in local legends and probably little known in later times beyond the confines of Argos. He is connected, however, with the general mythology of Greece by being represented as the father both of Îo and of Niobe. There are traces also of his having once been considered as the father of all mankind[2], and a famous poem is mentioned, the Phorônis, which would have told us more of what the Greeks believed about him. His mother, Melia, the ash-tree, may likewise contain a recollection of the fire, in very ancient times, having been obtained from the wood of that tree by friction, just as Agni is said to have been born alive from dry wood, Rv.

---

[1] Certain phonetic difficulties have been fully discussed by Kuhn (Herabkunft des Feuers, p. 27); and need not be discussed here again. Pott re-opened the question in Kuhn's Zeitschrift, ix, p. 342, but left it much as it was. We know now that there was even in Sanskrit a form bharanyu by the side of bhuranyu, which removes all difficulties.

[2] Plato, Timaeus, p. 22.

I, 68, 2 : Sushkát yát deva *gîváh gánishtháh*. If fire was represented as the first of men, or as the half-divine ancestor of families and clans, the firewood (Melia)[1] would naturally claim the place of the first mother, the ancestress of mankind.

His father Inachos was evidently meant for the river in Argos, on the shores of which Phorôneus established his settlements.

It might seem as if we did not gain very much by being able to connect Phorôneus with Bhura*n*yu, and by discovering in Bhura*n*yu a name of fire and its original meaning of vehement. And yet these are very important discoveries as connected with the general problem of mythology. Instead of leaving us with the bare statement that Phorôneus was the son of Inachos (river) and of Melia (ash-tree), we can now recognise in him one of the many names of fire ; we see in fact a god changed as it were before our eyes into a local hero, and we learn also that fire was recognised as the sine quâ non of social and civilised life. Fire was the first step in civilisation, and in the hymns of the Rigveda the enemies of the Âryas are spoken of as without fire, or as not keeping the fire (anagnitráh)[2]. It was from this point of view that Phorôneus could be looked upon as the founder of towns (ἄστυ φορωνικόν), and as the ancestor of the royal family of Argos, just as Agni in the Veda was conceived as Vi*sh*pati, the lord of clans, and as the ancestor of various families. In this way both his father and mother

---

[1] Kuhn takes Melia to be one of the Melian nymphs, originally a cloud holding the fire of lightning.

[2] Rv. I. 189, 1-4 ; Winternitz, Sarpabali, p. 25 ; M. M., Letter on Turanian Languages, p. 85.

become intelligible, and instead of an unmeaning myth, we get simple and natural ideas of the ancient world expressed in language that was equally simple and natural so long as it was rightly understood. Lastly, unless we chose to look on two such words as Bhura*n*yu and Phorôneus as the result of mere accident, or of two independent acts, we gain the conviction that before their final separation, the Aryan speakers possessed a common fund of mythological names, and thus learn once more the lesson that if on one side we must not look for an elementary deity of fire in Greece, we ought not on the other to try to discover either the river Inachos or the tree Melia in India.

Vulcanus. Ulkâ.

Let us now look back once more to Vulcanus and Hêphaistos. We found no god Ignis in Latin, corresponding to the Vedic Agni, nor do we find in the Veda a god having the name of Vulcanus. Still what we find, little as it may seem, is of some importance. The formation of the name Vulcanus is thoroughly Latin, nus being a Latin derivative. And in the base Vulca even so early a student of Sanskrit as Schlegel easily discovered the Sanskrit Ulkâ, a firebrand, a flame, a word which, as I showed in Kuhn's Zeitschrift of 1869, really occurs in the Veda under a slightly different form. There we read, Rv. IV, 4, 2: Âsandita*h* ví s*r*iga víshvak ulkâ*h*, 'Being unrestrained, O Agni, send out thy sparks in all directions.' This ul in ulkâ is, however, a contraction only of val or var, and it was Grassmann who in 1867 (K. Z., xvi, p. 164) pointed out a number of passages in the Rig-veda in which várkas occurs in the sense of fire or light. Rv. III, 22, 2 : Ágne yát te diví várkas prithivyā́m yát óshadhîshu apsú ā́ yagatra, 'O Agni, what light of thine is in heaven, on earth, in the plants, and in the waters!'

Rv. IX, 66, 21 : Ágne pávasva svápāh asmé várkah suvī́ryam, 'Agni, thou who art clever, pour upon us light and strength.'

Agni himself is called suvárkas (I, 95, 1), pâvakávarkas (X, 140, 2), sukrávarkas (X, 140, 2), and though other gods also are praised as possessing or giving varkas, yet Agni is most frequently represented as endowed with this peculiar glowing splendour. Thus, although we find no form exactly corresponding to Vulcanus, and have in fact no right to expect it, we cannot doubt that Vulcanus, who has no etymological background in Latin, received his name from an ancient Aryan word which survived in the Vedic varkas, and has possibly left some trace in the Greek ἤλεκτρον, and in the names of Êlektra and Êlektryone[1], so that we can see in language an unbroken chain between the Vulcan as worshipped by Etruscans and Romans, and the electric light so highly prized in our own houses.

Fêronia.

The Latin Fêronia also is connected with Bhura*ny*u and Phorôneus. The u of Bhura*ny*u is secondary, as we see from Bhara*ny*u, which is likewise given as an actual name of fire. In Phorôneus we have the primary vowel, and this appears as long in Fêronia.

---

[1] These words may, however, be derived equally well from a root ark, from which arka, sun, arkis, splendour. See Curtius, Grundzüge, p. 137.

The goddess Fêronia can hardly have received her name from the town of Feronia at the foot of Soracte, where her festival was celebrated at great annual meetings. It is more likely that the town received its name from her. Though little is known of her, yet there are several indications that point to fire as her original character. The Hirpi, priests officiating at her festivals, walked barefoot over burning coals, a feat performed to the present day by priests and sorcerers in several parts of the world, and lustrations are mentioned as performed by means of fire by these shepherd-priests. In the Veda also there is a legend of Bh*rigu* who, though roasted on coals, was not burnt. Other sanctuaries of Fêronia are mentioned near Trebula among the Sabines, near Luna in Etruria, and near Anxur or Terracina. Here the story is told that her grove was once consumed by fire, but that when the inhabitants came to extinguish it, the grove stood before them fresh and green. All this points to a goddess of fire, though the evidence is so incomplete that we cannot arrive at more definite results.

Hêphaistos and Yávisht*ha*.

But what is the etymological meaning of Hêphaistos? That it had a meaning there can, I suppose, be no doubt, for a word without an original meaning is an impossibility. The question is, can we still find its hidden roots, if not in Greek, at least in some of the fragments buried in the ancient treasure-house of the Veda?

Let us remember then that Agni is constantly called in the Veda the young god, yúvan, probably because he is always young, never fails (a*ga*ra), but always revives even after he seems to be extinguished. This thought is very clearly expressed in Rv. II, 4, 5 : Gurgurvân yáh múhur ấ yúvâ bhût, 'Agni who when old and worn out became always young again.' I, 144, 4: Dívâ ná náktam palitáh yúvâ agani, 'He who was grey by night was born young as by day.'

But not only was Agni called young, yúvan, he was frequently called yávishtha, the youngest, not so much in the sense of natu minimus, the youngest of the gods, as in that of very youthful and always vigorous.

How would this have been expressed in Greek? By the side of yúvan there is yávan as preserved in yávishtha. From this yav might have been formed an abstract *yâvyâ, and this in Greek would have been ἥβη, youth. This is a purely hypothetical form in Sanskrit, and still more hypothetical is the next form, namely ἥφη. Yet this form also is phonetically possible. There are few instances of a Sanskrit v being replaced by φ in Greek, but there is a well-known instance of v after s in svás = σφός, and that the change here is not necessitated by the preceding s, is proved by svâdu = ἡδύς, svap = ὕπνος, &c. Next it has been shown that the radical vowel is sometimes lengthened before the superlative suffix, as in drâghishtha, and that in Zend the final vowel of the base has sometimes been preserved before the same suffix, as in stâva-esta = Sk. sthavishtha. This would give us in Zend a possible form yâvaesta, and this would correspond letter by letter to Greek Ἥφαιστος. I am not so ignorant of the organic growth of the Greek language as to imagine that any ordinary noun or verb in that language could be accounted for in this roundabout way. Yet we have to admit again and again Greek and Latin words without an exact counterpart in Sanskrit. We have unus and οἴνη, but in Sanskrit there is no ena in the sense of one, but only eka. And in Hêphaistos we are dealing with a proper name, a mythological name, and we ought to take into account the very strong material evidence supplied by yávish*tha*, one of the constant epithets of Agni in the Veda. But though no scholar would give up the right of applying to proper names a different measure from that which we apply to all other words, I give my etymology for no more than what it is worth. It is a hypothesis and no more. Only I do not understand the triumphant air with which it has been announced that such a word as yâvyâ never existed. Who ever said that it did? Neither did svârâ exist for Hêre, though Svaryâ (Sûryâ) existed; nor Svarânâ, and yet we have Selêne. Such things require no repeating or explaining, they form the first steps in Comparative Philology. Nor do I see that we can ever give more than hypotheses when we deal with times so distant as that which gave rise to the first Aryan mythology. Still a hypothesis may grow stronger and stronger, and in our case it does grow stronger when we see how the same irregularities occur in the proper names of other mythologies also. We must not postulate what we have not proved our right to expect, and we have no right to expect that in ancient times proper names should have been miraculously preserved from the misfortunes to which we see them exposed at all times and in all countries.

Fire-totems.

We saw before by how easy and intelligible a process fire was changed into what we call a divine or half-divine person, who was supposed to have produced the fire, to have used it himself for various purposes, and to have taught its use to all the dwellers on earth. This process which we can watch in different mythologies, among Aryan people seems to me to leave nothing unexplained. The thoughts embodied in it are such as might arise in our own minds, if we placed ourselves on the level of that incipient civilisation which we have a right to presuppose among the early Aryan settlers in their common Aryan home, or even in the countries where they afterwards migrated, whether India, Persia, Greece, or Italy. However, if we are assured that there are some dark points left, and that these might be illustrated and rendered more intelligible by what are called fire-totems among the Red Indians of North America, let us have as much light as we can get. Totemism, such as we know it among the nomads of the Northern American continent, was a natural growth. There is humanity in it, and if but rightly understood, there is reason in it; nor do I see why the same human tendencies which led to a belief in real totems, should not have led now and then among Greeks and Romans to manifestations similar to those of the Five Nations. If we accept the accounts of students of Red Indian customs, a tribe that prided itself on the possession of fire, or on the possession of a knowledge of producing fire whenever it was wanted, would be distinguished by a totem or symbolic sign of fire, they would be called fire-men by their neighbours, and they would themselves look upon their totem of fire, whether in the form of an eagle (φλεγύας, black eagle) or a hawk or any other animal, as something sacred, something superhuman, which is not far from something divine. All this is perfectly intelligible even without the name of totem, a name that requires careful definition, whenever it is used for the purpose of comparison with customs among non-American tribes, or with a view of explaining them. Agni is called the hawk of heaven (Diváh syená, Rv. VII, 15, 4), the śakuna bhuraṇyu, and hiraṇyapaksha (Vâg. S. XVIII, 53), the swift bird, the gold-winged. We should say that these were poetical expressions for Agni in his character of sun or lightning; but if others think that it is helpful to call such names survivals of totemism, who would object?

The fire-totem, we are told, would thus naturally have become the god of the Indians, whether in the East or in the West, and being believed to have been the benefactor of their ancestors, he would himself be spoken of as the ancestor of their race. It is true that we have no evidence of any Aryan race having actually passed through this North-Indian process, but this need not prevent us from having recourse to it, supposing always that it could serve as an illustration of what would otherwise seem difficult to explain in Greek and Vedic mythology, namely the use of the same name for a god or half-god, for a king or ancestor of a whole race, and lastly for the race itself. Only whatever totemistic antecedents may be discovered behind Agni, we should be satisfied with knowing that Bhuraṇyu, for instance, was an epithet of Agni or fire in the Veda, that in Greek Phorôneus was changed into the inventor of fire, the founder of the Phorônic city, the ancestor of the Phorônic family, and lastly, the ancestor of the whole human race, so far as it could be seen within the narrow sphere of any settlement on Greek soil. There are several similar, if not quite identical cases in Vedic mythology.

Atharvan.

Thus, if we look for analogies, first of all in the Veda, we find that Atharvan, though never used as a name of Agni, was originally the name of a fire-priest (Athar, fire, Zend atar), and, like other names of the same character, became the name of a whole race, and of the ancestor of that race.

Aṅgiras.

Aṅgiras, again, originally a name of fire, is known in the Veda as the name of a family addicted to the worship of Agni, and likewise as the name of the reputed ancestor of that family.

And here I may add, at once, that though I fully agree that Aṅgiras meant originally fire, I have always felt more than doubtful when it was stated that Aṅgiras was the same word as the Persian angara (ἄγγαρος), a mounted courier, such as were kept ready at regular stages throughout the Persian Empire for carrying royal dispatches. It is true that Aṅgiras is a name of Agni, and that Agni was the messenger between gods and men, but this would hardly fit the word to be the name for an ordinary courier, even supposing that the Sanskrit Aṅgiras was correctly represented in Persia by Angara. And it should be remembered that the Persian word Angara could hardly have been known in Greece before the Persian war; it seems first to have been used by Aeschylos. The next argument in support of Angara being the same as Aṅgiras, and meaning messenger, seems to me to weaken rather than to strengthen the equation Angara = Aṅgiras. We are told that the Greek Angelos, a messenger, used at a much earlier time, was likewise a modification of the Persian Angaros. Is that possible? We have not only ἄγγελος, but ἀγγέλλω, ἀγγελία, &c., long before the Persian wars. Homer constantly uses ἀγγέλλω, and not in the narrow sense of acting as a mounted courier, but of announcing or reporting in general. Phonetically the transition from Angaros to angello would be irregular, and the idea that in our Angels we have lineal descendants of the Vedic Aṅgiras, pleasant as it may sound to some ears, will certainly have to be surrendered. The old etymology of ἀγγέλλω for ἀναγέλλω (see ἀγγράφω for ἀναγράφω) from ἀνα and γερ in γῆρυς, &c., though not without difficulties, is decidedly preferable, unless we choose to confess that the origin of angels is altogether unknown.

We now return to the question whether there are other names besides Phorôneus, Atharvan, and Aṅgiras, which show that Âryas of Greece and India possessed names for fire and fire-priests in common, before they separated.

Bhrigavâna.

There is the well-known epithet of Agni, viz. bhrigavânah, meaning brilliant: as in Rv. IV, 7, 4 :—

Âsúm dûtám Vivásvataḥ vísvâḥ yáḥ karshanîḥ abhí

Â gabhruḥ ketúm âyávaḥ bhrigavânam visó-vise.

'Men have brought on their bright banners the quick messenger of Vivasvat, who comes towards all men, who is brilliant to every house.'

Rv. I, 71, 4:—

Máthît yát îm víbhritah Mâtarísvâ grihó-grihe syetáh gényah bhût,

Át îm rágñe ná sáhîyase sákâ sán â dûtyàm bhrí-gavânah vivâya.

'When Mâtarisvan had produced him by attrition, the noble one who was brought to many places, came to every house. Then the brilliant (Agni) undertook the messengership (for the mortal) as for a mightier king, being attached to him.'

It seems that bhrígavâna was formed from Bhrígu, like vásavâna from vásu, but its meaning is not simply Bhrígu-like, but brilliant, shining.

This brilliant being produced by friction by Mâtarisvan, the messenger of Vivasvat, is clearly Agni. But in this case, as in that of Atharvan, we do not find Bhrígu any longer as the name of a god, but only as that of his worshippers, the old race of the Bhrígus. These Bhrígus are said to have discovered Agni (X, 46, 2), to have brought him to men (I, 58, 6), to have kept him in the wood (VI, 15, 2). They received him from Mâtarisvan (the wind), who lighted him when he was hidden (III, 5, 10). In later times the Bhrígus were chiefly known as a famous family in India, like the Aṅgiras and the Atharvans (Rv. X, 14, 6), and many Rishis, like Saunaka, and heroes, such as Parasurâma, were proud of belonging to it. When Krishna wants to say that he is or was the best of everything, he says that among the Rishis he was Bhrígu (Bhagavadgîtâ X, 25). In all this there may be hidden traces of totemism, though I must confess I cannot see them. The etymology of the name was known to the ancient Vedic interpreters, and Yâska (Nir. III, 17) says: Ar/ishi Bh*r*iguh sambabhûva, Bh*r*igur bh*r*ig-yamâno na dehe*s*ṅgâreshu, Aṅgirâ aṅgârâ, aṅkanâ, 'Bh*r*igu was born in the light, Bh*r*igu though being fried or scorched was not burnt in the coals. The Aṅgiras are the Aṅgâras (coals), they are so-called because they mark.'

Differing from Kuhn (p. 18) and others, I take dehe not as a locative of deha, but as the perf. pass. of dah, he was burnt. The root bh*r*ig or bh*r*ag*g* (bh*r*ig*g*ati) which means to roast, to fry, in Sanskrit, and from which Yâska derives Bh*r*igu, is, if not exactly the same, at least closely connected with other roots, meaning to shine or to blaze, such as Sk. bhrâ*g*, to shine, also bhârgas, splendour, Greek φλέγω (φλόξ), Lat. fulgere (fulgur), flagrare (flamma). To heat and to shine are cognate concepts, as in sûryas tapati, the sun shines, lit. the sun warms, and the act of frying was taken as an act of heating and broiling, not yet of cooking or boiling.

If Agni could be called bh*r*igavâ*n*a, brilliant, or Bh*r*igu, we can easily understand now how that name became the name of the ancestor of a race, being called the Bh*r*igus, because they possessed the Bh*r*igu fire, and Kuhn seems therefore to me quite right in comparing these Bh*r*igus with the Greek Phlegyes. Kuhn (p. 21) has collected the different forms of this name, such as Phlegys, Phlegyas, Phlegyeus, while Phlegyas is known as the name of a son of Ares and Chryse, a ruler of Phlegyantis near Orchomenos, who is said to have burnt the temple of Apollon, because his own daughter Korônis had through the god become the mother of Asklêpios. He was killed by Apollon with his arrows, and condemned to punishment in Hades. According to another legend, however, he was killed by Lykos and Nykteus (Lupus and Nocturnus), and is called the father or brother of Ixîon. Few scholars would deny that Phlegys is the correct representative of Bhrigu in Greek. Kuhn has also shown that there is a certain connection between the Phlegyes and Promêtheus, because it was in the home of the Phlegyes, in Panôpeus in Phokis, that Promêtheus is said to have found the earth from which he formed the first man. This is, as we shall see, an important point, and may help us in interpreting the character of Promêtheus, as a fire-god, in his various characters as discoverer of fire, benefactor of mankind by the gift of fire, nay maker of the human race. If others prefer to call Promêtheus a fire-totem, no one would object, if only it would help us to a better understanding of Promêtheus.

Promêtheus.

In trying to disentangle the mythological web that surrounds Promêtheus, we have to follow Kuhn, whose treatise on Die Herabkunft des Feuers is a master-work that has been criticised by many, though understood by but few. It is well known that I do not always agree with Kuhn, but my admiration for his real genius has never wavered, and I fully expect that his work will in the future receive far greater recognition than it has in the past.

Kuhn has shown that etymologically Promêtheus would represent the Sanskrit Pramanthu, the name of a person of whom little is known, but whose name is closely connected with pramantha, which means the stick used for drilling wood (terebratio), and producing fire from the wood. The root manth or math means to stir, to twirl, and particularly to produce fire by vigorously rubbing one wood against another. Atharvan, Mâtarisvan, gods and men, perform this action. Math is also used in the more general sense of shaking, tearing, treating with violence, rolling. An old noun math, n. sing. manthâs, means the stick used for turning milk into butter (mantha-da*n*da), but it also means wind and thunderbolt, the thunderstorm being compared with any noisy action on earth, whether churning butter, rattling a cart, or playing at nine-pins. In Greek the root math appears in μανθάνω, to learn. Kuhn thinks that to learn meant to appropriate with violence, to carry off knowledge; I think it would be more natural to assign to it the original meaning of rubbing, grinding, handling, studying (cf. m*ri*s, to stroke, to grasp, to consider, to study). But this is a point that cannot be settled, for the meaning of 'to grind' or 'to rub it in' in modern English would not help us much.

As to Prométheus for Promantheus[1], his original meaning was that of pramantha or pramâthyu, one who rubs and by rubbing produces fire[2], not one who robbed the fire from Zeus (p. 13). Popular etymology, however, soon discovered in Prométheus the clever producer of fire, the meaning of providens or prudens, nay assigned to Prométheus, Forethought, a brother Epimétheus, Afterthought. The

---

[1] A Zeus Promantheus is mentioned by Kuhn (p. 17) from Lycophron, p. 537.
[2] On p. 24 Kuhn seems to adopt the same view.

transition from Promêtheus, the producer of fire, to Promêtheus, the discoverer of fire, the fire-god, requires no further explanation after what we saw before in the case of Aṅgiras, Atharvan, Bhr*i*gu, &c. Even Savitr*i*, the sun, is said to have made the sun[1]. Mâtarisvan, the wind, who is said to have brought fire from heaven to earth, is in other places himself the fire. Though Mâtarisvan has no longer the meaning of wind in the Veda, it should be remembered that Mâtali, the charioteer of Indra, is the son of the wind, and Mâtarisvan was probably a name of the Wind-dog, and not, as Roth supposes, of 'the lightning, swelling (svan) in his mother (mâtari), i. e. in the cloud,'—an impossible form.

If we have once recognised in Promêtheus another form of Agni, a Titan who created the fire, who gave the fire to men, who brought this divine gift from the sky, we can better understand why he should share certain characteristics in common with Phorôneus, with Hêphaistos, with Mâtarisvan, with Bhr*i*gu, with Atharvan and Aṅgiras. Behind all these names there is the same thought, though modified according to circumstances. Promêtheus is not Hêphaistos nor Phorôneus. Hêphaistos, the god, stands highest, Phorôneus, the king, stands lowest, and between the two there is room for the Titan Promêtheus.

If then in Promêtheus also we have to recognise a fire-god and a hero who produced the fire, we should expect that like Phorôneus or like Agni himself, he should also be the first of men, the creator of men, nay in the end the creator of all things, bhúvanâ *g*anáyan, as we read in Rv. VII, 5, 7.

---

[1] Âsval. *S*rauta IV, 6, 3. Oldenberg, Rel. des Veda, p. 449.

And so he is. Prométheus is not only fabled to have fashioned the first human beings, he is also represented as the father of Deukalion, who after the deluge became the father of the whole Hellenic race.

We often see how mythological characters, starting from the same point, diverge afterwards in very different directions. What helps us in tracing them back to their common source is their performing the same acts, though in a different manner. No two characters can be more widely different than Prométheus and Héphaistos. But not only do both bring fire, but both perform the same office to Zeus by breaking open his head for the birth of Athéne, and again both offer violence to Athéne. Such coincidences cannot be ignored; they are full of significance, and tend to confirm the hypothesis that both were representatives of Agni, more particularly of Agni as the Deus matutinus, a frequent character of the Vedic Agni, the Agni aushasa, or the daybreak. What Prométheus shares in common with the two is the bringing fire to men, conferring benefits on them, and being represented as their ancestor, if not their maker.

Minys, Manu.

Starting from this Kuhn takes another step which has been much criticised, but which seems to me extremely well established. Kuhn shows that in India Manu also is the ancestor of the human race, and he appeals to Otfried Müller as having proved that Phlegyans and Minyans were only different names for the same race[1]. If then the Phlegyans were descended from Phlegys, i.e. Bhrigu, the

---

[1] O. Müller, Orchomenos, p. 179.

Mînyans would be the descendants of *Mînys, i.e. Manu. The phonetic difficulties of this equation have been so carefully considered[1], and, as far as I can judge, so completely removed by Kuhn, that I need not go over the same ground again. If scholars would only spend half the time on removing apparent phonetic difficulties which they spend on starting fresh ones, the progress of Comparative Mythology would have been much more rapid, and at the same time much more satisfactory. That Sanskrit a should be represented by Greek i is certainly not regular, but we have only to think of asva = ἵππος to see that it is possible even in appellative nouns. The long î of Mînos does not vitiate the equations Μανϝαντ = Μίνως and Μανϝα = Μίννα, and the fact that Mînos, like Prometheus, is sometimes represented as the father of Deukalion ought not to be overlooked. There is much confusion, however, in the stories about Mînos. Originally there was only one, but afterwards there were two, and it is not easy to keep them always apart. That both Mînos and Manu were famous as lawgivers need not mean more than that the ancient laws were naturally referred to the first ancestors or the ancient kings of certain countries. But though in some respects there is similarity between Manu and Mînos, and though in Sanskrit Manu and Bhrigu are closely connected, there is no trace of an igneous character in Manu, nor, as far as we can judge, in Mînos.

Manu.

When we come to know Manu in the ancient poetry of India, he is already man, the father man

---
[1] Beiträge, vol. i, p. 369.

(mánush-pitá), or, as we should say, the type of mankind. He has generally been interpreted etymologically as the thinker, from man, to think; but this has been declared to be far too abstract a name for the early periods of Aryan thought. Of course, the ancient mythological names may have passed through thousands of years and thousands of changes before they meet our view. If we want, however, for Manu a physical background, we can hardly find it in the fire, but rather, I think, in the moon. The moon was called the measurer of time, and it is possible, though I say no more, that the name Manu was coined originally, like the Greek μήν and μήνη, as a name of the moon. There is a curious but obscure passage in the Rig-veda, IV, 26, 1, beginning with the words, Ahám Mánu/ abhavam Súrya/ /a, 'I was Manu and I was the sun.' Here the meaning of moon suggests itself, but as the poet goes on to say he was also the *R*ishi Kakshîvat and Kavi U*s*anas, we cannot gain much information about the ancient meaning of Manu from this single passage. Nor do we gain much light from another verse, X, 62, 11, where we read of Manu's dákshinâ as sûrye*n*a yátamânâ. We should, however, remember the story of Sara*n*yû and Vivasvat, which tells us that when Sara*n*yû fled from Vivasvat, a substitute for her was given to him, who became the mother of Manu. Now Mannhardt (l. c., p. 298) already has remarked that when in popular stories we hear of a substituted wife, we may generally take her to be meant for the night or the winter. If then this substituted wife is the night, her child would naturally be the moon. It is a popular idea, unsupported though it be by observation, that as soon as the sun sets the moon rises, and rises just opposite the setting sun. Thus Heine writes:—

> Die glühend rothe Sonne steigt
> Hinab ins weit aufschauernde
> Silbergraue Weltmeer.
> Luftgebilde, rosig angehaucht,
> Wallen ihr nach; und gegenüber,
> Aus herbstlich dämmerndem Wolkenschleier,
> Ein traurig todtblasses Antlitz,
> Bricht hervor der Mond.

But whatever the distant antecedents of Manu may have been, in the Rig-veda he is the father, also the leader of men (grâmaṇîh, X, 62, 11). He was an individual Manu, and in the Satapatha-brâhmaṇa this Manu is represented as the man who escaped from the flood. He is called Vivasvat, but also the son of Vivasvat, i.e. Vaivasvata, and a legend represents him as the son of Âditya and his second wife Savarṇâ. Vivasvat is clearly a name of the sun, while the children, Yama and Yamî, have been taken by some scholars as the progenitors of the human race. All this shows the solar, and if solar, then igneous, character of the mythological Manu, and it also explains to a certain extent why Mâtariśvan is said to have brought Agni from the sky to the Bhrigus. But manu is also the regular appellative for man, though sometimes it is difficult to decide who is meant. When we read, Rv. I, 36, 19: Ní tvãm Agne mánuh dadhe gyótih gánâya śáśvate, we may translate either 'Manu placed thee, O Agni,' or 'man placed thee, O Agni, as a light for all people.'

Again, Rv. X, 63, 7: Yébhyah hótrâm prathamấm âyegé mánuh sámiddhâgnih, 'To whom Manu or man with lighted fire offered the first invocation.'

This is a very incomplete account of Agni, but the

outlines, as here given, are, I believe, correct, and can easily be filled out by further research. The thirty-second and forty-sixth volumes of the Sacred Books of the East contain a translation of more than half of the hymns addressed to Agni, and I regret that as the number of fifty volumes is not to be exceeded, the remaining hymns will not appear, at least not in that series.

Abstract Deities.

There is, however, one more lesson which the study of Agni should teach us, and which we should never forget in analysing other gods of the Veda. However high Agni may have risen as a god, as a benefactor and protector, nay as creator of heaven and earth, and source of light and life, he started originally from nature, from the visible fire on the hearth, or from the sun, or from the fiery meteor that descended from the clouds in the shape of lightning. What we know as a fact in this case we may safely extend to other cases. All Vedic gods, nay all Aryan gods, were in the beginning physical. I say in the beginning, for there came, no doubt, a time when the concept of deity being once formed and having become familiar, invisible and purely abstract objects also were raised to a divine status. Vâk, speech, for instance, though not visible, was audible, but Mrityu, death, was merely a postulated being, and yet he also is invoked as a deity. And these cases can teach us a lesson. Mrityu, death, was evidently a secondary deity and grafted on a primary deity, viz. Yama, the setting sun, and even Vâk, speech, shows in the distant background a physical foundation in the voice of thunder.

It has been supposed that all female deities are purely abstract creations. This is not so. Some of them have their physical prototypes, such as Âpas, the waters, whether on earth or in the sky, Ushas, the dawn, with the Apsarasas, P*ri*thivî, the earth, Sarasvatî, if representing the river, and with her I*l*â, Bhâratî, and possibly Mahî; Râkâ, Sinîvâlî, Kuhû and Guṅgû, phases of the moon; possibly Aditi, the Beyond, and P*ri*sni, the cloudy sky, the mother of the Maruts. Others, such as Yamî, Indrâ*n*î, Agnâyî, Varu*n*ânî, Asvinî, Sûryâ, Ara*n*yânî, are clearly derivative, not, however, Sarasvatî. Purely abstract goddesses, however, are Vâ*k*, speech, *S*raddhâ, faith, Aramati, devotion, and these must be assigned to a secondary phase of the Vedic religion.

I quite admit that Varu*n*a also has assumed a decidedly ethical and abstract character in the Vedic Pantheon, but I hold that in the beginning he must have been as concrete a deity as Agni or at least as Indra. Even if it should be questioned that like Ouranos he represented at first the sky, particularly the dark sky, there are sufficient traces left that point to him as the chief actor in the firmament of heaven. There can be no doubt that in later Sanskrit Varu*n*a is a decidedly physical god, how then could we suppose that he should not have been so from the beginning, or should actually have been taken over ready made from a more spiritual Semitic religion? In Post-Vedic literature Varu*n*a is clearly the god of the sea and of the Western quarter of the earth; is it likely then that in the Veda he was a purely spiritual deity without any physical antecedents? These antecedents may not be many nor very palpable, but we should remember that both in the Veda and in the Avesta the waters, Âpas, are mentioned as the wives of Varu*n*a and of Ahura, and that the place especially assigned to him is called âpyâ yoni, the watery place (Rv. II, 38, 9). Varu*n*a moves along with the waters (adbhi*h* yâti Váru*n*a*h* samudraí*h*, Rv. I, 161, 14); he is fire or the sun in the evening (sá*h* váru*n*a*h* sâyám agní*h* bhavati, Ath. IX, 3, 18); he actually created the night (mitrá*h* ahá*h* a*g*anayat, váru*n*o rátrim, T. S. VI, 4, 8, 3), and hence abides in the West. In the prayers addressed he is not always asked for spiritual blessings only, but for the very gifts which a god of the sky is able to grant. Thus in a prayer for rain we read, Rv. V, 63 :—

'Guardians of the Law, ye whose nature is truth, you mount your chariot in the highest heaven; O Mitra and Varu*n*a, whomsoever you protect here, to him the rain brings down the sweet water from heaven.'

I know full well that this decided view of the physical origin of the Vedic gods, with very few exceptions, has sometimes been questioned and even contemptuously derided, and that attempts have been made to prove the existence in the Veda of deities without any physical background. But however abstract the character of certain Vedic gods has become, it can always be shown that they have either been derived directly from certain physical phenomena, or have been grafted on primary gods of a decidedly physical character.

Savitri.

Let us take the case of Savit*r*i, the sun. First of all Savit*r*i in later Sanskrit is simply one of the many names of the real sun. It is quite true that there are passages, nay whole hymns, in which the solar character of Savitri is not very conspicuous, but this applies to other gods also, for instance, to Mitra and Varuna. To suppose therefore, as Prof. Oldenberg does, that Savitri was not from the first a name of a solar god or agent, but was meant for an exciting and moving power in general, a power that pervades the whole world, seems totally opposed to the general character of the Vedic gods. Abstract conceptions such as the exciter or compeller may be grafted on other gods, the sun, the fire, the sky, or Soma, the moon and the rain. We see this even in such names as Tvashtri, Dhâtri, Trâtri, shaper, maker, preserver. Tvashtri in the Veda changes places with Agni, nay with Dyaus, Agni is even called the son of Tvashtri, but I see no trace of an abstract deity, called the carpenter or the Creator (Tvashtri), without any physical antecedents.

After a time, no doubt, the original fulcrum of these names may fall away, and a deity remains, apparently without any physical background. We can often in the Veda itself watch that process by which a physical deity loses its original physical features and becomes apparently a purely ethical being. We saw how Agni, so distinctly a physical god, becomes in the end the Creator, the king of men, omniscient and omnipotent, without one trace of his igneous[1] origin being left, and we can see the same in the case of Mitra and Varuna. What we saw in the case of Varuna, we can likewise observe in the case of his companion Mitra. Of course it has been

---

[1] Physical Religion, p. 193.

denied that his origin was solar. Instead of taking him as a reflex of the sun, his origin has been sought for in the abstract idea of friend, or of all that was friendly and beneficent in nature. But where should we find a support for so abstract a concept? If the idea of god in the abstract had existed at that early time, such a name as friend or benefactor might well have been assigned to him. But whom could the ancients have meant if they addressed him as Mitra, as friend or benefactor, if not the sun? Different though their way of thinking may have been from ours, their logic cannot well have differed, they would not have used a predicate without a subject, expressed or understood. Even Prof. Oldenberg, while maintaining the existence of deities, abstract from the very beginning, seems to have felt this necessity of a visible object, as the starting-point of Mitra, and he therefore looks upon him as possibly an old fetish, nay he sees in his epithet, sarpi*h*-âsutim (Rv. VIII, 74, 2), an indication of this fetish having been anointed with butter (see also Rv. V, 3, 2). Here we see the danger of comparing heterogeneous myths and customs. First of all, an image or idol is totally different from a fetish, secondly a fetish, as far as I know, is not commonly anointed with butter, and thirdly, if Mitra were a mere fetish, why should not all the Vedic gods have descended from fetishes? Mitra was so clearly a solar deity that among the ancients at all events, that is, among those who believed in him and worshipped him, no one has ever dreamt of him as a fetish in the true sense of that word.

Nor has Savit*ri* by any means lost his solar characteristics altogether. If we compare, for instance, the hymns addressed to Sûrya, the sun, with those addressed to Savitri, we find the same solar elements in both. That the etymological meaning of Savitri was present to the minds of the poets is very clear from the frequent use of su and derivatives of su in the hymns addressed to him. Thus we read, Rv. V, 81, 2 :—

> Vísvâ rûpâ*ni* práti muñ*k*ate kavíh
> Prá asâvît bhadrám dvipáde *k*átushpade,
> Ví nâkam akhyat Savitâ várenya*h*
> Ánu prayâ*n*am Ushása*h* vi râ*g*ati. 2.
> Utá yâsi Savita*h* trî*n*i ro*k*anâ,
> Utá sûryasya ra*s*míbhi*h* sám u*k*yasi,
> Utá râtrîm ubhayáta*h* pári îyase,
> Uta Mitrá*h* bhavasi deva dhármabhi*h*. 4.
> Utá îsishe prasavásya tvám ókah ít,
> Utá Pûshâ bhavasi deva yâmabhi*h*,
> Utá idám vísvam bhúvanam ví râ*g*asi,
> Syâvâ*s*va*h* te savita*h* stómam ânase. 5.

'The wise (Savitri) takes all forms, he has sent (asâvit) prosperity to man and beast, the excellent Savitri has illumined the sky and shines after the procession of the Dawn. 2.

'Thou, Savitri, goest to the three bright places, and thou delightest with the rays of the sun, thou surroundest the night on both sides, and thou, O god, becomest Mitra by thy deeds. 4.

'Thou alone art the lord of creation (prasava), and on thy paths, O god, thou becomest Pûshan ; thou lightest up this whole world, O Savitri ; I, Syâvâ*s*va, have got this praise for thee!' 5.

Now, I ask, can there be a doubt that the poet conceived Savitri as a solar deity, as the agent behind the sun, and that he was fully aware at the same time that his name was derived from the root su in the sense of exciting, enlivening, or begetting. It is quite true that the name of Savitri, like every other name, is derived from a root which conveys a general concept, and that Savitri meant enlivener; but that predicate presupposed as its subject one object only, namely, the sun, and would for that very reason have never been applied to any other enlivener, whether the rain, or the moon, or the wind. After all, our own word for sun is probably derived from the same root su from which we have Savit*ri*, but no one doubts that it was meant as a name of the sun and of the sun only. If sunus in Gothic is the begotten (suta), sunna in Gothic can only have been meant for the sun as the begetter, the enlivener, as the Savit*ri*. In the hymn of the Rig-veda, Savit*ri* is felt as he who quickens nature and men, not as an unknown somebody, but most distinctly as the sun. In several passages his name Savit*ri* appears actually by the side of Sûrya. Thus when Savit*ri*, the Asura, is said to brighten up the sky, it is asked, I, 33, 7, where was then Sûrya? Again in X, 189, 4, when Savit*ri* arises, it is said that Indra saw the enclosures of Sûrya.

In V, 81, 4, we read that Savit*ri* goes to the heavens, that he is united with the rays of Sûrya, that he goes round the night on both sides, and that he is Mitra by night.

In X, 139, 1, Savit*ri* is called sûryarasmi, clad in the rays of the sun, and rising in the East.

Like the sun, Savit*ri* has his chariot, I, 35, 5, and his horses, VII, 45, 1. Like Sûrya he moves between heaven and earth, I, 35, 9; he is golden-handed, I, 35, 9, and golden-armed, I, 35, 10, golden-eyed, golden-haired, and golden-tongued. His armour is yellow, IV, 53, 2, his roads are called dustless, I, 35, 11, like the roads of other heavenly gods. Savit*ri* is constantly mentioned as rising with his rays (IV, 53, 2), as following the dawn, V, 81, 2, as before day and night, V, 82, 8, as stretching out his golden arms,

II, 38, 2; VI, 71, 1; 5. He goes up and down, seeing all things, he illuminates the air. He is even called the supporter of the sky, and praised for sending forth the chariot of the Asvins (day and night) before the appearance of the dawn. And though he is, no doubt, conceived chiefly as the life-giver, and thus as animating and exciting everything, he is also addressed as the comforter, as the pacifier, possibly as the giver of rest and sleep, IV, 53, 6; VII, 45, 1.

If a god drawn in such sharp outline and such living bright colours were supposed to have started from a mere abstraction, there would be few Vedic deities that would not have to share the same fate. The progress from the concrete to the abstract is clear enough, that from the abstract back to the concrete should be admitted with great caution.

It has been thought that there are other deities also in the Vedic pantheon which have sprung into existence without any physical support, as, for instance, Tvasht*ri*, Dhât*ri*, and Trât*ri*, but how different are they from the dramatic Savit*ri*! Their names express qualities or actions which may be ascribed to gods in general. But could we compare the pale and shadowy features of these deities with the vigour and brightness of Savit*ri*? It was long supposed that a Maker or Creator, a Supporter or Preserver, must everywhere have been postulated by the human mind, but the evolution of religious thought, as we can study it now in the Veda and elsewhere teaches a different lesson. The human mind laid hold at first of what was visible, and gradually discovered the invisible behind the visible. It began with what was concrete, and from it proceeded slowly to the discovery of what was abstract.

Even in the case of such gods as Dhâtri, creator, we may discover his physical fulcrum in Varuna[1]. We saw how some of the Vedic poets had suspected Agni in the background of Tvashtri, as well as of Vidhartri, III, 2, 3; 5; while in other places Tvashtri was actually represented as the father of Agni, I, 127, 9, nay as the father and the husband of Saranyû.

Reluctant as I always feel to differ from Prof. Oldenberg, Savitri seems to me to have been conceived throughout as an independent and visible god, visible in the sky as Agni was on earth, or Indra in the air, though, like them, afterwards endowed with a more sublime and abstract character.

Brihaspati and Brahmanaspati.

I doubt even whether we should treat such gods as Brihaspati or Brahmanaspati as merely abstract deities. Professor Roth took Brahmanaspati as an abstract deity in whom the action of the worshipper upon the gods is personified. M. Bergaigne (I, 299) changed him into ' un personnage divin qui symbolise l'action en quelque sorte magique des formules sacrées.' Hillebrandt saw in him a lord of plants and a lunar deity, while Oldenberg (Rel. des Veda, p. 66) explains him as the oldest king of prayers, the progenitor of all prayers. I must confess that I cannot enter into any one of these conceptions, and I doubt whether they would have been intelligible to the poets of the Vedic age. I retain my old opinion that Brahmanaspati was a god, grafted originally on

---

[1] Darmesteter, Ormazd et Ahriman.

Agni. (Rig-veda Samhitâ, 1869, p. 177.) The name Brihaspati or Brahmanaspati means, no doubt, Lord of prayer, and instead of Brihaspati we also find Vâkaspati, Lord of speech (thus showing that brih (word) must have had the same meaning as vâk), while in Brahmanaspati we can perceive the secondary meaning of Lord of the Brahman, i. e. of the priestly class.

I admit that these deities have assumed their own peculiar character, and have been very freely handled by priestly poets ; but I think we can still discover the fibres by which they cling to the stem on which they were originally grafted. Why should we not accept their names as originally names of Agni, just as Narâsamsa, Gâtavedas, and Vaisvânara? These names also were at first epithets of Agni, but they were afterwards invoked as independent personalities, as, for instance, Gâtavedas in I, 99, Narâsamsa in I, 18, 9 ; Vaisvânara in I, 59, &c.

If Brihaspati or Brahmanaspati seems to us to have assumed greater independence than these, this may be due to the priestly character assigned to them, as to Agni himself. Thus whenever a large number of deities had to be invoked, we often find Brihaspati in the same string with Agni, Indra, &c., and in one passage at least (X, 68, 9) Brihaspati is said to have found the dawn, the sun, and Agni, as if Agni were different from him. Here, however, Agni need not mean the god, but may be meant for the material fire, and I see that Ludwig takes it in that sense. In VII, 10, 4, however, Agni is actually invoked to bring near a number of gods, Indra with the Vasus, Rudra with the Rudras, Aditi with the Âdityas, and in the same way Brihaspati with the singers. In all passages like this where Brihaspati appears in company with the Aṅgiras, the original character of Br*i*haspati seems quite forgotten. It might be asked why Br*i*haspati should be looked upon as a name of Agni rather than of Indra, considering how some of his actions, more particularly his delivering the cows from the dark cave (of the night), seem to point to Indra rather than to Agni. But we should remember that Indra is far more frequently mentioned not only in the same string of divine names in which Br*i*haspati also occurs, but distinctly as Br*i*haspati's associate. Thus we find Indra and Brahma*n*aspati together in II, 24, 12 and VII, 97, 3; 9. Indra and Br*i*haspati in IV, 49; IV, 50, 10; 11; VII, 97, 10; 98, 7; VIII, 96, 15; Brahma*n*aspati is called the friend of Indra (I, 18, 6), and invoked with him as his ally (II, 13, 18), while Agni, so far as I am aware, is nowhere in the Rig-veda the actual associate and companion of either Br*i*haspati or Brahma*n*aspati, and this for a very good reason. As to the warlike character of Brahma*n*aspati, that no doubt would point to Indra rather than to Agni as his prototype. But we ought not to forget that Indra and Agni are twin-brothers, that they are often joined in their battles[1], that they both wield the thunderbolt and slay Vr*i*tra and perform other deeds of valour in common. Nay, by himself also Agni is said to have slain Vr*i*tra and *S*ambara, to have broken their strongholds, to be in fact vr*i*trahantama, the greatest of Vr*i*tra-killers. Hence there is nothing incongruous in all these exploits being ascribed to Brahma*n*aspati, while there are epithets applied to him which fit Agni only, and not Indra. Thus, like Brahma*n*aspati,

---

[1] M. M., Science of Language, ii, p. 613. Muir, v, p. 219.

Agni is pre-eminently the priest, Brahmâ (II, 1, 3), the Hotri, and the messenger between men and gods. If Agni is Narâsamsa, so is Brahmanaspati (I, 18, 9; X, 182, 2). If he is sadasaspati, lord of the house, so is Brahmanaspati (I, 18, 6). Both are called kavi, praketas (II, 23, 2), maghavan (II, 24, 12), sabheya or sabhâvân (II, 24, 13), saptâsya, seven-mouthed or saptarasmi (IV, 50, 4), Aṅgiras and Âṅgirasa (VI, 73, 1; IV, 40, 1; X, 47, 6).

It was in translating Rv. I, 38, 13, that the identity of Brahmanaspati and Agni impressed itself upon my mind most strongly.

The poet says, 'Praise Bráhmanaspáti, the lord of prayer, Agni, the brilliant, who is like a friend' (cp. I, 75, 4).

Here Bráhmanaspátim may be taken almost as an epithet of Agni, like darsata, brilliant; nor do I see any reason why it should be taken in a different sense, for even if we took Mitra as the name of the god (Agni being frequently identified with Mitra[1]), the meaning of the whole verse would remain the same.

Thus Ludwig translates: 'Agni, der schön wie Mitra ist!' If there were any doubt, other passages would remove it. Thus in II, 1, 3, we read: 'Thou, Agni, art Indra, a bull among (all) beings; thou art the wide-ruling Vishnu, worthy of adoration. Thou art the Brahman, a gainer of wealth, O Brahmanaspati.' This has generally been called modern syncretism[2], but there is an ancient syncretism also which points back to the common origin of gods who

---

[1] See Bergaigne, Rel. Véd., iii. p. 134 seq.
[2] Cf. Ait.-Brâhm. I, 1, 1, Agnir vai sarvâ devatâh, &c. Nirukta, vol. iii, pp. 387, 390.

afterwards became distinct. Besides, in our passage, Agni, though identified with other gods, is really invoked by the name of Brahma*n*aspati in the vocative.

And again, III, 26, 2: 'We call to our help the bright Agni, Vaisvânara (beloved by all), the praiseworthy Mâtarisvan, B*r*ihaspati, the wise invoker, the guest, the swiftly moving, that he may come to man's worship of the gods.'

As Agni is here called Mâtarisvan, B*r*ihaspati also is called Mâtarisvan in Rv. I, 190, 2, while in I, 128, 2, Mâtarisvan is said to have brought Agni to men.

I doubt whether Professor Oldenberg has taken all these passages into consideration when he declared in his last work (1895) that we must accept B*r*ihaspati as a purely abstract deity. There is no doubt that some of our evidence would admit of a different interpretation, but if we weigh the whole evidence carefully, the balance clearly inclines towards the side of the Agni-origin of B*r*ihaspati. I do not like to quote Sâya*n*a as an authority on such matters, but he too, in his commentary on V, 43, 12, is fully aware that Agni is indeed B*r*ihaspati (Agnir eva B*r*ihaspati*h*), and was so taken by native scholars.

With all this I am far from maintaining that all the Vedic worshippers when they invoked Brahma*n*aspati, or when they offered him sacrificial gifts, were fully aware that he was originally the fire, or the god of fire. He had become one of the many traditional deities, and in India no questions were asked about his antecedents, whether physical or ethical. When the people of the Veda invoked Agni (I, 189), saying, 'Lead us to wealth on a good path.

Drive away from us sin which leads us astray!' they did not mean the fire that was burning before them on the hearth, and yet they continued : 'Protect us with thy unwearied guardians, thou who flamest in thy beloved seat.'

This must suffice, and I trust it will be sufficient to enable all competent judges to form their own opinion as to whether the principles which I have laid down for the guidance of students of the Science of Mythology are justified by the illustrations given in the preceding pages or not. These principles may be summed up in a very few words.

The first principle is that there must be reason in mythology, and this principle, even where it cannot yet be substantiated in every case, should be retained as a postulate for the guidance of all students of Comparative Mythology.

The second principle, very much like Locke's principle of Nihil in intellectu quod non ante fuerit in sensu, is that there is nothing in the ancient gods of Aryan mythology that was not suggested by nature. Naturally, later historical influences or even misunderstandings are not excluded.

The third principle is that though coincidences between the myths of cognate languages are interesting and sometimes instructive, they cannot fully prove the common origin of myths, unless the names connected with them admit first of analysis, and econdly of comparison.

Comparison of Myths in unrelated Languages.

As a corollary, I should like to mention that comparisons between the customs and myths of races unrelated in language require a very accurate knowledge of their dialects as now spoken, or as spoken in former times, to prevent accidents like that of Tuna mentioned in the beginning. If coincidences between customs and myths of different uncivilised races, or between uncivilised and civilised races, can be clearly established, they may become extremely useful to the psychologists as proving or disproving tendencies supposed to be inherent in human nature, such as, for instance, the sense of shame. If, however, no such rationale can be discovered in them, we should still, no doubt, take note of them, as possibly indicating contact or even a community of origin where hitherto we should not have ventured on such a hypothesis. But beyond this we dare not go for fear of darkening rather than clearing up the ancient history of the human race, and the ancient growth of human thought. Let us take a case which in one sense at least may be said to belong to the domain of mythology.

Belief in another Life.

A belief in another life is found, as is well known, among the lowest as among the highest of human beings. Here the wish has clearly been father of the thought, and we need not look further to account for whatever coincidences may be pointed out. But when we find descriptions of heaven and hell, with punishments and rewards almost, nay altogether identical, what shall we say? Surely no more than that what was possible in the South was possible in the North, with this one reservation, it may be, that the climate of the country may react on the climate of heaven or hell. Next to this comes the belief in the migration or what is commonly called the transmigration of souls. As early as the time of the Upanishads, that is before the rise of Buddhism, we find a minute description of the migration of the soul through animal and even vegetable bodies, and very soon the idea that the new body depends on merit (karman) accumulated in each previous existence. As this migration seems to have no end, it is naturally represented as a circle or a wheel, the common emblem of eternity. If then these ideas occur not only in India, but likewise in Egypt and Greece, nay even among some of the uncivilised races of the world, what shall we say? Shall we say that these thoughts which spring up almost before our eyes in the ancient literature of India must everywhere have been borrowed from India? Or shall we say that they formed part of the original Aryan heirloom of thought, like Dyaus and Zeus, the sky or the god of the sky? If borrowed, how were they borrowed, considering that they were familiar to the earliest Greek philosophers or prophets? If they existed before the Aryan Separation, how did they travel to Egypt; and if they were of native growth in Egypt, how did they reach India? I see no answer to all these questions, no escape from all these difficulties, unless we admit that what was possible in India was possible in other countries also, that what occurred to the minds of Indian *Ri*shis may have occurred to the minds of Pythagoras and Pherekydes also, just as the numerals, particularly the decimal numerals, nay as the names for gods and god, were elaborated slowly and securely among savages as well as among Greek philosophers.

Suppose, however, that we found one single name

for hell or heaven, for the circle of existence, for merit or demerit, the same in India and Greece, in Egypt and Mexico, in the Arctic and Antarctic regions, would not the whole case be changed at once? Should we hesitate for one moment to say that the name was borrowed, and therefore its contents also?

If we found the Indian Naraka, hell, in Greek, if we found the Egyptian Amenti in Mexican, if we found the Finnish Tuonela or Manala in Patagonian, who would deny a real historical intercourse between the inhabitants of those countries in spite of all our former unbelief? But until that is done, as it has been done, even, if as yet, imperfectly, in the case of the Aryan mythologies of India, Greece, Italy, of the Teutonic, Slavonic, and even Celtic nations, it seems to me far more important for the folklorist to discover and accentuate the differences between apparently similar traditions than to dwell on the general similarity of some of their features. If we can understand why human beings in different parts of the world, and at different periods of the history of the world, should agree, we ought to be able to explain also why in the more minute details of their traditions they differ as they do.

I hope that in what I have said of the different schools of Comparative Mythology I have not spoken too strongly;—but we have a sanctuary to defend. We may all make mistakes, and who is there that is not conscious of his ignorance in following the new discoveries made from day to day in Babylon, Egypt, Phenicia, in India and in Persia, to say nothing of Mincoupies or Mincopies and Athapaskans? But whatever we do, we should do it seriously, not with a light heart. There are landmarks in the earliest history of the world that should not be moved at random. Conscious as I feel of my many shortcomings, I may assert one thing at least, that I have been guided throughout by the spirit of truth, and that whether in laying down the principles of the Science of Mythology, or in illustrating them by examples taken from Vedic-Greek mythology, I have never forgotten the grave responsibility which every student of the history of mankind ought to feel.

INDEX.

A, its pronunciation in Sanskrit, 314.
Ablaut, the explanation of the, 323, 339.
Abstract deities, 150.
— — derived from epithets of mythological deities, 151.
— — Finnish, 273.
— — supposed, in the Veda, 817.
Abstract ideas among savages, 291.
Accent, its influence on verbal and nominal bases, 337.
Accents, and comparative philology, 320.
Achelôos, Hêrakles' fight with, 616.
Adam and Eve, compared with Yama and Yamî, 215.
— — origin of men from, not an Aryan idea, 569.
Ἀδελφή, sagarbhâ, 49.
Aditi in the Veda, 57.
— supplanted Svârâ, 505.
— Oldenberg on, 556, 557.
— the Unbound, the Infinite, 556.
— wife of Tvash*tri*, 557.
Âditya, a name of the sun, 171.
— (sun), Yâska on, 485-487.
— see also Sûrya.
Âdityas, seven, in the Rig-veda, 551.
— their names, 551.
— Oldenberg on the, 552.
— and Amesha-spentas, 552.
— meaning of the name, 555-558.
Aëthlios, the race-horse, son of Zeus and Protogeneia, 524.
Afanasief, on riddles, 80.
Agamemnon explained as the ether, 73.
Agara, not aging, 116, 130.
Ag*as*, the Goats, explained by totemism, 201.
Agents, male and female, 116.
— physical, common epithets of, 116.
— the Devas physical, 208.
Aglaia, 'resplendent,' wife of Hêrakles, 772.

Agni, not restricted to one phenomenon, 45, 130, 132, 147, 479, 566.
— the god of fire or light, 45, 56, 780-817.
— usha*sya*, 46.
— the 'mover,' 114.
— different meanings of, 115.
— real meaning of, 117.
— the son of strength, 130.
— having two mothers, 130.
— the lord or friend of the house, 131.
— the son of heaven and earth, 131.
— the son of the waters, 131.
— the rising of the sun caused by the kindling of, 131.
— created heaven and earth, 132.
— as the light in the sun, 141, 147, 567, 656, 661, 790.
— and Indra, both gods of light, 144, 827.
— all the gods are, 146, 790.
— the lightning, 147.
— golden-bearded, 148.
— why represented as a horse, 209.
— the purifier of cattle and men, 212.
— his place on earth, 475.
— represents all phenomena on earth, 478.
— Yâska on, 479-483, 486.
— wives of, 482.
— follows his sister, 532.
— founder of towns, &c., 567.
— = Rohidasva, 593.
— and Rohita, 656.
— three births of, 656.
— threefold character of, 661.
— and Apollon, 688, 702, 705.
— a deliverer of the Dawn, 772.
— god of fire, 781.
— as a name of fire, 783.
— in India and Persia, 784-791.
— as a deity only found in the Veda, 784.
— ignis, ogn', 784.
— name of, absent in the Avesta, 785.

Agni, his name Aryan, but not as a deity, 786.
— the fire on the hearth, 786.
— names of, 787.
— his cosmogonic character, 788.
— as Tvash*tri*, 791.
— Br*i*haspati and Brahma*n*aspati, 825.
— Narâsa*m*sa, Gâtavedas, and Vaisvânara, 826.
— and Mitra, 828.
— the priest, 828.
— see also Indrâgnî.
— called yúvan, yávish*th*a, 802.
— the hawk of heaven, 805.
Agnis, the five, in India and Persia, 785, 786.
Agriology of the future, 231.
Agryâ, the Dawn, 725.
Ahanâ and Athênê, 378, 405, 726.
Ahans, the two bright ones, day and night, 558, 561.
Ahi, the serpent, slain by Indra, 758.
Ahti or Ahto, Finnish water deity, 269.
Ahto, see Ahti.
Ahura Mazda and Varu*n*a, 125, 547.
— — — Darmesteter on, 782.
— — created Mithra, 126.
Ahura mazdâo, the sky, 156.
Ahura and Mithra, 782.
Aia, the West, 437.
Aiakos, Aigina, and Zeus, 518.
Aidôneus, carrying off Kore, 536.
Aigina, Zeus the lover of, 518.
Aijeke vetschera, Finnish, the hammer of Ukko, from Zend vazra? 281.
Aikâgryam, concentration of the mind and the senses, 224.
Air, Finnish deities of the, 268.
Aisa, Fate, an abstract deity, 151.
Aisopos and Aithiops, 398.
Aithra (clear sky), mother of Theseus, 525, 637.
— the captive of the Dioskouroi, and the slave of Helena, 526.
Akka, or Eukko, mother, Finnish goddess, 262.
Akmon, 507.
— = Vedic asman, stone, 508.
Akmonidai, 508.
Akria of Argos, the Dawn, 725.
Alêtis, a name of Fortuna, 778.
Alexander, 52, 61, 62.
Alkmênê, representative of the morning, 524.
— mother of Hêraklês, 520, 612, 613.
'Αλληγορία, description of one thing under the image of another, 73.
Allelotheism and Henotheism, 146.

Allelotheistic character of Vedic gods, 531.
Altaic tribes, five classes of, 256.
Amenti, Egyptian, 833.
America, solar mythology in, 163.
Amesha-spentas and Âdityas, 552.
Ämmarik, the Gloaming (fem.), in Finnish mythology, 267.
Amphîon, the daily sun, parig*m*an, 522.
— married to Niobe, 643.
— and Zêthos, the twin sons of Zeus and Antiope, 522, 578, 642.
Amphitryon, husband of Alkmênê, 612, 613.
— and parig*m*an, 614.
Am*ri*tas, immortals, their origin, 116, 137.
Anadyomene, or Aphrodite, 172, 731.
Analogical School of Comparative Mythology, 117, 180, 234.
Analogy, its influence on language, 318.
— and its limits, 394.
Ancestors, invoked to pray to God (Chkaï) for their relations, 243.
— of one family and of mankind, 806.
Ancestral spirits, Finnish ideas as to, 273.
— — conceived as mischievous, 274.
— — always distinct from gods, 274.
— — Wotjakian invocations of, 466.
Ancestral worship, its place in mythology, 150, 443.
— — Herbert Spencer's theory of, 202.
— — of the Zulus, 203.
— — alone cannot account for mythology, 443.
Andaman islanders, nature-worship of the, 158.
Andra in Avesta, and Indra, 756.
Andromeda, delivered by Perseus, 616.
A*n*giras, Pers. angara, and ἄγγελος, 806.
Angué-Patay, prayer of women to, 470.
Angué-Patiaï (the same), wife of Chkaï, virgin and mother of his eight children, 238.
— — defending the creation against Chaïtan, 241.
— — the same as Védiava, the Divine Mother, 242.
— — invoked at the birth of a child, 244.
An-heru, the sun as parting heaven and earth, 166.
Animal worship, Artemis and, 733.
Animism, general term, 7.
— as an interpretation of mythology, 155.
— what does it mean ? 207.

INDEX.   837

Animism, in the Benedicite, 215.
Anna Perenna, festivals and legends of, 720.
Antarikshaprâ, 506.
Anthropomorphic development, 148.
Antiope, daughter of Nykteus, mother of Amphîon, 522; and Zêthos, 642.
Anubis swallows his father Osiris, 167.
Âpas, the waters, wives of Varuna and Ahura, 819.
Apellon, see Apollon.
Aperta, old Latin name of Apollon, 681, 686.
Aphareus, father of Îdas and Lynkeus, 637.
Aphidnai, Ahidanâ? 602 n.
Aphrodite, 85.
— or Aphrogeneia, a name of the Dawn, 130, 728–732.
— and Semitic Ashtoret, 216, 385.
— not = Sk. Abhrâd-itâ, 217.
— Bechtel's etymology of, 385.
— the sister of the Erinyes, 610.
— mother of Helena, 640.
— and Nemesis related, 640 n.
— the bright sun rising from the waves, 682.
Apollodoros, the Mythographos, 103.
Apollon, his solar character, 46, 74, 123, 685–726.
— and Artemis, 91.
— the rays of the sun, the flowing hair of, 99.
— more prominent than Hêlios, 164.
— Apellon, Aploun, 370.
— etymologised by Aeschylus, 372.
— Bechtel on, 384.
— his birthplace Dêlos, the bright East, 514.
— wider meaning of, 604.
— and Hêrakles, parallelism between, 618.
— and Hermes, 681, 685.
— etymology of, 688.
— sends death, 688.
— Krêtan Ἀβέλιος, i.e. Hêlios, 693.
— his servitude to Admêtos, 699.
— among the Hyperboreans, 700.
— destroyer and healer, 701.
— and Rudra, 701, 702, 703.
— and Agni, 702, 705.
— and Mars, 707, 710, 723.
Apples, see Golden Apples.
Âpri-hymns, deities of the, 480.
— — in seven of the ten Mandalas of the Rig-veda, 490.
Âptya = Trita Aptya, 663.
Ápyâ yôshâ, the Water-woman, comp. Aphrogeneia, 565, 731.

Ares explained as unwisdom, 74.
— Bechtel on, 385.
— and Mars, 724.
Argeiphontes, or Hermes, 91.
— etymology of, 679.
Argo saved by the Dioskouroi, 639.
Argonautic expedition, 631.
Argynnis, Sk. arguni, Dawn, 371.
Ariadne, and Thêseus, 773.
Arion, a horse, born of Dêo, 538.
Arkades and Arkas, 520.
Arkadians, had they a bear for their totem? 199.
Arkas, son of Zeus and Kallisto, 519, 733, 737.
Arkas, Arkades, Arkadia, connected with arktos? 738.
Artemis, a goddess of the moon, 85, 89, 735–743.
— and Chione, and story of Niobe, 177.
— Bechtel on, 385.
— her birthplace Ortygia, 514.
— sends death like Apollon, 688.
— called Propylaia, 693.
— presiding over births, 697, 736.
— myths and cults of, 732–743.
— totemistic interpretation of the cult of, 732–735.
— and Kallistô, 733, 737.
— maidens clad in bear-skins dance round, 734, 738.
— her parents, 735, 741, 743.
— sister of Apollon, 735, 743.
— goddess of the chase, 736.
— specially worshipped in Arkadia, 737.
— her name, 741.
— where worshipped, 742.
Artemis, or Selêne, 782.
Arthur, King, 61, 62, 110.
Arturus, Duke of the Silures, 64.
Aryaman in the Veda, 57.
— a name of the sun, 171.
Aryan mythology, what is called primitive in, 13.
— family, common myths of the, 21.
— civilisation, 185.
— and non-Aryan languages, comparison of, 189.
— and non-Aryan mythologies, comparisons of, 192.
— and Semitic mythologies, 213.
— vowels, 312, 316.
— vowels and their legitimate changes, 336.
— mythology suggested by nature only, 830.
Aryapatnî = Devapatnî, 772.
Âryas and Iroquois, 186.
Ascoli on gutturals, 350, 353, 356.

Ascoli on ἕβδομος and ὅγδοος, 395 n
Ashtoret and Aphrodite, 216.
Asklēpios, son of Apollon, 701.
Âsmân, Persian for sky, 508.
Asôpos, father of Aigina, 518.
Asru and δάκρυ, 396.
Assimilation. J. Schmidt on, 345.
Astarte and Aphrodite, 732.
Asteria, the starry sky, 514.
Astynome, for Semitic Ast Naama, 216.
Asura, living, 116.
— Varuna, or Ahura mazdâo, 156.
— name of Varuna in the Veda, 783.
Asuras and Devas, old and new gods, 446, 447.
Asvâ, the dawn, 48.
Asvinau, see Asvins.
Asvins and Helena, 48.
— the two, in the Veda, 48, 50.
— as two kings, 48, 134.
— at the marriage of Sûryâ with Soma, 94, 559, 582.
— explained as the morning and evening stars, 133.
— morning and evening, light and darkness, &c., 133, 138.
— derived from asvâ, dawn, 134, 542, 564.
— the lovers of Sûryâ, 138.
— and the Lettish God-sons, 433.
— descendants, or men of Dyaus, 529, 559, 580.
— birth of the, 539, 541.
— darkness and light, inseparably united, 541.
— identified with Dyâvâ-prithivyau, Ahorâtrau, &c., 541, 544.
— their relations, 558.
— and other dual gods and heroes, 558-651.
— names and legends of, 559.
— Yâska on the, 565, 603, 608.
— the children of Sindhu or the sea, 565.
— meaning of the myth of the, 565.
— other names of the, 579.
— and the Dioskouroi, 580, 600.
— as temporal gods, 583.
— their achievements, 583.
— rescue Vandana, 590.
— bring to light hidden gold, 590, 594.
— restore Vishnâpû to Visvaka, 592.
— replace leg of Vispalâ, 592.
— as helpers in general, 592.
— restore eyes of Rigrâsva, 593.
— their true and undefined character, 600.
Athapaskans, 833.

Atharvan, fire-priest, and name of a race, 806.
Atharva-veda, its age and importance, 461.
Athêne or Athêna, daughter of Mêtis, 72.
— produced from the head of Zeus, 72, 530, 725, 793.
— explained as wisdom, 74.
— Bechtel's etymology of, 378.
— and AhanÂ, 378, 405, 655, 726.
— and Zend atar, 408.
— and Hermes, 682.
— the Dawn, 725-728.
Atli in Norse mythology, 64.
Âtman, the Self, the root of all gods, 475, 476, 478.
Atotarho, Iroquois chief, 70.
Atri rescued by the Asvins, 589.
— Saptavadhri and Vadhrimati, 595.
Attila, king of the Huns, 64.
Aufrecht, 628.
Auge, a name of Ilithyia and the Dawn, 697.
— 'sunlight,' 772.
Augeias, stable of, and the dark stable kept by Vritra, 620.
Auguria taken by an army on its march, Ihering on, 460.
Aurora, Ἠώς, Ushâs, 116.
Avesta, myths of the Rig-veda and, 2.
Ayava, Sk., dark half of the moon, aia? 438 n.
Azyrava, goddess of the Mokshanes, 241.

BAAL, a Semitic Sun-god, 162.
Bâbu rezati, 'to saw the old woman,' 718.
Bahrâm from Vritraghna, 694.
Bantu languages, prefix-repetition in the, 191.
Barâ (Hebrew), to create, 511.
Barard, M. Victor, on Greek gods as derived from Semitic sources, 216.
Barth on the physical character of the Vedic gods, 445.
Bartholomew, various forms of, 401.
Bastholm, 28.
— on nature-worship, 159.
— on the feeling of shame, 289.
Bechtel, Indogermanische Lautlehre, 344.
— on the etymology of Dionysos, 372.
— on the etymology of Kerberos, 374.
— his mythological etymologies, 374.
— on Tritogeneia and Trito, 376.
Becoming of letters, 333, 353, 395.

INDEX.

Beehive, the world as a, 239.
Bees, considered as the most intelligent of insects by the Mordvines, 239.
Belief in another life, 831.
Bellerophon, his mother Eurymede, 524.
— serving the king of Lydia, 618.
Belos, Semitic, 219.
Benedicite, Animism in the, 215.
Benfey on the migration of fables, 110.
— on proper names and phonetic laws, 387.
— on γελᾶν and gval, 499.
— on gaghghatis, 500.
— winter solstice, 594.
— and Kerberos, 628.
Bergaigne on Vivasvat and Yamî, 575.
— Religion Védique, 755 n.
Berini on the Tonsure Ceremony, 230 n.
Berkholz, Dr., 431.
Bhaga, a Vedic god, 57.
Bhagavadgîtâ on the tapas, 223.
Bharanyu and Phoroneus, 501.
Bhrigavâna, epithet of Agni, 807.
Bhrigu, Yâska on, 809.
Bhrigus, a race of fire-worshippers, 808.
— = Phlegyes, 809.
Bhugyu Taugrya rescued by the Asvins, 591.
Bhuranyu, a name of fire, 115.
— = Phoroneus, 796.
Blaggaï, or 'children of accidental meeting,' in Mordvinia, 240.
Bleek, 41.
— on South-African Languages, 191 n.
Bloomfield, Prof., 53.
— Contrib. to Interpretation of the Veda, 628.
Boa, Tungusic name for god, and Persian Baga, 281.
Boar, a symbol of thunderstorm, 620.
Body and soul, Mordvinian ideas about, 252.
Bopp on the Sanskrit vowel a, 315.
— and Comparative Philology, 343.
Brahman, masculine and neuter, 250.
Brahmanaspati, an abstract deity? 825–830.
Bréal on Hercules and Cacus, 766.
Brihaddivâ, wife of Tvashtri, 557, 560.
Brihaspati, a Vedic god, 57.
— and Brahmanaspati, are they abstract deities? 825–830.
Brisêis and Brisaya, 413–416.
Brown, Robert, jun., on Dionysus, 218.
Brugmann's six series of vowel-change, 341.

Buga, Supreme Being of the Tunguses, 161.
Buller, Sir Walter L., 68 n.
Bunis, spirits of the Tunguses, 272.
Burnouf, Eugène, 2.
— on Feridun and Thraêtaona, 672.
Buto or abomination in Polynesian islands, 8.
Buttmann, Mythologus and Philologus, 195.

CACUS AND HERCULES, myth of, 766.
— etymology of, 768.
Callaway, Bishop, on the religion of the Zulus, 25, 28, 33, 203, 232.
— — 183, 206.
Campbell, J. M., on spirit-worship in India, 150 n., 161 n.
Canizzaro, 27, 34, 50.
Cannibalism and stories of Kronos, 71.
Capita, the Dawn, 725.
Carnival, burying the, 719.
Carpini on the Tatar religion, 160.
Cartwheel used for healing diseases, 465.
Casanowicz, Religious Ceremonies in the Talmud, 694 n.
Castor and Pollux, Castores pl., 581.
Castrén on Finnish mythology, 25, 105, 233, 258, 261, 277.
— on the Natigai and Nâtha, 161 n.
— on the nature-worship of the Tunguses, 161.
— on the Altaic tribes, 256.
— on Ahto and Ahti, 270.
— on Köpelit and other Finnish names of spirits, 275.
— and Georgi, 279.
— on foreign influences on Finnish mythology, 281.
Cerus manus, 511.
Chaïtan, Mordvinian god of evil, 241.
— Soltan's fight with, 241.
— created the evil spirits, 249.
— or Satan, 250.
— created by Chkaï, 250.
— and Chkaï, and the creation of the world, 250.
— — reconciliation between, 251.
— — constant struggle between, 252.
— thrown into hell, 251.
— as representing the fire under the earth, 251.
Chalcis derived from Sem. Kart, 216.
Change of place or sthânas of the consonants, 310.
Charis, daughter of Zeus and Hêre, 130.

Charites and Haritas, 95, 514, 729.
— Hermes leader of the, 682.
— Apollon's relation to the, 700.
Charlemagne, 53, 61.
Charmazd (Ormazd), as a name of Chkaï, 254.
Cheiron, instructor of Jason, 436.
Child, prayers at the birth of a, 243, 244.
Children, rites connected with the birth, &c. of, 229.
— 'of accidental meeting' in Mordvinia, 240.
— of sun, moon, and stars, 266.
Chimarloa or Simargla, Mordvinian evil spirit, 250 n.
Chimavas, Mordvinian goddess, 'mother of the sun,' 236.
Chim-paz (Mordvinian, the sun), sacrifice of a red bull to, 469.
Chione and Artemis, and story of Niobe, 177.
Chi-Paz = Inechké-Paz, 235.
Chkaï, Mordvinian solar god, 235.
— and Narou-ava, the mother of wheat, 237.
— his wife and daughter Védiava, 238, 242.
— his wife Angué-Pataï, and his eight children, 238.
— creation of, defended by Angué-Pataï against Chaïtan, 241.
— his wife Azyrava, 241.
— prayers to, 242.
— moral character of, 242, 249.
— as the god of spiritual light, 243.
— lord and creator of the world, an invisible and omnipotent god, 249.
— cannot do wrong, 249.
— his punishments turn to blessings, 249.
— and Chaïtan, 249.
— the Erzjanes allow no sacrifices to, 250.
— created Chaïtan as his companion, 251.
— the Milky Way the towel of, 253.
— called Charmazd, 254.
— horse-sacrifice to, 469.
Chkei (the same), Mordvinian god of the sky, 261.
Chormusda, a name of the Mongolian Tegni, 254.
— = Hormasd or Ahura Mazda, 281.
Chriemhild, 64.
Christian influences on Mordvinian mythology, 255.
— names, phonetic corruptions in, 365.
Chronos, time, for Kronos, 14.

Chryséis, 'golden,' wife of Hêraklês, 772-773.
Chthonioi, 46.
Cinq, Lat. quinque, 188.
Circumcision in many parts of the world, 290.
Civilisation, Dawn of, Mariette, 7 n.
Clouds as cows, 92.
Cocoanuts, South Pacific stories about, 5.
Codrington, Dr., on totems, 7.
— — referred to, 28, 33, 36.
— — on the Melanesians, 206.
Comparative Mythology, the beginnings of, 1.
— — the ethnological and philological schools of, 4.
— — founded on a comparison of names, 17.
— — controversies in, 20, 44.
— — summary of results of, 21.
— — the three schools of, 177.
— — analogical method of, 234.
— — ethno-psychological method of, 286.
— — does not depend entirely on Philology, 780, 781.
— Philology at Leipzig in 1838, 302.
— — the new school of, 318.
Comte on fetishism as primitive religion, 196.
Consonants, importance of, 348.
— discoveries in the realm of, 350.
Coreans, mourning in white, 205.
Couvade, the custom of, 289.
Cow means dawn, 92, 98.
— — cloud, 92.
— black and white, or night and dawn (Russian), 98.
Cows, meant for the days of the year, 90, 92, 763.
— three kinds of, in the Veda, 761.
— conquest of, 764.
Cox, Sir George, 181.
Creation-story in the Edda, 248 n.
— stories of the Mordvinians, 248, 250.
— of mountains, 251.
— of man, Mordvinian accounts of the, 252.
— of woman, 253.
— of the world from an egg, in the Kalevala and Khândogya-Upanishad, 282.
Cromlechs in Cornwall and in the Dekhan, 600.
Cross, see Crucifix.
Crucifix called a fetish, 195, 196, 197.
Cruel rite, 230.
Cuba, goddess who helps children to cry, 151.

INDEX.

'Culture-hero,' Hêrakles a, 52.
Cunina, a goddess who helps children to sleep, 151.
Curtius, 32.
— and his pupils, 317.
— on proper names and phonetic laws, 387.
— on Kronos, 510.
Cyrus, 180.

DADHIKRÂ in the Veda, 57.
Dahlmann on Henotheism in the Mahâbhârata, 140 n.
— on savages, 220.
Daksha, his twenty-seven daughters, 42.
Danae, mother of Perseus, etymology of, 524.
Danaides, myth of the, and the sieve of Uutar, 268.
Dante uses Giove for God, 66.
Dânu and the Dânavas, Δανάη and, 525.
Daphne and Phoibos, 3.
— Ahanâ, Dawn, 403, 636, 771.
— euhemeristic explanation of the story of, 442.
— Apollon's love for, 698, 770.
Daphnis, son of Hermes, 682.
Dardanos, Jasion, and Harmonia, 524, 578, 645.
Darija, the Gloaming (Erzjanian), 464.
Darmesteter, James, Études Iraniennes, 102.
— on Athêne and Zend atar, 408.
— on Varuna and Ahura Mazda, 782.
Darwin, 16, 38.
Darwinism, 7.
Dâsapatni, the imprisoned rivers, 771.
Dâsas, the aborigines of India, 760.
Dasra, name of an Asvin, 580.
Dasyus, or black natives of India, 212.
Dâtâ vâsûnâm, 'giver of good gifts,' 180.
Dawn of Civilisation, Mariette, 7 n.
— Sun and, 41, 47.
— feminine, 46.
— her red gown, 83.
— as a cow, 90, 92, 200, 432, 761, 773.
— Sun and, in Lettish songs, 93, 96.
— her two brothers, the Morning and Evening Stars, 95.
— Sun, Day, and Morning, as members of the same family, 95.
— — — — among the Slavonic races, 95.

Dawn, the sister of the Sun, hurls the golden apple, 97.
— the wife and daughter of the Sky, 107, 432.
— as a mare, 200, 542, 564, 728, 773.
— Mordvinian myths of the, 246.
— the luck of the day, 264.
— in Finnish mythology, 267.
— in Lettish songs, 432.
— as the mother of twins, 562.
— several dawns or agents of the, 564.
— the Water-woman, ápyâ yóshâ, 565, 731.
— Moon and, 627, 742.
— weaving and unweaving of the, 683.
— as horse, dog, cow, bird, &c., 728.
— names of the, and wives of Hêrakles, 773.
— in her relation to man, 774.
— Fors, Fortuna, 774.
— see Eos, Ushas.
Day and Night, twin-brothers, 138.
— — brothers and children of the sky, 166.
— — sisters, one bearing the other or being born of her, 167.
Days represented as cows, 90, 92.
De Brosses and Fetishism, 194.
Death or winter, carrying out, 715.
Decharme on Athêne, 727.
Dêianeira, wife of Hêrakles, 616.
— = Dâsyanâri, 773.
Deities and heroes, the agents behind certain phenomena of nature, 44.
— the dual or correlative character of, 48.
— see Abstract deities, and Gods.
Dekanawidah, Iroquois chief, 70.
Dêlos, birthplace of Apollon, the bright East, 514, 585, 696.
Deluge, the idea of it among widely separated nations, 220.
Dêmêter, 46.
— and cannibalism, 71.
— Dêmô and Dêô for, 368.
— Zeus, and Kore, 512.
— the Earth, 530-533.
— = Gê-mêter, Mother Earth, 535.
— and Jasion, 536.
— as Dêô, changed into a mare, 537.
— = Dyâvâ mâtâ? 544.
— epithets of, 544.
— and Jason, 646.
Demigods, common origin of gods and, 105, 107.
Demons, representing sicknesses, 276.
— slain by Indra, 747, 758.

842   INDEX.

Dêo for Dêmêter, Sk. Dyâvâ? 368, 537, 545.
— changed into a mare, 537.
— and Poseidon, 538.
De Saussure on Sanskrit roots, 328.
— on ri, li = ορ, ολ, 418.
Despoina, daughter of Dêo and Poseidon, 538.
— identified with Persephone, 539.
Deussen on Tapas, 222.
Deva, 43.
— derived from dâ, 57.
— bright, and god, 69, 116, 129, 171, 179.
— true meaning of, 118.
Devapatni, the god-wives, and Indra, 771.
Devas, θεοί, dii, tivar, their origin, 112, 138.
— and Dyaus, 117.
— what are the, 117.
— bright agents, 119, 136, 137.
— their names in modern Sanskrit or in Zend, 121.
— complementary, 122.
— not restricted to one single phenomenon, 132.
— the forces of nature, 135.
— human feeling of dependence on the, 136.
— Dr. Mehlis on the, 143.
— ancestor-worship preceded by the worship of, 202.
— and Asuras, 446.
— see also Gods.
Devatâ, meaning of, 473.
Deverra, companion of Mars, 713.
Dhâtri, an abstract deity, 820, 824.
— and Varuna, 825.
Dia, wife of Zeus, mother of Peirithoos, 523.
Diaktoros, or Hermes, 91.
Dialectic varieties in prehistoric Aryan speech, 333.
Dialects antecedent to classical speech, 310, 356.
Differences in traditions as important for study as similarities, 833.
Dii or Divi, and Devas, 138.
Dikshâ, mystic power derived from, 223.
— Oldenberg's explanation of the, 227.
— and Upanayana, 227, 231.
— a new birth, 227.
Diomêdes, mares of, 621.
Diônê (Sk. *divânâ), the mother of Aphrodite, 522.
Dionysos and Semele, alleged Semitic origin of, 217.
— etymology of, 272.

Dioskouroi and Divo napâtâ, the Asvins, day and night, 49, 98, 376, 516, 578, 580, 601, 636.
Dioskouroi, and the twin brothers Amphion and Zêthos, 522.
— Helena, and Aithra, 526.
— legends of the, 633-642.
— their fight against Thêseus, 637.
Dipavansa, the Nighantu mentioned in the, 474.
Dirke, Lykos, and Antiope, 643.
Diseases, origin of, 252.
Dius Fidius, originally a name of Jupiter, 151.
Divi or Dii, 138.
Divyah svâ, the heavenly dog, 629.
Dobrizhoffer on sun-worship in America, 163.
Dog, man's soul confided by Chkaï to a, 252.
— punished with having to wear a fur, 252.
— the heavenly, the sun or moon, 629.
Dogs at the doorway of the lower world, 240.
Donar, who lives in the thunder-mountain, 101.
Don Quixote, 61, 62.
Drakon, Pýthon, 759.
Dual or correlative character of deities, 48.
— deities, Vedic, representing light and darkness, &c., 145, 521.
— (twin) gods and heroes, 558.
— — Greek and Roman, 577, 609, 633.
Dviga, or twice-born, origin of the name, 227.
Dvita and Trita, 662, 665.
Dyaus, the shiner, the agent of the bright sky, 45, 120, 164, 171, 264.
— and Zeus, 50, 128.
— called deva, bright, 129.
— superseded by Indra, 142, 757.
— Dr. Mehlis on, 143.
— not mentioned by Yâska, 492.
— reign of, 492.
— history of, 492.
— and Varuna, antecedent to Agni and Indra, 492.
— a deity in the Atharva-veda, 493.
— connected with Prithivi, 494.
— feminine, 494.
— manifold aspects of, 502.
— children of, 529.
— identified with Tvashtri and Indra, 560.
— father of Sûrya, 653.
— sky, as a feminine, 783.
Dyaush-pitar, Ζεὺς πατήρ, Ju-piter, 177, 179, 493, 498.

INDEX. 843

Dyâvâ-prithivî, Sky and Earth, 271, 492, 495, 530.
Dyu, see Dyaus.

'EAΩN AND VASÛNÂM. 180.
Earth, the wife of the Sun, 237.
— as wife and daughter of the god of heaven, 242.
— deities of the Fins, 270.
— conceived as a mother, 271.
— Erzjanian goddess of the, 464.
— goddesses representing the, 530-545.
East and Easter, from root vas, 171.
"Εβδομος and ὄγδοος, Ascoli on, 395 n.
Echidna, name of a monster, 627, 759.
Echion, one of the Gigantes, 759.
Eclipse, due to Chaïtan, 251.
Eclipses of the moon in Finnish mythology, 267.
Edda (Older), date of, 65.
— creation story in the, 248 n.
Egyptian gods, animal forms of, 17.
— solar deities, 162, 165.
— religion, and totemism, 202.
Ehni, Dr., on Yama, 574, 576.
Eileithyia, a name of Hère, 152.
— and Eleuthyia, 370, 697.
— see Ilithyia.
Eirène, peace, an abstract deity, 151.
Ekata, Dvita, and Trita, 662, 665.
Elektra, the Dawn, 524.
— mother of Harmonia, also called Hêmera, 645.
— and Elektryone, etymology of, 800.
Elektryon, father of Alkmêne, 613.
Eleusinian mysteries, 537.
Eleutho, original form of Ilithyia, 697.
'Ηλύθιον, from ἐλυθ, 'l'avenir,' 697.
Emerson on the days, 264.
Enalia, name of the Dawn-Charis, 731.
Endymion, Selênê's love for, 90.
Entstehung der Götterideale, Kekulé, 110.
Eône, wife of Hêrakles, and Êos, 772-773.
Êos, the Dawn, 89.
— a woman, 116.
— true meaning of, 117.
— = Ushas, 376.
— sister of Hêlios, 652.
Epicharmos on nature-gods, 156.
Epiphany, Feast of the, in Italy, 719.
Epôpeus and Antiope, 642.
Erechtheus and Erichthonios, 368.
Êrigone derived from Erek Hagim, 216.
— the dog of, 675.

Erinyes, why they are avengers of crimes, 610.
— Saranyû, Nemesis, 641.
Erinys, Bechtel's etymology of, 377.
— a name of Dêo or Dêmêter, 539, 545.
— and Saranyû, 540, 541, 543, 609-612, 641.
Eriounios, name of Hermes, 91.
Eris, the golden apple of, 97.
Ermak-Kov, the mountain of money, Chaïtan imprisoned in, 251.
Eros, love, an abstract deity, 151.
Erse, the dew, daughter of Selêne, 90.
Erymanthos, the boar of, 620.
Erytheia, isle of, the Far West, 621.
Erzjanes, and Mokshanes, the two divisions of the Mordvines, 236.
Erzjanian riddles and myths, 10c.
Etelätär, South-wind, Finnish deity, 269.
Ethnological evidence, uncertain character of, 205, 219.
Ethno-psychological School of Comparative Mythology, 177, 178, 181, 286.
Etymological or Genealogical School of Comparative Mythology, 177.
Etymologies of mythological names, 20.
— and Comparative Mythology, 21.
— words with different, 392.
Etymology uncertain, 50.
— words without any, 58.
— a great help to Comparative Mythology, 781.
Etzel, husband of Chriemhild, 64.
— identified with Attila, 64.
Euboia, 'rich in cows,' 773.
Euhemerism, 153.
Euhemeros on mythology, 74.
Eukko, see Akka.
Europe, 506.
Eurôpia, name for Hêre, 506.
Εὐρύ, wide, 506.
Eurybia. Euryke, &c., 772.
Eurymêde or Eurymêle or Eurynome, mother of Bellerophon, 524.
Eurynome, mother of the Charites, other names of, 371.
— the Dawn, 513.
Euryphaessa, the Dawn, 88.
— = Theia, 652.
Eurytion, the shepherd, slain by Hêrakles, 622, 627.
Evil spirits, belief in, 211.
— — fear of, 229.
— — more than good ones, 241.
— — created by Chaïtan, 249.

VOL. II.   E e

INDEX.

FABLES, migration of, 109.
Fabula, how did it arise? 72.
Faith, the word for, Aryan, 448.
Fauni and Vedic Dhuni, 713.
Faunus, tutelary deity of agriculture, 713.
Faust, 61, 62.
Fay, Edwin W., on Lêto, 218 n.
— on θεός, 391.
— on phonetic laws, 412.
Female deities as abstract creations, 818.
— — and their physical prototypes, 818.
Feridun = Traitana = Thraêtaona, 2, 672.
Fêronia, a goddess of fire, 800.
Festivals, from the necessity of establishing a kind of calendar, 457.
Fetish, original meaning of, 194.
Fetishism, an ill-defined term, 7, 194.
— supposed to be primitive, 158.
— among the Fins, 189.
— De Brosses and, 194.
— Comte on, 196.
— a late phase of religious thought, 278.
— its proper place in mythology, 443.
Feu de St. Elme, the fire of Helena, 517.
Fick's etymology of Poseidon, 379.
Figona or Hi'ona, name of spirit in San Cristoval, 207.
Finnish deities, Castrén's four classes of, 258.
— minor deities, 263.
— mythology, the materials for, 256.
— — summary of, 277.
— — foreign influences on, 281.
— religion, according to Georgi, 270.
Finno-Ugrian Society, Journal of the, 235.
— — tribes, five classes of, 256.
Fins carry little stones in their pockets, considering them lucky, 189.
Fire, enigmas on the, 101.
— Mordvinian god of, 238.
— and the sun, 266.
— in Finnish and Vedic religion, 266.
— gods of, and fire-priests and ancestors of human families, 806.
— see also Agni.
Fire-priest in Russia, 784 n.
Fire-totem of Red Indians, 804.
Fires in the Veda and Avesta, 785.
Folk-etymologies, 57.
Folklore, its importance for mythology, 104.
Fontenelle, 9.

Fontenelle, quoted, 14.
Forchhammer on Python, 698.
Foreign influences on Finnish mythology, 281.
Forest spirits of the Fins, 271, 273.
Fornjöt, son of, the wind, 86.
Fors, Fortuna, the Dawn, 774.
— etymology of, 779.
Fravashis, worship of the, 150.
Frazer's 'Golden Bough,' 31.
Frederick the Great, battlefields of, 79.
Friday as holy-day, Mordvinian legend, 237.
Funeral ceremonies of the Fins, 274.
Future life, Finnish ideas as to a, 274.

GÂHUSHA (cf. Ζέφυρος), rescued by the Asvins, 591.
Gaia and Dêmêter, 533.
— and Ouranos, their offspring, 533.
Gaidoz, M., 37.
Ganapâtha, and Comparative Philology, 410.
Gandharva, another name of Vivasvat and Dyaus, 565.
Garanus, a name of Sancus, 767.
Garuda, Garutmat, 87.
Garutmat, heavenly bird, name for sun, 87.
Gâtavedas, 'knowing all things,' 480.
— first an epithet of Agni, 826.
Gender, how it influences mythology, 39, 46.
Genealogical School of Comparative Mythology, 177, 178.
Georgi on Finnish mythology, 270.
Gershâsb = Keresâspa = Krisâsva, 2.
Gervinus, 19.
Géryones, and his herd of oxen, 622, 627, 765.
Gestiblindr, riddle of, 86.
Ghoshâ, given a husband by the Asvins, 596.
Gill, W. W., 5, 25, 28, 33, 36, 183, 247 n.
Giove, used by Dante for God, 66.
Gladstone, on Greek mythology explained by the Bible, 214.
Gmdiri-Mumi,Thunder-Mother,Wotjakian), 466.
God, concept of, 65.
— committing crimes, &c., 69.
— the idea of, developed from Zeus, 149.
Gods, really agents behind the phenomena of nature, 21, 74, 819.
— their names the most important material for Comparative Mythology, 21, 117.

INDEX.

Gods, manysidedness of ancient, 49, 502.
— with intelligible names, 88.
— demigods, and heroes, common origin of, 107.
— interference among the, 135.
— ethical excellences of, 148.
— concept of, must precede the deification of human beings, 154.
— distinction between spirits and, 278.
— the thirty-three, 475.
— of the earth according to Yâska, 480.
— of the air, according to Yâska, 483.
— of the sky, according to Yâska, 485.
— by birth and by creation, 488.
— earlier and later, in the Rig-veda, 492.
— and God, names for, slowly elaborated, 832.
— see also Devas.
God-sons, the two, Morning and Evening Stars, 94, 98.
— in Lettish mythology, 433, 594.
Golden apple, the sun, 98 n., 435.
— apples, the, 93.
— — Montenegro song of the, 97.
— — the Dawn crying over the fallen, 433, 435 n.
— — of the Hesperides, 436, 622, 624.
— boat, the setting sun, in Lettish mythology, 433.
— — of Hêlios, 652.
— fleece, 83, 436.
— — and the woollen cloth of the Sun-daughter in Lettish songs, 438.
Good and evil, Mordvinian ideas about the fight between, 251-254.
— — reconciliation between, 251.
Grassmann, 32.
— on exceptions to Grimm's Law, 306.
Greek views on the meaning of mythology, 73.
— mythology, and Mordvinian riddles, 101.
— — polytheistic family-organisation, 137.
— — foreign influences on, 739.
— gods, anthropomorphic development of, 148.
— poetry, solar ideas in, 167.
— gods derived from Semitic sources, 216.
— religion and mythology, independent of Semitic, 219.
— mythological names, dialectic varieties in, 400.

Greek and Italian gods, 707.
Grimm, 31.
— the Brothers, and Teutonic mythology, 104, 108.
— on Ablaut, 325, 339.
— on sacrifice and prayer, 458.
Grimm's Law, 304.
— — exceptions to, 305.
— — a case of Nebeneinander, not Nacheinander, 305.
Gruppe, Prof., 32.
— his view of Aryan mythology, 288.
— on religion as exported from India, 528.
— on Kerberos, 630.
Guna and Vriddhi in Sanskrit, 313, 327.
Gutturals, Palatals, and Linguals, 350.
— — use of the terms, 358.
Gýmir, dwelling of, the sea, 86.

HADES, 46.
— the sun that has set in the West, 615.
— Zeus, Poseidon, 657.
Hagen, 63.
Hahn, 25, 28, 33, 181, 183.
— testing the memory of the people of Albania, 79.
— 'Sagwissenschaftliche Studien,' 109, 649.
— on twin gods and heroes, 649, 650.
Hair-cutting, rites connected with the first, 230.
Hale, Horatio, 25, 28, 34.
— — on a 'disease of language,' 69.
Haltias, Finnish spirits or genii, 271.
— of human individuals, 272.
Hamsa, swan, a name of the sun, 515.
Hara Berezaiti, the mountain surrounding the earth, 127.
Haris or Harits, and Slav. Zoris, 95.
Haritas called deva, bright, 129.
— and Charites, 129, 501, 514, 729.
— the rays of the morning, 130.
— the seven ruddy horses of Sûrya, 653.
Harmonia, daughter of Zeus and Êlektra, 524.
— Dardanos and Jasion, 645.
Haryasva = Indra, 593.
Hasta of the Fetiales, explained as a fetish, 194, 196, 197.
Haupt on Comparative Mythologists, 20.

E e 2

Hayonwatha or Hiawatha, Iroquois chief, 70.
Heaven and Earth, husband and wife, 138, 220.
— the Earth his wife and daughter, 242.
Heavenly gates, 692.
Heicks, Th., on Helena, 108 n.
Heidreck, King, 86.
Heine, H., on Dawn, 84.
Hekate and Hekatóbolos, 369.
Helena and the Asvins, 48.
— the Dawn, Vedic Saramâ, 48, 49, 108, 515, 637, 640, 674.
— the Moon (?), 108.
— a goddess, 108, 632.
— etymologised by Aeschylus, 372.
— the Dioskouroi, and Aithra, 526, 634.
Hellheim, a Finnish parallel of the Scandinavian, 276.
Hélios, brother of Selêne, 41, 88.
— the sun, 56, 88.
— the boat, and the herds of, 89, 763.
— his wife and children, 90.
— true meaning of, 117.
— in mythology, 164, 652.
Ἥλιος from svar, 172.
Hélios, Mêne, and Hestia, Aryan words, 377.
— Bechtel's etymology of, 378.
— the light that follows the Dawn, 782.
Helle (Svaryâ) and Phrixos, 83, 438.
Henotheism, the name, 138, 140.
— and Polytheism, 139.
— in the Mahâbhârata, 140 n.
— Allelotheism a result of, 146.
— in Finnish mythology, 263.
— in the Veda, 758.
Henry, Prof. Victor, 32, 80.
— — on Kyavâna and Sisyphus, 589 n.
Héphaistos, and Zeus and Hêre, 72.
— a fire-god, 89, 791, 795.
— birth of, 530.
— and Aphrodite, 730, 794, 795.
— assists at the birth of Athêne, 793.
— and yávishṭha, 801.
— — Promêtheus, 813.
Herakleides or Herakleitos, the Mythographer, 103.
Herakleitos, on the seasons, 77.
Hérakles, Alexander, Charlemagne, 52.
— a 'Culture-hero,' 52.
— his solar origin, 52, 424, 439, 520, 612-633.
— historical, 63.
— the sun's death in the fiery clouds, 172.

Hérakles and Hercules, 390, 766.
— vanquishes Kerberos and Orthros, 415.
— and the apples of the Hesperides, 436.
— Iphikles, and Alkmêne, 578, 612.
— etymology of, 612, 632.
— labours of, 617-633.
— adversaries of, 623.
— liberates the cows, 765.
— names of wives of, 772.
Hercules, Herculus, and Hérakles, 766.
— and Cacus, 766.
Hêre and Zeus, 71.
— (*Svârâ', the bright sky, 85, 504-506.
— as the moon, Plutarch on, 123.
— her name Ilithyia, 152, 697.
— Bechtel on, 380.
— and Svârâ, 382, 501.
— from vas, to shine ?), 504.
— called Európia, 506.
Hermann, G., on Kronos, 510.
Hermes, 46, 91.
— dialectic varieties of the name, 368.
— and Sârameya, 369, 377, 673-685.
— Bechtel on the etymology of, 380.
— son of Zeus and Maia, 517, 684.
— his real character, 677.
— and Apollon, 680, 685, 764.
— and morning goddesses, 682.
— his parents, 684.
Herodotus on θεός, 57.
— on Greek mythology, 104.
— on the religion of the ancient Persians, 156.
— — of the Libyans, 156.
Heroes, 65.
— gods, demigods and, 105, 107.
— and physical gods, 269.
Heros, etymology of name, 65 n.
— from Sk. sâra, sap, power, 65 n.
— eponymos made the son of Zeus, 519.
Herr and frau, things addressed by, and Teutonic mythology, 272.
Herse, the Dew, beloved of Hermes, 682.
Hesiod, his story of Mêtis and Athêne, 72.
— and Homer, systems of mythology based on, 103.
— on Themis, 152.
— first to name Kerberos, 630.
Hêsíodos, a Boeotian name, 398.
Hesperides, the golden apples from the garden of the, 93, 436, 622, 624.

INDEX. 847

Hesse Wartegg, E. von, on the Coreans mourning in black, 205.
Hessians or Chatti, had they a cat for their totem? 199.
Hestia, from Sk. vas, to shine, 195, 382.
— Aryan origin of, 377.
— in Greece, the deity of fire, 784.
Hiawatha, Iroquois chief, 70.
Hiisi, Finnish forest devils, 273.
Hillebrandt, Prof., on Yama, 572.
— Vedische Mythologie, 755 n.
Hindu grammarians on accents, 321.
— sacrifices, Oldenberg on, 325.
Hi'ona or Figona, name of spirit in San Cristoval, 207.
Hiongnu (Huns), nature-worship of the, 161.
Hippolyte, the Sun-daughter, the girdle of, 439.
— and the Amazons, 621.
Hiranyahasta, son of Vadhrimati, 595.
Hissarlik, Schliemann on, 64.
Historical traditions, 78.
History and Myth, 62.
— appeal to, 155.
Hobgoblin, etymology of, 275 n., 366.
Holda or Frau Holda, dialectic varieties of, 400.
Homer and Hesiod, systems of mythology based on, 103.
— mythology before, 110.
— Schelling on, 111.
Homines alali, 190.
Hopkins, Professor, his views on totemism, 8.
— Religions of India, 185 n.
— on Tapas, 222.
Horse-sacrifice, Mordvinian, 469.
Horus, the child of Osiris and Isis, 162.
— the sun, stories of, 165.
— son either of Osiris, or of Râ, 166.
— Sut devoured the eye of, 167.
Hruodlandus, 64.
Hübschmann on the Ablaut, 339.
Human race, feeling of solidarity of the, 67.
— — origin of the, Aryan idea of the, 570.
— feeling of dependence, 136.
— feelings with regard to the panorama of nature, 167.
— sacrifices, Mordvinian, 470.
— — for Artemis, 735.
Huxley on the Deluge, 220.
Hydra of Lerna, 619.
Hyllos (sûrya), son of Deianeira, 773.
Hyperboreans, Apollon among the, 700.
Hyperion and Euryphaessa, 88.
— father of Helios, 652.

Hyperion, the light that follows the Dawn, 782.
Hypnos, sleep, an abstract deity, 151.
Hypokoristic or coaxing names, Greek, 367.
Hyponoia of mythology, 73.
— of ancient myths and customs, 178.
— of Aryan myths, 179.

ÎDA AND ZEUS IDAIOS, 658.
Idâ or Ilâ, Vedic deity, 57.
— daughter and wife of Manu, 242.
Îdas and Lynkeus, cousins of the Dioskouroi, 637.
Ihering on the auguria taken by an army on its march, 460.
Ikshvâkus, explained by totemism, 201.
Iku-Turso, see Turso.
Ilâ, see Idâ.
Ilithyia, assisting at Apollon's birth, 696.
Ilmatar, the daughter of Ilma, the air, in Finnish, 268.
Ina and Tuna, story of, 4.
— means moon, 6.
— or Sina, legend of, 36.
Inachos, father of Phorôneus, 798.
Incantation, see Prayer.
Incest among the gods, stories of, 532, 573.
Indji, last conqueror of the Mordvines, 254.
Indo-Iranic period, 16, 447.
Indra, the agent of rain (indu), 45, 115, 131, 751, 757.
— in Vedic and Aryan mythology, 50, 57, 89, 743, 772.
— folk-etymology of, 57.
— different meanings of, 115.
— not restricted to one manifestation in nature, 131, 132, 605.
— the most powerful of the Devas, 132, 757.
— as the champion of the blue sky, 141.
— a god of light, 144.
— his nose and helmet, 148.
— explained as a totem, 200.
— why called a bull, 200, 209.
— his place in the air, 475.
— represents all phenomena in the air, 478.
— Yâska on, 483-485, 486.
— son of Dyu, 496.
— begetter of heaven and earth, 497.
— the son of Tvashtri, 560.
Indra-Haryasva, 593.

Indra and Thunar or Thôrr, Mannhardt's comparison of, 744.
— his fight with demons, 747.
— the conqueror of Vrítra, 754.
— supreme, 757.
— liberates the cows, 764.
— and Ushas, 769.
— as deliverer of women (rain), 771.
— the rain-giver, 782.
— and Zeus, sprang from the same source, 782.
— and Bríhaspati and Brahmanaspati, 825.
— and Agni, 826.
Indrâgni, Indra and Agni, compound deity, 145.
Inóchké-Paz, Mordvinian god of the day or sunlight, 235.
— Mordvinian god of fire, 238.
— the good souls sent to, 239.
Infinite, the perception of the, 292.
Ingle, Scottish, 784.
Inmar, Wotjakian god, prayers to, 466, 467, 468.
Inti, chief god of the Incas, the sun, 163.
Îo, daughter of Phorónous, 797.
Iourtava, Kardan-siarhka dwelling together with, 245.
Îphigeneia, Artemis as, 743.
Iroquois stories, 70.
— and Âryas, 186.
Isis, the Dawn, 162.
Ivan, a star, sun and moon his parents, 41.
Ixion, the solar wheel, 523.

JANUS, 46.
'Ιασίων and 'Ιάσων, 436.
— son of Zeus and Êlektra, 436.
Iasion or Jasion killed by the thunderbolt of Zeus, 436.
— and Dêmêter, 536.
Jasion, Dardanos, and Harmonia, 645.
'Ιάσων, son of Aison and Polymede, 436.
Jason and Jasion, and Vivasvân, 436, 646, 648.
Jâson, not a shortened name, 369.
— instructed by Cheiron, 436.
Jâson or Iason = Sk. Vivásvân, the sun, 436, 437, 439.
Jâson, the healer, 437.
— the Argonaut, 437.
— and Pelias, 526.
— and Médeia, 648.
Jehovah, as a name of God, 66.
Jemshid = Yima-Kshaêta, 2.
Jeudi, dies Jovis, 58.

Jewish influences on Mordvinian religion, 255.
Jones, Sir William, his attempts at Comparative Mythology, 528.
Jourtazyrava, Mordvinian goddess of the household, 241.
— goddess of the house or of the inglenook, 244.
— prayer addressed to, 244.
Jumala, Finnish name for the gods, 116.
— chief god of the Fins, 259.
— in the plural meaning god in general, 259, 261.
— the Creator, 260.
— of purely Ugrian descent, 260.
— the sky, 260.
— from jumu, thunder, 260.
— meaning God, 261.
— and Ukko, 262, 263.
Jungbrunnen, and the saisava pool, 588.
Juno, names of, 152.
— the Mater Matuta, 152.
Jupiter, Dius Fidius, Sancus, 151.
— Dyaush-pitar, Ζεὺς πατήρ, 179.
— the lesson of, 375.

KA or ancestral spirits in Egypt, 150.
Kabeiroi and Dioskouroi, 639.
Kadmos and Harmonia, 647.
Kalevala, the golden apples in the, 94, 94 n.
— and Finnish mythology, 258.
— the mundane egg in the, 282.
Kali, the waning moon, his youth renewed by the Asvins, 591.
Kallixte, a name of Artemis, 737.
Kallisto and her son Arkas, 519.
— changed into a bear, 733, 738.
Kalma, Finnish ruler of the ancestral spirits, 276.
Kalman-inpi, daughter of Kalma, 276.
Kalydonian chase, 631.
Kamadyu, Vimada, and the Asvins, 595.
Kapoet, spirits eating the moon, 267.
Kar, originally skar, Zend kar, 511.
Karalune weeps = it rains, Lit., 85.
Kardan-siarhka, Mordvinian god of the hearth, 245.
— — prayer addressed to, 245.
— — invoked on entering a new house, 245.
Kardas-siarko = Kardan-siarhka, 245.
Karna, son of Prithâ and the sungod, 180, 616.
Kastor, Polydeukes, and Helena, 48, 578.

Kasyapas, had they a tortoise for their totem? 199, 201.
Katachthonioi, 46.
Kathenotheism or Henotheism, 140.
Kavandha, a demon slain by Indra = cloud, 753.
Keijuiset, Finnish name for ancestral spirits, 275.
Kekulé, Entstehung der Götterideale, 110.
Kélou-paz or Kélou-ozaïs, Mordvinian god of the beech-trees, 244.
Kema (kindred) in the Polynesian islands, 8.
Kentaurs, cloud and storm-gods, 620.
Kerberos = Sarvara, 46, 374, 630, 677.
— 186, 627.
— etymology of, 374.
— and Orthros, 416.
— and Hérakles, 424, 623.
— and Sarvari, night, 628.
— without a name in Homer, 630.
— first named by Hesiod, 630.
Keremet, places of Haltia worship in Finland, 273.
Keresâspa = Krisâsva, 2.
Kerynean doe, the golden-horned, the moon, 439, 620, 625-627.
Khormuzda or Tengri of the Mongols, 160 n.
Koi, the Dawn, in Finnish mythology, 267.
— and Ämmärik, Dawn and Gloaming, as lovers, 267.
Komaitho, daughter of Pterelâos, 613.
Kööpelit, Finnish name for ancestral spirits, 275.
Kore, daughter of Zeus and Dêmêter, 512.
— the annual vegetation, 536.
Korych, or Owl, Mordvinian evil spirit, 250.
Koryphasia of Messena, the Dawn, 725.
Korytos, husband of Êlektra, 645.
Koudazyrava, Mordvinian goddess of the stable, 241.
Kouzma, the Mordvine who collected a ritual of sacrifices, 269, 272.
Κραίνω (κράντωρ), Sk. kṛi, to make, do, 510.
Krek on Russian religion, 215 n.
Krôtan bull vomiting fire, 621.
Krisâsva and Keresâspa, and Gershâsb, 2.
Kritti, hide, 511.
Kronos and his children, 13.
— for Chronos, 14.
— etymology of, 14, 74, 507.

Kronos and cannibalism, 31, 71.
— and Polynesian folklore, 36.
— compare Sut, 167.
— the stone swallowed by, explained as a fetish, 194.
— a god without a history, 507.
— from Κρονίωνες, 507, 546.
— connected with κραίνω, to perform, 510.
— rendered by Perficus, 510.
— the husband of Rheia, 514 n.
— son of Gaia, 534.
— and Zeus, 534.
Kshaêta (Yima) and Jemshîd, 2.
Kshana, a moment, 512.
Kudai of the Tatars, the Persian Khodâi, 281.
Kuhn and his critics, 19.
— 31, 32.
— on stages of mythology, 54.
— on solar and meteorological myths, 144.
— on abstract deities, 152.
— on Hermes and Sârameya, 369.
— on Yama, 568.
— on Apollon, 702, 703.
— on Bhrigu and Phlegyas, 809.
— on Prometheus, 810.
— on Manu and Minys, 813.
Kui, the blind, father of Ina, 6.
Kummun Ukko, or Ukko of the hills, 262.
Kuu, Finnish god of the moon, 265.
— sons and daughters of, 266.
Kyavâna made young by the Asvins, 587.
Kypris and Kyprogeneia, 368.

LADA (Lykian), Lady, Lêtô, Latona, 218.
Lakshmi, Happiness, an abstract deity, 151.
Lang, Mr. Andrew, 3, 27, 32, 181.
Language, its influence on mythology, 37.
— and thought, 37, 68.
— mythology a disease of, 38, 68.
— — Mr. Horatio Hale on, 69.
— the origin of the Devas a process of, 113.
Languages, sexless, poor in mythology, 41.
— comparison of Aryan and Non-Aryan, 189.
Lar, Buttmann on, 195.
— a Mordvinian kind of, 245.
Lautverschiebung, 353, 356.
Lêda, the grey dawn, 515.
— wife of Tyndareôs, mother of the Dioskouroi, 634.

Lêda and Nemesis, 641.
Leipzig, battle of, 79.
Lemmäs, Finnish deity who cures wounds, 273.
Lemminkäinen, the hero, mixed up with Ahto, 269.
Lempo, Finnish god of love, 273.
Lepsius on nasalisation, 336.
Lêto or Latona, etymology of, 216, 514, 515.
— the Night, mother of Apollon, 514, 696.
— Apollon and Artemis, 585.
— Night or Earth, 685.
Letters in Sanskrit and other Aryan languages, 396.
Lettish songs, Sun and Dawn in, 94.
— mythology, 430-434.
Leukippides and the Dioskouroi, 636, 637.
Leukippos, 'White-horse,' lover of Daphne, 636.
— son of Eurypele, 773.
Libyans, Herodotus on the religion of the, 156.
Liekkiö, Finnish deity of grass, 271.
Lightning conceived as laughing, 499.
Linguistic or Genealogical School, 178.
Linguo-palatals in Sanskrit, 351.
Lippert, 28.
Lituanian mythological riddles, 85.
Local names, and phonetic rules, 363.
— — loss of meaning entails change of form in, 364.
Lokapâlas, Yama one of the, 572.
Lönnrot on Finnish mythology, 233.
— on Jumala, 260, 261.
— on Lemminkäinen, 269.
Lottner on exceptions to Grimm's Law, 306.
Lower World, Finnish idea of the, 276.
Loxias, epithet of Apollon, 704.
Luceria, a name of Juno, 151.
Lucetia, a name of Juno, 151.
Lucetius, a name of Mars, 711.
Lucina, a name of Juno, 151, 697.
Lucknow, siege of, 63.
Lucretius on the Mater Matuta, 152.
Luna, 56.
Luonnottaret, or the lovely maidens of the air, 268.
Lustrum facere, burying the cycle? 720.
Lycian inscriptions, the word Lada in, 218.
Λυκοκτόνος, a name of Apollon, 93 n.
Lykastos and Parrhasios, twin heroes, 649, 651.
Lykios, 'luminous,' son of Toxikrate, 774.

Lykos and Antiope, 642, 644.

MAA-EMÄ, Finnish Terra-mater, 271.
— the wife of Ukko, 271.
— is an Akka, 271.
Macdonell, on Indrâgni, 145 n.
Maera, or Maira, the dog of Érigone, 675.
Magic and witchcraft, sacrifice and, 458.
Mahâbhârata and Râmâyana, their antecedents, 447.
Mahî, Sk. Dawn or Earth, and Maia, 684.
Mahishmatî, 45.
Maia, the mother of Hermes, 517, 684.
Maine, Sir Henry, on the slippery testimony concerning savages, 29.
Mainof on Mordvinian mythology, 236.
— — sacrifices, 463, 469.
Mama Quillu, deity of the Incas, the moon, 163.
Mamuralia, celebration of the, in Rome, 721.
Mamurius, 714-725.
— not connected with Mars, 714, 722.
— Veturius, representing the dying year, 714-723.
Mana, or Kalma, 276.
— a supernatural force, Polynesian term, 294.
Manala, name of the Finnish Hades, 276.
— 'what is beneath the earth,' 276.
Manalaiset, Finnish name for ancestral spirits, 275.
Manes, abstract deities classed with them at Rome, 151.
Mangaia, philosophical ideas on the universe, among the people of, 291.
Mâni, the moon, son of Mundilföri, 40.
— and Sol, in the Edda, 651.
Mannhardt, 31, 83, 184, 594.
— German. Mythen, 86 n., 744.
— on the 'pectines solis et lamiae turres,' 96 n.
— on Lettish mythology, 431.
— on Dawn and Gloaming, 563 n.
— on the golden apples, 624.
— on solar myths, 744.
— on Indra and Thunar, 744.
Mannun Eukko, Mother of the Earth, 262.
Manu, and his daughter and wife Idâ, 242.

INDEX. 851

Manu, a son of Vivasvat, 559, 816.
— = Minos, 671.
— Vaivasvata and Trita, 671.
— = Minys, 813.
— the type of mankind, 815.
— the moon? 815.
Märchen, Dr. Hahn on, 109.
Marco Polo on the religion of the Tatars, 160.
Mardan, Wotjakian god, 467.
Marena (Slav.), Winter as an old woman, 717.
Maria, the Sun-daughter (Lettish), and her woollen cloth, 438.
Mariette, Dawn of Civilisation, 7 n.
Marija, the Dawn (Erzjanian), 464.
Mars and Apollon, 707, 710, 723.
— and Marut, 712.
— representing the return of spring, 723.
— and Ares, 724.
Maruts, 46.
— Sk., Pali Maru, used for gods in general, 117, 259.
— as agents in thunder, lightning, and rain, 120.
— sons of the sky, 138.
— helpers of Indra and Agni, 145, 753.
— double aspect of the, 212.
— the sons of Dyaus, 529.
— and Rudras the same, 605, 706.
Mastyr-Kirdy, lord and ruler of the world, name of Soltan, 241.
Mastyr-Paz, Mordvinian god, 239, 240.
Mâtali, son of Mâtarisvan, 812.
Mâtarisvan, 57.
— wind or fire, or bringer of fire, 812.
Matsyas, explained by totemism, 201.
Matuta, a name of Juno, 152.
Mayer, R., on natural forces, 69, 112.
Medousa, Perseus sent to fetch the head of, 616.
Megha, cloud, from mih, to moisten, 113.
Mehlis, Dr., on solar and meteorological myths, 143.
— on Hermes, 678.
Melanesians, the, by Dr. Codrington, 8 n.
— Anthropology and Folklore, 206.
Mélia, 'ash-tree,' mother of Phorôneus, 797.
Melikertes, Semitic. 219.
Menander on the nature-worship of the Tukius, 161.
Môn-an-tols of the Celts, explained as fetishes, 194.

Mêne, the moon, 88, 89.
— Aryan origin of, 377.
Menoitios, 627.
Metaphorical expressions, Erzjanian, 101.
Meteorological and solar interpretation, 141.
Mêtis, first wife of Zeus, mother of Athênê, 72, 152.
Metrodoros of Lampsakos on Agamemnon, 73.
Mielikki, wife of Tapio, Finnish forest deity, 271.
Milky Way, the towel of Chkaï, 253.
Miller, Orest, on riddles, 80.
Milton's Ode on the Nativity, 62 n.
Mincopies or Mincoupies, 833.
Minor deities of the Fins, 263.
Minos = Manu, 671, 814.
Minyans, descendants of Minys = Manu, 813.
Mithra, in Zend, the sun, 121.
— invoked with Ahura, 126.
— the lord of wide pastures, 126.
— before the sun, and the lord of the sun, 127.
— not among the Amesha-spentas, 552.
— and Ahura, the divine couple, 782.
Mithra-Asura, 783.
Mitra, the Sun, in the Veda, 45, 57, 121, 122, 171, 821.
— the agent of the bright morning, 120.
— the sun the eye of, 120.
— wider meaning of, 120, 604.
— no longer the sun, but a high being, 124.
— and Varuna, or the two Mitras, or the two Varunas, dual deity, 125.
— — close connection between, 547.
— calling man back to his work, 125.
— Agni identified with, 146, 147, 828.
— explained as a totem, 200.
— friend, and sun, 547.
— Oldenberg's view of, 821.
Mitrâ = Mitra-Varunau, 122.
Mitrâ-Varunau, dual deity, 57, 122.
— the divine couple, 782-783.
Mjölnir, the thunder-hammer of Thunar, 745, 750.
Mnemosyne and Moneta, 767.
Mohammedan influence on Mordvinian ideas, 250.
Moira, Fate, an abstract deity, 151.
Mokshanes and Erzjanes, the two divisions of the Mordvines, 236.

Moluches, sun-worship of the, 164.
Moneta and Mnemosyne, 767.
Montenegro song of the golden apples, 97.
Moon, a calf, with the Slaves, 40.
— its gender, 40, 47.
— Sun and, in mythology, 40, 47, 96.
— the Sun its father, 41.
— Sun, and Rain, as brothers, 41.
— the Sun its brother, 41.
— falls in love with the Morning-star, 41.
— why he is consumptive, 42.
— the daughter of the Sun given to the, 94, 434.
— the horses of the, 98, 101.
— — — in Lettish myths, 434.
— is bald-headed, 99.
— receives the souls of the departed, 239.
— in Finnish mythology, 267.
— and Dawn, stories of, running together, 627, 742.
— is visvarûpa, 667.
— see also Soma.
Mordvines, two divisions of, 236.
Mordvinia, illegitimate children in, 240.
Mordvinian riddles, 92, 101.
— gods solar, 235.
— — agents of nature, 255.
— mythology, 235.
— — and Vedic mythology, 245.
— prayer, 238.
— philosophy and religion, 247, 248.
— religion, foreign influences on, 254, 255.
— sacrifices, 462-472.
Morning-star, the Moon falls in love with the, 41.
Morning and Evening-stars, the two God-sons, 94.
— — — brothers of the Dawn, 95.
— — — the horses of the Moon, 98.
— — — in Lettish myths, 434.
Mother of Wheat or Narou-ava, 237.
Mountains, creation of, Mordvinian account of the, 251.
— — Russian belief as to the, 251 n.
Mrityu, Death, grafted on Yama, 817.
Muir, on Henotheism, 140 n.
Müller, Otfried, on Kallisto, 519, 733.
Mundane egg in Kalevala and Upanishads, 282.
Mundilföri, Sun and Moon his children, 40, 651.
Munnu, Finnish deity who cures eye-complaints, 273.

Munro, Prof., on the union between Sky and Earth, 496.
Mużjem Mumi, Mother Earth, Wotjakian, 465.
My defenders, 26.
Μυκῆναι, and Phenician machanah, 216.
Mylitta and Aphrodite, 732.
Myriantheus, 593 n.
Myrkvi = murk, mist, 86.
Myrrha, 4.
Myth and History, 62.
Mythographi, the Greek, 103.
Mythological and historical elements, 51.
— names, freedom in analysing, 397.
— — local or dialectical character of, 397.
— — prehistoric, 403, 409.
— — comparisons, limits of, 500.
Mythologus and Philologus, Buttmann, 195.
Mythology of uncivilised races, proper use of, 7.
— fermentation of, 21.
— the influence of language on, 37.
— how gender influences, 39.
— its importance to philosophy, 44.
— its origin, and its later development, 51.
— anomalous, 53.
— stages of, 54.
— study of, changed, 59.
— its scientific character, 59.
— the true problem of, 66.
— as a psychological problem, 71.
— the hyponoia of, 73.
— Greek views on the meaning of, 73.
— ethical and physical interpretations of, 74.
— enigmatic language of, 85.
— no system, 103.
— the original elements of, 110.
— can the a priori view of its evolution be verified? 149.
— definition of, not exhaustive, 149.
— ancestor-worship not a part of, 150.
— primitive Aryan, 153.
— different interpretations of, 153.
— necessity of accounting for, 175.
— composite character of, 441.
— and epic poetry, 673.
— Genealogical and Ethno-Psychological Schools of, 732, 739.
— see also Comparative Mythology.
Μῦθος, word and myth, 21, 39.
Myths in unrelated languages, comparison of, 830.

NÂGAS, had they a serpent for their totem? 199.
Names of deities, their importance, 45.
— anomalous mythological, 55.
— Vedic, 57.
— influence of riddles on mythological, 85.
— of gods, intelligible, 88.
— of gods, enigmatic, 92.
— of the Dawn and the wives of Hêraklês, 772.
— value of, 781.
— must admit of analysis and comparison to prove the common origin of myths, 830.
Napoleon, the old woman on, 79.
Naraka, Indian Hell, 833.
Narâsamsa, 57.
— first an epithet of Agni, 826.
Narcissus, 4.
Narou-ava, the Mother of Wheat, Mordvinian goddess, 237.
— Friday the day of, 237.
Nâsatya, one of the Asvins, 580.
Nastasija, Erzjanian goddess, 464.
Nâtha, Sk., and the Nâts, connected with the Natigai, 161 n.
Natigai, Ongot, Nâts, 161 n.
Natigay, Tatar god of the Earth, 160.
Natural forces, words for, 112.
— — R. Mayer on, 69, 112.
— phenomena worshipped not as such, but as agents, 264, 265, 269, 277.
Nature, human feelings with regard to the panorama of, 168.
Nebeneinander more important than the Nacheinander in the growth of language, 305, 311, 334, 354.
Nechkendé Tevtèr, Mordvinian goddess of the bees, 239.
Nêleus and Pelias, Poseidon and Tyro, 648.
Nemean lion = Leôphontes, Doôphontes = dâsahantâ, 619.
Nemesis, mother of Helena, 640.
New Zealand myth of setting sun, 594.
Nibelungenlied, 63, 64.
— date of, 65.
Nichké-Paz, the son of God, came to act as ruler on earth, 253.
— rebellion against him, 253.
— mixed up with St. Nicolas, 255.
Nida, Sk., from ni + sada? 300.
Nighantus presupposed by Yâska's Nirukta, 473.
— mentioned in the Dipavansa, 474.
Night, fem., 46.
— and moon, 47.

Night, and clouds, 415.
Nikhâta, dug in, 590, 594.
Nila, a king, 45.
Ninya (hidden), applied to Agni, 81.
Niobe and Chione, 177.
— daughter of Phorôneus, 797.
Nirriti, 57, 590.
Nomina agentis, the names of the gods can only be, 113.
Nostos in Greek, and Nâsatya, 581.
Nouriamava, Mordvinian goddess, 239.
Nouriamava-Aparotchi, Mordvinian goddess of agriculture, 240.
Nouziarom-Paz, Mordvinian god of the night, 239, 240.
Num, Supreme Being of the Samoyedes, 161.
— (Finnish), sky, god, thunder, 260.
Numerals in Pan-Aryan period, 16.
Nut, heaven, 162.
— Seb and, heaven and earth, 166.
— and Seb parted by Shu, 166.
Nyassa people, on the moon as bald-headed, 99.
Nykteus, father of Antiope, 642, 643.
Nyktimus, father of Phylonome, 649, 651.
Nyx, the night, 56.

ODIN AND TŶR, 128.
Od-koöuava, the mother of the new-moon, Mordvinian goddess, 236.
Odkoüozaïs, Mordvinian lunar god, 239.
Ododam or totem, 198.
Odysseus and Hermes, 683.
Oidipous and Laios, 526.
Oinone and Aigîna, 518.
Ôkeanos, 90.
Oldenberg, Professor, Hopkins on, 9.
— on the physical character of the Vedic gods, 153 n., 445.
— and the Genealogical School, 184.
— Schrader on, 187.
— on savage remnants in Vedic religion, 209, 228.
— on Tapas, 222, 223.
— on Hindu sacrifices and savage rites, 225.
— on the Dikshâ, 227.
— on Varuna, 547-555.
— on the Âdityas, 556.
— on Yama, 576.
— on Indra, 752.
— Religion des Veda, 755 n.
— on Mitra, 820.
— on Savitri, 820.
— on Brihaspati, 825.
Olle Fritze, 79.

INDEX.

Olympos, the abode of Zeus, 657.
'Omne obscurum pro magnifico,' 92.
Ongot, supreme spirit of the Tunguses, 161 n.
Ophion, one of the Titans and Gigantes, 759.
Orchomenos derived from Erek Hagim, 216.
Ormazd or Ahura Mazda, 126.
— and Ahriman, and Chkaï and Chaïtan, 254.
Orsini, had they a bear for their totem? 199.
Orthros and V*ri*tra, 421-425, 757, 759.
— dog of Eurytion, 622, 627.
Ortygia, birthplace of Artemis, the returning morn, and Sk. vartikâ, 514, 585.
Osiris, the sun, 162, 167.
— Râ, and Horus, 166.
— Sut devoured the head of, 167.
— swallowed by Anubis, 167.
Osthoff quoted, 17, 22.
Otava, the great bear, Finnish god, 265.
— sons and daughters of, 266.
Oultsé-Paz, Mordvinian god of the flocks, 239.
Ourania, name of Aphrodite, 731.
Ouranos and Varu*n*a, 216, 387, 390, 416-421, 545.
— and Gaia, their offspring, 533.
— and Ouraniones, 547.
Ozaïs, Mordvinian spirit or little god, 241.

PAASONEN, H., on riddles of the Mordvinians, 92, 100.
— on the Erzjanians, 463.
Pada, Anga, and Bha bases, 323, 328.
Pâda, foot, 592.
— fourth part of anything, 592.
Paiêon or Paian, identified with Apollon, 702.
Päivä, Finnish god of the sun, 265.
— sons and daughters of, 266.
Päivän poika, son of the Sun, or the fire, 266.
Paksia-Patiaï, Mordvinian goddess of the meadows, 240.
Palaiphatos, the Mythographer, 103.
Paley, F. A., on Greek mythology explained by the Bible, 214.
Palladium, explained as a fetish, 194, 196, 197.
Pallas, father of Selêne, 89.
— Athênê, Dawn, 89.
Pân, son of Penelope, 683.
Pan-Aryan period, 16, 447.
— — dialects in the, 356.

Pancake tossing in India, and in England, 228.
Pandurang, edition of Gaudavaho, 607 n.
Pa*n*i, 57.
— cows stolen by, 761.
Pâ*n*ini's Ga*n*apâ*th*a, 410.
Panope, 'all-seeing,' a wife of Hêrakles, 772.
Panu, fire in its divine character, in Finnish, 266.
Parallel development of Indian and Greek gods, 499.
Parâv*ri*g, 593.
— outcast, 594.
— no name corresponding to, 594.
Parganya, the rain-cloud, 46, 57, 605.
— from a root meaning to sprinkle, 113.
— not restricted to one phenomenon, 132.
Parigman, and Amphitryon, 614.
Pârvatî, her worship in Vâkpati's time, 606.
Pata*n*ga, bird, 87.
Pater matutinus, 46.
Patroklos, 64.
Pedu and the horse Paidva, given by the Asvins, 597.
Peijot, Finnish name for ancestral spirits, 275.
Peirithoos, son of Dia, 523.
Pekehé-ozaïs, Mordvinian god of the lime-trees, 244.
Pelasgos derived from Peleg, 216.
Pêleus and Thetis, wedding feast of, and the apple of Eris, 97.
Pelias and Nêleus, children of Poseidon and Tyro, 578, 648.
Pellervo, Finnish guardian spirit of the ploughed field, 271.
Penelope, the beloved of Hermes, mother of Pân, 682.
Perficus, name for Kronos, 510.
Perkun, Lettish god, 434.
Perkuna, supreme deity of the Lets, has his wedding in the West, 94.
Perse, Perseis, Persephone, and Prithâ, 617.
Persephone, 46.
— or Kore, 536.
— death-bringing, 536 n.
— and Proserpina, 767.
Perseus, 180.
— and Akrisios, 526.
— a solar hero, 615.
— serving Polydektes, 618.
Persian influence on Mordvinian religion, 254.
Persians, religion of the, 156.

INDEX.   855

Peru, solar mythology in, 163.
Phaidra, 'brilliant,' wife of Thêseus, 773.
Phenician influence on Greek religion, 647.
Pherekydes and the transmigration of souls, 832.
Philosophical ideas in Mordvinian religion, 247.
— — among the South Sea islanders, 247.
— — in the Veda, 247.
Philosophy and mythology, 44.
— and religion, Mordvinian, 248.
Phlegyes = Bhrigus, 809.
Phoibos and Daphne, 3.
— Bechtel's etymology of, 383.
— and Apollon, 688, 696, 710.
— Phoibos Apollon, 782.
Phonetic rules, as applied to proper names, 298, 362.
— — discovery of, 299, 304.
— — restricted evidence for, 301, 409, 412.
— — and the new school of Comparative Philology, 318.
— — not natural laws, 388.
Phonetics, 296.
— true value of, 331.
Phorôneus = Bhuranyu, 796.
Phylonome carried off by Ares, 649.
Physical basis of the Ugro-Finnic mythologies, 283.
— — of all mythologies, 284.
— mythologies of Aryan nations, general similarity of the, 833.
Picus or Picumnus, 713.
Pid, Sk., from pi-sad ? 300.
Pieria and Pierides, 101.
Pikku-mies, the dwarf, a Finnish water-spirit, 270.
Pilumnus, companion of Mars, 713.
Pisâkas, evil spirits, 212.
Pischel on Asvins and Dioskouroi, 600.
Pitris, worship of, 150.
— or ancestral spirits, Pretas, 213.
— and the moon, 267.
— or fathers, and Yama, 572.
Plant-legends, two classes of, 4.
Plato on θεός, 57.
— on the gods as representing phenomena of nature, 74 n.
— on nature-gods, 157.
Plouton for Pluto(n), 46, 646.
Ploutos or Plutos, son of Dêmêter, 46, 536, 646.
Plutarch on Greek mythology, 74.
— on Zeus and Hêre, 123.
Pollux and Polydeukes, 581.
Polydektes, a name of Hades, 615.

Polydeukes, Kastor and, 578.
Polymêle, mother of Jâson, other names of, 371.
Polynesian folklore, Kronos and, 36.
— myths of heaven and earth, 166.
Polytheism, Henotheism and, 139.
Polytheistic family-organisation, 137.
Pontia, name of the Dawn-Charis, 731.
Pork, prohibition of, among the Mordvines, 255.
Poseidon, dialectic varieties of the name, 368, 399.
— and Potidan, etymology of, 379, 658.
— and Dêo in equine form, 538.
— and Tyro, Pelias and Nêleus, 648.
— Hades, Zeus, 657.
Pott, and Grimm's Law, 306.
— on Greek proper names, 367.
Pourgas, Mordvinian storm-god, 240, 244.
— a kind of Indra, 246.
— the bridegroom of Syria, 246.
— has become a connection of the people at large, 247.
Pourguiné-Paz, see Pourgas.
Pragâpati (the sun), 45, 56, 89.
— the gods incensed against, 532.
Πραπίδες, etymologies of, 393.
Pravrikta used of Rebha, 594.
Prayer, Mordvinian, 238.
— at the birth of a child, 243.
— and sacrifice, 453.
— for curing an illness, Erzjanian, 464.
— after a thunderstorm, Erzjanian, 465.
— Wotjakian, 465.
— Mordvinian, 470.
Preller on Kronos, 36.
Prellwitz on etymology of hero, 65 n.
Pretas, different from the Pitris, 213.
Priests, seven classes of, in the Veda, 455.
Principles of the Science of Mythology, 830.
Prisni, 57.
Prithâ connected with Perse, Persêis, &c. ? 617.
Prithivi, Earth, as a mother, 46.
— the Earth, in Dyâvâ-prithivî, 495.
— the Earth, as a goddess, 530.
— meaning earth, 783.
Prithvî, prithivî, broad, 88.
Prodikos of Keos on nature-gods, 156.
Prokris from προΐξ, dew, 772.
Promêtheus as a fire-god, 810.
— and the Phlegyes, 810.

Prométheus, Promantheus, and pramantha, 811.
— the creator of men, 813.
— and Héphaistos, 813.
Proper names, etymologies of, 20.
— — phonetic rules as applied to, 298, 362, 387.
— — in Greek, 366.
— — of gods and heroes, 367.
— — dialectic varieties of, 368.
— — local character of, 397.
Propylaios, name of Hermes, 91.
— and Apollon, 692.
Proserpina and Persephone, 536 n., 767.
Protogeneia, the Dawn, mother of Aethlios, 524.
Psyche, soul, an abstract deity, 151.
Psychological or Ethno-Psychological School of Comparative Mythology, 177, 178.
Ptereláos, made immortal by a golden hair, 613.
Purûravas, the sun, 590.
Puseyism, 7.
Pûshan, 57.
— a name of the sun, 171.
Pythagoras, and the transmigration of souls, 832.
Pythagoreans, precautions observed by the, 224.
Python, Apollon's fight with, 698.
— = ahir budhnya*h*, 760.

QUINQUE, Aryan pankan, kankan, 188.

RÂ, Egyptian name of the sun, 162.
— Osiris, and Horus, 166.
Rain, Sun, Moon and, as brothers, 41.
— a traveller, 78.
— conceived as women, 771.
Râkâ, 57.
Rakshas, evil spirits, 212.
Rasâ, the river crossed by Saramâ, 675.
Rawlinson, Canon, on Lada and Lady, 218.
Reason must exist in mythology, 830.
Rebha, 594.
— the winter sun, 594.
Recaranus, name of Sancus, 767.
Religion des Veda, Oldenberg, 755 n.
— Védique, Bergaigne, 755 n.
Renouf, Le Page, on savages, 29.
— — — on Egyptian solar deities, 162 n., 165 n.
Rheia, originally the Earth, 514 n.
Rhode, Erwin, on Kerberos, 630.
*R*ibhu, 57.

Riddles, 80.
— origin of, 80.
— he who cannot guess them shall have his head cut off, 82.
— in the Old Testament, 82.
— Finno-Ugrian, 83.
— Russian, 83, 84.
— and the names of gods, 92.
— of the Mordvinians, 92.
— African, 99.
— on the thunder, 100.
— Erzjanian, 100.
— on the sky, stars, and moon, 100.
— on the sun, 100.
— Mordvinian, 101.
*Rig*rasva = Red-horse, 593.
— eyes restored by the Asvins, 593.
— slaughtered 100 sheep, 593.
Rig-veda and Avesta, myths of the, 2.
— age of the, 455.
— hymns, the Pantheon of the, 488.
— — earlier and later gods in it, 492.
— chronological divisions in the, 489.
— system in the succession of hymns of the, 490.
— Samhitâ and Pada texts of the, 491.
Rivers, holy, and receiving sacrifices, 269.
— offended when chained by a bridge, Roman idea of, 269.
— invoked as mothers, 467.
— as streams of rain, 753.
Rodasyau, 57.
Rohidasva = Agni, 593.
Rohi*n*î, wife of Soma, 42.
Rohita (sun), 45.
— a sun-god in the Atharva-veda, 655.
— and Agni, 656.
Roman Catholic relics, explained as fetishes, 195.
Romans covering their heads when praying, 224.
Romulus and Remus, 180.
Roots, origin of, 114.
— threefold differentiation of, 308.
— weakening and strengthening of, 326.
— nasalisation of, 337.
Roscher on Apollon and Mars, 707.
Rückert, 83.
Rudra, 57.
— the agent of the thunderstorm, 120, 607, 706.
— double aspect of, 212.
— terror of, not prominent in the Veda, 224.
— Tryambaka, pancakes thrown up for, 228.
— and the Rudras, 605.
— as Siva, 606.

Rudra, as healing diseases, 607.
— lightning of, 607.
— 'bright tawny bull,' 607.
— 'red boar of the sky,' 607, 620.
— and Apollon, 701, 702, 703.
— Kaparda, 703.
Rudras, sons of the sky, 138.
Rumina, a goddess who helps children to take the breast, 151.
Ruotperht and Robert, 366.
Russian belief as to the origin of mountains, &c., 251 n.

SABALA AND SARVARA, 628.
— the speckled, the day, 628, 630.
Sacrifice and prayer, 453.
— Sanskrit words for, 454.
— and magic, 458.
Sacrifices, Mordvinian and Wotjakian, 462.
Sacrificial ceremonies of the Wotjakes, 468.
Sagarbhâ, ἀδελφή, 49.
Sagard on North American religions, 163.
Saihs (Goth.), Lat. sex, Sk. sha*t*, 188.
St. Augustine, 62.
— Paul on rain and seasons, 77.
Saiva, spirits of the Laps, 272.
Saivo, Finnish, and Gothic saivala, 281.
Salii, festivities of the, 722.
Samâvartana, the pupil's returning home from his Guru, 231.
'Samlath and Semele, 217.
Samoyedes, religion of the, 161.
Samson, solar character of, 215.
Sancus, originally a name of Jupiter, 151.
— Recaranus, and Hercules, 767.
Sanskrit, its importance for Comparative Philology, 320.
Sâra, sap, ἥρως, power, 65 n.
Saramâ. 57.
— and Helena, 108, 516, 640.
— Sara*n*yû, the Dawn, 673.
Sârameya and Hermes, 369, 675.
Sârameyau, the two dogs in Yama's abode, 571.
Sara*n*yû, 57.
— Saramâ, Helena, 516.
— Vivasvat, and the Asvins, 539, 541, 559, 560, 815.
— the Night, 540.
— and Erinys, 540, 541, 543, 609-612.
— the Dawn, 541, 564.
— daughter of Aditi, 557.
— her metamorphosis into a mare, 566.
— and Nemesis, 640.

Sara*n*yû and Vivasvat, story of, 815.
Sarasvatî, 57.
Sarvara = Kerberos, 46, 375, 677.
— and sabala, 628.
Sârvara and sâvara, 628.
Sarvari, night, and Kerberos, 628.
Sarvarika and savara, barbarian, 628.
Sarvarîpati or Sarvarîsa, name of the moon, 628.
Sarvarîsa or Sarvarîpati, name of the moon, 628.
Saturnalia or festa calendarum, 594.
Satyavat, the waning moon, 48.
Savage races, study of, 24.
Savages, 23.
— Le Page Renouf on, 29.
— Sir Henry Maine on, 29.
— decadent races, 174.
— supposed to be primitive, 197.
— their customs made use of for the interpretation of Vedic rites, 222, 224, 226, 228.
— their myths and customs have no historical antecedents, 226.
— abstract ideas among, 291.
— their ideas about death and sunset, 574.
Sâvara and sârvara, 628.
— and sarvarika, barbarian, 628.
Savarnâ, wife of Manu, 816.
Savitrî and his daughter Sûryâ, 41.
— a solar god, 45, 48, 171, 818-825.
— and Savitrî, 47.
— Sûrya as, pervades all living things, 118.
— superseded by Agni, 142.
— made the sun, 812.
Savitrî, 47.
Saws about weather, 77.
Sayce on Semele and 'Samlath, 217 n.
Sayu, her cow filled with milk by the Asvins, 597.
Scheffer, Coelum Poeticum, on Solarism, 157.
Schelling, 44.
— on Homer, 111.
Schleicher and the Ursprache, 310.
Schliemann, 64.
Schmidt, J., on Assimilation, 345.
— — on ορ, ολ = ri, li, 419.
Schrader, 187.
— on Oldenberg, 188.
Schroeder, v., 123 n.
— — on Apollon, 688.
— — on Apollon-Agni, 702, 705.
Schwartz, 31.
— W., on Greek mythology, 103 n.
— — on the brothers Grimm, 104, 108.
— — on gods and heroes, 105.
'Science of Thought,' 38, 68, 114.

Sea, dwelling of Gŷmir, 86.
Seasons, weather and, 75.
— sationes or sowings, 76.
Seb, the earth, 162.
— and Nut, heaven and earth, their child the sun, 166.
— — parted by Shu, 166.
— the earth, also meaning goose, 166.
Segare la vecchia, 'to saw the old woman,' 718.
Selene, her brother Helios, 41, 88, 652, 782.
— the Moon, 56, 90.
— her love for Endymion, 90.
— her fifty daughters, 90.
— and Helena, 108.
Semele and Dionysos, alleged Semitic origin of, 217.
— her death before the brilliancy of Zeus, 520.
— and Stimula, 767.
Semitic and Aryan mythology, 213.
— origin of Greek gods, M. Barard on, 216.
Senart, M., on solar myths, 144.
— on Agni, 788.
Sentinus, he who gives children their senses, 151.
Serpent-worship, Aryan, 598.
Serpents in the sky and air, enemies of light, 598.
Seven sisters, rivers or dawns, 92.
Sex (Lat.), Sk. sha*t*, 188.
Shâhnâmeh, mythology in the, 53, 64, 672.
Shaman, not connected with the Buddhist Samana, 210 n.
Shamanism, not a religion, 162.
— supposed traces of it in the Veda, 210.
Shamans, their practices to work themselves into a state of excitement, 222.
Shame, ethnic psychology and the sense of, 289.
Sha*t* (Sk.), six, 187.
Shawnees, solar worship of the, 163.
Shooting stars called the serpent of fire, 252.
Shu parts Nut and Seb, 166.
Sibylla, Artemis as, 743.
Sidati, Sk., does it represent sisadati? 300, 334.
Sidero, mother of Tyro, 648.
Siecke, 47 n.
Siegfried, solar hero, bondman to Günther, 63, 180, 618-619.
Sigurd (Siegfried), 63.
Silures, Arturus, Duke of, 64.
Simargla, Mordvinian evil spirit, the Persian Simurgh? 250 n.

Sin, Babylonian moon-goddess, 36.
Sina, see Ina.
Sinivâli, goddess of the first day of the new moon, 57, 592.
Sisters, ten, 92.
— seven, 92.
Six, Goth. saihs, Lat. sex, Sk. sha*t*, 188.
Skanderbeg jumping on horseback from the tower of his fathers, 79.
Sky, enigmas on the, 100.
— father and lover of the Dawn, 107.
— worship of the, among primitive races, 260.
— tree, Lettish, 434.
Slavonic mythology, sun and moon, &c., in, 40.
— sun-myths, 95.
Sleeping on the earth, 229.
Smith, Robertson, on Semitic religion, 214.
Snow as a bird, 87.
Sôl, the sun, daughter of Mundilföri, 40.
Sol, 56.
— and Mani, in the Edda, 651.
Solar myth, Herbert Spencer on the, 3.
— and meteorological interpretations, 141.
— and vernal myths more important and primitive, 142.
— ideas in Greek poetry, 167.
— gods, Mordvinian, 235.
— myths, Egyptian, Babylonian, Chinese, 284.
— — matutinal and vernal ideas in, 585.
— heroes, servitude of, 618, 699.
— horse, 666.
— deities, apa-var in the sense of uncovering applied to, 690.
Solarism everywhere, 155.
Soltan, solar god of the Mokshanes, 240.
Soma, worship of, in Indo-Iranic period, 16.
— Moon, and Sûryâ, 41, 95.
— married to the twenty-seven daughters of Daksha, 42.
— Vedic name of a god, 57.
— offered to Indrâgni, 145.
— Moon, the rainer, 208.
— held by Tvâsh*t*ra Visvarûpa, 667.
— the rain, 755.
— see also Moon.
Son becoming the murderer of his father, a solar idea, 525.
Sonne, 32.
Sonnenwende, 594.
Sophocles speaking of Hêlios, 167.

INDEX.

Soshonis, had they a serpent for their totem? 199.
Soul and body, Mordvinian ideas about, 253.
— returns to Chkaï by the Milky Way, 253.
Souls of the blessed, changed into stars, 239.
— of the departed received by the moon, 239.
South Pacific legends, 4.
South Sea islanders, their philosophy, 247.
Southey, on the sun, 170.
Spencer, Mr. Herbert, 3.
— — his theory of ancestral worship, 150, 202, 443.
Sphinx, 82.
— riddle of the, found among the Mordvinians, 102.
Spirit-worship in India, Mr. Campbell on, 150 n.
Spirits, good and evil, among the Mordvinians, 240.
— distinction between gods and, 278.
— see Evil spirits.
Sraddhâ, Faith, an abstract deity, 151.
— — etymology and meanings of, 448.
Srotriyas and cultivation of memory, 185.
Stars, goats, with the Slaves, 40.
— unknown friends, 78.
— called orphans (of the Sun-daughter), 96.
— the children of Sun and Moon, 96.
— and moon, enigma on, 100.
Stimula and Semele, 767.
Stymphalides destroyed by Hérakles, 620.
Styx, a Finnish parallel of the river, 276.
Subterrestrial gods of the Fins, 279.
Sukanyâ, wife of Kyavâna, 587.
Sukkamieli, Finnish goddess of love, 273.
Sukra, 57.
Sun, masc. and fem., 39.
— a cow with the Slaves, 40.
— and Moon in mythology, 40, 138.
— — as father and son, 40.
— — brother and sister, 41.
— — and rain as brothers, 41.
— — love-stories of, 41, 47.
— the mother or daughter of the Dawn, 41.
— called a swan or bird, 87, 201.
— the golden apple, 94.
— and Dawn, in Lettish songs, 94.
— gives her daughter to the Moon, 94.

Sun, Dawn, Day, and Morning, confusion between them as members of the same family, 95.
— — — — among the Slavonic races, 95.
— the white horses of the, 95.
— always feminine in the Slavonic myths, 95.
— the housewife, 96.
— enigmas on the, 100.
— human feelings with regard to the, 169.
— Southey on the, 170.
— man's dependence on the, 170, 172.
— names of, 170.
— and sky, intimately connected, 172.
— called a horse, 201, 542, 597.
— a wheel as representing the, 201.
— the shiner, or the wanderer, the strong man, the swift bird, 208.
— regard for the, among the Mordvines, 236.
— Earth the wife of the, 238.
— and fire, 266.
— conceived as a stone in Sanskrit, 509.
— and Dawn as horse and mare, 563.
— dying or 'following in the track of the,' 574.
— conceived as an egg, 635.
— gods representing the, 652-725.
— chariot of the, 653.
— triple character of the, 656.
— three steps of the, 661.
— Gothic sunus, 'begetter, enlivener,' 823.
— see Âditya.
Sun-daughter, the Dawn, 96.
— (Sûryâ, lektra`, her bridegroom, 98.
— in Lettish mythology, 433, 594.
Sun-tree in Finnish mythology, 438, 438 n.
Suna, 57.
Sunakas, explained by totemism, 201.
Sunâsirau, 57.
Sundi-Mumi, Sun-Mother, 466.
Suonetar, Finnish goddess of muscles and veins, 273.
Superstitions, modern, 189.
Sûrya, m., the Sun, 39, 45, 56, 171.
— and Sûryâ, 47.
— true meaning of, 117.
— not restricted to one phenomenon, 132.
— superseded by Agni, 142.
— in mythology, 164, 652, 653.
— from svar, the Greek ἥλιος, 172.
— his place in the sky, 475.
— represents all phenomena in the sky, 478.

VOL. II.   F f

Sûrya, son of Heaven and Earth, 496.
— follows the Dawn, 532, 770.
— a white horse, 653.
Sûryâ, fem., Sun, 39, 47.
— daughter of Savit*ri*, 41.
— her marriage with Soma, 95.
— daughter of Sûrya, 138.
— and the Asvins, 138, 573, 582.
— the Sun-daughter, Lettish parallel to, 434.
Sut, god of darkness, 166.
— devoured the head of Osiris, or the eye of Horus, 167.
Suvetar, the same as Etelätär, 269.
Svar, gen. suras, sun and sky, 172.
— sun, the shiner, 208.
Svar-bhânu, demon causing eclipses of the sun, 654.
Syâma, the dark, the night, 628, 630.
Syncretism and Allelotheism, 146.
Syria, carried off by Pourgas to be his wife, 244, 246.
— the Dawn, Mordvinian goddess, 246.
Syriava, story of Pourgas and, 244.

TADEBEJO, Finnish name for ancestral spirits, 274.
Tadebejos, spirits of the Samoyedes, 272.
Tähti, star or pole star, Finnish god, 265.
— sons and daughters of, 266.
Taivahan Ukko, or Father of the Sky, 262.
Talâtala and Tartaros, 669.
Talbot, Fox, on Dian-nisi, 218.
Talmud, Relig. Ceremonies in, 694 n.
Tanûnapât, 57.
— a name of Agni, 788.
Tapas, meanings of, 221, 223.
— Oldenberg on, 222.
— and Tapasvin, modern and ancient authorities on, 223.
— Bhagavadgitâ on, 223.
— means aikâgryam, 224.
Tâpasa, the Vedic ascetics, and the Shamans, 222.
Tapio, Finnish forest-god, 271.
Taramaakiaki, sea-weed, 36.
Taramahetonga, south-wind, 36.
Tara*ni*, sun, and T*ri*ta, 655, 662.
Tartaros and T*ri*ta, 668.
Tavun-ozaïs, Mordvinian god of swine, 255.
Tchim-Paz, Erzjanian name for Chkaï, 236, 248.
— see Chkaï.
Tchouvan, first Tsar of the Mordvines, 254.

Tegni, Mongolian god, also called Chormusda (Ormazd), 254.
Tekanawita, see Dekanawidah.
Ten sisters, the fingers, 92.
Tengri, Mongolian name for the gods, 117, 272.
— supreme god of the Mongols, 160 n.
— Turkish god of the sky, 261.
— the same as Tegni ? 426.
Teraphim, explained as fetishes, 196.
Terhenetär, mist or fog, Finnish goddess, 268.
Terra, 56.
Theia, the Dawn, 89.
— mother of Hêlios, 652.
Themis, the old goddess of justice, 151, 152.
— daughter of Hêlios, 152.
— — Uranos and Gaia, 152.
Theogony, the true, 135, 171.
Θεοί, and Devas, 138.
Θεύs, derived from θη, 57.
— discussions about, 302.
— and deva, deus, 390, 394.
Theriolatry and totemism, 7, 199, 201.
Thêseus, 180.
— his mother Aithra, 525.
— and the birth of the morning, 526.
— double of Hêrakles, 621, 773.
— fight of the Dioskouroi against, 637.
Thetis, wedding feast of Pêleus and, 97.
Thirty-three gods, 475.
Thörr, see Thunar.
Thraêtaona = Traitana, 2, 672.
Thridi, name of Ódinn, 671.
Thunar milks his heavenly cows (the clouds), 93.
— or Thôrr, Indra compared with, 744.
— his fight with giants and demons, 747.
Thunder, enigmas on the, 100.
— the old man beyond the great water, 101.
Thyria, a nymph beloved by Apollon, 693.
Thyro, a nymph beloved by Apollon, 693.
Tiele, Prof., 32, 34, 36.
— on the physical character of the Vedic gods, 445.
Tien, Chinese god of the sky, 261.
Tivar, and Devas, 138.
Totem, clan-mark, 198.
— of fire, 804.
Totemism, an ill-defined term, 7, 198.
— Professor Hopkins on, 8.
— among Polynesians and Melanesians, 8.

INDEX. 861

Totemism, supposed to be primitive, 158.
— its proper place in mythology, 443.
Totems, Dr. Codrington on, 7.
Toumo-ozaïs, Mordvinian god of the oak-trees, 244.
Traitana and Thraêtaona, and Feridûn, 2, 672.
Transmigration of souls, 832.
— — in India, Egypt, and Greece, 832.
Trâtri, an abstract deity, 820, 824.
Tree-worship, Finnish, 273.
Triptolemos, the inventor of the plough, 536.
Trita and Tarani, 655, 662.
Trita or Trĭta, the last light of the sun, 661–673.
— fell into a pit, 663.
— Âptya, i. e. abiding in the waters, 663.
— a far-off deity, 663, 664.
— his fight with Tvâsh*tr*a Visvarûpa, 667.
Trito, Tritogeneia, and the Vedic Trita, 376.
Tritogeneia, &c., names of Athêne and Trita, 670.
Trĭton (Greek) and Sk. T*r*ita, 670.
Trophònios, name of Hermes, 91.
Troy, siege of, 631.
Tukius (Turks), nature-worship of the, 161.
Tuna, chief of the eels, 4.
— the brains of, the white kernel of the cocoanut, 5.
— of the cocoanut, 36.
Tunguses, nature-worship of the, 161.
Tuonela, the Finnish Hades, 276.
— the road to, 276.
— or Manala, Finnish, 833.
Tuonelan Ukko, or Ukko of death, 262.
Tuoni, or Kalma, 276.
— means death, 276.
— and Thánatos, 276, 281.
Turso or Iku-Turso, a dangerous water-spirit, 270.
Tuulen tytär, daughter of the wind, a Finnish 'Windsbraut,' 269.
Tvâsh*tr*a Visvarûpa, Trita's fight with, 667.
Tvash*tri*, his wife Aditi or B*r*ihaddivâ, 557, 560.
— progenitor of Sara*n*yû's children, 559.
— a name of Dyaus, 560.
— is Visvarûpa, 668.
— Agni as, 791–794.
— Agni, Dyaus, 820.
— is he an abstract god? 824.

Tweggi, Thridi, and Ódinn, 671.
Twin deities, representing light and darkness, &c., 521, 524.
— — see Asvins, and Dioskouroi.
— gods, see Dual gods.
Tylor, 27.
— on solar and meteorological myths, 142.
Tyndareôs, father of the Dioskouroi, 633.
Typhâon, a hurricane, 505.
— power of darkness, 627.
Typhon, Apollon's fight with, 698.
— Typhâon, Typhôeus, slain by Zeus, 759.
— etymology of, 768.
Tyr and Odin, 128.
— and Dyaus, 129.

UGRO-FINNIC mythologies, the physical basis of the, 283.
Ukko, the old venerable father, Finnish god, 262.
— god of the thunderstorm, 262.
— and Jumala, 262, 263.
— the Luonnottaret, his daughters, 268.
— his wife Maa-emä, 271.
Uljana, Erzjanian goddess of the earth, 464.
Uni, Finnish god of sleep, 273.
Unkulunkulu, 24.
— the great-grandfather, 203.
— the sky? 204.
Untamo, Finnish god of dreams, 273.
Upanayana, represented as a new birth, 227.
— and puberty, ceremonies of savages, 230.
Ural-Altaic tribes, five classes of, 256.
Ursprache, Schleicher on the, 310.
— attempt at reconstructing it, wrong in principle, 311.
Urvasi, 57.
— or Aditi supplanted Svârâ, 505.
— and Mitrâ-Varu*n*au, 548.
— the Dawn, 590.
Ushas, the shiner, 115.
— different meanings of, 115.
— or Ushâsâ, a female deity, 116.
— true meaning of, 117.
— the Dawn as an agent, 120.
— Dawn, her perpetual youth, 132.
— daughter of Dyaus, the Sky, 138, 529, 726.
— a lovely maiden, 148.
— he or she who lights, 171.
— Êos, Aurora, 376.
— sing. or plur., mother(s) of Sûrya, 653.

F f 2

Ushas, and Indra, 769.
— as a kind of Fortuna, 775.
— the Dawn, 782.
Uutar, mist or fog, Finnish goddess, 268.

VADHRIMATÎ, given a son by the Asvins, 595.
Vagitanus, the god who helps children to cry, 151.
Vahni, a name of fire, 114.
Vaisvânara, first an epithet of Agni, 826.
Vâk, Speech, an abstract deity, 151, 818.
Vâkpati on the worship of Pârvatî, 606.
Vanaspati, Vedic name of deity, 57.
Vandana, 590, 594, 595.
— rescued by the Asvins, 590.
Vanna-issa, Ukko's name among the Ests, 262.
— the Old Father, and Koi and Ämmärik, 267.
Varana by the side of Varuna, 417, 546.
Varma-Paz, Mordvinian god of the air and winds, 240.
Vartikâ (Ortygia), the quail swallowed by the wolf, 93, 514, 584.
— delivered by the Asvins, 584.
Varuna, god of the sky, changed into the god of the waters, 50, 818.
— Vedic name, not etymologically transparent, 57.
— the agent of the evening sky, 120, 121, 545-555.
— wider meaning of, 120, 132.
— the moon the eye of, 120.
— greater than Mitra, 125.
— not restricted to the moon, 134, 554.
— Agni identified with, 147.
— and Ouranos, 216, 387, 390, 416-421, 545.
— Wackernagel's etymology of, 390, 417.
— and Varana, 417.
— and Dyaus, antecedent to Agni and Indra, 492.
— not a recent god, 546.
— supposed Semitic origin of, 547.
— and Mitrâ-Varunau, 547.
— is Ahura in the Avesta, 547.
— his ethical character, 549.
— his connection with the water, 555.
— rivalry between Indra and, 757.
— and Ahura Mazda, Darmesteter on, 782.
— his physical character, 818.

Varuna, abstract character of, 818.
— at first a concrete deity, 818.
— in post-Vedic literature, 818.
— see Mitra and Varuna.
Varunâ = Mitrâ-Varunau, 122.
Vas, to shine, 195.
Vas-ar, Sk., morning, 171.
Vâsâtya and Nâsatya, 608.
Vasishtha, the offspring of Mitrâ-Varunau, 548.
— or Purûravas, the sun, 590.
Vâstoshpati, a Mordvinian, 245.
— or Agni, and Asva, children of Saranyû, 559, 576.
Vasûnâm and ἐάων, 180.
Vatsas, had they a calf for their totem? 199.
Vâyu, wind, not mythological, 56.
— 'the blower,' 113.
Veda, survival of primitive mythology in the, 7.
— Henotheism in the, 140.
— philosophy and mythology in the, 247.
— in what sense is it primitive? 427-430.
— Contributions to the Interpretation of the, by Prof. Bloomfield, 628.
Vedava or Vedazyrava, mother of the sun and goddess of the water, 243.
Vedazyrava or Vedava, 243.
— goddess invoked at childbirth, 243.
Védiava, Earth, wife of Chkaï, in Mordvinian mythology, 238.
— and the egg, Chkaï stepped on, 242.
— or Védiazyrava, the same as Vedava or Vedazyrava? 243.
Vediazyrava, other name of Azyrava, 241, 242.
— or Védiava, the goddess of water and rain, 242.
— the same as Angué-Patiaï, 242 n.
Vedic mythological names, 57.
— mythology, remnants of a mythological fermentation found in, 22.
— — traces of anthropomorphic development in, 148, 477.
— — and Mordvinian mythology, 246.
— — antecedents of, 440.
— — and other Aryan mythologies, relation between, 451, 527.
— — more modern ingredients in, 452.
— deities, their character predominantly physical, 444.

INDEX. 863

Vedic deities, Yâska's classification of, 472-488.
— — the three classes of, 473-488.
— — indicated in the Brâhmanas, 475.
— — not restricted to one locality, 487.
— — their allelotheistic character, 531.
— — comprehensive character of, 604.
— literature, age of, 446.
— hymns, ceremonial ideas in, 452.
— Sanskrit, advantages of, for mythological studies, 783.
— mythological names still retaining their meaning, 783, 784.
— — — losing their meaning, 784.
Vedische Mythologie, Hillebrandt, 755 n.
Ved-Paz, Mordvinian god, 240.
Veen Ukko, or Ukko of the water, 262.
Verethraghna and Vritrahan, 756.
Véria-Patiaï, Mordvinian goddess of the fruits, 240.
Vernal and solar myths more primitive, 142.
— ideas in solar myths, 585.
— sun, birth of the, 714.
Ver-nechké-vélén-Paz, Mordvinian god, 239.
Verner's Law, 307, 320.
Vesi, water or water deity in Finnish, 269.
Vesta, from Sk. vas, to shine, 195.
— deity of fire, 784.
Veturius Mamurius, see Mamurius.
Vico, 9.
Vidhartri and Agni, 825.
Vimada and Kamadyu, and the Asvins, 595.
Virâg (sun), 45.
Virchow, on language and thought, 38.
Viriazyrava, Mordvinian goddess of the woods, 244.
Vishnâpû and Vishnu, 592.
— restored to Visvaka by the Asvins, 592.
Vishnu (sun), 45.
— Vedic name not etymologically transparent, 57.
— and Vishnâpû, 592.
— his three steps, 661.
Vispalâ, 592.
— leg replaced by Asvins, 592.
Vis-patni, epithet of Sinivâli, 592.
Visvaka, Asvins restore Vishnâpû to, 592.
Visvakarman, maker of all things, not mythological, 56.

Visvarûpa and Tvashtri, 794.
Vitumnus, he who gives life to children, 151.
Vivásván and Ἰασίων, 436.
— and Jâson, 437.
Vivasvat, a name of the sun, 171.
— the bright day, and Saranyû, and the birth of the Asvins, 540, 541, 559, 560, 565.
— a priest, 582 n.
— = Vivanhat, 672.
— and Saranyû, story of, 815.
— a name of Manu, 816.
Vohu manô, and Λόγος θεῖος, 553.
Voltsé-Paz, see Oultsé-Paz.
Vowel-system, Aryan, 312.
Vožo, Wotjakian goddess, 467.
Vrika, rescued by the Asvins, 591.
Vrishabha or bull, name of Indra, 7.
Vrishàkapi, Vedic name not etymologically transparent, 57.
Vritra and Vritras, evil spirits, 212.
— and Orthros, 421-425.
— coverer, genius of darkness, 694.
— older than Indra, 756, 758.
Vui, spirit, definition of, 207.
Vulcanus, survives in mythology, rather than Ignis, 85.
— a fire-god, 791.
— and Sk. ulkâ, 799.
Vu-murt, Wotjakian water-spirit, 467.

WAITZ, on ethnological evidence, 28.
— on fetishism, 194.
— on physical gods of the Naturvölker, 284.
Water deities of the Fins, 269.
Weather, the, and the Seasons, 75.
— saws about, 77.
Weber, 628.
Welcker, on Kronos, 14, 510, 512.
Wellamo, Ahto's wife, 270.
Welthaum, and the Lettish sky-tree, 435.
Werther, mixture of history and poetry in, 61, 62.
Wetterbaum, and the Lettish sky-tree, 435.
— and sun-tree, 438 n.
Wheel as representing the sun, 201.
Whitney and M. M., 318.
Wichmann, Yrjö, on the Wotjakians, 463.
Widows, self-immolation of, how to be explained, 289.
Wieland, the smith, his 700 gold rings, 763.
Wind, the heavenly child, 78.

INDEX.

Wind, son of Fornjöt, 86.
— enigma on the, 101.
Winter and snow, enigmas on, 100.
— to kill, 593.
— or the dying year, 716.
Winternitz on Aryan serpent-worship, 598.
Wôdan and Thunar, 744.
Wolf, meant for darkness or night, 93.
— the grey, catches the stars in the sky, 93.
Women employed by the sun-god Chkaï, 236.
Wongs or fetishes of African tribes, 189.
Words, ideas fixed by, 42.
Wormingford, etymology of, 363.

XANTHIS, wife of Hêraklês, 772, 773.

YAMA AND YIMA, 2.
— the setting sun, 45, 563, 566, 573, 574.
— Vedic name not transparent etymologically, 57.
— was he Adam? 215, 569.
— and Yamî, 215, 562, 566.
— as Agni, 375, 566.
— the twin, born of Saranyû, 558, 560, 562, 565, 566.
— discussed, 562–577.
— as the firstborn and the first to die, 568.
— the type of mankind, 569.
— as the ruler of the Departed, or as Death, 571.
— one of the Lokapâlas, 572.
— collector of men, 573.
— and Mṛityu, 817.
Yamau, the twins, 541.
Yami, Vedic name not transparent etymologically, 57.
— and Yama, the pair of twins, 559, 562, 566.
— the moon, 576.
— an afterthought, 577.
Yâska on the manysidedness of the Vedic gods, 133.
— on the Asvins, 133, 565, 603, 608.
— classification of Vedic devatâs, 258, 472–489.
— age of, 474.

Yâska, his Pantheon, and that of the Rig-veda hymns, 491.
— on the story of Saranyû and Vivasvat, 540.
— his mythology, 608.
Yasodharâ, Buddha's wife, other names of, 370.
Yâtudhânas, evil spirits, 212.
Yávish/ha and Hêphaistos, 801.
Year, celebrations of the birth of the new and death of the old, 714.
Yima = Yama, 2.
Yule on the Supreme Spirit of the Tatars, 160 n.
— on the Natigai, 161 n.
Yzit, Tatar name of spirits, from yazata? 281.

ZAUBER, meaning of the German word, 459.
Zêthos and Amphîon, 642.
— married to Aêdòn, 643.
Zeus and Dyaus, 23, 50, 128, 375
— — differences between, 502.
— Helena, daughter of, 49.
— as a name of God, 66.
— Hêre, and Hêphaistos, 71, 504.
— degradation of, 106.
— his physical and moral character, 106.
— as the sun, Plutarch on, 123.
— the greatest and best, 149.
Ζεὺς Γελέων and Dyaús smáyamânaḥ, 499.
Zeus Euryopa, the wide-seeing Zeus, 506.
Zeus as the husband of Dêmêter, begetting Kore, 512.
— the wives of, 513–527, 530.
— as a swan approaching Lêda, and haṃsa, the sun, 515.
— children of, 529.
— and Kronos, struggle between, 534.
— as a swan, the father of the Dioskouroi, 635.
— Poseidon, and Hades, the three Kroniônes, 657.
— and Indra sprang from the same source, 782.
— forehead of, the East, 793.
Zori, Dawn and Gloaming, Slavonic, 95.
Zulus, the religion of the, 203.

THE END.

www.ingramcontent.com/pod-product-compliance
Lightning Source LLC
Chambersburg PA
CBHW022143300426
44115CB00006B/315